DISCOVERING SOCIOLINGUISTICS

Discovering Sociolinguistics

From Theory to Practice

Dick Smakman

First published 2018 by
RED GLOBE PRESS

Red Globe Press in the UK is an imprint of Springer Nature Limited, registered in England, company number 785998, of 4 Crinan Street, London, N1 9XW.

Red Globe Press® is a registered trademark in the United States, the United Kingdom, Europe and other countries.

ISBN 978–1–137–51907–8 paperback

This book is printed on paper suitable for recycling and made from fully managed and sustained forest sources. Logging, pulping and manufacturing processes are expected to conform to the environmental regulations of the country of origin.

A catalogue record for this book is available from the British Library.

A catalog record for this book is available from the Library of Congress.

Contents

Introduction

Book synopsis

Discovering Sociolinguistics introduces readers to the field of Sociolinguistics and hands them the tools to start their own sociolinguistic research project. The first two parts of the book present this broad field and the second two parts lay out the practicalities and steps needed to do actual sociolinguistic investigations. The book is introductory in nature and covers the common core of topics and theories in the field. It gives much attention to cultural variation and examples from across the world.

Audience

This book is for students and budding researchers from any cultural or linguistic background who are interested in taking up sociolinguistic research, updating their theoretical knowledge, and/or expanding their methodological skills. It also helps lecturers supervise sociolinguistic research projects and develop an introductory course in this discipline.

Motivations

The first of four motivations underlying this book is that it is difficult for starting researchers and for students to transform the information in existing introductory books into their own investigation. While these researchers and students will want to design their own research methodology, they are faced with a wide range of theoretical and methodological options but no instructions as to how to go from observing patterns in language use to building a theoretical and methodological framework. *Discovering Sociolinguistics* presents steps from observing language variation to designing a custom-made methodology and analysing data practically and theoretically.

The second motivation for this book is that existing introductions to the field are not only becoming more complete and state of the art but also longer and more specialised. As a result, they are often difficult for those who merely want to discover the outlines of the field. *Discovering Sociolinguistics* gives such overviewable outlines. For those who wish to specialise, suggestions for further reading are given at the ends of the theoretical chapters and on the companion website, at www.macmillanihe.com/companion/smakman.

Thirdly, introductions to sociolinguistics tend to divide the attention paid to languages and situations on the basis of the availability of research. This leads to an overrepresentation of research inspired by the schools of thought in the Anglo-Western regions and to relatively much attention being paid to

English in its many shapes and forms. *Discovering Sociolinguistics* tries to keep this cultural bias to a minimum. While respecting (and discussing) main-stream traditions, this book takes a broad international view of the field. As a result, fewer elaborate explanations of research on Englishes from all over the world and more examples from cultures, languages, and sociolinguistic systems outside this realm are given.

The less balanced selection of research that starting sociolinguists generally face also underlies the final challenge that this book tries to meet. Selected investigations in mainstream introductions tend to be based on a limited set of methodologies, and the full scope of methodological options that are available remains undiscussed. This means that the reader is left to their own devices when choosing a methodology. *Discovering Sociolinguistics* puts forward a broad range of methodologies to choose from as well as the motivations for choosing one or the other, and it explains how each methodology can help answer cer-tain sociolinguistic questions.

Book structure

This book consists of four parts. Parts 1 and 2 discuss the field. They draw a picture of the historical, theoretical, and cultural space in which language use occurs. Parts 3 and 4 are geared towards the practical side of research and pro-vide the tools towards empirical sociolinguistic research.

Part 1 Introducing Sociolinguistics introduces the field. This first part tries to draw a picture of how the field came to be (Chapter 1) and what the latest challenges and developments in it are (Chapter 2). It also explains the concept of language variation and how it leads to a myriad of ways to view and refer to language (Chapter 3). Culture as a sociolinguistic variable is also introduced (Chapter 4).

Part 2 Understanding Sociolinguistics delves into the theories and concepts of today's field. It starts with describing the individual speaker who makes all kinds of language choices in the sociolinguistic space in which they reside and move around on a daily basis (Chapter 5). Language ideology and the ensuing language norms are then discussed, both generally (Chapter 6) and from the viewpoint of 11 major cultures in the world (Chapter 7). The next two chap-ters deal with the ways language is viewed by ordinary language users. The difference between lay and expert opinions and the research fields that deal with this distinction are first dealt with (Chapter 8), and after that the nature and workings of lay attitudes are discussed (Chapter 9). Two core themes in Sociolinguistics that are generally treated separately are then presented: age (Chapter 10) and gender (Chapter 11). The final chapter of the second part of the book deals with the importance of sociolinguistic variation in the field of Second Language Acquisition and the many interests that these two fields increasingly share (Chapter 12).

Part 3 Processing Sociolinguistics gives the basic steps and information needed to design, organise, and execute a research project, and to write it down in a report. It starts by explaining the very first exploratory and conceptual steps towards selecting a methodology (Chapter 13). It then gives an outline of a typical sociolinguistic research report (Chapter 14). The next two chapters provide technical information that is needed in many of the available methodologies in the field but that is not part of every researcher's or every student's academic background; for those who need them, the basics of Statistics (Chapter 15) and Sociophonetics (Chapter 16) are given.

In *Part 4 Doing Sociolinguistics*, 20 methodologies are explained. For each of these, a practical example of a possible research project is laid out in some detail. Methodologies are described to deal with three ways in which language can appear: language that is already available (Chapter 17), language that needs to be elicited (Chapter 18), and language that occurs naturally and is viewed as part of a larger system of communication (Chapter 19). The final chapter explains how language attitudes can be researched (Chapter 20).

Terminology

Terminology is in most cases highlighted and explained in the text and in the text boxes. In the Glossary, you can find a list of terms whose meaning is not explained elaborately in the text or text boxes. The Index contains an overview of sociolinguistic terminology that can be found in the book and of the places, languages, and peoples across the world that are discussed. Statistical and phonetic terminology is not included in the Glossary and Index. Statistical terminology can be found in Chapter 15, while phonetic terminology can be found in Chapter 16. The main text sometimes contains some pronunciation examples, but these are usually easy to understand without further phonetic knowledge. Consulting the International Phonetic Alphabet (IPA) overview in Section 16.2.1 helps the reader understand the specific use and meaning of certain phonetic terms.

Companion website

The website that belongs to this book provides tools for teaching and researching. It contains extra references to research, more writing and research tips, more statistical help (guide to SPSS), as well as exercises, teaching materials (lesson plans and PowerPoint slides), and relevant clips. These resources can be accessed at www.macmillanihe.com/companion/smakman.

Acknowledgements

The following people have provided valuable examples, helped with the editing and proofreading of this book, and/or given other types of guidance: Max van Arnhem, Sandra Barasa, Albertine Bosselaar, Bert Botma, Irene Cenni, Florian Coulmas, Natalia Edisherashvili, Aone van Engelenhoven, Carmen Ebner, Kapitolina Fedorova, Thomas de France, Viktor Friedman, Patrick Heinrich, Jos Hornikx, Viktorija Kostadinova, Silvia Kouwenberg, Frank van Meurs, Sofia Mitsova, Jiří Nekvapil, Shobha Satyanath, and Cassie Smith-Christmas. Thank you very much! Any inconsistencies or any lack of precision or nuance are, of course, still the author's responsibility. The people at Palgrave have been great, and I hope to work with them again.

PART I

INTRODUCING SOCIOLINGUISTICS

The first four chapters of this book introduce the historical, linguistic, and cultural space in which the field of Sociolinguistics has developed and is currently continuing to mature. After introducing the beginnings of the discipline (Chapter 1) and its current state (Chapter 2), the ways language can be viewed from a sociolinguistic point of view and the terminology that goes with these ways are discussed (Chapter 3). This first part ends with an introduction into culture as a factor to be reckoned with in explaining language choices (Chapter 4). This first part provides the reader with the background knowledge to understand the workings of the field and the many aspects it covers.

Early Sociolinguistics

The Birth of a Field

1.1 Introduction

Sociolinguistics is the study of language use in a social context. Before the name 'Sociolinguistics' started being used regularly in the 1960s, research involving the social aspects of language had already been done. In the nineteenth century in particular, the awareness of the disappearance of dialects triggered an effort to describe these dialects and the cultures of which they were a part. At the same time, awareness was growing of the psychological aspects of language in communication. In the second half of the nineteenth century, a broader discussion was also taking place concerning whether language was part of the Natural Sciences or the Humanities. All of this laid the foundations of the field of Sociolinguistics.

The current chapter lays out the natural evolvement of Sociolinguistics from separate academic disciplines such as Linguistics, Dialectology, and some of the Social Sciences. It describes how it was the natural outcome of these disciplines finding each other and combining forces, and it gives examples of research that took place in various countries.

1.2 Separate disciplines

The description of language was traditionally done by linguists and dialectologists. While linguists focussed more on the formal properties of languages (**syntax** and **phonology**, mainly), dialectologists described the language use (vocabulary and pronunciation, mainly) of ordinary people. Unlike linguists, dialectologists focussed on language that was uncodified, that is, not written down in dictionaries, grammar books, and all kinds of historical descriptions. Linguists tended to view the considerable variation in the way individuals speak as less relevant – as 'noise' – because this variation was considered as superficial compared to deeper linguistic structures, and as less predictable and systematic. Dialectologists did show an interest in speaker-related aspects, but this was usually limited to speakers' social status in a community (based on their profession) and their geographical origin. This interest was mainly driven by the desire to find and document local and regional language characteristics.

These two fields were largely separated in the nineteenth century but what they had in common was that they attempted to describe 'language' (the resource) rather than 'language performance' or 'language use' (how the resource is applied). Language use by individuals was mainly seen as one of many aspects of human behaviour and therefore part of disciplines like **Sociology**, **Anthropology**, or **Psychology**. The latter fields were even further removed from traditional Linguistics than Dialectology was and paid little attention to language.

EXAMPLE

Early awareness

While Linguistics, Dialectology, and the Social Sciences were largely separate fields, there was nevertheless a latent awareness of a common core. As early as in the late nineteenth century, the German linguist Philipp Wegener (1880) suggested a psychological study of accents and of word choice from a stylistic point of view. He also suggested that dialectologists pay more attention to word choice in different social settings. Wegener (1885) used the term *Sprachleben*, 'language life', to refer to the social aspects of language.

1.3   Early sociolinguistic activity

1.3.1 Dialectology

Although Sociolinguistics was not explicitly acknowledged as a field, much of the language-related research that was done in the nineteenth and first half of the twentieth century can retrospectively be classified as sociolinguistic. Nineteenth-century research of this type was mainly dialectological. Many dialects and other smaller languages were thoroughly documented, amongst others in England (Wright 1898–1905) and, for instance, France (Guilliéron and Edmont 1902–1910). Greenberg (1996), in addition, explained that there is a considerable amount of dialectological research on the territory of former Yugoslavia, going back to the nineteenth century. Coulmas (2013) mentioned that in Japan and India, too, rich traditions existed that are now relatively unknown. All of these dialectological studies were mainly descriptive and laid bare regional and historical patterns rather than giving social explanations for language variation. Dialectology in Japan was mostly pursued by **folklore** scholars who put more emphasis on the study of local customs and less on the use of language (Tachibana 1943 [1936]), and similar motivations could be found elsewhere.

1.3.2 Early sociolinguistic activity

In the twentieth century, more sociolinguistic aspects appeared in research in various places. In a country like Russia, sociolinguistic studies developed in the 1920s, albeit on a very modest scale and aimed partly at **language planning**, according to Brandist (2003). Research focussing on language variation appeared incidentally, like research into the use of new words in Russian (Selishchev 1928), slang as an identity marker in the language of Russian school children (Polivanov 1931), and socially stratified differences in the language of Ukranian workers (Danilov 1929). As a final Russian example, Shpilrein et al. (1928) did an experimental study of the lexicon of Red Army soldiers.

In the mid-1930s, the Japanese linguist Tanabe published the book *Gengoshakaigaku*, 'Sociology of Language' (Tanabe 1936), which described the viability of a separate discipline combining language and social aspects. The concept of *Gengo Seikatsu*, 'language life', was (and is) used to refer to, amongst others, language as an instrument in a socio-cultural and historical setting, as an activity of speakers and listeners (Coulmas 2011). Differences between the ways the social classes in Buenos Aires (Argentina) pronounced certain Spanish consonants were investigated by Guitarte (1955) and Barrenechea (1951). In the Netherlands, the situation in the northern bilingual province of Friesland was studied by Boelens and Van der Veen (1956) while Weijnen (1946) laid bare patterns of beliefs about dialects in the south of the country. In the United States, Kurath (1949) did extensive dialectological work with a strong sociolinguistic angle. India was favoured as a destination for sociolinguistic researchers in the 1950s and 1960s; most notably the American linguist Gumperz (1971) and the Indian philologist (i.e., historical linguist) Pandit (1955).

More such sociolinguistic activity took place in scattered places across the globe, but it was not necessarily categorised as sociolinguistic but as dialectological, anthropological, historically/theoretically linguistic, or sociological.

1.3.3 Constraints

In some countries, sociolinguistic traditions were slowly becoming a reality but for various reasons these more local traditions did not spark a broad interest or a start of a new unified discipline. Many of the ensuing publications remained below the radar of international attention for various reasons, including the low international power of academic fields from certain regions. Moreover, these publications were not always written in an internationally understandable language and thus remain(ed) inaccessible to most.

Furthermore, the social and official acceptability of describing the realities of language variation varied across countries. Until the fall of the socialist governments, scholars interested in socially conditioned language variation were often constrained by ideologies. In countries such as Russia and China, the political situation impacted the nature and degree of research into language variation. As an illustration, the previously named Russian scholar Danilov had to officially disclaim his results as going against Marxist theory. The works of the psychologist Lev Vygotsky (1896–1934), which are relevant in discussions on the socio-psychological aspects of language use, were banned in the

Soviet Union until 1956 and were only translated and published after his death (Vygotsky 1962, 1978). So, academic freedom was constrained in some places.

FOCUS ON...

Modern constraints

Political effects on academic progress are not something of the distant past. Greenberg (1996) explained how Dialectology was used in the service of nationalism in the period leading up to the Yugoslav Wars of Succession (1991–2001). Besides linguistic characteristics, ethnic and religious boundaries were proposed as the main dividing lines between languages, which affected the objectivity of analyses. A political system may also affect the opportunities to actually generate data. The fieldwork done by Xu (1992) in Baotou, China, for instance, involved a genuine risk of being apprehended and questioned.

1.4   Merging disciplines

1.4.1 Social and psychological aspects of language

Motivated by the loss of dialectological variation and not hindered by political forces, Western dialectologists could freely continue to pursue their academic interests. These Western researchers made observations on the social **stratification** of various language **styles** using a technique referred to as Linguistic Geography (see 3.3.3 and 17.3). Researchers from the various disciplines gradually found each other in the study of the sociopsychological and sociocultural aspects of language. Societal tendencies brought about this shared interest as did certain ground-breaking publications, like the one by Ferdinand de Saussure (1857–1913). This Swiss philologist taught a course (in French) called *Course Générale de Linguistique,* 'A course in General Linguistics' (De Saussure 1978 [1916]). De Saussure asked himself a number of fundamental questions:

> Must linguistics then be combined with sociology? What are the relationships between linguistics and social psychology? Everything in language is basically psychological, including its material and mechanical manifestations, such as sound changes; and since linguistics provides social psychology with such valuable data, is it not part and parcel of this discipline? (6–7)

The distinction made several times in this chapter between 'language' and 'language use' is strongly associated with De Saussure. His distinction between *langue* ('language') and *parole* ('speaking') is relevant from a sociolinguistic perspective; 'language' is the system, the principles of language, whereas 'speaking' refers to the use of the language by individuals.

Awareness can also be seen in publications in which the words 'sociology' and 'linguistics' were coined. The English anthropologist Thomas Callan Hodson wrote an article called 'Socio-linguistics in India' (Hodson 1939), and the American linguist Eugene Nida mentioned 'sociolinguistics' in a book on **morphology** (Nida 1949). The American linguist Haver Currie produced the most famous early instance of this coined word, namely in a journal article entitled 'Projection of sociolinguistics' (Currie 1952).

1.4.2 Linguistics and Dialectology

By the mid-1950s, certain circles had become aware of the unnecessary divide between Linguistics and the discipline that tried to include characteristics of speakers, Dialectology. The Polish-born American linguist Uriel Weinreich (1954) even called for a 'unified theory of language on which both could operate' (388). In the wake of this awareness, a broader interest arose in the socio-cultural and psychological aspects of language use. A specific example of a sociolinguistic investigation that helped to lead the way to the establishment of the field of sociolinguistics was the one by the American Joshua Fishman (1958), who studied the alternation between the 'in'-like (/ɪn/) and the 'ing'-like (/ɪŋ/) pronunciation in the progressive suffix (i.e., the endings in words like 'working' and 'going') in the speech of children in the North-East of the United States. Another early sociolinguistic investigation, albeit with an educational angle, is the one by Richard Allsop (1958), a native of Guyana (South America), on the English language in the former colony British Guyana. An educational angle to language variation was also applied by the British sociologist Basil Bernstein, who produced a string of publications in which the connection was made between language perception and social class and between language use, social class, and educational success (Bernstein 1958, 1959, 1960, 1965). Two investigations in the United States by the American William Labov crucially contributed to the international recognition of the field, namely a study on dialect feature choices by the inhabitants of the island of Martha's Vineyard (Labov 1963) and a study on social and situational language variation in New York City (Labov 1966). These two studies (see 5.3.1, 7.4.8, and 18.6.2) are seen as important stepping stones towards the acknowledgement of Sociolinguistics as an organised discipline. Koerner (1991) envisaged the work by William Labov as the synthesis of various lines of research from several generations of researchers from various fields.

Other names that are often mentioned as being at the root of modern-day Sociolinguistics other than William Labov are Basil Bernstein (see 6.3.3), Dell Hymes (see 4.4), John Gumperz (see 18.5.1), Charles Ferguson (see 6.3.5), and, for instance, Joshua Fishman (see 1.4.2 and 3.5.4), some of whom have been mentioned in this chapter already. Koerner (1991) referred specifically to the publication of the proceedings of two American conferences on **ethnography** and language variation in the mid-1960s (Bright 1966; Gumperz and Hymes 1964). At these conferences, some of these scholars had the opportunity to present their findings to each other and the scientific community. Variationist and Interactional Sociolinguistics were the main approaches, that is, the study of the correlates between social and linguistic factors and the study of the language as used in interaction (see 2.3.2 and 18.5). Because of the linguistic and cultural background of these researchers, a powerful Anglo-Western signature was given to the field (see 4.2).

1.5   Conclusion

An important part of the development of an academic field is understanding where its origins lie. What were the reasons for its coming to existence and how have these reasons developed over time into the rise of the field? The sources of Sociolinguistics are diverse, both theoretically and methodologically. It is a relatively new field, which arose from the awareness that various existing independent disciplines could be combined.

There is a discrepancy between the time when the name 'Sociolinguistics' started to be used and the actual rise of the field. Sociolinguistic activity was taking place in various countries (more than are mentioned in this chapter) before this name came into common use. These investigations and the growing awareness that was behind them largely stayed restricted to these countries. It wasn't until the early 1960s that the circumstances were right for a more explicit and international acknowledgement of the field.

STUDY QUESTIONS

1. Is Sociolinguistics more of a theory or a methodology?
2. When did Sociolinguistics start?
3. What do you know about the sociolinguistic tradition in your country of origin?

FURTHER READING

Focussing mainly on Western philosophical and critical academic developments, Koerner (1991) discusses the history of Sociolinguistics and gives overviews of how intellectuals and researchers influenced each other. Malkiel (1976) discusses the role of dialectological research in Romance languages in Europe as an important predecessor of modern Sociolinguistics. The volume edited by Ammon et al. (2004) contains a set of articles on both Western and non-Western sociolinguistic activity from before the 1960s.

Sociolinguistics Today

The Modern Study of Language in a Social Space

2

2.1 Introduction

Language varies from person to person and from moment to moment. Every individual speaks differently from every other individual. No one is completely consistent in the way they speak at different points in time. At the same time, everyone's language has much in common with that of many others and patterns can be found in the way individuals produce language under certain circumstances. Forces causing language variation are people's personalities, their personal characteristics (like gender and age), their intentions, their degree of literacy, their social lives, and all kinds of specific circumstances in which they use language on a daily basis. More broadly, these forces include the cultural, economic, political, and historical space in which language is produced. Modern Sociolinguistics describes the nature of such language variation patterns and the forces determining them.

This chapter introduces the discipline of modern Sociolinguistics. It first explains what today's sociolinguists are interested in and what they actually do. After that, it explains how this relatively new discipline has since its inception become increasingly identifiable as a separate field. It then presents the directions in which the field is currently moving and various challenges and opportunities that modern-day sociolinguists face. Finally, the purpose of Sociolinguistics is explained, especially its potential to contribute to linguistic theory and to raise awareness amongst ordinary language users as to the effect of language variation on their daily lives.

2.2 Sociolinguistics

2.2.1 What are sociolinguists interested in?

Sociolinguists like to study any type of language variation, be it individual or grouped, controllable or less controllable, conscious or less conscious, intentional or less intentional. Oftentimes, this is variation that is not obvious and patterned but, instead, is not too noticeable and is seemingly unsystematic. Generally, these researchers are not too eager to call variation meaningless or random unless there is evidence that it is in fact unpredictable and free from any type of symbolic or stigmatised value and that it is used beyond any degree of consciousness or control. Research generally focuses on language patterns that are produced, evaluated, or perceived in certain situations.

The research interests of sociolinguists are very broad. To them, speaker-related characteristics do not only include predictable ones – like age, gender, or **ethnicity** – but also speakers' intentions and motivations. The setting in which the language is produced is also viewed from many angles: historical, cultural, economic, and even political. Language-related characteristics of interest to sociolinguists include pronunciation and word choice, most notably, but also hard to grasp aspects such as pragmatics (the untold meanings of utterances when used in a certain way in a certain situation) and intonation patterns. These three elements of interest (speaker, setting and language use) come together in Sociolinguistics.

2.2.2 What do sociolinguists do?

So, what does this come down to in practice? Sociolinguistic research tries to lay bare correlations amongst speakers, settings, and language uses. Research is geared towards understanding the basic question of how language functions as both a practical and symbolic tool in communication. The practical, core function of language is exchanging information, while the symbolic function lies in giving our audience hints as to how we feel; we express our identity and mood as well as our motivations and intentions. We can express these explicitly in the content of what we say or we can express them less explicitly in **speech style** (through choice of words, prosody, or, perhaps, silences). To try and understand this symbolic function, all kinds of social and linguistic factors need to be described and all kinds of communicative settings need to be taken into consideration.

A wide range of investigations is possible. One could, for instance, investigate the social and communicative circumstances under which an admixture of languages is produced by individuals; this admixture is called codeswitching (see 3.6). Finding language varieties that can be defined on social (other than linguistic) grounds is also a common topic of research. Other themes that sociolinguists study are how people express their individual identity or the identity of the group they belong to through language and also how one language becomes more socially dominant in a speech community than another. The study of language use as found in new media, such as Facebook and Twitter, is a more recent interest of researchers. The effects of language policy on language use and the study of slang language are interests as well. The final example of a research theme is the **power** and prestige (or lack thereof) that is associated with certain ways of communicating. These examples demonstrate the broad range of approaches and interests of the field, which at the same time consistently takes language use as its specific focus.

Listening tests, surveys, corpora, interviews, and many more methodologies and sources are used in these investigations (see Chapters 17–20). Sociolinguists tend to approach the same subjects in various ways, through various methods. This principle – called 'triangulation' – leads to a broad range of methodological approaches. Combined with the naturally broad range of topics, this principle makes for a very lively field of investigation; one that constantly tries to stay on top of ongoing developments by finding new techniques and theoretical explanations of language use in changing societies and by linguistically versatile individuals.

2.2.3 Waves of research

In its short lifetime, the field of mainstream Sociolinguistics has already known three waves, and we are currently in the third one. During the first wave, the correlation between language and speaker/listener characteristics was the dominant interest. The nature of the communicative setting and the power relationship between 'interlocutors' (i.e., the people talking to each other) were typically also factored in. During the second wave, more efforts were made to discover the reasons behind these correlations. Members of communities (i.e., people who have something in common, including language or language features) were treated as active agents who decide on the nature and intensity of variation. That way, researchers tried to grasp the mechanisms behind variation and change more than first-wave researchers did. Groups of speakers were still an important focus in this second wave.

KEY CONCEPTS

Essentialism

'Essentialism' refers to the view that people have a fixed set of basic attributes, including language, that determine their identity. In the Social Sciences, such an approach is generally considered flawed, because of the common lack of homogeneity of groups, the fact that individuals vary their behaviour constantly, and the fact that speakers may associate with more than one group. Modern Sociolinguistics also challenges essentialist views in which certain socially definable groups with certain characteristics (for instance, biological or cultural) show a relatively predictable and stable behavioural pattern (Bucholtz 2003).

The third wave emphasises the notion that the members of a community practise and learn and are instruments in the construction of identities. Individuals are considered to define, construct, and take on identities through language while being constantly influenced by contact with speakers from their own and other **social spaces**. The Belgian sociolinguist and linguistic anthropologist Jan Blommaert (2010) summarised the change in

research focus as a 'shift from language to resources' (181), so from describing the language to describing the way individuals apply it and then finding
out why language is the way it is. He also mentioned a shift away from the
Saussurian approach (see 1.4.1) of language being tied – to time, to place, to
a set of speakers sharing qualities, and to local functions – to the approach
of language as a means towards mobility and meeting all kinds of personal
wishes. In these new spaces, the traditional meanings of linguistic signs are
becoming detached from their static meanings, and meanings are themselves
reconsidered. Meanings then become situational and context-dependent.

FOCUS ON...

Cognition

Meyerhoff (2011) mentioned another trend in modern Sociolinguistics,
namely the cognitive approach, with researchers exploring and combining
production and perception rather than merely looking at the language people produce. If you know how an individual evaluates and perceives language
and language structures, then this can be used as a factor to explain their
language choices.

2.3   Today's Sociolinguistics

2.3.1 Still a diverse field

Because of its history in both the Humanities and the Social Sciences,
Sociolinguistics has since its beginnings been a diverse field. More so than
many other linguistic subdisciplines, it combines approaches. Experimental
settings in controlled laboratory environments are inspired by applied
psychological research, Sociology and Social Psychology have contributed
several theories and methodologies, and Anthropology-inspired ethnographic
techniques are often used as well. History, politics, and culture are taken into
consideration as factors determining language as well. Nevertheless, the field
falls unequivocally into the Linguistics arena and uses linguistic variation as
its main inspiration.

Over the decades, approaches have arisen that are considered typically
sociolinguistic, which means that the field has matured considerably as
an independent discipline. Related fields have also arisen that are inspired
by the more social and cultural aspects of language variation. These go
by several names; for instance, **Linguistic Anthropology**, Ethnography of
Communication, Sociocultural Linguistics, and the Sociology of Language.
The dividing lines between some of these fields and Sociolinguistics are
sometimes hard to draw.

> **KEY CONCEPTS**
>
> **Sociology of Language and Sociolinguistics**
>
> Sociology of Language studies the effects that language variation has on **society**, with society as the object of study. Sociolinguistics studies, amongst others, the effects that society has on language and takes language as its main point of interest.

2.3.2 Types of Sociolinguistics

Types of Sociolinguistics are described here. It should be clear that these subfields to a degree look more like methodological approaches than theoretical fields. Individual researchers will have their own style and preferences – they attach more value to certain types of findings than to others and have their own preferred methodological and theoretical styles.

The most conventional (and 'old') type of approach is Variationist Sociolinguistics, which pays attention mostly to the correlations between social and linguistic variables. Methodologically, variationist researchers will often try and find people producing spontaneous and natural language; for instance, on television or in shops. They will then document this language, find out about characteristics of the speakers, and subsequently correlate the linguistic and social factors. These sociolinguists are interested in both 'synchronic variation' (in the present time) and 'diachronic variation' (occurring over time). Interactional Sociolinguistics uses discourse analysis (see 18.5) to study how language users create meaning via social interaction. This subfield is interested in intercultural miscommunication and communication between people who are somehow different (like men and women) and in another topic that is relevant when individuals communicate with each other, namely politeness. Audio- and video-recordings of people interacting function as important sources of data in this type of approach. (Social) Constructionist Sociolinguistics is another (yet more recent) subfield and involves paying much attention to the meaning (rather than just the patterns) of language variation. Language choices of individuals in specific contexts and how these lead to identity formation are important interests of this subfield. Power relations amongst speakers are also a major focus, especially as part of social theories (how societies as well as individuals in societies operate) and of cultural theories (how cultures and people in cultural settings operate). Interviewing people is an important research tool for constructionist sociolinguists, because the researcher wants to find out about motivations. The three types of Sociolinguistics are interested in ethnographic approaches, which are methodologies involving behaviour within a group of people within a certain cultural context.

KEY CONCEPTS

Macro-/Micro-Sociolinguistics

Another distinction that is often made is between Macro-Sociolinguistics and Micro-Sociolinguistics. The former investigates how language varieties are distributed. Language varieties as a whole are the object of study and how they are grouped. Language planning is part of this level of thinking about language variation. The latter type of Sociolinguistics looks at individual speakers, groups of speakers, separate words and sounds, and other low-level variables, and it tries to find behavioural and other patterns.

2.3.3 New developments

Globalisation and superdiversity

So, while Sociolinguistics traditionally looked to groups of people and their speech habits, nowadays a more individualised and situational approach is additionally applied. Globalisation is taking place, which refers to the effects of increased contact and integration amongst people from all over the world. There is a strong awareness that in a globalising world, with increasing mobilities, speakers should be viewed as individuals with highly versatile skills and specific motivations, who choose their own customised paths in life. While it might be estimated that a majority of people in the world stay more or less in one regional or socioeconomic space throughout their lives, the percentage of highly individualised life trajectories not part of those fixed and predictable circumstances is increasing. Due to this, people's exposure to languages and speakers outside their (comfortable and familiar) original social realm is becoming more common. The individual is confronted more often than before with the effects of the way they speak (because it deviates from how others around them speak) and may feel the need to express personal identity more. Modern-day sociolinguists try to capture these individualised language choices. The term 'superdiversity' (Vertovec 2007) is often mentioned in this context and refers to the fact that nowadays levels of diversity in certain places (especially urban ones) are higher than ever before; culturally, ethnically, and in many other ways (and linguistically as a result).

Blommaert and Rampton (2011) observed a **paradigm** shift in Sociolinguistics and suggested that Sociolinguistics and Anthropology should theoretically and methodologically engage with superdiversity and the social changes it is based on. Superdiversity is based on the assumption that today's mass migrations lead to a degree and type of diversity that cannot be compared with that of earlier periods of migration. The category of 'migrants' is now less easily outlineable and does not have fixed sociocultural features. Many of them see the whole world and not their own regional or local space as a potential place where their personal, professional, and academic development could take place. They are not necessarily economic or political refugees, although that is an often made association. More so than before, migrants maintain close contact with their homeland – digitally and through travel – and mix and mingle with migrants with other ethnic backgrounds and with natives from the country they live in. They use and combine all kinds of styles and languages in a systematic way, depending on the nature of the audience and specific circumstances.

KEY CONCEPTS

Languaging

Research into superdiversity is associated with 'languaging', which refers to humans producing language as part of the effort to achieve their goals and deal with complex social activities. It is associated with language learning and language use, where learners engage in language-related activities together and learn to use language that way (Swain 1985). In multilingual contexts, 'translanguaging' is often used to refer to this phenomenon; multilingual language users strategically employ multiple semiotic resources to achieve their goals, including their full multilingual repertoire (Garcia and Wei 2014). In the ensuing process of using, mixing, and choosing between languages, a new discourse entity arises, one could say.

Reinterpretations of language, communication, and speaker groups

Blommaert and Rampton (2011) explained how languages, communication, and speakers may be viewed differently. Rather than looking at languages as ideological constructs that are historically tied to the **nation state** (Spanish or Russian as belonging to Spain and Russia, for instance), one could view language as 'individual linguistic features with identifiable social and cultural associations' (4). Communication can also be interpreted less predictably, namely not as a system but as a set of communicative practices. It changes from setting to setting and should be studied in each of these. Knowledge of language is merely a resource that individuals borrow from. The meanings of words vary per situation, and meaning itself is not just communicated through language but also through other means, like gestures or signs (see 6.2). Communication setting is also fluid in that it combines features that the speaker has picked up from all kinds of experiences, including global experiences. These are mixed with more personal and localised styles, and this is done systematically. Groups of speakers, finally, are nowadays also viewed differently. Entities called 'speech community' (group of people whose language shares many features) or '**ethnolinguistic** group' have been superseded by entities like 'communities of practice' (see 5.5.2), 'institutions', and 'networks' (see 5.5.1), which presume a degree of mobility and flexibility in language use.

Power as a factor   **FOCUS ON...**

These days, the awareness of changed demographics bringing about new types of identity formation has led to variation being considered as part of a power paradigm. The writings of the French sociologist and philosopher Pierre Bourdieu, especially in his book 'Language and Symbolic Power' (Bourdieu 1991), have intensified awareness of the notion that language is used as a power symbol in interactions. Power, then, is 'discursive', meaning that our practices of using language – i.e. our 'discourse' – express and shape it. This motivation behind language use is often seen in an 'oppressor versus oppressed' paradigm, a system of thought in which one party dominates the other. Some have power and they often dominate those who do not. In this view, the widely acknowledged proper way to speak a language is used not only as a means to signal membership of the powerful group but also as a means to stay in that group – with all its privileges – through symbolic linguistic distinction. It is also used to keep others out.

Impact of technology on the individual experience

The globalising individual is digitally and technologically mobile, besides geographically and socially. LaGrandeur (2014) explained how there is an increasing intertwining of human and intelligent technology, in which the two are becoming like subsystems in a larger system. Elliott (2016) added that the massive technological transformations and the increased mobility that are currently unfolding have led to a 'metamorphosis of identity' (7). He described how we live in an age of 'fascination for the renewal, recalibration and reinvention of identities' (2) and that identity formation nowadays is shaped and reshaped at the level of the 'affective, fantasy-driven, desire-laden investments of the human subject.' (14). Danesi (2016) explained how modern developments are even changing communicative competence.

New methodologies

The more traditional variationist approach of defining groups of speakers on the basis of characteristics or sets of characteristics is as alive as ever. Nevertheless, with the waves of research have come shifts in methodology, and more traditional methodologies have come under critical scrutiny. The labelling of people and their language utterances leads to clear results but fails to provide answers in many cases; it merely points out and does not explain. Another drawback of this approach is that a complicated creature like a human being is reduced to a handful of labels and all kinds of circumstances (personality, specific mood, specific situation) are simply ignored, although these may be the main determinants of the language produced. Based on numerical output based on the correlations of social labels and linguistic output, all kinds of generalisations about the effects of gender, age, social background, and other characteristics come out of these investigations. Statistically significant differences often seem to emphasise differences which may in fact be relatively subtle (both groups use a form a lot but one uses it slightly more often).

There is currently increasing attention for big datasets, such as written and spoken corpora, which are often available online. Large language corpora are used to draw statistically relevant conclusions on lexical and grammatical choices by certain populations, and these findings can help traditional variationist research, which runs the risk of drawing conclusions pertaining to large groups in society on the basis of small sets of participants or language items. Speech corpora are also being constructed in which 'ordinary' speech is recorded for research purposes (see 17.2). Besides this quantitative broadening of datasets, the possibility of indepth analysis has become available due to technological advances. Acoustic measurements (see 16.3.2) and statistical testing (see Chapter 15) are easy to perform and have made analyses more systematic and reliable. Online testing tools and social media as research tools are also very accessible. Ease of travel makes visits to far-away communities more feasible.

There is also the increasing attention for more qualitative approaches that explore in more depth why speakers speak the way they do. Finding out speaker motivation can be done by talking to speakers, interviewing them. Observing natural speech by becoming a participant in communities is another popular method of research that really digs into the life of the individual speaker rather than describing a group from a distance. Blommaert and Rampton (2011) pointed out that the context in which communication takes place as well as the meaning of language and symbolism in a certain context should not be assumed but determined through investigation. This means that communication settings and the typical nature of groups of people should be researched, not merely the language. These approaches are in line with the one taken by Heller (2007), who considered language use to be a process in which languages are not whole, independent systems but linguistic resources that speakers draw from under specific circumstances. To study language, then, social practice, **ideology**, and social organisation need to be studied in relation to language.

New interests and terminologies

Research into new areas is not only leading to new methodologies but also to new terminology. Besides the interest in superdiversity and globalisation, there is a constant extension of the field into the study of topics like new media, digital communication, literacies, and creativities of individuals. The language of individuals, in particular online language and language used in urban contexts, is currently being rediscovered. Modern-day researchers are trying to find patterns and explanations for the language they encounter and are developing new definitions, needed to come to grips with what is encountered. A few examples are: 'self-styling', 'language policing', 'ideospace', 'reflexivity', 'authentication', 'languaging', 'translanguaging', 'polylanguaging', 'linguistic appropriation', 'translocality', '(language) crossing', 'cool', 'self', and 'other'. Some of these terms are borrowed from other academic fields. Each of these in their own way illustrates new ways of thinking about differences between individual speakers under different circumstances and about variation in the language of individuals. All of these terms are discussed in this book (see the index of this book for specific references).

2.4   The purpose of Sociolinguistics

2.4.1 Role within Formal Linguistics

The social approach to language is different from the one that is traditionally applied in **Formal Linguistics**. Formal linguists often view language as a closed system, that is, one that is written down in books, is static, and that changes with time mainly. The language referred to could be called 'Modern Hindi', 'Rumanian', or 'Middle English', or it could denote a group of dialects that share features or a specific dialect from a town, area, or island. The forces that change the language in question are usually searched for in language itself, like the nature of related languages. When it comes to low-level sound change, surrounding phonemes and place of a sound in the syllable are often used to explain change. Another point of consideration for formal linguists is the general tendency of word meaning, grammar, and pronunciation to undergo change as well as the ease with which certain sound clusters are pronounced. Linguists usually investigate descriptions of languages and language systems as noted down by scholars over the centuries. Such descriptions and the analyses based on them have been successful in laying bare patterns in historical language change; however, they also tend to overlook the interactional aspect in linguistic change, which is discussed here.

Thomason and Kaufman (1988) elaborately explained how 'language contact' (people with different languages or styles talking to each other; see 3.4.1) leads to linguistic change and how mainstream Linguistics has come late to this knowledge. They demonstrated how investigating language from a sociolinguistic point of view is fundamental in explaining language change. Existing analyses about the forces bringing about language change might be complemented by a sociolinguistic approach; one focussing on speakers as actors who change language rather than assuming that language apparently changes itself. Variation is the start of this line of thought, because differences between people's daily language use lie at the heart of low-level language change. People do not just start speaking slightly differently en masse but instead individuals at some points in time pronounce something differently from the rest or slightly adjust the meaning of a certain word, and those small adjustments may be copied by others. Sociolinguistic research, especially that which focuses on the finer aspects of language, such as pronunciation, can lay bare **intra-speaker variation** (in the speech of an individual) and **inter-speaker variation** (between speakers) that speakers themselves are not aware of but that is likely to be a low-level trigger of change. Language change could be viewed as being the result of many individuals using language in various (patterned) ways in daily communication. Language is passed on intergenerationally, and every generation finds itself speaking slightly differently from the previous one, which means that somehow in the totality of daily communication changes occur during our own lifetimes. These changes are not solely motivated by the language itself; an individual does not necessarily consciously choose a certain language form on the basis of ease of articulation, for instance. In fact, they often pronounce things differently from what would be easiest for them. The reason why they do this is because one way of saying something has a certain effect in the conversation or because it accentuates a certain aspect of their personality or background.

FOCUS ON...

Limited effects of language contact

Gumperz (1967) associated people who are in constant contact over longer periods of time but do not adopt each other's speech patterns with highly stratified societies like the caste societies of India. However, in less rigidly stratified societies, close contact may also not lead to assimilation. The pronunciation of speakers of Dutch as it is spoken in the Netherlands and in neighbouring Flanders would start to sound similar if the intensity of contact between people and mutual exposure were the main determinants. However, research in the Dutch-speaking area (Van de Velde 1996) showed that speakers in these two areas tend to maintain or even enhance the differences, despite close mutual contact.

This is not to say that Sociolinguistics has so far acted outside the realm of Linguistics. In fact, as Walker (2010) explained, while well-known theoretical linguistic theories like **Optimality Theory** and **Minimalism** have hardly shaped the directions in which sociolinguistic theory has moved, sociolinguists are contributing to linguistic theory. This is demonstrated by Cornips (1998), who made a connection between the social variation of syntactic structures and syntactic theory. Meyerhoff (2011) added that formal linguists are for their part recognising and taking an interest in language variation the way sociolinguists approach it.

2.4.2 Explaining the unexplained

Formal Linguistics has failed to explain why everyone does not speak the same language by now. Sociolinguistics appeals to those who ask themselves the important question of why people don't start sounding like each other more and more if education keeps spreading messages as to what is correct and incorrect in language. Traditional media like television and radio, furthermore, are said to accelerate homogenisation of languages. Nevertheless, despite all these forces that would logically lead to mutual linguistic sameness, people still often choose not to sound like each other or abide by the norm.

Besides understandability of messages, there are, apparently, other forces at work that make people want to sound different from other people. As Joseph (2010) pointed out, 'If communication were the only function of language, we could expect all mother-tongue speakers of English or any other language to sound more or less the same' (9). In other words, people want to be understood and blend in, but at the same time they don't always want to wholly assimilate to their environment. Social assimilation is not the only force at work, social distinction is as well. Besides facts, speakers constantly express affect. This is a part of communication that is difficult to fathom, and much sociolinguistic work still needs to be done to understand it.

2.4.3 Practical applications

Other than theoretical contributions, there are very practical ways in which sociolinguistic knowledge can be useful. It helps us understand why people use language in different ways and that this is not automatically a result of intelligence or skill. It also helps us teach children that what is generally considered good language is not necessarily richer or more systematic linguistically but simply the variety that is chosen as a practical communication tool.

The practical application of sociolinguistic research receives more interest in some societies than in others. Rickford (2016), in fact, assessed that the prevalence of theory over application is particularly strong in Western and relatively developed regions like North America, Western Europe, Japan, New Zealand and Australia. In other regions (Rickford gave the Caribbean and West Africa as examples), the application of linguistic research to tackle educational and nation-development issues is much more common.

In court, the detailed study of intonation and word choice may reveal that certain speaker types are systematically treated differently and that in general power relations that exist in society at large are active in the legal system as well, and usually at the expense of the traditionally weaker members (Eades 2010; Lippi-Green 1994, 2012). Another field of interest is education in a broad sense (Lawson and Sayers 2016); traditional teaching contexts like schools, but also public education projects, like museums. The authors in the Lawson and Sayers volume explained the potential of the influence of sociolinguistic research on professional practice in all kinds of organisations, like the police, as well as the impact on language policy.

There are more such practical applications, and many of them come down to raising awareness, amongst others about the language between doctor and patient and between teacher and pupil (Bernstein 1961, 1964). This is how Sociolinguistics can be viewed; as a scholarly science that reveals patterns that deepen our understanding of how people communicate. By demonstrating how power relations are revealed in language style, other than in information communication, Sociolinguistics can be a way to create awareness of bias and prejudice when it comes to how language is used and abused and how it is perceived and misperceived. Ultimately, it is a science that looks for patterns in human behaviour and tries to understand them.

2.5   Conclusion

This chapter has provided a bird's-eye view of the field of Sociolinguistics and the activity and thought that takes place in it. Because of its interdisciplinary background, the field draws from a broad range of methodologies and theoretical angles, while its focus is limited to explaining language use (of groups and individuals).

The field of Sociolinguistics has developed rapidly under the influence of changes in the world and developments in scientific awareness. While early sociolinguists focussed on groups of speakers who had social and linguistic features in common, there has been a shift to viewing language as a tool that individuals use to achieve communicative and symbolic goals and that they vary amongst communicative contexts. Language is seen as a way to exert and maintain power. Language, communication, and speaker groups are seen as highly fluid rather than static entities. Knowing about the mechanisms behind these entities is insightful for many theoretical and practical reasons. At the same time, the essentialist approach, which looks at language as an entity rather than a process and which presumes the existence of boundaries between languages, is still very much alive. These two approaches are not necessarily at odds with each other.

STUDY QUESTIONS

1. Can you come up with examples that demonstrate where Sociolinguistics ends and Sociology of Language starts? Where do you draw the dividing line? Which criteria do you use? Is it a hard and fast dividing line?
2. To which degree is there such a thing as 'noise' in language production from a sociolinguistic perspective? Is there variation in the way sounds or words are produced that is completely meaningless in every possible way? Can you give an example?
3. Which languages do you speak and which styles? Which do you speak in which context?

FURTHER READING

Textbooks

The introduction to Sociolinguistics by the New Zealander Miriam Meyerhoff (2011) pays much attention to theory and to social aspects and contains many lively and down to earth examples and explanations. Mesthrie et al. (2010) also comes highly recommended and has as an advantage that several authors (from South Africa, the United States, and the United Kingdom) wrote it. The introduction to the field by the German Florian Coulmas (2013) focuses on the choices that individual speakers make under different circumstances and in doing so takes a relatively culture-independent approach.

Monographs, handbooks, and other textbooks are also available. Examples are Ammon et al. (2004), Bell (2013), Danesi (2016), Friginal and Hardy (2014), Meyerhoff and Nagy (2008), Mallinson et al. (2013), and Friedrich and Diniz de Figueiredo (2016). Each of these has its own specific approach – like multilingualism (Meyerhoff and Nagy), corpus research (Friginal and Hardy), digital communication (Friedrich and Diniz de Figueiredo) – while at the same time discussing the field as a whole. An overview of theoretical debates can be found in Coupland (2016). These books are sometimes difficult to read.

Many introductory books are strongly based in mainstream, Anglo-Western tradition and are written and inspired by a relatively small group of Anglophone scholars. They often tend to draw examples from the cultures that the authors are from. It is therefore worthwhile trying to find an introduction to Sociolinguistics from the country or region you are interested in. Examples of such specific sociolinguistic introductions are the one on the Arab region by Albirini (2016), the handbook on Hispanic Sociolinguistics compiled by Díaz-Campos (2011), the edited volume on sociolinguistic aspects of Singaporean society by Evangelos and Kuo (1980), the introduction to Chinese Sociolinguistics by Dil (1976), and the edited volume on South African Sociolinguistics by Mesthrie (1995). Alternatively, general introductions into the field written in a more local language are an option for researchers who want more information on a certain region. For example, Chaer and Agustina (2010) and Nababan (1993) are suitable for those interested in a book in Bahasa Indonesia about general Sociolinguistics and Indonesian Sociolinguistics. Another example is the Russian introduction to the field by Švejcer and Nikol'skij (1978). Such regionally focussed introductions contain many insightful examples from the region. They are generally relatively traditional in their approach, applying Variationist Sociolinguistic principles mainly and taking dialects and other forms of language as well as groups of speakers as their main point of departure.

Journals

The most well-known international journals available are in English, and important ones are *Language in Society*, the *International Journal of the Sociology of Language, Language Variation and Change, Discourse and Society*, the *Journal of Linguistic Anthropology*, and the *Journal of Sociolinguistics*. The *International Journal of the Sociology of Language* is known for covering a particularly wide range of regions and languages and catering to a particularly international audience of authors. It may well be that the topic you are interested in is covered in one of their volumes. Journals in other languages are available too, such as the *Journal of Chinese Sociolinguistics*, which is mostly in Mandarin Chinese. Descriptions of many interesting local situations are available in articles in such journals. An example is Dular (1986), which is in Slovenian and which deals with a specific language situation in Slovenia and is published in *Slavistična Revija*, 'The Slavonics Journal'. Such articles often contain an abstract in English. Those interested in a certain area or language can look for articles like that. Unfortunately, the international journals are not usually available through Open Access but require an expensive subscription. Asking a colleague who works for a university where subscriptions to such journals is common (this is not true for all universities) is recommended; directly asking the author for a copy is another option.

Books on Applied Sociolinguistics

As for the practical application of Sociolinguistics, Lawson and Sayers (2016) provide an overview of international research projects that have contributed to understanding language variation and that have even led to practical and positive outcomes. In Trudgill (1984), a number of experts discuss how sociolinguistic findings can be of real-life value. These two books pay much attention to the methodologies that are part of such investigations.

Language Variation

The Many Shapes of Language

3.1 Introduction

The language that is codified in dictionaries, grammars, pronunciation guides, and schoolbooks deviates strongly from language in its most natural and original habitat, namely daily spoken and written communication. Sociolinguists distinguish between such a language norm and day-to-day language and in fact tend to be most interested in the latter. They need to be able to describe all kinds of uncodified and often very individual language uses. This requires the use of specialised terminology.

This chapter presents the various shapes that language use can take on and the terminology to point to these shapes. Terminology is introduced to refer to types of language use, both by groups and individuals, and the chapter explains the various connotations each term has. The coming into existence of the language shapes as well as how they interrelate (and often overlap) is explained as well. The important category of dialects is discussed next: how they are embedded in society, how their shapes and interpretations change, how they have been researched so far, and which new types have arisen.

3.2 Ways to refer to language use systems

3.2.1 Terminology

The choice of terms to denote language signifies the author's stance or approach to the language or language-related topic that they are describing. Some ways to refer to systems of using the available language tools (which could be called 'language use systems') denote ways that groups of speakers speak. Other terminology refers to more individual language use systems. Some terminology emphasises variation within the language of groups and of individuals, while other terminology presents language as a fixed system and pushes the importance of intra-speaker and inter-speaker variation to the background.

The word 'variety' is possibly the most-used term that refers to ways to use language and is a neutral way to denote the language use system to which individuals and groups adhere. A variety is typically a language that can be identified by speakers themselves and by others as being distinct in subtle or not so subtle ways from other varieties. The term can be used generically to avoid unwanted distinctions between less codified and more codified languages ('dialects' and 'standard languages' are all 'varieties', and so are, for instance, occupational varieties involving jargon).

Some of the terms include the syllable 'lect', which refers to a set of linguistic phenomena that can be recognised as an entity. A 'sociolect' is a variety defined on the basis of social grounds and is associated with a group of people who share certain qualities. For instance, in a Tamil-speaking region in India there are two sociolects, namely Mudaliyar and Iyengar. Mudaliyar is spoken by a lower caste than Iyengar, as the latter caste is associated with scholarliness. This is a social (rather than a regional) difference between the groups. There are also internationally known sociolects, like so-called 'Valley speak', or 'Valspeak', as well as 'Surfer talk', which are typical of younger speakers in Southern California in the United States (Macías et al. 2018). 'Hyperlect' is a name sometimes used for a certain sociolect, namely posh speech (Honey 1985). Poshness refers to a sociolect that is characterised by distinctive word choices and ways to pronounce certain sounds and certain words. A 'regiolect', which often has a name, is defined on the basis of geographical criteria. Latgalian, as spoken in Eastern Latvia, is a regiolect. An individual's unique language system, i.e., one's personalised variety, is often referred to as an 'idiolect'.

The term 'idiolect' is closely related to the word 'vernacular', which refers to the language used for everyday communication, i.e., a spontaneous language that comes naturally. The latter term is often also used to refer to a group's indigenous language, especially if that deviates from a wider language norm. 'African American Vernacular English', an urban vernacular from the United States, fits that particular meaning of the term. The word 'code' is used mostly in a context where the variety referred to is socially meaningful and individual speakers could consciously or subconsciously switch from one code to another (see 3.6), depending on the social information that they wish to communicate.

3.2.2 Style

Individuals will not simply switch on their sociolect or perhaps their regiolect and consistently use it in accordance with written and unwritten rules, irrespective of the situation and to whom they are talking. Instead, they will vary the use of these language use systems in specific ways, and they could even systematically mix systems under certain circumstances. The resultant variation is called 'stylistic variation'. The term 'style' refers to ways of speaking that are a result of accommodation of the language of the speaker to, amongst others, social circumstances (like degree of formality), qualities of the person to whom they are talking (e.g., the social status of that person), or goals of the conversation (e.g., persuading or discouraging). For now, it is important to distinguish between the use of a language use system and the application of stylistic variation within that system. Note that switching from one system to another might also be a stylistic choice.

> **EXAMPLE**
>
> **Speech levels in Indonesia**
>
> Stylistic variation can take on unexpected forms. Meyerhoff (2011) explained the phenomenon of different so-called 'speech levels' in some Indonesian languages, where a stylistic adjustment to social norms may lead to the replacement of words in one's speech so as to speak one of the three speech levels (low, middle, and high). The choice depends on the social status relative to one's own of the person to whom one is talking. The vocabulary could for stylistic reasons actually be replaced completely while the sentence structure remains the same.

3.3 Dialect

3.3.1 Definition

The word 'dialect' typically refers to a language from a certain region, city, town, or village. It is often contrasted with a larger and codified language. Dialects are traditionally placed at the far end of a 'dialect continuum' that ranges from the language norm to linguistically related language varieties that strongly deviate from it. Such a continuum may cross national borders. Dialects may deviate from that larger language to such an extent that they are less understandable to those who don't speak them as a native tongue but who do speak the **norm language** or another dialect. Some countries are known for having many mutually difficult-to-understand dialects (for instance, China and India), while others are known for having relatively few widely diverging dialects in view of the geographical spread of language varieties, due to all kinds of historical reasons (for instance, Russia and Australia). Between the dialect and the norm language, intermediate varieties may exist, like *Obecná čeština* ('Common Czech') in the Czech Republic or *Tussentaal* ('in-between language') in Flanders – used in informal communication or as a neutral **lingua franca** amongst speakers with various degrees of command of the norm language or a dialect and which over the generations grew into the native tongue of speakers.

Dialects can take on unexpected forms and do not always need to be part of a predictable dialect continuum. The Transcarpathian dialects of the Ukraine, for instance, are not only very different from Standard Ukrainian (a Slavic language) but also very different from neighbouring dialects and from surrounding Slavic and non-Slavic languages. These dialects carry linguistic elements from Hungarian, German, Polish, Slovakian, Russian, Romanian, and Yiddish.

FOCUS ON...

Nation-building and the recognition of dialects

Usually, there is tension between territorial nationalism and linguistic diversity. In some countries in South Asia, for instance, nation-building has typically focussed on dominant and monocultural nationality, while at the same time interacting with a reality that is multicultural. Country borders are often ideologically equated with cultural and ethnic borders and also with linguistic borders. In Japan, if speakers fall within the political borders of the country, then their culture and language tend to be treated officially as being Japanese, irrespective of linguistic distance or relatedness to Japanese culture and language. For example, the Ryukyus islands, between mainland Japan and Taiwan, were an independent kingdom until 1872 when Japan annexed them. The Ryukyu languages were from that moment on treated as Japanese dialects, despite being linguistically deviant from Japanese.

3.3.2 Connotations and associations

The words 'dialect' and 'accent' come with very strong connotations. Accent is, simply, a reference to pronunciation, but this word is often (incorrectly) used in popular discourse to refer to the deviation of someone's pronunciation from that of the norm language. To some people, comments like 'you have an accent' or 'you speak a dialect' are suggestive of deviations from the norm language that are almost like a medical condition. Others take pride in their regional origin and don't mind – and in fact prefer it – if someone can hear where their geographical roots lie. To linguists, dialects denote fully-fledged linguistic systems that develop naturally from generation to generation. It should be noted that while the norm language often has the higher status and is by some considered to be the more logical and 'better' tongue, traditional dialects most commonly form the basis of norm languages, may be linguistically more consistent (less meddled with by language prescriptivists), and often predate the norm language.

The stereotypical speakers of dialects are rural people, as is reflected in the description of typical dialect speakers (in a European setting) as given by Chambers and Trudgill (1980), namely the so-called 'NORMs' (Non-mobile Older Rural Males). A popular association of dialect speakers is that they live away from the city in a relatively secluded area. However, the term 'dialect' is nowadays increasingly used to also refer to varieties that are typical of cities. Goeman (2000) put forward the urban equivalents of NORMs, the MYSFs (Mobile Younger Suburban Females). This group will typically be more likely to speak a more urban dialect or a dialect that is between that of a large city dialect and a broader language norm.

3.3.3 Drawing dialect borders

Linguistic Geography generally refers to drawing borders between uncodified spoken smaller languages. Often referred to as Dialect Geography, it has its origins in the study of characteristics of regional dialects. The fear of rural dialect disappearance in countries across the world led to efforts to describe them, mostly in the nineteenth and twentieth century (see 17.3). Empirical studies, especially European ones, involved descriptions of the speech of older speakers who were not too mobile and were assumed to be representative speakers of dialects. With these descriptions, dividing lines between dialects, called 'isoglosses', were made apparent. Various aspect of dialects – most notably the pronunciation of words or the way to refer to objects (tools, tree types, etc.) – can be geographically delineated. By viewing the geographical positioning of isoglosses and particularly the areas where they bundle together, researchers can separate different regional dialects and smaller subdialects. These linguistic divisions often coincide with political, ethnic, religious, or with physical boundaries such as rivers, mountains, and deserts. On the basis of a combination of historical and empirical research, dialect atlases have been created for many regions in the world. These maps visually describe dialects and dialect groups.

EXAMPLE

Dialect research

The French dialectologists Jules Guilliéron and Edmond Edmont composed a questionnaire of about 1,900 words and phrases. Edmont then undertook surveys in 639 places in France using this questionnaire. He took to the road and travelled from one place to the next, by bike or public transport, and in every town he asked dialect speakers to indicate how certain things were pronounced locally or what the local word was for certain objects. With these data, and after years of travel, he and Guilliéron were able to draw a series of maps of French dialects, called *Atlas Linguistique de la France*, 'Linguistic Atlas of France', which was published in several editions (Guilliéron and Edmont 1902–1910). These maps are still regarded as reflecting important dialect divisions in France today.

Traditional 'regional dialectology' (the study of the geographical spread of dialects that uses the mapping of individual linguistic features) and 'social dialectology' (the study of linguistic variation that is dependent on the groups the speakers are members of and their participation in those groups) are no longer practiced only through traditional methods. Modern-day variations of these disciplines have arisen. One way is to enter known data on modern dialects (word use and pronunciation mainly) into a computer programme and determine how many changes a certain language item needs to undergo before it is equal to an equivalent language item of a geographically adjacent community of speakers (Heeringa et al. 2015; Beijering et al. 2008). The idea is that rather than looking at a linguistic item as a whole, it is broken down into parts, and the researcher checks how many changes the version of one dialect needs to undergo to become like the equivalent of the adjacent dialect. Rather than hard and fast dividing lines on the basis of whole words or whole phonemes distinguishing one dialect from another, more detailed transitions between one dialect and the next can be drawn when number of changes and degree of change are factored in.

Drawing borders between languages of all kinds of shapes and sizes is sometimes difficult. Such borders are usually drawn on the basis of a combination of characteristics: geographical ones (rivers, mountains, deserts) and, for instance, linguistic, political, historical, cultural, and ethnic ones. Stell (2014) found racial, socio-historic, and regional dividing lines between language varieties in Namibia but in a situation in which speakers of various races and backgrounds would live side by side, albeit often in separated communities. Because of this variation in criteria and because simple dialect continua (see 3.3.1) are not a rule, such borders are often fluid.

EXAMPLE

Real versus traditional dialect borders

Morgenstierne (1961) investigated the languages of India and reacted to what he found on earlier dialect maps. About the Dardic dialect groups he said that 'there is not a single common feature distinguishing Dardic ... from the rest of Indo Aryan languages .... Dardic is simply a term to denote a bundle of aberrant Indo Aryan hill languages ....' (139). This shows that well-known dialect borders are often obsolete and based on unclear assumptions of earlier times.

If linguistic and other criteria are used to create dividing lines, then actual speakers might still disagree. Speakers of the Burmese dialects of Rakhaing, Intha, and Tavoyan, for instance, are geographically cut off from central Burmese, and speakers of these dialects view themselves as having a non-Burmese linguistic identity. Speakers of the Palaung varieties – as spoken by about half a million in a large region covering parts of Burma, China, and Thailand – by contrast, claim to speak one and the same language, although these dialects are not mutually intelligible (Müller and Weymouth 2016). Even linguists may disagree on the location of language borders, despite claiming to use facts to support their stance. The very existence of the Macedonian language as something apart from Bulgarian has been debated by Macedonian and Bulgarian linguists, with opposing sides using the same dialectal data to support their view. The same thing is true for the question of whether Kašubian, a language spoken within the Polish borders, is distinct from Polish.

3.3.4 Global dialects

Future research into the geographical distribution of language varieties will need to pay attention to a changing reality that includes an increased geographical mobility of people. While in the past regional origin was looked at rather statically, with people simply being from a certain region or town, it is becoming more common for people not to have a straightforward geographical background, because they moved around during their early years. This affects an individual's language. Examples include expatriate children, whose parents typically move to a different part of the world at some time during the child's formative years or who move regularly. The lives of these so-called 'global nomads' put ways of looking at geographical variation in a new perspective. These people live an international lifestyle, are highly mobile, and are not strongly emotionally or practically bound to a certain town or region. Their lifestyle is typically Western (Elliott and Urry 2011) even if they do not live or travel in the West. The children of these global nomad families can often be typified as 'third culture kids' (Pollock and Van Reken 2009), which refers to children raised in a place and culture (the 'second culture') that is different from that of their parents (the 'first culture'). These children develop their own, unique culture, the 'third culture'. So, while the parents may have some connection with a country and culture, these children move between cultures while developing their personal linguistic and cultural identity.

Global nomads are often associated with English but they might also speak another transnational language, like Arabic, Spanish, Portuguese, Malay, or Swahili, depending on the regions in which they travel. They are typically multilingual. Global nomads do not usually adhere to the identity of native speakers in the country of origin of these languages (like Spanish identity if they speak Spanish) or the identity of speakers around them in the place where they happen to live. Instead, they draw their language norm from a more global norm that is more difficult to define.

3.4   New languages

3.4.1 New-dialect formation

Dialects may have been in an area for a long time, but they can also form within a few generations. Not only new dialects that arise in cities fall into this category but also dialects spoken by speakers in places where at one point there were no speakers. For instance, speakers may live on formerly drained land, like the Fens area in Eastern England, or in the 'new city' of Brasilia in Brazil. They may also live in a new town like Dronten, which is built in a polder (land reclaimed from the sea) in the Netherlands. The people moving into these places bring with them a certain language background. Modern Dialectology is interested in how the language of consecutive generations of speakers in these places develops. This is the study of 'new-dialect formation'. Research by the British sociolinguists David Britain and Peter Trudgill is a good example of this. They investigated pronunciation features of speakers in the Fens area mentioned earlier. The investigators found that so-called 'reallocation' took place. First, there were two ways to pronounce a certain vowel sound (because of the different regional backgrounds of speakers) in the new settlements. Rather than the two merging into one vowel for all speakers, the two variants of such a variable survived and each became typical of either a linguistic (phonological) context or of two different degrees of social status (Britain and Trudgill 2005). In other words, the variants were reallocated, that is, given a new social and/ or linguistic function. Kapteijn and Scholtmeijer (1998), furthermore, investigated the previously mentioned new town of Dronten in the Netherlands and found that this is the place in the country where the national norm language is highly dominant because people with various backgrounds meet there, live side by side, and adjust their language to a consensus norm of unmarked speech. So, 'levelling' has taken place (see 6.3.4).

KEY CONCEPTS

Language contact

If large groups of speakers regularly speak with people who speak other languages or dialects, then this contact may lead to changes in either language and/or to intermediate language varieties. This contact between speakers is called 'language contact'. Hindi, the official language of various states in India, for instance, is in contact with the many local Indo-Aryan languages. This co-existence has resulted in new regional varieties of Hindi. These new varieties are distinct from Standard Hindi as it is used in television news reports and in nationwide print.

3.4.2 Creoles and pidgins

Contact situations may be the result of migration, with one language usually being more dominant than the other and intermediate mixed languages coming to existence, called 'pidgins' and 'creoles'. Pidgins are newly formed varieties (of, for instance, French and a regional African language) that are linguistically primitive. Creoles evolve from pidgins, are more advanced linguistically, and they have native speakers – the offspring of pidgin speakers, who grew up speaking the mixed language and developed it further. Speakers of pidgins and creoles often live in a highly multilingual situation and will need to mix languages so as to accommodate the speakers around them, who might speak the pidgin, the creole, the dominant language that provided most of the vocabulary (the 'lexifier'), or the original language of the incoming immigrants, which is less dominant linguistically (the 'substrate').

The use and formation of creoles are highly varied. As an example, there is an Aboriginal community in Northern Australia, called Lajamanu, in which an indigenous language, Warlpiri, has been combined with English and with a language that is already a blend of Warlpiri and English from an earlier time. The outcome is a 'new' language, called 'Light Warlpiri'. The use of this new language is subject to certain unique rules, according to O'Shannessy (2005). Speakers under thirty years of age use this language to talk not only to each other but also to elders, but the elders do not speak Light Warlpiri (although they will understand it quite well).

Although creolisation and pidginisation are often associated with slaves developing all kinds of mixed languages and with past developments over generations of speakers with various backgrounds, it is still happening today. There is, for instance, a pidgin called Gulf Pidgin Arabic, which is a link language that is sometimes used in the highly diverse city-state of Dubai amongst speakers with various backgrounds, including non-Arab ones (Bakir 2010).

3.4.3 Urban dialects

The Dubai example is a good illustration of how all kinds of new dialects are formed from old ones in inner cities, where people with different language backgrounds live. The most common situation is where young people with different language and cultural backgrounds come together and gradually develop their own expressions and pronunciations and become identifiable as a group. The urban space can be referred to as 'ideospace', in which various language ideologies are formed and contested (Phyak 2015). The 'new' sociolects emerging from such spaces may consist of features from several languages as well as general conceptual ideas about what an urban ('street') language should sound like. Cornips and De Rooij (2013) demonstrated how such groups of speakers in adjacent neighbourhoods (in the Netherlands) may be distinct regarding the usage and meaning of a certain word of phrase, which points to the formation of subvarieties by such groups.

It should be noted that while cities may be diverse, the linguistic effect hereof may be limited. Superdiversity does not automatically translate into close networks across ethnolinguistic boundaries (Coles and Walsh 2010). Instead, the norm may be 'parallel social lives involving public tolerance, yet little meaningful interaction' (1322). Superdiversity (see 2.3.3 and 4.4) does not necessarily lead to 'super' language contact if various groups lead separate lives.

3.4.4 A new life for old dialects

The final important circumstance for a new language to come to existence mentioned here is if (usually younger) speakers use a minority language or a certain dialect towards identity building. They may use sounds and words from the language to assert their identity without actually speaking the language properly. The speakers in Corby, England, or the speakers on the island of Martha's Vineyard are good examples of this (see 5.3.1). They started revitalising features of a dialect that was intergenerationally shifting in the community.

3.5   Disappearing languages

3.5.1 Language shift

Some language varieties run the risk of ending up with no speakers. They may be endangered because they exist alongside a bigger and more dominant language with a more official status, for instance. Individual speakers, from generation to generation, take over the dominant language and become both hesitant and less able to pass on the minority language to their children. Minority languages do not necessarily have to have only a few speakers or be spoken on remote islands or in secluded areas. The Náhuatl language and the Yucatec Mayan language in Mexico, for example, have about 1.5 and 1 million speakers, respectively.

FOCUS ON...

Language concealment

It should be noted that if minority languages are not heard in public life, in places where a more dominant language exists, that does not mean that the minority languages are dead or that they are shifting across generations. Research in Timor-Leste, East Indonesia, and the East Indonesian diaspora in the Netherlands brought forward a phenomenon labelled 'language concealment'. According to Van Engelenhoven and Van Naerssen (2015), this phenomenon occurs when a minority group of speakers decides to refrain from using their own language when they are not in their minority community. Margaret and Van Engelenhoven (2001) suggested that the disappearance of a language from society may be an attempt of speakers of the minority language to preserve cultural knowledge.

3.5.2 Causes of language shift

Language shift has several causes and these causes usually operate in unison. First of all, languages may be very small, like the many Himalayan languages in South America. One can choose not to speak a 'small' language because few other people speak it. Secondly, a language may not have a written system, which makes transmission more difficult. Pileni, a language spoken by about 1,500 inhabitants of a number of small, remote, and almost inaccessible islands in the easternmost area of the Solomon islands, is an example of such a language. It is described to a degree but not in extensive grammar and vocabulary books that might be used to pass it on to future generations. Thirdly, a small language may be caught up in all kinds of societal transformations (like politics, mobility, immigration, changing livelihood patterns, urbanisation, and conflict), which distracts attention from the plight of the shifting language and from its importance. The fourth cause mentioned here is an ideological one, namely the low status of many shifting languages and the high status of the dominant language.

FOCUS ON...

Status of minority languages

While outside the community a smaller language may have a low status, within a diglossic community the shifting language may have a high status and actually be associated with authority (Smith-Christmas 2016).

Language ideology refers to a system of ideas and beliefs about languages that guides individuals' language choices and ultimately those of larger groups of speakers. This may or may not be influenced strongly by policy (Spolsky 2009). Language policy is another important cause (and number five on our list) for the fate of smaller languages. The examples given here will show how policy can be in place but have little effect on the situation, while policy may also have very practical effects.

In Bangladesh, for instance, the official dominance of Bengali as the state language is threatening the over thirty languages spoken by small communities in that country. In Nepal, by contrast, a one-nation-one-language policy was replaced in 2007 by a guaranteed equal status of all languages spoken in this linguistically rich country. However, no laws were passed to implement any change or measures to protect or revitalise languages, making the protection a symbolic one. Similarly, the Mexican government endorses the multilingual state but does not support the interests of speakers of languages other than Spanish (Terborg and Velázquez 2018). There are also examples of language policy actively stimulating smaller languages and leading to action. In Scotland, Gaelic Medium Education was established in the 1970s, for instance. The Gaelic Language Act of 2005 recognised Gaelic as an official language of Scotland and enabled the establishment of *Bòrd na Gàidhlig*, the Gaelic Language Board. This board coordinates and funds language planning initiatives within Scotland. Furthermore, in Serbia an official role is given to the language rights and needs of minority groups in primary and secondary education. Minority languages in this country – such as Roma, Hungarian, and Slovakian – are actively endorsed as is Serbian as a second language for those who don't speak it as their native tongue (Filipović et al. 2007).

A common principle in societies is that there is one dominant language, which ideology automatically turns other languages into 'lower' languages and causes shift and less diversity. The United Nations and UNESCO nevertheless support linguistic diversity and societal multilingualism. The European Charter for Minority and Regional Languages, with its subdivision of languages into various degrees of acceptance, have classified languages as having degrees in their right to exist (Sano 2001). If this ideology spreads, then the threatened smaller languages may stand a better chance of survival by gaining more status (Duchênes 2008). The emancipation of minority languages could be adopted as part of a new ideology, and governments can play a role in this, said Maher (1997).

3.5.3 Why research a disappearing language?

Describing language shift may create awareness of the erosion (Wolfram 2004b). There are also academic and cultural reasons for such research. Language shift is sociolinguistically interesting from a variationist point of view because there may be 'aggressors' of language shift; perhaps specific people (of a certain age or people with certain types of motivations) are more inclined to use and pass on the dominant language rather than the endangered one than others are. It is not always clear who the aggressors are or which people have positive attitudes to the survival of smaller languages or dialects. Lundberg (2007), as an illustration, found that the (Slovenian) students who participated in his research were quite optimistic about the chances of long-term survival of dialects, which goes against the common assumption that younger people have less interest in the survival of dialects and are passively letting them disappear. It may also be that this optimism is merely a sentimental optimism towards dialects that they know are disappearing.

Language shift is culturally relevant because it undermines the preservation of linguistic and cultural knowledge. Language shift itself can be seen as impoverishing change in culture. In line with this, and speaking in a time of budding awareness of dialect erosion, the German poet and philosopher Johann Gottfried von Herder (1744–1803) said that the existence of diversity within a national culture is an enrichment of that national culture and a sign of civilisation. Minority cultures and languages can in this view be seen as part of the national culture rather than an intrusion. Minority languages can be viewed as a source of enrichment, or simply as inextricable parts of a larger culture and bearers of much cultural information (stories, myths, religious dogmas, thought patterns) and local and regional wisdom. Speaking them gives one access to this information and to documents written in the language in question.

3.5.4 Language revitalisation

Fishman (1964) suggested a number of practical steps towards maintaining or revitalising shifting languages. Revitalisation is nevertheless not usually achieved. Heinrich (2010) mentioned several problems surrounding language revitalisation: selecting a language variety (which of the varieties of a certain dialect is the 'correct' one?), developing it (writing a grammar and a dictionary and expanding the vocabulary, where necessary), and adjusting it to modern communicative needs. Such fundamental issues make revitalisation a complicated process, which often takes places in a time when the dominant language is growing in importance. At the same time, new-dialect formation processes may be taking place, in which only some aspects of the old and disappearing dialect may play a role. This may undo the chances of a full return of the shifted language.

The chances of survival of the language of smaller groups of speakers is often expressed through 'ethnolinguistic vitality', which Giles et al. (1977) defined as 'that which makes a group likely to behave as a distinctive and collective entity within the intergroup setting' (308). Vitality depends on the status of a language, demographic factors including number of speakers and geographical spread, and government support. According to a report by UNESCO (2003), the development of orthography may also contribute to vitality, especially if it is taught or used in schools. The norm language usually has the highest vitality.

3.6 Codeswitching

3.6.1 Definition

Codeswitching occurs when a speaker alternates between more than one language within a single conversation. The switch from one language to the next (and back) can be between two sentences (for instance, the sentence 'If you produce a typo on your application letter, *işe alınmazsın*'; the last two words mean 'you will not be hired' in Turkish) or within a sentence ('*La onda* is to be ten minutes late'; the first two words mean 'the in-thing' in Spanish). Another technique is to insert a single word or phrase, as in the sentence '*Er ist da, tú sabes*', which means 'He is there, you know'; the bit before the comma is German (the main language used), and the bit after the comma is an inserted Spanish phrase. One could even start a word in one language and end it in another as in this sentence from Bamankan (a language spoken in Mali), in which some French is mixed: '*O tuma, i ka theme kun poselen do mun kan?*', which means 'So what was your topic about?'. The verb '*poselen*' has as its base the French verb '*poser*' ('to be about') and ends with the Bamankan verb ending '*len*' (Minkailou and Abdoulaye 2016).

While in some societies using one language at a time is the norm, in many highly multilingual regions using more than one language in a conversation is the norm rather than an exception. Many African countries are typically associated with this norm, and so is a place like Jamaica. The number of languages involved in codeswitching is not restricted to two, although that is the most common scenario. Three is also not uncommon, while Finlayson and Slabbert (1997) found a group of urban speakers in South Africa who used no fewer than seven languages in informal conversations, including Afrikaans, Zulu, and English. In less multilingual areas, patterned codeswitching may also take place – for instance, if two national language norms exist. In the town of Hemnesberget in Norway, so Blom and Gumperz (1972) found, alternating between Bokmål and Ranamål, the two national standards in Norway, was patterned and predictable amongst local people on the basis of social situation.

Switching from one style to another, or switching from one degree of deviation from the language norm to another, fits into the codeswitching paradigm. In other words, switching between a formal and informal style, or between dialect and a regiolect in the middle of a conversation are instances of codeswitching, just like switching between two very different languages.

3.6.2 Motivations and functions

A switch from one language or style to another can have a social function and it can index group membership, identity, or anything else the speaker wishes to forefront, like status or ethnicity. There are also very straightforward practical reasons, like quoting people or clarifying something, but these are sociolinguistically less relevant. Speakers in diglossic communities who codeswitch know how the system works and use it on a daily basis; how codeswitching depends on who they are talking to and the situation they are in, most of all.

Many theories have been postulated to come to terms with this common phenomenon, and some of these border on the sociolinguistic. An important theory is the Markedness Model (Myers-Scotton 1998). This model posits that language users practise codeswitching when there is no obviously unmarked language choice and do so to explore possible language options. Myers-Scotton treated code choices as a function of position negotiation of speakers; the negotiation of rights and obligations. She argued that any code choice indexes existing norms in society and that the degree of markedness depends on these norms. Wéi (1998) and Auer (1998) emphasised the negotiation and formation of the meaning of the conversation as motivations for switches. Some researchers have placed codeswitching in the context of Accommodation Theory (see 5.4.4), i.e., a method of systematically adjusting one's language use to the person one is talking to (Giles and Smith 1979; Giles and Powesland 1975). The desire of individual speakers to either emphasise agreement or difference between themselves and their interlocutor is an important motivation to codeswitch then (see 3.6). Fishman (1958) and Blom and Gumperz (1972) looked at conversation topics and the social settings in which speakers are located as determinants of codeswitching. Grosjean (1982) presented a list of factors influencing language choice; amongst others, the competence of participants in conversations, the general background of participants, degree of formality, and intimacy of the situation.

3.7 Conclusion

This chapter focussed on the various shapes language can assume in daily communication, and these shapes can be called 'language use systems'. A range of terms to discuss those systems has developed. For Sociolinguistics, the term 'style' is a particularly important one, as it involves subtle and meaningful language choices.

Dialects are the most well-known language use systems that are deviant from the norm language. While the language norm is commonly associated with the city, dialects are popularly associated with non-urban regions and with speakers who are less mobile. Urban dialects exist as well, so the current chapter has shown, and some of these (namely the newly created ones) are particularly sensitive to change and fluidity. The language norm and dialects have different types of statuses, and this affects the longevity of dialects; dialects are oftentimes under threat because of the high status that the norm language has.

The concept of dialect is changing in modern times, because multilingualism and geographical mobility are becoming more common, and this changes our view and knowledge of how both rural and urban dialects are formed and should be studied. New dialects take shape and will continue to do so as a result of people with different language backgrounds communicating and making stylistic choices on a day-to-day basis for, amongst others, identity purposes. This identity function breathes some new life into old dialect forms, as they can be used as identity markers in a time when that function of languages seems to be becoming more important. Codeswitching is part of a paradigm of language choices, as people can codeswitch consciously for all kinds of reasons that are not communicative but symbolic.

STUDY QUESTIONS

1. What was your definition of 'dialect' before reading this chapter? In what way has your definition been narrowed or broadened?
2. Do you know of any dialects in your country that can be considered 'new dialects'?
3. It is often said that the number of languages is declining, and the proof of this is that small languages stop being used on a regular basis. At the same time, the number of new (mixed) languages and all kinds of styles seems to be growing. In the end, is the world becoming linguistically richer or less rich?

FURTHER READING

Simpson (1993) describes how people perceive and evaluate language variation and how this affects their language and general behaviour. Chambers and Trudgill (1998) explain in detail how traditional and modern dialectological approaches can be combined. Boztepe (2003) contains an overview of the various interpretations of codeswitching and the theories attached to it. A useful book on style-shifting is the one by Hernández-Campoy (2016).

The Language of Culture

Practices and Belief Systems as Sociolinguistic Variables

4.1 Introduction

Each society type has historically developed its culture under different natural and other circumstances. Groups of people over the ages developed methods of making a living and had different ways to form communities and settlements. An important distinction between various traditional societies was whether they were dependent on hunting, animal-keeping, horticulture, or agriculture. The role of men and women and the power relations between the sexes in societies in particular were determined by these conditions. Different belief systems developed under these circumstances and were passed on and adapted by new generations. Cultural differences are the result of this. Culture refers to a way of thinking and its visible expression through art, way of life, moral codes, habits, or traditions. Culture is also present in communication habits and in language use.

The current chapter addresses culture as a factor in communication. An important motivation behind this chapter is discussed first, namely the tendency of sociolinguistic theory to be based on an Anglo-Western cultural model. Then, the concept of society type will be addressed by laying out three approaches towards typologising cultures in the world. These are efforts to categorise society types on the basis of empirical research. Next, modern tendencies that affect the communication within cultures across the world today will be discussed.

4.2 Anglo-Western bias

Coulmas (2013) noted that in spite of the universal nature of language variation, Sociolinguistics is in the main a science that approaches concepts within a Western paradigm. After Sociolinguistics was put on the international map in the 1960s, scholars looked forward mainly and an Anglo-Western research tradition boomed from that moment on and it still keeps going today.

The United States in particular keeps playing a leading role. In fact, Koerner (1991) noted that nowadays a widespread assumption among United States scholars is that Sociolinguistics actually started in their own country.

In Anthropology, the Western world is sometimes referred to through the acronym WEIRD, which is an acronym for 'Western, Educated, Industrialised, Rich, and Democratic' (Henrich et al. 2011). The available introductory books into the field, which aim to synthesise sociolinguistic patterns and draw generalisations, often place this world at the basis of argumentation, and as a result they suffer from a Western bias and even a bias towards theories drawn from situations in which English is involved. This is no surprise because a majority of the authors of the most well-known international introductions to Sociolinguistics are themselves from an Anglophone culture, as illustrated by Meyerhoff and Nagy (2008) and Jenkins (2009), and English is the most widely and diversely spread language. Socioeconomic and other factors have led to an overrepresentation of researchers, authors, and editors in the field from the United States, Britain, and Europe and to an enormous availability of research on Englishes across the world. Journal publications on sociolinguistic patterns across the world cover a wide range of languages and speech communities but the authors are often part of the mainstream culture. Smakman (2015) concluded on the basis of the authorship of articles in international journals over the past few decades that while the Anglo-West constitutes less than one-fifth of the world's population it generates well more than four fifths of the publications in the field. Asia, by contrast, constitutes more than half the world's population but produces only one in every ten sociolinguistic articles.

FOCUS ON...

Terminological adjustment

The Anglo-Western dominance is illustrated by the fact that outside the Anglo-West, academic terminology from the mainstream arena is used as a terminological basis. Kimura (2011) explained how in Japan academic terms are usually imported from the Anglophone West and given new denotations and connotations to fit the Japanese language situation.

This situation inevitably leads to a Western predisposition in introductory books. Theories constructed outside this realm often fail to contribute to mainstream theorisation. The constant flow of sociolinguistic output from the Anglo-West makes this situation hard to reverse. A growing self-assurance of areas outside the Anglo-Western territory and a higher number of publications from these areas would ideally change this trend and democratise non-mainstream Sociolinguistics.

Other than that, there is an increasing awareness that the world and the languages that coexist in it are changing. Traditional assumptions on the function and shape of language in societies – with the nation state and national language as basic components – are reconsidered not only because of the growing knowledge of societies that do not fit this model but also because the language use in well-known society types is changing and becoming part of a more global language-variation system. This growing awareness may be key to change.

KEY CONCEPTS

Social constructionism

'(Social) constructionism' departs from the concept of social constructs. These are ideas and notions that are obvious to those who accept them, but they may not necessarily represent reality because they are inventions of societies. Gender is such a construct, as it represents attempts by societies to construct feminine and masculine identities. What 'language' or even what 'age' encompasses is dependent on cultural perspectives and is not fixed for each culture.

4.3 Cultural patterns in the world

4.3.1 Cultural models

Some cultural descriptions focus on visual characteristics like art, attire, and even culinary habits, while others focus more on underlying belief systems as expressed through moral choices. The current chapter deals only with the latter and with communication style as a cultural expression and reflection. Pioneering work in categorising cultural characteristics was done by the American anthropologist Hall (1959, 1976). Since then, more investigations have been done that have yielded models to categorise world cultures. Three of these are described here. Other models exist as well, but these three are particularly helpful for you to make sense of the language(s) or style(s) in the culture(s) you may want to study, because they are based on research (large-scale surveys) and are very explicit about which countries or regions fall within a certain cultural realm.

1. World Values Survey

The World Values Survey (WVS 2015) refers to a series of investigations about human values and beliefs. This survey started in 1981. The WVS addresses how people in various cultures value fundamental aspects in life such as religion, happiness, materialism, gender roles, freedom of choice, self-expression, tradition, and authority. This survey is still continuing today, and so far respondents in more than 100 countries have participated as informants. On the basis of the responses in the surveys, Halman et al. (2008) and Inglehart and Welzel (2004), amongst others, helped to subdivide cultures in the world into nine categories: (1) Confucian, (2) South Asia, (3) African-Islamic, (4) Latin America, (5) English-speaking, (6) Catholic Europe, (7) Protestant Europe, (8) Orthodox, and (9) Baltic.

On the website of the World Values Survey Association (www.world valuessurvey.org), these nine cultures are visualised through a model based on human values. Two value scales are visualised on which countries are plotted: Survival – Self-Expression and Traditional – Secular-Rational. More details and descriptions are provided on the webpage. It should be noted that not all countries in the world are mentioned in the graph and that different distinctions between cultures have over the years come to existence. The assumption of the researchers has been that certain aspects of cultures are subject to change. This overview is updated every few years on the basis of new insights and cultural changes that are taking place.

2. The Hofstede Model

Together with the aforementioned Hall, the Dutch organisational psychologist Geert Hofstede was one of the pioneers in describing cultures. He investigated how culture influences values in the workplace. The findings were based on information provided by employees of a large multinational in the late 1960 and early 1970s with branches in 50 countries across the world, and these data were later extended to more countries, amongst others by looking at new research data by other researchers. Despite the weakness of the age of much of the data (especially when bearing in mind cultural changes in the last 50 years), these cultural dimensions are still commonly used. Hofstede's results have appeared in several publications – like Hofstede (1980) and Hofstede et al. (2010) – and summaries are available on a website (Hofstede n.d.).

Hofstede distinguished between six dimensions on which cultures can be placed and gave the following definitions on the website (Hofstede n.d.): Power distance, Individualism, Uncertainty avoidance, Long-term orientations, Indulgence, and Masculinity. These are explained in detail on this website. It should be noted that the masculinity dimension is not the degree to which men or women are dominant in society. Instead, it refers to the appreciation of stereotypically male or female behaviour. The countries in the world are qualified on the basis of all of these criteria. For a few countries, data are lacking. On the website https://geert-hofstede.com/countries.html, which is updated regularly, you can mutually compare cultural differences between up to three countries.

3. The Lewis Model

The World Values Survey and Hofstede's model reveal to us how groups and individuals view things, and it is up to the reader to decide how this can affect language and communication. British linguist Richard Lewis also attempted to categorise world cultures but included some very general communication tendencies in his model.

The Lewis Model was developed in the 1990s (Lewis 1996), and the data were drawn from questionnaires and surveys across 68 nationalities. The model charts countries triangularly in terms of the tendency towards types of communication, which are labelled Reactive, Linear-active, or Multi-active communication. These are explained in detail on Lewis' website (www. crossculture.com). Although Lewis' model is not geographically oriented, strictly speaking, there are certain clear regional tendencies. The visual model Lewis provides shows that the English-speaking world and the Germanic countries are most closely associated with Linear-active communication styles. Reactive styles are mostly typical of Asian countries, especially China and Japan. Multi-active communication styles are more scattered across the globe.

FOCUS ON...

Language as part of culture

Hockett (1958) named a number of features that are an intrinsic part of the design of language; amongst others its interchangeability (people can be senders or receivers), the option of speakers to correct and self-monitor their language, and the ability to refer to things that are not present in space and time. Eller (2016) observed that many of these design features are also features of culture in general and that the skills that make culture possible also enable language. He specifically referred to symbolism and symbolic thinking as a connecting feature of both language and culture. The symbolic value of language usages is arbitrary, because there's usually a limited (or no) natural relationship between a symbol and its meaning, like the meaning of raising a number of fingers in the air in a certain way, sticking your tongue out, or using an intonation pattern. They are not intrinsically rude, encouraging or friendly. Culture determines the conventions hereon, just like it determines the symbolic values of things like clothes and rituals.

4.3.2 Applying the models

A challenge in dealing with culture is that cultural descriptions of large societies ignore all kinds of highly prominent low-level differentiations within these societies. A single culture can span several countries (such as is the case for the Saami culture in the Nordic countries), and within countries multiple cultures may co-exist (such as Muslim, Christian, and Kurdish culture in Iraq). Generalistic approaches also ignore the individual's relationship with the culture they grew up in. Meyerhoff (2011) reminded us that sociolinguists should be self-critical when incorporating culture in their research and making such distinctions. She referred to work by Morales et al. (1998), who found that qualifying individuals as either 'individualistic' or 'collectivist' could not be used to predict politeness strategies by these individuals under various circumstances. Indeed, one should be reluctant to use binary distinctions as straightforward analytical models. Wierbicka (1996) even talked about 'the straitjacket of binary categories' (338).

The models described here should be viewed critically, but they are nevertheless very useful. The models can be used in an ad hoc manner if the data that you have generated show certain patterns. For instance, if you come across dominant behaviour of one of the sexes in certain social contexts, then you can ascertain how Hofstede's model describes the masculinity or femininity of the culture of the language you are describing. If you come across many silences in conversations, then you might want to check whether your speakers' culture falls into the 'Reactive' communication style as described by Lewis. Besides this, you can use the models to think up tasks and questions in your investigations. If masculinity and silences are indeed prototypical features of the culture you are describing according to one of the models, then you could include an interview question hereon when collecting data. In any case, these models should be used for general guidance and inspiration rather than as hard and fast models that will apply to your specific speaker or speaker set.

4.4 Modern trends

Despite much internal variation within regions and countries, the trends that have come out of the investigations presented here will be very recognisable to individuals across the globe. However, while the basic culture type that societies belong to will be widely felt to be alive and active, modern trends sometimes make the original culture less visible. To make cultural descriptions more complete, certain aspects that are typical of modern times need to be taken into consideration. Four important ones are described here.

1. Industrialisation versus westernisation

Inglehart and Welzel (2005) made the claim that people's world views change when they as individuals and the society around them undergo socioeconomic development. Many societies today are swiftly becoming industrialised and on the surface seem to have similar goals, namely economic ones. Energy, machines, and information are dominant determinants of power relations, besides the original societal hierarchical structures. New economic powers may even overrule the old powers.

Elliott (2016) and Elliott and Lemert (2009) associated modernist Western culture with dynamism, speed, change, short-term thinking, and self-making (which tendencies are illustrated in the rise of short-term contracts, multiple careers, and continuous down-sizing in companies and institutes). Elliott (2016) was convinced that the growing rise in individualism and the 'growing cult of reinvention' (72) is increasingly global in scope. However, even if a certain business attitude may be spreading globally in a very visible manner, this does not mean that non-Western industrialising societies are also becoming more Western in their communication styles. Instead, they seem to be developing a style in which the old culture is part of the new, industrialised culture. A style to communicate with other industry-based societies is part of their developing repertoire.

2. Globalisation

'Cultural globalisation' refers to the extension and intensification of social relations through the transmission of ideas, meanings, and values around the world (James 2006). Although it is commonly associated with today's widespread

---

FOCUS ON...

Religion and economic power relations

An important distinction nowadays is between societies in which religion is officially endorsed and those in which institutionalised religion is dwindling and increasingly separated from state affairs and the public space. Male and female relations are in particular affected by this. In countries where religion is prominent, gender roles correlate strongly with power relations; for example, in Arab countries. In many Western countries, on the other hand, gender equality is an official government aim. This difference in policy affects communication patterns strongly.

---

exposure to the Internet, popular culture, and international travel, it goes back many centuries and was set in motion through the historical processes of economic exchange and colonisation (Nederveen Pieterse 2003). All of these phenomena have the effect of carrying cultural meaning to other countries in the world and of circulating culture. This circulation makes it easier for people to enter into social relations with those that live in other countries and cultural spheres. In addition to sharing and mixing at the information and materialistic level, these tendencies also contribute to the formation of shared norms (Steger and James 2010). According to Eller (2016), globalisation and universal access to cultural images is associated with the 'One-world culture' concept (312), which is the idea that people are becoming more culturally similar. The most obvious basic society form that influences this globalisation, according to Fukuyama (1992), is Western democratic capitalism.

Another view of the situation is captured in the term 'glocalisation'. This term is a combination of the words 'localisation' and 'globalisation' (Robertson 1995) and refers to a tendency of local worlds interconnecting in a global world (Schuerkens 2004). This phenomenon is illustrated by so-called Metropop Fiction from Jakarta in Indonesia. The authors of this artform combine the Jakarta vernacular with English words and phrases and avoid the use of the standard language, Bahasa Indonesia. This is a possible effect of globalisation but does not lead to an international style of language use. Glocalisation indeed contests the idea that globalisation inevitably leads to uniformity.

KEY CONCEPTS

Translocality

The term 'translocality' refers to the notion that today's local cultures are connected to surrounding cultures and that their existence and definition in fact depend on each other. This means that cultures need to be viewed as outward-looking and as part of a larger complex of cultures (Westinen 2011) rather than independent and unique identities.

3. Mixed cultures

Not everyone belongs to a single culture. Increasing numbers of people move away from the region where they were born in order to make a wealthier, safer, or more interesting life for themselves elsewhere. Speech communities are thus broken up and parts of them are redistributed, oftentimes across neighbourhoods in cities (high densities of people with similar regional and cultural backgrounds in specific neighbourhoods). Together, the resultant new communities make up increasing numbers of speakers whose language is from various geographically scattered areas and whose native language and culture are challenged on a daily basis. The children of these people grow up in a culture that is not their parents' and may feel less connected to their birth ground than those who come from several generations of people living in the same culture. This group and their offspring could be considered a separate culture and are becoming more common.

KEY CONCEPTS

Metro-ethnicity

The British sociolinguist John Maher (2005) proposed the phenomenon of 'metro-ethnicity', defining it as 'a hybridized "street" ethnicity deployed by a cross-section of people with ethnic or mainstream backgrounds who are oriented towards cultural hybridity, cultural/ethnic tolerance, and a multicultural lifestyle in friendships, music, the arts, eating and dress' (83). In this view, individuals play with ethnicities (and not necessarily their own) and are not so sentimental about the purity of ethnic language. Maher called this playing with ethnicity for aesthetic effect 'cool' (89). In India, for instance, the mixing of English and Hindi ('Hinglish') is part of everyday speech in large cities like Mumbai. It has a strong identity function that neither pure English or Hindi serve and speakers with various backgrounds employ it for that purpose.

---

4. Intercultural communication

Intercultural communication means communication between one culture and another, between people with different understandings and assumptions of the world and of language use. It could also involve more than two cultures. In socially differentiated societies, individuals tend to have multiple identity options and tend to construct their own, unique personality (Giddens 1991; Kraus 2006), and these can be hybrid and situated in a context of superdiversity (Vertovec 2007; Bhabha 1994), as discussed in Section 2.3.3. These phenomena make cultural traditions more manifold and less clearly outlined, and they make intercultural communication problematic as a study object, according to Koch (2009). In such a context, cultural groups are symbolic and constructed in the minds of people rather than a natural entity (Anderson 1983; Koch 2009). An added challenge in investigating the language of such groups is that they are intrinsically subject to change and innovation and to the dynamism of modern lifestyles rather than directly and predictably based in existing traditions.

Despite the reasonable objection that intercultural communication is too diverse to be studied as an object, there is nevertheless a tradition in Sociolinguistics to find patterns. The first framework to approach the question of intercultural communication was designed and elaborated in the 1960s and 1970s by the American anthropologist and linguist Dell Hymes. Hymes put forward the idea of Ethnography of Communication (Hymes 1964), which theory was at an earlier stage of development called Ethnography of Speaking. It is the analysis of communication in which social and cultural beliefs and practices are taken into consideration of members of a smaller community or of a larger culture. Hymes' ideas can be viewed as a methodology which lends itself very well for communication in which more than one cultural pattern is present. Intercultural communication studies are increasingly incorporating the above-named superdiversity, hybridity, and self-made identities in communicative settings by applying Hymes' research principles.

4.5   Conclusion

It is safe to assume that a thorough understanding of the sociolinguistic intricacies of language varieties is reserved for native speakers of those varieties. Gould (2000) said that 'reality does not speak to us objectively, and no science can be free from constraints of psyche and society', and he spoke of a 'conceptual lock' (276); one can't switch off one's own cultural experiences when analysing those of others. Even reading about language situations or experiencing them first-hand will not provide outsiders with a full understanding. Nevertheless, it is good to study cultures that are not native to you because an outsider often notices things that do not strike the native as exceptional or interesting.

This chapter has tried to raise awareness of culture as a factor in Sociolinguistics. Culture is an active current that influences individuals and larger communities and should be taken into consideration when describing language use patterns. In this chapter, culture is defined on the basis of shared characteristics such as ethnicity, customs, and beliefs. It was explained that it can be defined regionally in many cases.

This chapter has proposed some practical tools to place any language variety in a broad cultural framework. When studying language use, the sociolinguistic researcher can use these tools to come to grips with underlying cultural patterns of the language under investigation when preparing methodologies or generally interpreting findings. The challenge that researchers face who want to use such a model is that each model provides different criteria and categorisations. An additional issue is the enormous variation within the categories. It should also be noted that individuals and groups of individuals are to varying degrees affected by their culture, and it is important to find out the relationship they have with their culture rather than assuming that cultural descriptions fully apply to them and affect their language accordingly.

It should be noted that cultural groups can also be defined in less predictable ways. People who share activities or people of the same gender can, for instance, also be treated as cultural groups. The chapters on age and gender in this book can be read with this in mind.

STUDY QUESTIONS

1. Which of the three methods of determining cultural patterns in regions and countries across the world appeals to you most? Why? What are strengths and weaknesses of each of them?
2. How would you incorporate the strong diversity that is currently becoming more common in the world in an investigation into language-use patterns?
3. If Anglo-Western theories are of such high quality, should we not keep taking those as the point of departure to form theories for the regions outside the Anglo-Western region?

FURTHER READING

Chapter 7 will demonstrate how culture affects language. That chapter looks at the relationship between language and status. The companion website at www.macmillanihe.com/companion/smakman contains general descriptions of important (large) cultures in the world. In addition, researchers are advised to find cultural descriptions of the region or perhaps speech community that they are describing; the more specific, the better. These may not be in English, like the one by Baeza Ventura and Zimmerman (2009), which offers perspectives on the profiles of Central American culture in an age of globalisation and transnational processes. This book is written in Spanish. Another example is Mallia (2012). Written in Maltese, this book offers historical and modern aspects of Maltese culture. Other such books are available as well. A technique has been suggested to analyse ways of speaking through so-called cultural scripts (Goddard and Wierbicka 2004). Cultural scripts are assumptions about what is bad and good and what one should or should not do, especially when speaking (Wierbicka 2002), and this approach can be very insightful. Joseph et al. (2001), furthermore, describe the Western linguistic tradition. The first two chapters of Blommaert (2010) explain and illustrate the workings of globalisation very clearly; how these affect our daily lives linguistically and how these effects are all around us. More on communication in intercultural settings and between cultures can be found in Croucher (2017) and Clyne (1994). The latter pays attention to the less affluent nomadic worker in intercultural communication.

PART 2

UNDERSTANDING SOCIOLINGUISTICS

The following eight chapters present the theoretical developments in the field of Sociolinguistics. The opening chapter covers factors that cause individual speakers to vary their language (Chapter 5). Language ideology is discussed next; first generally (Chapter 6) and subsequently from the standpoint of 11 major cultures across the globe (Chapter 7). The next two chapters explain how ideologies and other factors affect ordinary people's perceptions and evaluations of language variation. The way lay perceptions and evaluations are viewed and researched by experts is first explained (Chapter 8), and after that the mechanisms behind the language attitudes that they reflect is outlined (Chapter 9). The next two chapters discuss the common sociolinguistic themes of age (Chapter 10) and gender (Chapter 11). Sociolinguistic variation in language-learning contexts is explained in the final chapter (Chapter 12) of Part 2. Together, these chapters provide the most well-known explanations of why certain people produce and experience language the way they do in certain circumstances.

Speaker Agency

Language Choices in a Sociolinguistic Space

5.1 Introduction

In the Social Sciences, human 'agency' refers to the ability of an individual to act independently and make their own free choices. Agency is exhibited in the degree to which individuals can act for themselves in the face of influential social structures and other relatively fixed circumstances (Barker 2005). A central interest of today's sociolinguist is the individual and the opportunities they have and take to make language choices in the midst of all kinds of circumstances. Coulmas (2013) indicated that Sociolinguistics is about 'what it is that speakers do with their language(s); how they pass them on to following generations; how they allow them to be influenced by other languages; how they adjust their speech to that of their interlocutors; and how they interact with speakers of other idioms.' (xii). To find this out, speakers first and foremost need to be looked at as individuals continuously triggered by a plethora of influences. The choices each of them makes under these circumstances explain the broader workings of language variation.

   This chapter discusses four influences on the language from the perspective of individual speakers: who we are, how we view ourselves, how we view others, and who we associate with. Characteristics of people are discussed first (i.e., who we are). First of all, these are features we are born with and that cannot usually be changed, such as age, sexuality, and the way our vocal tract is built. Furthermore, these are features that are imposed in our early lives but that can often be changed in later life, such as social position and place where one lives. After that, identity as part of language is explained (i.e., how we view ourselves) and why we communicate with others in certain situations the way we do (i.e., how we view others). The final type of explanation of an individual's language use that is discussed is membership of one or more groups of people with whom we share certain language features (i.e., who we associate with).

5.2 Who we are

5.2.1 Physiology

Speakers have certain characteristics that they are born with: their so-called 'core identity' (Friedrich and Diniz de Figueiredo 2016). Our physiology, for one, is a strong determinant of our lives. People vary in the degree to which their bodies function satisfactorily and in the degree to which their bodies are considered attractive in the society where they live. Their bodies affect their self-worth, happiness, and how they undergo experiences. Inevitably, their bodies determine the way they speak.

An important characteristic one is born with is one's biological gender. Most speakers will sound male or female, whether they want to or not. Pitch and voice quality are the main factors distinguishing a male from a female voice, and the effects of these characteristics are often salient. Such differences, however, are not absolute. An individual's physical attraction to one, both, or neither of the sexes hangs together with their gender and may correlate with the way they use language. However, like gender, it does not affect language use in an absolute way.

Age is another independent and predictable aspect of our bodies. Speakers' voices change with time, due to age. Inevitable features of old age are creakiness, a lower pitch, a slowing down of the speech rate, and the voice becoming tremulous (Chambers 2009). These natural changes affect the way people's language comes out and is perceived.

Race is also not subject to change because we are born with it. Race affects the oral and nasal structures and as a consequence the voice quality (Xue and Hao 2006). There are indications that listeners can identify race when people are speaking, and breathiness and such subtle aspects like the moment when the vocal cords start vibrating when someone speaks have been found to constitute such cues for listeners (Newman and Wu 2011). On the basis of such features, it is said that there is, for instance, a 'black' and a 'white' way of speaking American English (Labov 1972b; Bernstein 1972). However, absolute, or even strong, differences in language use due to race-related physiological factors are unlikely, and reliably distinguishing speakers with different races on the basis of their natural voice qualities is probably impossible. Any correlative difference of people with a certain race can usually be traced back to the language of ancestors and of other speakers in the social circles that people frequent, rather than being the result of the way their vocal tracts are shaped. This is illustrated by the fact that the many Chinese children adopted in northern Europe cannot be recognised as being Chinese on the basis of their voice quality; they don't sound 'Chinese' or 'Asian' when they learn to speak. They are most likely to sound like their parents, siblings, and friends.

The ability to use, control, and stylise language is part of the talents that you are born with. It is sometimes claimed that during your lifetime you will not pronounce the same sound in exactly the same way, at least from an acoustic point of view. The content and structure of many sentences you produce in life are unique. Many of the longer sentences you produce are also subject to a certain unpredictability and might have come out differently under different circumstances (different word order, word choice, etc.). This is because one does not have perfect control over one's speech tract and general language ability. The resultant type of variation is very subtle and may largely pass below the radar of consciousness of both speaker and listener but it may affect how language is perceived. This imperfect control also affects the degree to which people can adjust their language to their wishes. One cannot imitate all speech styles, especially not at a later age. Meyerhoff (2011) reminded us that it is 'harder to change your vowels than your address' (166) and that this is due to developmental restrictions. These are different for each individual.

5.2.2 Early lives

Other characteristics that influence language are instilled through place of birth and general conditions and circumstances in life, especially during one's early childhood. Social position and geographical origin are characteristics of individuals that are not biological but are part of their early youth. The language as spoken in the place where one was born and/or grew up will have a lasting effect on one's language throughout one's life. To various degrees, individuals can change social status during their lives, but the social position that one was in during one's formative years will strongly affect one's behaviour, thinking, and language for the rest of one's life. Changing the effect of regional origin on one's language is possible too, but limitations exist in that respect as well.

5.2.3 Research approach

Gender, sexuality, age, and race are usually researched and discussed as a part of a larger set of factors or in a context of behavioural roles. Gender research tends to focus on prototypical roles that men and women play, and sexuality is researched within that context too. Age is often looked at from a social point of view, namely as stages in people's lives. Chapter 11 discusses gender and sexuality and Chapter 10 discusses age. Race is not usually treated separately in research. Instead, ethnicity is a variable often used. An 'ethnic group' shares a combination of features, such as nationality, race, language, cultural origins, and culture-based customs or traditions. Ethnicity is an aggregate of characteristics that in unison act more convincingly than race alone. Social and regional background are notoriously difficult to test because of the increasing social and geographical mobility of people nowadays. Through questionnaires, efforts are nevertheless made to determine these features.

5.2.4 The workings of 'who we are'

In addition to qualifying people on the basis of characteristics, such as biological gender, regional origin, or ethnicity, it is also relevant to know to what degree people actually associate with these characteristics. One may be from a certain town but not associate with it, one may be proud of a certain ethnicity or have no special connection with it, and one may also exploit one's ability to play with language or not. Variation herein is dependent on experiences and, for instance, personality. The mood of the speaker at a certain moment is an added factor affecting language. One might also add more difficult to measure features such as imagination, creativity, ambition, sensitivity, and intelligence as well as all kinds of other characteristics to this list of features one is born with and that develop under all kinds of circumstances. Imaginative and creative people might play with language more. So might speakers who are highly sensitive to subtle language cues and their self-image.

The effects of all of these characteristics on language and how they are perceived by others are deep and lasting, but individuals may ignore (maintain), accentuate, suppress, or change the language use they acquired naturally in their youth. They regulate their own speech (which is called 'self-styling'). Speakers are themselves in charge of their language choices and to varying degrees actively engage in polishing them to meet their needs. It should be noted though that speaking a certain way is necessarily intentional and it may not be an effort to express something (Benwell and Stokoe 2006).

EXAMPLE

Personality

Fox and Sharma (2018) discussed two brothers in a London (England) neighbourhood whose general lives and background were identical in many respects (such as education, place of birth, profession, and even type of spouse). The two brothers spoke very differently, with one of them favouring a more traditional style than the other. The authors explained how the sensitivity to certain experiences in particular was an important factor. The boys had at some point gone through some different experiences in their youth. One brother was confident and extraverted, while the other was shy and introverted, and this difference had likely influenced how they reacted to these experiences. The effect of the difference in experience on language could have been less if their personalities had been different.

5.3   How we view ourselves

5.3.1 Identity

The speaker characteristics mentioned so far to a large degree affect how you view yourself and how people view you. This partly shapes your 'identity', which refers to the ideas individuals have about what makes them different from others. Bucholtz and Hall (2010) presented a broad definition of this phenomenon, namely 'the social positioning of self and other' (18). This 'self' and 'other' may be redefined through interaction (Cornips and De Rooij 2013). In discourse, people tend to view themselves in relation to others; 'othering' is the process of perceiving or portraying someone else as fundamentally different, for instance by talking about them or describing them (Baumann and Gingrich 2004).

Danesi (2016) reminded us that an individual's sense of identity is strongly influenced by the language(s) they acquire in their childhood. He distinguished between various types of identity and referred to the one determined by language as 'linguistic identity' (156), which thus exists alongside other identities. So, in addition to influencing language use, speaker characteristics such as age, social position, and gender are themselves identity markers (and so people have an 'age identity', a 'social identity', and, for instance, a 'gender identity'). According to Block and Corona (2016), the current consensus on identity is that it is 'multilayered and complex' (509–510), which means that its different dimensions cannot be treated in isolation. These identities interrelate in various ways and together form an individual's overall identity.

Le Page and Tabouret-Keller (1985) believed that identity is largely something you do, rather than something that you are born with. Coulmas (2013) added that individual linguistic identity is partly given and partly adopted. Individuals may choose to show an identity, and they may choose to do this subtly or conspicuously and choose to foreground certain identities at the expense of others. Language identity may be foregrounded or not.

Identity on Martha's Vineyard

A good example of research exploring identity is William Labov's investigation of local speakers on the island of Martha's Vineyard (an island just off the North East coast of the United States). In this famous investigation (Labov 1963), he found that islanders often pronounced certain vowels, namely those in words such as 'mouth' and 'price', in a way that was typical of the island. Labov assumed that this showed their identification with a Martha's Vineyard

---

FOCUS ON...

Non-linguistic aspects of identity

Language is an important identity marker of groups and individuals but hardly ever acts alone in this sense. It usually marks identity in combination with a myriad of other characteristics, even unexpected ones. In Toksook Bay in Alaska, dance is an important identity marker (John 2015). Marriage, mourning, and other ceremonies are important markers of group identity amongst Gurezi immigrants in the Valley of Kashmir in the Western Himalayas (Ahmed 2014). For the latter group, woollen cloth is another marker of identity, especially a distinctive woollen cap. Identity expressions and reflections are everywhere; from the brand name on your glasses to the bumper sticker on your car and your fashion sense. Such visible identity markers create expectations about how people speak.

lifeway. He even found that some of the younger men used the more local pronunciation, especially those who did not intend to leave the island and therefore identified with the local culture.

5.3.2 Borrowed identities

Sometimes, speakers choose to adopt the language identity of another group. This is called 'crossing' or 'language crossing'. Speakers of Standard Colloquial Sudanese Arabic, for instance, have been observed to cross to a variety spoken by a highly marginalised group known popularly as Shamasha. This group speaks a highly marked street language (Awadelkarim 2013). A lighter form of a borrowed identity was found by Dyer (2001) in the English town of Corby. Although this town is about 400 miles away from Glasgow, Glaswegian pronunciation features are sometimes heard there. Dyer found that younger male speakers from Corby were borrowing pronunciation features from their Glaswegian ancestors, who moved from Glasgow (Scotland) to Corby some generations earlier to work in the steel industry. Normally, those features would disappear after a few generations, but for identity purposes some speakers chose to start using them again as a 'badge of local belonging' (55), that is, being a true Corby local.

FOCUS ON...

Identity-driven diversification

The need of speakers to show their identity when language homogenisation is taking place is illustrated by the use of the Nagama language. This language is spoken in a small state, Nagaland, in the North East of India. It is used as a lingua franca in this state in which more than 20 mutually less intelligible languages are spoken. Although it is a common language, it nevertheless acts as an 'ethnolinguistic marker', as it reveals people's origin. An individual's village and clan can even be detected in the way this language is spoken (Satyanath 2015). This stylistic variation acts as an important and conscious signal of ethnolinguistic identity (Satyanath 2016), especially amongst older speakers.

5.3.3 Identity-based theories

Several theories to explain language choices by individuals based on the principle of identity have over the past few decades arisen. Three important ones are described here.

I. Social Identity Theory

Social Identity Theory states that an individual identifies with more than one identity. The Polish-born Brit Henri Tajfel (1974) is associated with this theory and distinguished between identities that are mostly personal and those that are mostly associated with a group. Social Identity Theory suggests that we identify most strongly with a certain persona depending on the communicative and social situation. Individuals perceive any interaction as either communication between two groups or two individuals. In other words, we associate most strongly with a group identity in intergroup communication, and when we identify most strongly with an individual identity then we perceive the communication as interpersonal communication. When a personal identity is most salient, then an individual's communication is constrained by idiosyncratic and personal traits and by the moment when the conversation takes place. If the individual feels that they are in an intergroup communication setting, then there will be less variability in their style, because they will speak in accordance with the in-group communicative rules and be steered less by personal motivations and characteristics.

2. Speaker Design Theory

A more recent theory that tries to explain the effects of identity on stylistic choices is Speaker Design Theory, which is concerned with attention paid to oneself when one is speaking. The British linguist Nikolas Coupland (2001) suggested that speakers are triggered by how they want to present themselves as identifying with a certain group. Speaking is thus a so-called 'act of identity', in accordance with which we sometimes put salient features of a certain language variety into our language, so as to signify that group association or some other kind of association. The perceived symbolism of such small language choices may be very powerful. One of the principles in this approach is that speakers, when talking, paint a positive picture of themselves by accentuating the positive and eliminating the negative.

3. Indexicality

'Indexicality' is an even more recent approach to explaining the workings of identity and language. A way to express one's identity is to use language that indexes a certain identity. Indexicality is a concept introduced by the American philosopher Charles Sanders Peirce (1839–1940). An index, so Peirce (1932) explicated, is a sign that denotes a causal connection with what it refers to, i.e., a result or cause of the sign. For instance, fever is a symptom of a certain disease; so, we could say that fever (=visible) is indexical of a disease (= invisible).

Your index finger is the one next to your thumb, and it is often used to point at things. The verb 'to index', i.e., 'to point to', is commonly used within the field of Semiotics (see 6.2). The concept of indexicality has relatively recently started to be applied to Sociolinguistics; most notably by Silverstein (2003) and Eckert (2008). From a sociolinguistic perspective, indexicality refers to the way an observable linguistic fact can be indexical of social identities in the same way, for instance, that clothing can. Language features can thus be semiotic signs associated with such identities. The allocation of such associations is sometimes referred to as 'enregisterment'. All kinds of identity characteristics (race, gender, etc.) intersect in this classification experience. Geeslin and Long (2014) gave some examples from various languages of 'facts about the origin and personal characteristics of the speaker' (9); people who are not native speakers of these languages may have some imperfect knowledge of these facts and start playing with them. Silverstein (2003) argued that linguistic features may index more than one meaning, that meanings may overlap, and that these meanings may be competing. Over time, new meanings develop out of the older ones, and these may eventually replace these older ones. The language producer and receiver may or may not agree on the meanings. Individuals can play with these evocations of images; either the very direct, factual images or more subjective ones that are the outcome of the speaker's own ideological stance towards certain connections between language items and what they symbolise. This playing can be at the level of isolated language features (a word, a sound) or it might be at the level of codes (a whole language variety), which is an approach that Bassiouney (2015) took in discussing language choices and codeswitching in Egypt.

KEY CONCEPTS

Polylanguaging

In highly multilingual contexts, speakers sometimes use features associated with different languages, even without speaking these languages. This is referred to as 'polylanguaging' (Jørgensen et al. 2011). In a similar vein, Blommaert (2010) discussed the semiotic (symbolic) use of parts of a language (such as a word or a phrase, or sound) without necessarily speaking that language; he called these symbolic parts of language 'bits of languages'.

For instance, someone could use the highly variable and socially loaded post-vocalic 'r' in Mandarin consciously; for instance, to index a certain urban, ambitious, and trendy lifestyle. To listeners, this reference may come across as it was intended by the speakers, but it may also be interpreted as simply a traditional local Beijing feature. The intended meaning of the speaker may be different from that of those addressed. Vaicekauskienė (2007), furthermore, found that Lithuanian with a high concentration of English borrowings is fairly unanimously associated with males under the age of 35 living in a city. Another example is if the Georgian expression *ar arsebobs* – a phrase used to show surprise; 'no way!' – is uttered in Tblisi, the capital of Georgia. It evokes images of the Vake neighbourhood in this city (associated with a high social status), youth, and poshness. In Mexico City, female customers on outdoor markets may be addressed as *marchanta* (or the diminutive *marchantita*) and males as *marchante*. Such forms of address cannot be heard in a supermarket or regular shops. This way, these forms of address index the context of the street. Furthermore, people using such forms of address are likely to have a traditional background, so it also indexes speaker characteristics (Terborg and Velázquez 2018). An example involving language choice is the use of Ukrainian or Russian in the Ukraine. This choice has a powerful symbolic impact and directly reveals a certain cultural loyalty.

KEY CONCEPTS

Stereotype, marker, indicator

Labov (1972c) introduced the concepts of 'stereotypes', 'markers', and 'indi-cators', which also deal with features that somehow stand out in people's speech and whose perceptual salience causes opinions. Stereotypes are lan-guage features (words or sounds, mainly) that are subject to strong listener opinions and are sometimes even used for mocking and impersonations. Speakers are aware of producing such features. Speakers are less aware of producing markers, although these features also have an effect on listeners' evaluations. Indicators are linguistic variables that speakers are even less aware of. This theory pays less attention to the possibility of a fluid set of associations and the nature of associations, while it contributes perceptual salience and strength of association as relevant factors.

5.3.4 New types of identity

Identity theories should logically be applicable to social spaces that are digital and should consider the fact that access to mobility and technology is fast developing. In view of the radical changes in the natures of identities due to the rise of online identities, Elliott (2016) called for a new social theory of identity. Papacharissi (2011) demonstrated the need for a new identity theory by referring to the construction of virtual identities in new media that to varying degrees resemble real-life identities. This leads to multiple identities for individuals, and these new identities and their workings are of a very different nature than what current theories cover. Not only online commu-nication but also multicultural communication in a globalising world calls for a satisfactory theory. Such a theory should situate the new experiences of the individual in a perspective of globalisation and should incorporate the abrupt changes that have led to the intensification of individualisation (Elliott 2016).

5.4 How we view others

5.4.1 Expressing how one feels about one's interlocutor

When people speak, they are temporarily experiencing a relationship with their partner in speech or their audience. In addition to adjusting their speech to per-sonal identity needs, speakers also adjust to their (known or presumed) audi-ence or the person they are communicating with. The named relationship is affected by the non-linguistic and linguistic messages that the speaker sends out to others, and these reveal how they feel about their audience or interlocutors. These are discussed here.

5.4.2 Politeness

'Politeness' is usually interpreted as the actions targeted at socially accommodating the person one is communicating with and avoiding social discomfort. Whether speakers are trying to act in accordance with politeness rules determines their speech behaviour in conversations strongly. The challenge in dealing with politeness is that while at some general level politeness is universal, it is also strongly culture-bound. Shouting during a quiet dinner or saying nasty things may be impolite in most cultures, but being quiet in a conversation is a sign of respect in one culture while in other cultures this might be perceived as being impolite or even passively aggressive. Ironical or euphemistic language may in one culture be considered obnoxious while it is a sign of friendliness in another culture.

Face

In an effort to capture the difficult topic of politeness, the U.S. linguist Penelope Brown and the British linguist Stephen Levinson tried to lay out the main components and processes of this social phenomenon (Brown and Levinson 1987). Although much work on this topic has been published since, including by Brown and Levinson themselves, this innovative publication is the most well-known in the field and has served as a guideline. In this publication, 'deference' (meaning 'courteous respect') is taken as a sign of politeness. Another central issue is the phenomenon called 'face', which term was borrowed from Social Psychology. The Canadian sociologist Erwin Goffman (1967) had described this concept and had been inspired by research from China, where face had had a longer history than in the West (Hu 1944; Lu 1960). The idea is that in communication we try not to 'lose face' and we always try to 'maintain face' and, if necessary, 'save face'. This goes for ourselves (we don't want to be embarrassed) and for our interlocutor (we don't want to embarrass anyone we are talking to). Face is a self-image that we thus try to protect and it is considered quite vulnerable. Brown and Levinson (1987) discussed three important factors that determine politeness: social distance, power, and imposition. People are generally more polite to people they do not know so well (and are thus socially distant) and to people who have greater power. In situations where much potential or actual imposition is felt, the attention paid to politeness is also greater. Asking for the time is less of an imposition than asking for money.

Entering a conversation entails the risk of face threat. So-called 'speech acts' can threaten face. Such acts are language utterances that 'do something'; in producing a speech act, you are doing something by saying something, in addition to just saying something. Apologies and wagers are well-known speech acts. From this idea of the speech act comes that of the 'face-threatening act', a so-called FTA. An FTA can potentially threaten a speaker's face (a promise, apology, thank-you, or a slip of the tongue) or the interlocutor's face (a warning, criticism, order, or a request). When face (yours or the one of the person you're talking to) is under threat, then you can do nothing or do several things (say or do something) to minimise the damage, that is, save face.

There are two types of face, 'negative face' and 'positive face', and these can be explained through needs. Negative face is the need to interact without your interlocutor constraining you. It is the need that speakers have to be autonomous and the need not to be embarrassed. This can be achieved, for instance, by showing deference. Positive face, on the other hand, is the need for a reaction from your interlocutor, such as reassurance, approval, appreciation, and positive feedback. This can be achieved, for instance, by being very friendly.

Brown and Levinson's model has been challenged and/or refined since it first appeared. Scollon and Scollon (2001), for instance, proposed a model of politeness including the phenomena of 'involvement' and 'independence' as motivations to be polite. Involvement refers to a person's 'right and need to be considered a normal, contributing, or supporting member of society' (46). Independence, on the other hand, refers to an 'individual's right not to be completely dominated by group or social values, and to be free from the impositions of others' (47). More recently, some scholars have taken a different turn, namely through the study of disagreements and impoliteness (Locher 2004; Culpeper 2011).

Cultural variation in politeness

An important assumption in mainstream Politeness Theory is that politeness allocates a central role to the speaker as an individual with certain rights and wishes. From a global perspective, however, this is by no means a rule. In fact, the most numerically dominant societies in the world do not seem to abide by this principle. Asian societies in particular are generally more group-oriented in applying politeness (Eelen 2001; Van Engelenhoven and Van Naerssen 2015). Asians can be said to pay relatively much attention to the hearer's negative face wants (not constraining that hearer). Even within the West, a broad politeness theory does not hold very well. Speakers from the European Mediterranean, for instance, are known to apply the technique of positive politeness, in which the interlocutor's face is emphatically enhanced (Sifianou and Antonopoulou 2005; Cenni 2015) through compliments.

EXAMPLE

Hungarian politeness

Expressing politeness in Hungarian involves the use of *tetszik,* 'pleases (you)'. You could, for instance, ask the polite question 'How are you' as *Hogy tetszik lenni?,* which literally comes down to 'How does it please you to be?' This illustrates that very idiosyncratic politeness tools exist.

Honorifics

A good example of the polite use of language is the honouring of the relative social status of other speakers. The language forms that go with this are called 'honorifics'. Thirteen forms of the first person personal pronoun 'I' exist in Thai, depending on who is being addressed. In French, Dutch, and, for instance, German, there are two ways of saying 'you', with one showing more politeness and respect than the other. The number of honorifics per language is indicative of the culture in which it is embedded, but it does not mean that cultures or languages that have fewer honorifics are less polite or have fewer degrees of politeness. English, with its one way to form the second person pronoun ('you'), has other methods of being polite. Calling the queen 'you' in a conversation with her is unmarked, but by saying 'your majesty' you can still express politeness and respect. It is also common to curtsy to the queen in the United Kingdom. In Belgium, where French and Dutch are the two most dominant languages, it is less common to greet royals through such a subtle respectful bow. It would on the other hand be unacceptable for Belgians to address their royals with '*tu*' or '*jij*', the informal second-person forms of address in, respectively, French and Dutch. So, this all means that politeness is a composite of linguistic and other communicative acts.

5.4.3 Silences

Although their functions have been described and analysed by some – for instance, by Jaworski (1992) – silences are often ignored in linguistic research because they do not contain any grammar or pronunciation. Incorporating silences in a linguistic theoretical framework is hard. Yet, they are crucial parts of communication. Silences are often near a moment when 'turn-taking' (one person stops speaking, the other one starts) could take place, a so-called 'transition-relevant place' (Sacks et al. 1974). Conventions about turn-taking moments and the meaning of silences are highly dependent on culture, and it is probably as easy to embarrass someone from another culture or put them at ease through silences as through actual words. In some cultures, silence is an integral part of conversations, while in others it is considered less desirable and may in fact be frowned upon and cause discomfort. Silence can be used to show the speaker that you are really listening, and it may show respect, but it may also have opposite effects.

Examples of countries that are known to use silence relatively often are Finland and Norway. Cultures that are relatively silent can furthermore be found in parts of the Far and Middle East and amongst the original peoples of Canada and the United States. The Japanese are also associated with relatively much silence in conversations. Silence in such cultures may be perceived as evidence of trust, confidence, agreement, and, for example, harmony. 'Backchannelling' (which means saying 'I see' or 'Mmmm', to show that one understands something or to urge the speaker to keep talking) is also less common in these cultures. It is even (jocularly) claimed (Lehtonen and Sajavaara 1985) that Finns will only backchannel out loud when slightly intoxicated. Relatively silent conversations can be associated with so-called 'high-considerateness styles' (Tannen 1990), in which long pauses occur and in which overlapping speech (two people talking at the same time) is frowned upon, while the subject is not changed easily.

In more loquacious cultures, so-called 'word cultures', speedy turn-taking and few or short silences are more likely to occur. Silences are sometimes charged with meanings such as indifference, resistance, mistrust, and sometimes even hostility (Agliati et al. 2005) in these cultures. Examples of such cultures are the European part of the Mediterranean and South America. The prototypical speech style of Jewish communities in the United States city of New York also falls into this category. Suggestions have been made that the avoidance of silences by these speakers is aimed at avoiding face threat (Tannen 1986). This can be referred to as 'high-involvement style' (Tannen 1990). This speech typically contains no or very few pauses, much backchannelling, changes of subject, and speakers explicitly showing an interest in the other.

5.4.4 Accommodation

Central to (Communication) Accommodation Theory – which was proposed by the psychologist Howard Giles (Giles 1973; Giles and Smith 1979) and later updated and finetuned (Giles et al. 1991; Griffin 2009; Giles and Ogay 2007) – are 'convergence' and 'divergence'. The assumption is that speakers tune into the conversation and the needs of both themselves and their interlocutor and that this tuning is noticeable in their language. This way, they show their attitude to the person they are talking to. Convergence refers to accommodation to the speech of the person one is talking to. This speech behaviour accentuates what the two talkers have in common linguistically. So, the two talkers may be adopting each other's word choices to a subtle degree, for example. As a result, they will sound a little bit more like each other. Liking the interlocutor and wanting to be a little bit like them is considered the motivation behind this. Conversely, divergence refers to an adjustment to the speech of the interlocutor in the opposite way: one accentuates the differences and creates more social distance between oneself and the other speaker by not attuning to the interlocutor and even trying to sound different.

KEY CONCEPTS

Anti-language

Distinction through language use is not an exclusive prerogative of speakers of majority languages. Minority speech communities that wish to set themselves apart from the established society may also speak with distinction, namely through so-called 'anti-language'. This refers to emphasising differences between the minority and majority language (Halliday 1976). This can be done through lexical choices mainly, whereby certain features of the minority language or social dialect are formed by the substitution of new words for old ones (Montgomery 1994). Minority language speakers who are part of a subculture and show subversive behaviour are most prone to this phenomenon.

5.4.5 Audience Design

Bell (1984) introduced the theory that holds that style depends primarily on audience. It distinguishes between various levels of listenership in addition to an audience that one is directly addressing and who know that they are the intended audience. Bell added to this design people overhearing other people speaking and people eavesdropping. A possible audience is assumed, such as the one that radio presenters might have when presenting a programme. The latter are referred to as 'imagined audiences'.

Audience Design Theory suggests that speakers in various ways adjust their language to these very near and real audiences or the very distant and even imagined audiences. The suggestion is that differences in the way individuals speak (i.e., intra-speaker variation), are influenced by whom the speakers are addressing or who might be overhearing them or eavesdropping. The awareness hereof is the force behind the speakers modifying their speech.

FOCUS ON...

Individual decision trees

When an individual talks, how they view themselves, the other, and the situation are quickly taken into consideration. In line with this idea, Meyerhoff (2011) presented trees (123–124) depicting what Hawaiian students said they bore in mind when they were faced with the choice to use either Pidgin or Standard American English. In deciding to use one or the other, they asked themselves, for instance, where they were (with family or perhaps at school), whether they knew the addressee speaks Pidgin, and whether the situation was formal or not.

5.5   Who we associate with

5.5.1 Social networks

We tend to communicate most with people we have much in common with. Our web of social relations is called our 'social network' (Granovetter 1973). It is a group of people that is predominantly interconnected through social contacts. With some people we have more frequent contact than with others, and the intensity and quality of interaction will also vary. Some networks start early in life and some start later, and this also affects the strength of the network. The individual speaker adjusts their speech to this direct social environment and is affected by it. The more intense and stable the network, the more an individual will adjust their speech to it.

The most well-known early investigation into social networks was by Milroy and Milroy (1978). This investigation was on the speech in a Belfast (Northern Ireland) neighbourhood. They distinguished between dense and more loose networks and found that close-knit networks are where most vernacular speech is used. Networks in their investigation were mainly based on religious affiliation (Protestant or Catholic) and neighbourhood. But the effects of all kinds of network-related factors turned out to be as important as these two features; for instance, one's family size, the frequency of visits to neighbours, weekly hobby activities, and degree of care for the weaker members in a network. To find out the effects on language of these factors, extensive interviews and a systematic scoring system for each of the network-related behaviours were used.

Today, new types of networks are becoming more common. The Belfast study represents a very traditional network, which is constrained by geography and by socioeconomic sameness. Digital communities are nowadays equally common and their number and size are growing. People are often part of more networks than before because of this. Gaming communities and digital social network communities contain friends and acquaintances, and networks overlap and interconnect to almost extreme degrees. Everyone in the world seems only a few handfuls of online friends away from most other people in the world. The number, size, and complexity of networks of highly multicultural and multilingual immigrants is also growing, especially in cities. The members in these digital and urban communities are less obviously connected than the members in traditional networks, who often share a common language, social position, ethnicity, and culture. How the language of the members of such highly diverse communities works still requires considerable research as is the case for research into online communication.

5.5.2 Community of practice

Groups of people who share some skill, interest, or set of norms are called a 'community of practice' (Eckert and McConnell-Ginet 1992), which is below the level of the social network when it comes to size. You may share religious practices with a small group of people, professional ones with colleagues, or sporty ones with your baseball team. You meet often with these people, perform a joint activity, and temporarily work towards the same goal. While doing this, you will tend to use similar, possibly jargon-like vocabulary as well as other speech characteristics. Your social networks are more stable than your communities of practice, so the assumption is (Eckert and McConnell-Ginet 1992). In communities of practice, you actively engage in community-specific acts, surrounded by like-minded other people, while the social networks that affect your daily language do so less directly but more permanently. Online communities are often more like communities of practice than stable networks.

5.6 Conclusion

When people talk, the information they put across is directed by many forces not directly related to the content of the message but by characteristics that are simply a part of these speakers. Their bodies are built a certain way and these bodies develop in certain ways. Vocal tracts have a certain shape and the way our bodies are built affects the way we view ourselves. Social and regional origin and how they develop after our early lives also play an important role. We have an opinion about how we view ourselves and others and about our role in groups that we associate with.

To varying degrees, these factors affect an individual's language choices – from moment to moment and in different social settings. However, the unpredictability of language use lies in the fact that some speakers work harder in suppressing or accentuating certain characteristics that they have. Some speakers are highly concerned about their identity, while others are not. Some people attach much importance to politeness, others don't. Some people use their abilities to stylise their language while others do so less. So, in the end, language choice – rather than fate – is the most important force, and each individual uses the linguistic resources at hand in their own way and towards their own goals.

A question that is equally important as the intended message is its perception. The interpretation of the subtle cues by listeners may be the one that the speaker expected or intended or it may not. It is in this juxtaposition of sender and receiver interpretation that the key lies to harmonious communication as well as the explanation of miscommunication.

STUDY QUESTIONS

1. Can you indicate to what degree you still speak the way you did when you were a child? In which ways and why have you changed your speech?
2. Describe your own linguistic identity.
3. What are the differences and agreements between the politeness system as described in this chapter and the politeness system that you abide by?

FURTHER READING

The first chapter of Elliott (2016) gives a state of the art interpretation of the phenomenon of identity in a social context. Joseph (2004) discusses language and identity in detail and includes ethnicity and religion as factors. Lakoff and Ide (2005) contains an overview of politeness systems in the world as well as relevant research that is available. It focuses mostly on non-Western systems and is written by experts from all over the world. Watts (2003) illustrates politeness using a range of real-life examples and tries to present a new view of politeness and impoliteness. Barton and Tusting (2005) give a series of interesting studies on social networks.

What is Good Language?

Language Norms and Ideology

6.1 Introduction

When people hear the word 'language', they are likely to think of two things. First, language is the system that people use to communicate. It is something inside their brain, a cognitive skill that they use every day to pass on, receive, and process information. Their second interpretation is likely to be that of the national language, a codified construct; there is 'Finnish', the language of Finland, and Standard Arabic, the language of the Arab region. At schools, the two interpretations come together. Children are taught the canonical, correct language and, depending on their skills, they can do well in reproducing it (produce correct grammar, use a rich vocabulary) or not do so well (produce mistakes, have a small vocabulary).

This chapter elaborates on these two basic interpretations of the 'language' phenomenon. It first introduces what language in its broadest sense means as a skill in a communicative setting. It then introduces the language norm that large groups of people abide by; the various ways that this norm is embedded in societies and people's lives and the power that it can have.

6.2 Language

Language is a communication system that mainly utilises speech and writing and that enables people to exchange messages. Sociolinguists in particular tend to look at communication in a sense that is broader than the linguistic and involve the study of signs to describe this exchanging of messages. A sign is something that stands in for anything other than itself and could refer to gestures, for instance. It also refers to various cultural, social, and situational contexts in which language is uttered. One might even include **kinesics** (facial expression and body language) and **proxemics** (body posture and movement) in this analysis of human communication in a broad sense. Spoken and written language is part of this larger system of meaningful signs and thus carries only part of the intended and perceived meaning. This large system of communicatively meaningful signs is often referred to as 'Semiotics' (Crystal 1995).

Ferdinand De Saussure (see 1.4.1) is associated with Semiotics; the study of signs as they operate in communication. The idea is that word meaning depends on the value assigned by humans. This meaning tends to change and vary. It depends on the way language is used and where the sign appears. For instance, the word 'cool' painted on a façade of an air-conditioned bar in Bangkok (Thailand) will be interpreted differently from that same word shouted out enthusiastically by a schoolgirl skateboarding with friends in downtown Tromsø (Norway). Which of the dictionary meanings applies most, and which exact connotations, depends on a myriad of signs. The culture in which it appears is a strong determinant of meaning, as is whether it is a first or second language of the person producing the utterance, and the form in which the language appears (on a sign or spoken) also influences meaning. In addition, the way the letters are ordered on the Bangkok façade as well as the intonation patterns and hand gestures the Tromsø schoolgirl uses all combine to create meaning.

FOCUS ON...

Sign language

Semiotic signs in communication do not refer to gestures in sign language. This is an actual language that applies gestures out of basic necessity. The fact that it is a fully fledged language is shown by the various degrees and types of official recognition and of codification that sign languages all over the world have received. In some countries, there is an officially recognised national sign language (a state language), such as in Malta. In Thailand, furthermore, Thai Sign Language is acknowledged as a national language of deaf people. Sign languages are part of a global system of related and less related languages. Sign language users have access to a rich sociolinguistic system in which they can express meaning and, for instance, irony and excitement by gesturing in a certain way. The gestures themselves are subject to semiotic interpretation, as they depend on context and the other factors mentioned here, just like aspects of spoken and written language do.

6.3   The language norm

6.3.1 Good language

In speech communities, ideas tend to exist as to what the right way to write and speak is, i.e., ideas about the language norm. Within countries, the norm is usually institutionalised and spread through the educational system, and it is used in government. Usually, the language norm is visible and audible on a daily basis in public life. The rules are codified through grammars and dictionaries and are often also available in pronunciation descriptions and in usage guides (instruction books on how to use language). After the norm has come to existence, it may become so widely embraced that it results in a widespread ideology, resulting in large groups of people feeling that the language norm is 'normal' and in deviations from it being viewed critically. In industrialised nation states, especially Western ones, the language that is in accordance with the ideology – and could be called the 'norm language' – is referred to as the 'standard' language (Foley 2003; Kachru 1976). The standard language concept works particularly well in societies with language norms that gradually came to existence over a few centuries, with one dialect surfacing as the most dominant one (because powerful people spoke it). The language norm may in some countries also be referred to as the 'official' language or 'national' language.

The 'norm language' in each country has a unique history. The dialect or sociolect (see 3.2.1) of an economically and/or politically dominant group of speakers, who often live in a certain (usually urban) area, often gradually becomes the norm for a larger area or is simply proclaimed as the norm. In each society, this language norm is important and fixed to a different degree. For some societies, it is an important part of nation building and of communication amongst people with different language backgrounds, as is the case in the large culturally and linguistically diverse archipelago of Indonesia, while in a small country such as Denmark it does not serve that function but is simply a neutral communication tool and a symbolic norm with a high status. The language norm in Indonesia (a large archipelago with extreme linguistic, geographic, ethnic, and other variation amongst its people) has no fixed pronunciation. In fact, the pronunciation depends strongly on the language background of the speaker and often leads to misunderstandings amongst speakers with different backgrounds. The written norm is also adhered to relatively loosely. In a country such as Denmark, the written system and the pronunciation are much more fixed and a higher percentage of speakers apply broad language norms in daily life.

FOCUS ON...

'Norm' versus 'most widely used'

A codified, institutionalised language may not be the most common language in an area. In Kashmir, a region in the north of the Indian subcontinent, the mother tongue (Kashmiri) of 5.6 million speakers is mainly an oral home language. The official state languages – Sanskrit, Urdu, English, and Persian – are mainly used in official realms. Sometimes, an official language is hardly used as an actual, living language. Portuguese is an official language of the former Portuguese colony of Macau (China), for instance, although few Macau natives actually speak it, and it is not the language of politics or administration. Some official languages do not have many native speakers, especially not when it comes to daily communication, such as is the case with Standard Arabic, which is usually taught more or less as a second language at schools. In several northern European countries, on the other hand, the language commonly heard in the public space is an understandable variant of the norm language, and it is common for people to speak this as a native tongue on a daily basis.

Norm languages are described and prescribed to different degrees. In some countries (for instance, the Arab region) the language norm is largely restricted to the written form, while in some countries, (for instance, England) detailed descriptions exist of how to pronounce and not pronounce the norm language.

6.3.2 The status of deviations from good language

It is very common for people to be very fond of the norm language in their society, and this fondness may take on judgemental shapes. Bourdieu (1991) said that all linguistic practices are ultimately measured against the theoretical norm. The power of the norm lies in its associations with, for instance, a high status. This is the case in Egypt, where Eltouhamy (2016) found associations of the national language norm with leadership, professionalism, and smartness. Hogan-Brun and Ramonienė (2005), furthermore, showed that attitudes towards Standard Lithuanian are overall favourable, especially when it comes to competence associations. This is called 'overt prestige' (see 11.5.4). Giles and Billings (2004), however, noted that there is also a certain acknowledgement that deviations from the norm also carry prestige although this prestige is less explicit and outspoken; they are tacit values ('covert prestige'; see 11.5.4). The prestige of deviations from the norm may be visible in associations with traits relating to solidarity, integrity, benevolence, and social attractiveness (Giles and Powesland 1975). This was found, amongst others, in Switzerland (Hogg et al. 1984) and Ireland (Edwards 1977). Research by Šimičić and Sujoldžić (2004) also showed that while the explicit norm (in Croatia) is associated with competence, deviations from it were associated with social attractiveness and thus also carried a certain type of prestige.

FOCUS ON...

Claiming norm-language proficiency

The symbolic value and power of the norm language is illustrated by the fact that it is common for speakers who do not have it as their native tongue to proclaim speaking it nevertheless. A popular tendency among some residents of Hindi states in India is to report Standard Hindi as their mother tongue despite having home languages that are quite distinct from this language. So, a resident of the central Indian district of Bhopal may claim that Hindi is their mother tongue although they are in fact native speakers of the Western Hindi dialect called Bundeli (spoken in central India) and do not use Standard Hindi.

6.3.3 Deficits, codes, and difference

In the Anglo-Western tradition, theories have been developed to explain differences between the language of members of different status groups. (Verbal) Deficit Theory is based in a Western class system and refers to the idea is that children growing up in a lower social-status group have a less adequate command of grammar and vocabulary to express complex ideas. This is presumed to be the result of a host of parental practices and environmental circumstances and practices, which have a negative impact on language proficiency. The ensuing less information-filled style has been associated with the concept of Restricted Code, which is different from the Elaborated Code, which style is more explicit and linguistically rich. The hypothesis is that children from a lower social-status group have a command of only the Restricted Code, while those from a higher social-status group have the ability to use both and, in addition, know when to use which. These codes were proposed by Bernstein (1964). This researcher did not invent or propose (Verbal) Deficit Theory and was not an explicit supporter of it, but he is often associated with it nevertheless.

An alternative view is Difference Theory, which was explained, amongst others, by Baratz (1969) and Labov (1965). This theory presumes that the language of the various social classes is different in nature rather than in quality. Like (Verbal) Deficit Theory, it accepts that there is variation in income, learning, and parenting environment, but it presumes that these do not necessarily lead to underdeveloped cognitive or communicative skills. Proponents of this theory pointed out that certain allegedly 'deficient' aspects of, for instance, African American Vernacular English are in fact linguistically well-structured and systematic (Labov 1972b). The difference is that the structure is not in accordance with the prescribed language norm. It is thus linguistically different but not linguistically deficient.

6.3.4 Qualities of the language norm

The norm language has a unique position in society compared to other varieties. Certain types of speakers typically use it. It is spoken in certain places and social contexts in particular. Few generalisations can be made about this, but about standard languages in particular some tendencies can be found in the literature.

The qualification 'regionally neutral' is a common feature of the standard language, and it was famously proposed by the Danish linguist Otto Jespersen (1925). One can also take into consideration the historical position of the language and the way it is treated in society (Stewart 1968) for the norm language often has a history of being described and debated. One could also look at whether a language has gone through certain stages of development, which is what Haugen (1966) and Van der Wal and Van Bree (2008) did. These stages are: selection (which of the dialects that exist is to become the norm?), codification (writing down the rules), elaboration (spreading the norm amongst speakers), and acceptance (influential and, after that, less influential speakers embracing the norm). A language that has gone through these stages can then be qualified as 'standard'. One could, finally, emphasise which people use the language, which is what Finegan (2007) did. Newsreaders and politicians, for instance, are known to use the standard language.

KEY CONCEPTS

Standardisation versus levelling and mixing

'Standardisation', the steps a language goes through towards becoming a standard language, is not the same as 'levelling', which is a term often associated with it. Levelling refers to similar language varieties becoming more alike when speakers of these varieties communicate (Dillard 1972). Through this process, these varieties assimilate and become even more mutually alike. Some associate levelling as being the result of standardisation tendencies, with people avoiding marked features and seeking to use more broadly accepted forms. 'Mixing' is a stronger form of speakers influencing each other and creating new language. It refers to a new language arising from the linguistic features of two other (usually very different) languages. The common language that is the end result of levelling or any other process whereby similar languages meet and a new one comes to existence is a 'koiné' (Dillard 1972). An example of a koiné is Los Angeles Vernacular Spanish (Macías et al. 2018). This variety is the outcome of contact amongst varieties of Spanish in the Latino communities in Los Angeles. New languages coming out of such processes are discussed in Section 3.4.

In industrialised nation states, the characteristics that are assigned by ordinary speakers to the standard language can be divided into two types (Smakman 2012). On the one hand, there is the view of this language as being typical of the happy few (the 'exclusive standard language'), while there is also the view that it is the language that socially connects people in a country (the 'inclusive standard language'). The latter interpretation involves a more varied and liberal application of the language rules. In certain Western countries, this distinction doesn't work very well. In predominantly monolingual societies with 'imported' national languages, such as Australia (English from the United Kingdom) and Argentina (Spanish from Spain), the notion of exclusiveness in this sense is less relevant and the socially and communicatively cohesive function is usually the main function of the norm language in such places.

6.3.5 Norm languages in multilingual contexts

The norm-language paradigm in multilingual societies is usually more complex than it is in societies with one obvious language that functions as the norm. Smakman and Barasa (2016), for instance, explained how there is often no exclusive norm language in postcolonial multilingual societies, as standardisation may mainly or only have a communicatively and socially cohesive (i.e., inclusive) function and is not usually used as a distinctive means in daily communication.

Mesthrie (2015) explained how conditions taken for granted in certain mainstream models (which tend to focus on standard languages) do not apply in many colonised countries. He referred, amongst other things, to the absence of a written language tradition for certain languages, which makes codification difficult. The assumption of there being only one leading language is another issue. In formerly colonised countries, the language imported by colonists may share the position of language norm with another language, as is the case in Kenya, where Kiswahili and English are the two official languages. Each of these languages may have a different practical function in public discourse (which are fulfilled by one and the same language in the standard-language paradigm), with the colonial language being associated with the more prestigious and ceremonial functions (the more 'exclusive' functions) while the more indigenous official language is for a wider range of communicative functions (the 'inclusive' functions). A slightly different situation exists in the city-state of Dubai, where English functions as the language of communication with the rest of the globalising world and as default lingua franca within the city, while only Arabic is the official national language. As is the case in other places where Arabic is spoken alongside English, Arabic is associated with the private and with Islamic tradition, while English is associated with the professional world, modernity, and with modern technology and science (Findlow 2006). Although only one language is official, both languages in their own way have a norm-like status and perform functions of the norm language.

FOCUS ON...

The size of lingua francas

A widespread assumption is that a lingua franca is a 'large' language or a majority language. In Burma, however, the Jinghpaw language is the trade language used by a major ethnic minority group, the Kachin. Within this ethnically and linguistically diverse people, this language is a lingua franca. Within the country as a whole, this language is nevertheless a minority language, with its one million speakers.

In diglossic cultures – where two languages exist side by side, with many people speaking both as a native tongue –, so Smakman and Barasa (2016) explained, a style involving codeswitching may serve as a kind of language norm, since it is a reality in both the formal and informal domain. Typical speakers of this 'codeswitched language' can even be heard on television (although news anchors will not codeswitch and will instead speak in what is perceived as a less natural monolingual style). There are also adapted languages (oftentimes from a formerly colonial language); they are adapted by speakers to accommodate local meanings and habits and generally incorporate the cultural and linguistic needs of the local community. In several ways, these are the real norm languages in these countries and the native tongue for increasing numbers of speakers. Kachru (1976) was one of the first to assign status to these 'nativised' languages, and Banda (1996) and Jenkins (2009) also discussed them as a tangible entity and norm to be reckoned with. These could be French that deviates strongly from French as it is spoken in France because it is wrought with a pronunciation and lexicon that is typical of the home culture (for instance, in Nigeria). It contains all of the cultural intricacies that speakers need to position themselves as belonging to the society at hand (Nigerian culture) and not the culture belonging to the colonial language (French culture). The codeswitched and nativised languages perform functions that are typically assigned to the norm language. Jaffe (2004) suggested giving more rights to such mixed codes.

KEY CONCEPTS

High language and Low language

Ferguson (1959) laid the foundations of the study of 'diglossia' in so-called diglossic communities. He distinguished between two languages in a community; 'High' and 'Low'. The Low language (also called 'L-language') has less prestige than the High language (also called 'H-language'). The latter is usually the most dominant language and is used in formal contexts, while the former is used for more informal functions. Oftentimes, the Low language has been around longer in the community. The Low language is usually most susceptible to language shift (see 3.5.1). Examples of Low languages are Komi and Udmur, as spoken in Central Russia. Today, almost all the speakers of these languages are bilingual, and these languages are generally not used in official domains. They also suffer from mixing with the High language, Russian (Edygarova 2014).

Monolingual versus multilingual countries

Whether a country is monolingual or multilingual depends on whether there is a general tendency towards using one language across the country in official communication and in the public space. There are degrees to which countries are multilingual or monolingual. A country such as Japan is highly monolingual, both officially (through prescribed policy) and realistically (in the public space). Using a language other than Japanese is relatively problematic in this country, even in the centres of the largest cities. South Africa, on the other hand, with its 11 official languages, is multilingual in the official domain, and in everyday life one is also likely to encounter more than one language. In between these two extremes is a country like the Czech Republic, with a monolingual ideology and even reinforced linguistic homogeneity (Sloboda 2010), while visible linguistic diversity in daily life is growing because of immigration in the past few decades, especially in an internationally oriented city like Prague (Drbohlav 2011). Russia is another example of this mismatch between a monolingual policy and the realities of language competencies and usages amongst ordinary speakers, especially in the city of Moscow.

6.3.6 The cultured language

The language norm has a history that is different from that of other language varieties. It is assigned certain specific functions, and it has an idealised grammar, lexicon, and pronunciation. Indeed, so Thomason and Kaufman (1988) explained, norm languages are often to a degree the product of language construction rather than evolution. Obviously, such interference by authorities will affect the naturalness of the language in question. In China, for instance, a hybrid language, combining traditional and modern features, was constructed as the norm language. *Putonghua* (the Chinese name for Mandarin Chinese) is a mix of northern Chinese dialects and is influenced by Mongolian (as spoken in the region of Mongolia) and Manchurian (as spoken in North East China). Because of this background, such a model can be qualified as artificial.

This idea that the norm language sometimes comes across as stilted is strengthened by the fact that it is often not the first language of speakers, so that some speakers need to try hard to speak it. The norm language is most likely to be subject to language cultivation, according to Nekvapil (2010). This author defined 'cultivate' in this context as 'refine,' or 'improve something by making small changes' (251).

This extraordinary background of many norm languages also leads to other qualities. Coulmas (2011) associated the standard language with monotony and clarity. Smakman (2012, 2006) found that his respondents (from seven different societies across the world) described the norm language as suffering from a degree of blandness. Bassiouney and Muehlhaeusler (2018), furthermore, referred to the standard language in Egypt as lacking character, and Wolfram (1991) referred to Standard American English as 'colourless' (210).

The polishing of language may lead to a variety that distinguishes a certain group of speakers. It becomes their sociolect. Certain distinctive speech styles can, for instance, be qualified as 'posh', which means 'cultivated' or 'highly distinctive'. Hagen (1990:34–35) referred to the posh variety as 'super standard'. This style is expressed through a certain manner of speaking and of positioning the vocal tract. This style is typically associated with England and some mainland European countries with centuries-old traditions of inherited wealth and status. The phenomenon of distinctive speech can be found elsewhere as well, albeit in a different form. In St. Petersburg, for instance, there is a cultured style of speaking that is typical of the old intelligentsia. It is associated with a high status (although not necessarily with wealth). Young academics sometimes use this speech to assert their identity. As an example, the letter combination *ch* in words such as *konecho* ('certainly', 'surely') and *chto* ('what') are pronounced as they are spelled, which is marked. Another example relates to a variety called 'Engsh'. In Kenya, this urban youth slang variety evolved among younger speakers of the more affluent Nairobi neighbourhoods and is associated with distinctiveness (Abdulaziz and Osinde 1997).

6.3.7 Media and the language norm

There are other reasons for this perceived unnaturalness of the language norm than the ones described here, and these are related to the media. In broadcasting media, which are associated with the standard language, presenters are often instructed to speak in a certain way and use certain words and phrases, although they wouldn't normally use them (Shioda 2011). The type of Portuguese that is promoted by Brazilian TV networks does not have any native speakers (Gluszek and Hansen 2013), in fact. Also, in early broadcasting, presenters needed to speak clearly in order to be understood by their audience (Van de Velde 1996), which tendency may have left its traces in today's norm-language pronunciation, such as associations of clear enunciation and a good speed.

The media are known to influence communication, and this is often seen in the context of a larger tendency referred to as 'mediatisation' (Livingstone and Lunt 2014), which comes down to a broad influence of the media on institutions and society. When it comes to language, the media have a special relationship with the norm language in that they pass on both traditional and innovative language norms. While the media today are traditionally associated with 'good' language in many countries, according to Inoue (2011) destandardisation processes are currently reinforced by them, and he mentioned Japanese broadcasting as an example. In other countries, such tendencies are also noticeable. In the United Kingdom, for example, the well-known variety called Estuary English is commonly heard. This variety is typically spoken in the region on both sides of the Thames river estuary (which runs through London to the North Sea) and is made up of a mixture of features, some of which are considered highly non-standard. The Dutchman Jan Stroop (1998) signalled something similar in the Netherlands, namely the rise of a type of Dutch in the media that bears certain vowel features that deviate from the norm and are reminiscent of an accent from the city of Amsterdam, the capital of the Netherlands.

These varieties may be innovative in nature and challenge the status of the traditional language norm. While traditional media, such as television and radio, are typically associated with promoting a single language, they are nowadays allowing or even stimulating substandard language uses. The British Broadcasting Corporation is increasingly often employing presenters with accents from Wales, Northern Ireland, Scotland, and regions within England. The substandard varieties considered suitable are often urban. In Egypt, an urban dialect (from Cairo, the capital of Egypt) has more or less become the norm on national television (Bassiouney 2009). Examples are also known of modern media stimulating variation, or at least exposing the audience to it, through popular culture; in (mainly Mandarin-speaking) China, Cantonese popular music from Hong Kong (so-called Cantopop) is very popular in the media, while in Indonesian media Javanese artists singing in Javanese languages are often heard.

6.3.8 Norms and the city

Changes in the norm do not necessarily spread according to a predictable mechanism that is often referred to as the Wave Model. This model suggests that change starts in one place and then gradually spreads to the nearest place and then the next; like a wave. This model does not take into consideration population densities and population centres, although these are in fact important factors in linguistic change. From large population centres, innovative

FOCUS ON...

Online norms

Online communication and other communication through texts (such as through mobile phones and smartphones) is subject to brevity constraints, amongst others because the screen does not allow more than a certain number of characters. Abbreviations (such as 'LOL' for 'Laugh out loud' and emoticons such as ;-) to denote a smile and a wink) are used to simplify and shorten messages, and these texts are known for a certain degree of informality and for containing emotion. People sometimes worry that younger people use such abbreviated and often informal language in more serious contexts. It is difficult to gauge whether this type of language is affecting other forms or whether informalisation is a general trend that acts independently and is restricted to certain types of communication. It is true though, that using emoticons in professional emails is by many considered acceptable, even in emails to people in one's professional field that one doesn't know yet (Friedrich and Diniz de Figueiredo 2016).

language is often spread across less urban areas, and this mechanism is referred to as the Gravity Model. The idea is that cities influence each other first, and the rural areas in between them come next in adopting linguistic innovations. Cities are where linguistically influential speakers live and speak, develop, and spread their own sociolect, which may eventually gain the status of a broader language norm.

Massey (2005) described cities as 'peculiarly large, intense and heterogeneous constellations of trajectories, demanding of complex negotiation' (154). Indeed, in addition to being the hubs of linguistic diversity, cities are the places where norm development seems particularly active, due to the intensity of communication amongst people with various experiences and intentions, which leads towards efforts to understand each other better. As an illustration, according to Tzitzilis (2001) and Kourdis (2004) local idioms and general language use in the diverse cities of Thessaloniki and Athens (Greece) are giving way to the standard language.

The final trend in urban contexts described here is the blurring of the distinction between the language norm and that of the city. In many cases, the original dialect of a specific city may in fact be associated particularly strongly with a national norm. In Egypt, for instance, the media broadcast almost exclusively in Cairene Arabic, to the extent that this city variety is adopted more or less as the national norm language. (This dialect is even functioning as a standard in other Arabic countries). It is associated with Egypt as a whole and with Egyptian identity, despite being characteristic of the city of Cairo. In other places, a standard and urban variety are also competing as the norm. Pedersen (2003), as an illustration, observed that in Copenhagen, the capital city of Denmark, not all features of the language of the educated middle classes but features typical of the more local type of Copenhagen speech were by younger ambitious speakers associated with standard speech. In Beijing too, local features are highly prestigious, especially amongst younger speakers, even if they deviate from the traditional standard style. In England, the speech that is typical of the capital city and the surrounding counties is by young and ambitious people, including educated ones, followed as a language norm and can be heard on television and radio (Coggle 1993).

FOCUS ON...

The changed city

Studying language in the city nowadays is not as easy as it was in the mid-1960s, when William Labov did his research in New York (see 7.4.8 and 18.6.2). He walked into department stores and on the basis of reasonable assumptions expected people to speak a certain way, and they often did. Nowadays, diversity in inner cities is such that walking into a large department store and expecting people you see to be native speakers of the language in the country where the department store is or to be from the city where you are doing your research is no longer a reasonable assumption.

6.4   Conclusion

The word 'language' is popularly held to refer to communicative ability, specifically the ability to write and speak a codified language; the language norm. Language norms can take on many shapes in countries and regions across the world and may be referred to as 'standard', 'national', or 'official', depending on their history and position in society. In many countries, this language is a cultivated form of what was originally a regional, local, or urban dialect, which developed into a sociolect of the powerful and privileged. In some countries, the coming to existence of the norm is less predictable, as more languages may be involved as candidates to perform the various functions that the norm language typically has. The status and treatment of the language norm in a society depends on its role as a national symbol and, for instance, its practical necessity. Traditional media and urban contexts are particularly influential as regards the shaping of the language norm.

STUDY QUESTIONS

1. What is your main association with the term 'language'?
2. What is the name of the language norm in your country of origin (standard, national, official language, or something else)? Why is it called that?
3. How detailed are the rules?
4. Is it widely used and can it often be heard in daily life?

FURTHER READING

The phenomenon of language ideology is described in the edited volume by Schieffelin et al. (1998) and in Irvine and Gal (2000). Joseph (1987) describes the rise of standard languages. The final chapter of Mesthrie et al. (2010) contains an excellent introduction to sociolinguistic aspects of sign language. Trudgill (2000) gives a description of the Wave Model and Gravity Model, which explain the geographical spread of linguistic change. Coulmas (2016) gives a lively account of the lives and influence of a range of historical figures who have left their mark on how language is perceived and treated in their society. An overview of various publications about the (Verbal) Deficit Theory is in Gordon (1981).

Language and Status across the Globe

Cultural Variation in Language Norms

7

7.1 Introduction

When William Labov did his research on the island of Martha's Vineyard (see 5.3.1), he presumed the existence of two language models. First of all, there was the authentically Vineyard way of pronouncing certain vowels. Secondly, there was a broader, mainstream norm, which was closer to the norm in the United States as a whole. Labov took the latter norm as an underlying reference point by qualifying Martha's Vineyard vowels as deviating from it, amongst others by using terms such as 'more raised' and 'more centralised'.

These two norms were associated with two groups of identifiable speakers. Labov specifically referred to local fisherman as examples of speakers with a 'real' island way of talking. So, these were speakers with a traditional and rural lifestyle, a manual profession, and perhaps not too highly educated or wealthy. The speaker group associated with the more mainstream norm was less narrowly defined but could be qualified as the opposite; more mainstream in their lifestyle, living in an urban or suburban setting, relatively educated and wealthy, and less likely to do manual work. The criteria to define these groups are thus related to lifestyle and a result of economic factors, most notably ways of making a living. Those who want to associate with high-status language will try to speak the way the latter group of people does.

This chapter demonstrates the Anglo-Western bias as explained in Section 4.2 by the describing the concept of the high-status group, whose language functions as a model to others, in various cultures across the globe. In these cultures, such groups are defined on different grounds, as this chapter will illustrate. The phenomenon of status will first be discussed as well as the specific use of the term 'status group'. Status as a phenomenon in a number of major cultures in the world will then be discussed. For each of these cultures, some research findings on the language of high-status groups will be discussed.

7.2 Status

7.2.1 Thinkers

Well-established societal hierarchies were the source of the theories by American sociologists Kingsley Davis (1908–1997) and Wilbert E. Moore (1914–1987) and by German thinkers Karl Marx (1818–1883) and Max Weber (1864–1920). Their theories typically applied to industrialised societies, especially in times when status-related group divisions were relatively clear and thus measurable in these societies. In non-industrialised and/or non-Western societies in particular, certain activists have shaped thoughts on how a society should be structured. The Guyanese political activist Walter Rodney (1942–1980) and the American civil rights figure Marcus Mosiah Garvey (1887–1940), for instance, have influenced ideas about class divisions on the island of Jamaica, while Nelson Mandela (1918–2013) influenced the way South Africans view social divisions in society. In India, the influential politician Bhimrao Ramji Ambedkar (1891–1956) addressed social inequality. Ideologies in today's societies are influenced by such thinkers.

7.2.2 Status groups

Hierarchical systems in which some have more status than others develop if people come together and form a community. Individuals have a certain status within a community, and communities have a certain ranked position amongst other communities, all within the larger social system. Social groups with different degrees of status might be called 'tribe', 'caste', 'class', or perhaps 'clan'. Each of these refers to a group of people who share certain lifestyle and social characteristics and who are associated with a certain degree of wealth, power, and privilege. Members of high-status tribes, casts, classes, or clans will be entitled to more of such benefits than lower-status ones. Language is a distinctive and symbolic tool in such hierarchical systems. There is a tendency for high-status speakers to have a role as model speakers to other groups.

Ash (2002) and Rickford (1986) emphasised that the lack of clear definitions regarding status-related issues makes research challenging. Dictionary definitions of status usually contain various aspects (Rundell and Fox 2002), two of which are relevant from a sociolinguistic perspective. First, there is the reference to 'rank'; both rank of individuals within a social framework and rank of groups relative to each other. The second is the one referring to respect and importance. In that interpretation, 'status' is a synonym of 'prestige'. The term 'social status' emphasises relative status in a system of groups that are socially definable.

The term 'status group' has been subject to various interpretations and uses since the German philosopher Max Weber put it forward in the late nineteenth century. In this chapter, it refers to a social stratum in which the members share lifestyle aspects and the prestige that goes with these (Bendix 1960).

7.2.3 Membership criteria

Tacit agreement on the nature and workings of power features and the kinship they evoke amongst people is part of the mechanism that upholds a status-group system. Race, belief, and custom determine the sense of group in tribes, while caste systems are based on inherited and unchangeable status. In these caste systems, religious denomination and marriage are amongst the factors that determine divisions. Class is most strongly associated with profession, income, wealth, and education. Aspects of class can be passed on from generation to generation to various degrees. A clan, finally, is defined on the basis of family relations. It is a kinship group or group of kinship groups that one is born into and which can trace its descent back to a common ancestor.

Some of these status groups are easier to join or abandon than others. The tolerance towards individuals being members of more than one status group also varies. Classes are more open to accepting members and letting them go, while tribes are less flexible in this sense. Castes are known to be the most unbending when it comes to new members entering or existing ones leaving, and dual membership is not part of the system. A clan can be entered through marriage and procreation and is difficult to exit.

Class, tribe, caste, and clan sometimes overlap. In different cultures they are associated with slightly different social entities, while within cultures they might co-exist and have a changing mutual relationship. In India, for instance, the distinction between tribes and castes is currently becoming less clear with time (Sharma 2007).

7.3   Language and status

7.3.1 Language as a symbol and a tool

People from different status groups speak differently. Holmes (2001) famously and straightforwardly said that 'Bank managers do not talk like office cleaners, lawyers do not speak in the same way as the burglars they defend' (135). In addition to performing this affirmation role, the language of the high-status group may facilitate securing privileges (Bernstein 1971). Pierre Bourdieu introduced the terms 'symbolic capital' and 'symbolic power' to deal with the fact that the ability and willingness to communicate in a certain way in the **linguistic marketplace** can influence one's position in society. Symbolic capital refers to all kinds of non-material resources, such as language skills, knowledge, experiences, and social relationships. If you have and control many of these resources and use them well, then you can gain much symbolic power over other groups. When it comes to language use as symbolic capital, the linguistic features to achieve this lie not solely in what you explicitly say to people but in the subtle vocabulary and grammatical constructions you produce. It lies in the use of certain phrases and sayings and in pronunciation choices that you make. Bourdieu used the term 'legitimate language' to refer to symbolic capital that leads to symbolic power – the official, prestigious language in a country, which in his case (French in France) is associated with education, culture, and history.

7.3.2 Status-group research

Early (Western) research used index scores to measure people's social status. Chambers (2009) explained how the variable of social status can be measured by assigning individuals a numerical index score on the basis of characteristics. Blishen (1971), Trudgill (1974b), and, for instance, Jameson (2011) put forward an array of (largely socioeconomic and network-related) factors to measure the status of groups in societies. Each speech community has its criteria and these could be measured through a straightforward questionnaire.

Despite some waning of the interest in status as a factor, grouped status divisions are still a major interest in Sociolinguistics across the world (Ash 2002; Battisti and Pires Lucas 2015; Mesthrie 2015; Satyanath 2015). A shift away from the (socioeconomic) class approach has been taking place. Attention is paid to individual speakers' identity, motivation, and life trajectories in explaining their status-related language use. Social status is treated as flexible, subject to change, and multifaceted. Surveys, interviews, and observation of language use are the most obvious research tools to supplement surveys aimed at indexation.

7.4   Status and language variation across the globe

7.4.1 Status-group systems and research

Status depends strongly on culture and lends itself particularly well for a separate look at how this factor affects language in different cultures. Here, status-related research from various regions in the world is described. The descriptions here, which are ordered on the basis of approximate number of inhabitants of the region discussed, will demonstrate how cultural systems lead to a different interaction of status and language. They also show that the availability of research in the various areas is very diverse.

7.4.2 China

The Chinese sociolinguistic situation with respect to status is characterised by a limited social mobility of most individuals, that is, the relative lack of opportunities to move away from one's status group. There is an official classless ideology. Nevertheless, a few large classes can be distinguished on the basis of wealth mainly. Massive urbanisation has led to the coming to existence of more fluid class boundaries.

Research on language and status is scarce in China. Systematic and large-scale research into class as a sociolinguistic variable is still at an early stage. Chen (1980, 1983) pointed to a correlation between language use and socioeconomic class, and Dai (1993) mentioned the topic of class in his introductory book on Sociolinguistics. Bauer (1984) used social class as one of the independent variables in his study and found an effect of education in the speech of Hong Kong speakers of Cantonese Chinese when they pronounce a certain sound (the syllable-initial labialised velar initial). Hong Kong was not part of China then but was culturally strongly influenced by this country.

Furthermore, Xu (1992) investigated social stratification in the use of nasal sounds in Mandarin Chinese using Labovian principles and methodologies. The correlation between status and language can also be seen in Chinese research into language and ethnicity, by, for instance, Zhang (2002).

7.4.3 India

India has a rigid status-group division system that includes castes that people are born into and cannot easily leave. Castes are associated with religion and profession, amongst other things. The social segregation this system brings along is less rigid in urban environments. A new class of entrepreneurs is currently forming in these cities, irrespective of caste.

In some ways, studying caste language use is easier than studying Western-based class language use. Castes are stable, clearly named, clearly separated from one another, and based on hereditary membership. With the current development of class overruling caste (Sharma 2007) and of ongoing urbanisation, however, studying the language habits that go with social status in India is becoming more challenging. The language of castes has been widely researched. John Gumperz was empirical in his approach and investigated the language of the inhabitants of a small North Indian village, Khalapur (Gumperz 1958). Phonologically, castes could be distinguished, so it turned out, and each caste even appeared to have its own distinctive vocabulary. Caste as a source of dialect variation in south India was addressed by Bright and Ramanujan (1964). McCormack (1966) attempted to lay bare the method of transmission of caste dialects. More recently, Boch (2010) discussed sociodialectal differences between northern and southern caste dialects. Even more recent is the status-related investigation by Sunny (2013). Sunny's findings suggested that caste and language interact. Satyanath (2015) mentioned a strong role of gender in such results and pointed out that research suggests that caste and class do not work in the same way, as caste may be less hierarchical than is often thought. The caste is usually more salient than social class, so she indicated.

7.4.4 Subsaharan Africa

Subsaharan status-group divisions are determined by factors such as tribal affiliations, belief systems, occupation, and family ties, amongst other things. Race and ethnicity play a dominant role. Status differences exist between and within groups. In particular, the highly visible contrast between the former European colonists, the more indigenous peoples, and groups that have come from non-European regions is indicative of status difference. These status relationships have been subject to change since the mid 1990s, since economic factors are playing an increasingly important role in generating status.

Class is an important factor in sociolinguistic research in the area, according to the South-African researcher Mesthrie (2007), who indicated that the clear dividing lines that Apartheid had maintained are changing and that language is an important component in this ongoing process. Nevertheless, relatively little research into class in relation to language use in southern Africa is available.

The same is the case in other parts of the continent. The challenge researchers face is separating class from ethnicity and gender. The colonial heritage of most African countries adds to the complexity of isolating the effects of social class. An example of class-based research in South Africa is that of Mesthrie (2007), who explored the English of young elites and tendencies of speakers to imitate middle-class speech patterns. Race was an important factor in this investigation.

7.4.5 Europe

Class-related divisions are common in Europe and usually go back generations. Family, education, profession, and economic factors are important status markers. Class mobility is increasingly common and the various classes welcome newcomers, making the dividing lines less obvious. Old classes are becoming less obvious, but divisions existent in the past are often still visible.

Europe has a long tradition of researchers and other experts discussing the correlation between language and status. The German linguist Philipp Wegener spoke about the differences between the language of the educated, the half-educated, and of farmers as something that deserves attention (Wegener 1880). European dialectological research from the nineteenth and early twentieth century also contains frequent references to social status (usually based on profession).

An Eastern European research tradition is currently developing. Kontra (2006), for instance, showed a correlation between upward mobility of Hungarians and the use of the standard language. Much more activity has taken place in the Germanic European area, with its long tradition of social-class research following the Anglophone tradition. Sociological techniques to research the language of status groups systematically started to be used frequently from the mid-1960s onwards, but in the decades before that activity in the field had already taken off. In the Netherlands, for instance, Boelens and Van der Veen (1956) investigated the language use in the bilingual province of Friesland and took class of children into consideration systematically. Loman (1972), furthermore, found very few qualitative differences between middle-class and working-class speakers in Norway. Research in neighbouring Sweden (Paulston and Tucker 2003) did yield a correlation between class and language use.

In Romance Europe, class has also been a common theme in sociolinguistic research for a long time. Tempesta (2000), for instance, revealed how in the Italian town of Puglia, network ties and social class, amongst several other factors, influenced the ratio of Italian and dialect, including the tendency to codeswitch or **codemix** between them. Grassi (2001) assumed that social status in Italy is diminishing in relevance nowadays and that it is allowing more flexible linguistic norms to the extent that even the educated classes (such as politicians) are using colloquial forms that are not common of their class. Wise (1997) researched borrowings by the French and concluded that some English borrowings were used by Frenchmen irrespective of the speaker's social class. Gadet (1989) found that in France a certain 'incorrect' relative pronoun, albeit a stereotypical marker of working-class speech, was also used by the intellectual elite.

7.4.6 South America

Old status-group divisions are slowly becoming less prominent in South America, especially the ones that came with the division between colonists (from Spain and Portugal) and the indigenous peoples. Inherited status is nowadays less common but the status system is not too flexible. Individuals are, in principle, socially mobile but poverty is passed on intergenerationally nevertheless. Neighbourhood, education, and whether one is urban or rural are important contributors to status.

In South America, the Labovian tradition was picked up with considerable enthusiasm and elaborated on, and class was included in some investigations. According to Battisti and Pires Lucas (2015), researchers are now trying to create socioeconomic indices based on the characteristics of speech communities in order to come to terms with class and language use. This way, these researchers are partly continuing the Labovian tradition.

Battisti and Pires Lucas (2015) said that South American studies in which individuals have been placed in classes are nevertheless rare. An example comes from Barbados (in the Caribbean) by Blake (1997), who dealt with dialectal difference stratified through, amongst others, class. Devoicing in palatalised fricatives in Spanish in Buenos Aires (Argentina) showed class stratification, so Guitarte (1955) and Barrenechea (1951) found. Bortoni-Ricardo (1985) applied an approach in which social networks were looked at and found a correlation between certain phonetic-phonological variables in Brazilian Portuguese in the speech of rural migrants in the city of Brazlândia. Brazilian research by Amaral (2003) showed that status of one's neighbourhood (city centre, inner suburbs, and outer suburbs) is the aspect that most significantly correlates with second-person singular verb agreement. Amaral (2003) applied indices of socio-economic status and distinguished between three social classes and found a higher frequency of verb agreement in the speech of individuals in the upper-middle class and a cross-over effect (see 7.4.8) between classes.

7.4.7 The Arab region

Remnants of tribal and caste divisions exist in the Arab region and form the basis of status-group divisions. Nobles and unskilled workers are at the far ends of the status-group system. There is a large middle class. Economic factors are becoming more important. Education is another important factor.

Most of the Arabic sociolinguistic research into social stratification comes from the North African region. In the region, Arabic serves as a lingua franca for the educated classes and exists alongside the old colonial languages. Both in their own way, these lingua francas carry considerable prestige. The role of Standard Arabic as a language that is not a common form of daily communication (Chambers 2009) makes studying the use of this language in relation to speaker status challenging.

In the area as a whole, class is very strongly interwoven with ethnicity and other factors, and therefore it is not the primary or only categorisation tool that researchers will apply. Examples are research by Al-Ali and Arafa (2010), who investigated patterns of variation in the use of three sounds (/θ/, /dʒ/, and /ð/) in Jordanian Arabic and found that speakers with lower education levels had a stronger tendency to adopt local variants while those with a university education were more likely to adopt non-local prestigious variants. However, level of education correlated very strongly with gender patterns. Indeed, gender is difficult to separate from class, according to Ibrahim (1986). Gender research from the area is widely available and through that variable status can often be derived (see Chapter 11).

7.4.8 The Anglophone world

The so-called Inner Circle, which is a set of countries in which English has for several centuries existed as the undisputed language in daily life (Kachru 1985), consists of the United Kingdom, Ireland, Canada, the United States, Australia, and New Zealand. The United Kingdom, and England in particular, used to have a famous and in many ways rigid class system, with a Working, Middle and Upper Class. Nowadays, the old class patterns are still visible but they are said to be replaced by a system with more than three classes (Savage et al. 2013), and the class separations are more flexible. Predetermined class in the United States exists but there is an overt rejection of such a system and much emphasis on social mobility (Beller and Hout 2006). New Zealand and Australia are increasingly class-conscious, despite their image of being classless societies (Murray 2006).

A wealth of research findings is available on the effects of status on language in the Inner Circle countries. Early sociolinguistic studies on the interplay between status differences and language use were done by Americans Raven McDavid (1948), and Haver Currie (1952). McDavid described the usage of the sound 'r' at the ends of syllables by speakers in South Carolina, and he observed status differences. Currie published a paper with a discussion on trends in Linguistics and also mentioned status. A high number of well-known investigations into status are from the Anglophone world, and these are sociolinguistically particularly interesting simply because the status of features of the same language in related cultures are studied in locations scattered across the world. For instance, the pronunciation of the ending 'ing' in English words (such as 'walking') was studied in England (Trudgill 1974b) and in New Zealand and Australia (Holmes et al. 1991).

The most well-known – and still influential – investigation into the effects of class on speech is the one by William Labov (1966). He investigated the relationship between the use of a notable feature of the New York city dialect (lack of 'r' at the end of a syllable, as illustrated in the words 'fourth' and 'floor'). He found that speakers who were likely to be more highly pegged on the social ladder were more inclined to pronounce these two words in the General American way ('r' pronounced) and those who were lower on this ladder were more inclined to apply a New York way of saying these words (without the postvocalic 'r' or replacing it with something else, like a vowel-like sound). Labov's research (see 7.4.8 and 18.6.2) sparked a tradition into correlations between the status of language features and the status of speakers.

Another illustration of the Anglophone research tradition is the investigation into the covariation between Australian English phonology and social class, which was done by Horvath (1985). He identified a continuum comprising four varieties, with social class being an important determinant. Twenty years later, the same researcher (Horvath 2005) concluded that palatalisation of the fricative in a word such as 'assume' (pronouncing the 's' deeper in the mouth) is more common amongst some speakers of a lower economic status, while Horvath and Horvath (2001), in their search for social variation in the tendency of speakers to turn the phoneme /l/ into a vowel-like sound, did not find that speakers were differentiated through social class.

KEY CONCEPTS

Cross-over

Someone's social status might be heard through their language. However, the so-called cross-over phenomenon (Labov 1972c) may give listeners the wrong impression. It refers to the tendency of some speakers to use more variants of the status group that is just above them than the members of that group do themselves. Gumperz (1958) indeed showed that in some cases lower-status groups may imitate the habits of higher ones (and this leads to the higher prestige group finding new linguistic ways to distinguish themselves).

7.4.9 Indonesia

The Indonesian archipelago is so ethnically, culturally, and geographically diverse that it is difficult to generalise on an overarching status-group system. There is considerable social stratification, but it is sometimes difficult to pinpoint what determines one's status. Economic, political, ethnic, and religious factors play an important role. There is a ruling class that inherited its wealth and power and there are a few other elites, but these do not form a coherent group, as they include powerful generals but also captains of industry. The lower stratum is also diverse, with ethnically and religiously separated groups. In addition to these, there is also a range of middle-class groups (Dick 2015; Dick et al. 2002).

Class-related sociolinguistic research in Indonesia is difficult. First of all, there is the ununified nature of classes, making any class-related generalisations hard. Secondly, the nation is building its national culture at the moment, making class effects highly transitional. Status-related research from Indonesia is, as a result, not too widely spread. Some class-related research is available that tends to focus on language choice. Kurniasih (2005), for instance, found that children from middle-class backgrounds prefer Indonesian (the national language) to (the more local/regional language) Javanese, more so than children from working-class backgrounds did. Another example is Goebel (2005), who investigated two neighbourhoods with different socioeconomic profiles in the central Javanese city of Semarang and noted down social class effects in language choice.

7.4.10 Russia

Considerable differences in wealth exist in Russia. There is a strong discrepancy between status and traditionally relevant factors such as educational level and wealth. One's position in economic exchange strongly determines one's status. A high education and much wealth do not necessarily lead to status and if they do then it is a different kind of status for each. There is now a small group of millionaires, who hold much of the country's wealth. There is also a political elite and there is an intellectual elite. In addition to these, there is an independent group of successful businessmen, such as bankers. Each forms a status group. According to Fedorova (2018), most Russians will refer to themselves as middle class. The average worker does not have access to the many available goods.

Fedorova (2018) gave a detailed account of all the historical, political, ideological, and cultural reasons why sociolinguistic research in Russia is highly challenging. Some Western publications were nevertheless translated into Russian – see, for instance, Chemodanov (1975) – and modest attempts to describe social variation were made (Panov 1968; Krysin 1974). During the 1980s, ideology relaxed a little but variationist methodologies, and especially those dealing with social class variation, remained rare. A practical problem in the region is finding linguistic variables to research, because certain variables will turn out not to be social but regional (Krysin 2000). There is nowadays a firm standard language ideology, which marks deviations from the language norm as undesirable (Fedorova 2018). As a result, Russian sociolinguistic research, including that which focuses on a sensitive topic such as class, is in a highly exploratory stage.

Some sociolinguistic research that touched on social class differences was done by a number of Moscow linguists, who recorded everyday 'kitchen dialogues' and discovered differences between Standard Russian and colloquial speech, especially in syntax (Zemskaya 1973, 1983; Zemskaya et al. 1983, 1990). Zhuravlev (1988) used syntactic indices and related these to social difference. Fedorova (2018) claimed that social variation in Russia can be found in syntax more than in phonology, which goes against the mainstream assumption that subtle pronunciation and lexical differences are often at the core of expressing social difference. Most studies on social variation in Russian deal with lexical differences, and even variables that seem phonological – for example, palatalised versus non-palatalised consonants before /e/ in loanwords; see Larionova (2015) – are actually typical of specific words only.

7.4.11 Japan

Today's social situation in Japan is changing from the inherited and ideologically based classless society to a socially divided society. A prolonged recession, which has been going on for 30 years, has created a top social layer of newly rich (through new media and information technology, mainly) and a class of jobless people at the other end. In between are several other social layers. Wealth and hard work are amongst the qualities that give one status. Social hierarchy discussions are sensitive, as they tie in with discussions on minorities and their languages and with immigration.

Japan abides by the ideal of an egalitarian, classless, and monolingual build-up (Heinrich 2015). Heinrich and Masiko (2015) pointed out that it is safe to assume that considerable numbers of linguists purposefully avoid a controversial subject such as social class. They even talked about the 'belief in the myth of a classless and mono-ethnic Japanese society' (256). Because of this, Japanese sociolinguistic research into status language has never really taken off, although in the 1980s educational sociologists did initiate some research on how social class reflected in language. The few researchers focussing on status group differences pointed out unequal distributions of power between various societal fractions and related it to language. Hibiya (1988), for instance, found class variation in Tokyo Japanese. However, the degree to which ideology has affected this investigation and other investigations is unclear.

7.4.12 Minority communities

Status in smaller communities works in very different ways compared to status in societies that are based in nation-state or regional models. The criteria to attach prestige to language varieties or styles are highly varied. The actual existence of a fixed or dominant socially hierarchical structure in some of these societies is even debatable as the minority community members might actually belong to the majority community hierarchical structure.

The investigation by Gal (1979) in Austria – where in the 'language island' of Oberwart Hungarian was spoken by some speakers while the community was surrounded by German (and also Croatian) and was bilingually German and Hungarian – pointed to majority language use as an indicator of status. Dorian (1981) reached a similar conclusion in her study into a variety of Scottish Gaelic. Stanford and Preston (2009) concluded from a number of studies in minority communities that social classes in these communities tend to be relatively indistinct and not the source of linguistic stratification. In line with this, Smith-Christmas and Ó hIfearnáin (2015) explained how the sociolinguistic construct of class is difficult to apply directly to varieties of Gaelic. The variable 'social class', so they said, does not satisfactorily explain the language situation in the Gaelic areas. The Gaelic situation can in fact be described as one evidencing a high amount of linguistic variation in a socially relatively homogenous set of communities. MacKinnon (1977) went even further and described the Scottish Gaelic heartland community of Harris as 'classless' (171). Social classes in the Saami communities (Northern Europe), which is another set of minority communities, are also not very distinct, according to Aikio et al. (2015). Prestige and status might be drawn from their knowledge of the local culture and ways to provide livelihood, including its rituals and vocabulary and the ability to use dialects, so Aikio et al. (2015) indicated. So, prestige may lie in the use of traditional linguistic models of minority languages from certain areas if these are considered richer and purer than other varieties. Clark (1988), in line with this, gave an example of the high prestige of a certain dialect as spoken by the community of Montagnais Indians (United States). John (2015), finally, described how in the Yupik community in Alaska knowledge of a local dance carries prestige, because it shows knowledge of the local culture.

7.5 Conclusion

Studying topics such as social hierarchy and the status features that go with it is wrought with definitional and conceptual issues. The status of groups is difficult to separate from certain other variables, such as ethnicity and gender, for one. Also, it may be that functions typically united in one status group are actually taken up by more than one status group. Status of wealth and of education, most notably, may not be present in a single status group but in two separate ones, which means that two types of speakers and their languages may be prestigious but each in their own way. Furthermore, sociolinguistic research is still at an early stage of development in some places. This makes researching the status of groups as a distinct variable difficult, so this chapter has demonstrated. On top of that, the phenomenon itself is not so socially relevant or prominent in certain societies. In some places, there is more of a tradition to study the language of status groups than other places. In some places, this is ideologically and politically sensitive.

The factors determining status that a quick tour of some important cultures shows us go well beyond the most common systems that take socioeconomic features into consideration, such as wealth, education, and profession. The additional criteria to take into consideration that this chapter brought forward were, amongst others: ways to provide livelihood, urban-/ ruralness, family relations, religious affiliation, ethnicity, position in a former regime, cultural knowledge, marital status, network ties, position in economic exchange, and ability to use a certain variety (a certain dialect or the majority language). Many other criteria are likely to exist. Status features in groups of immigrants and expatriates, for instance, are difficult to assess. In such international communities, status features may not only include profession, education, and wealth but also knowledge of other cultures and of languages as well as amount of travel experience. It should be noted that there is a global tendency for economic success to become an overarching force determining status.

The Western literature has been particularly active in trying to explain differences between the language of different status groups; for instance, through theories such as Difference Theory (see 6.3.3) and the idea of covert prestige. From the Western realm, the idea has also arisen that language is used as not merely a symbol but also a tool. More research is needed to see to what extent these theories can be applied outside the West. An indexed system to determine status could incorporate more criteria in addition to socioeconomic ones, making cross-cultural comparisons possible.

STUDY QUESTIONS

1. Each individually, write down the three things that you most strongly associate with status.
2. Now, write down three aspects of the language of people with a high and a low status.
3. Which of the 11 society types described in this chapter is closest to yours and why? If you live in one of the societies described, do your intuitions agree with what is found in the literature from the society type that you are from? Please explain.

FURTHER READING

Chapter 4 discusses culture as part of Sociolinguistics. The companion website to this book, available at www.macmillanihe.com/companion/smakman, discusses specific cultures as well as the specific approach to status in these cultures.

The People's Language

Folk Linguistics and Perceptual Dialectology

8

8.1 Introduction

The American linguist Leonard Bloomfield (1944) referred to so-called 'secondary responses to language' (45) as traditional statements about language that are widely accepted, regardless of their truth or validity. Although such statements are 'loosely organized but fairly uniform' (45), Bloomfield advised against studying them seriously. Hoenigswald (1966), by contrast, said that we should not merely be interested in what goes on in language but also people's reactions to what goes on in language. In today's societies, populist views are increasingly becoming a force to be reckoned with. In Sociolinguistics, too, a trend of combining lay and expert views has been taking place.

This chapter looks at the phenomenon of linguists' interest in how non-linguists evaluate language and in what non-linguists believe to be true about language. It first describes the phenomenon of lay views about languages and lay perceptions of the workings of language variation. After that, this chapter presents certain common beliefs that non-linguists have about language and how it operates in a social context. Next, the two related fields that address non-linguists' language perceptions and evaluations are discussed, namely Perceptual Dialectology and Folk Linguistics, as well as research that has emanated from these fields. The chapter closes with the challenges that are part of trying to fathom lay perceptions and evaluations.

8.2 Lay versus expert approaches to language

8.2.1 Two almost opposite approaches

Sociolinguists view language in a social context through their own personal experiences and attempt to objectively observe and describe these experiences systematically. They then combine this with what they have read about other researchers' contributions to the field. They write this knowledge down in articles and books and exchange ideas about their findings with mostly a selected audience of fellow sociolinguists and with students. They will be hesitant to make suggestions towards changing language use.

Non-linguists, of which there are many more, tend to form and express their opinions on how language functions in society quite differently. Rather than viewing language from a distance and objectively describing it, they are generally triggered by specific language usages (a word, a grammatical construction, a sound, a pronunciation style) and subsequently feel inclined to express how they feel about these usages. They may also express and explain their ideas about what is good and bad about certain ways of using language as well as about the type of people they associate with certain usages. They are more inclined than sociolinguists to view language variation and change as intrinsically problematic and potentially harmful. Corrective actions and communication are more common amongst this group, in order for the 'right' way to produce language to prevail. The expressions of concern regarding the perceived decline of a language that go with this approach are associated with feelings of 'linguistic declinism'. This phenomenon can be placed in the broader context of the self-evident term 'linguistic complaint', which was introduced by Milroy and Milroy (1985) and which reflects a long tradition of critical attitudes to language variation and change.

FOCUS ON...

Online communication

Online writing habits and texting, with emoticons, abbreviations, and self-made acronyms, are often associated with a decline in literacy levels, according to Chatfield (2013). Tagliamonte and Denis (2008), however, concluded from their research amongst Canadian students that Computer-Mediated Communication is 'not the ruin of this generation at all, but an expansive new linguistic renaissance' (27).

8.2.2 Descriptivism versus prescriptivism

Linguists and non-linguists tend to disagree on some major points. The most basic division lies in the tendency towards 'descriptivism' (describing language use) and 'prescriptivism' (expressing ideas on how to use language). Associated with the latter is 'proscriptivism', which comes down to prohibiting people to produce a certain form. Linguists tend to depart from a stance of descriptivism, while non-linguists are more inclined to be prescriptive and proscriptive. Non-linguists tend to make a link between correctness and logic; something is correct because it is logical. Deviations from 'correct' are sometimes seen to point to a real problem (of linguistic logic, of consistency, or even of the intelligence of the speaker). Although no linguist is completely devoid of such ideas, they nevertheless tend to look at comments about language as mainly reflecting all kinds of sentiments about certain people and about society. They know that systematicity and logic are not the best of arguments to prove that something is right or wrong in language, because languages are not always the most consistent of systems. Languages even allow for much variation within the norms of correctness – called 'exceptions' or 'strong forms' at schools. Linguists will more likely acknowledge that there can be more than one way to say something acceptably.

KEY CONCEPTS

Language policing

A lesser known form of regulation is that coming from some unofficial pre-scriptive authority. Such corrective action is sometimes referred to as 'lan-guage policing'. This authority could, for instance, be one or more individuals that are respected members of a community of practice. An interesting example of language policing in this sense was presented by Mitsova (2014), who found that on a certain Bulgarian humorous internet site, the use of a specific North-Western Bulgarian dialect in posts was compulsory, and play-ing with the use of words and phrases from the dialect was subject to very strict rules that were actively enforced by self-proclaimed authoritative users monitoring the online network.

8.2.3 The formation of two sets of norms

Halliday (1977) described how a child does not only start using language but also starts to talk about it. At school, this unimpaired and natural approach to language is interrupted and overruled by the classroom situation, in which categories, classes, rules, and regulations bring about a fundamental ideological change in the child's image of language. What started as a resource, namely the language habits of the family and neighbourhood, turns into a set of culturally codified rules of the classroom, especially rules regarding what's right and what is not. Halliday (1977) compared this to the approach to language in the late classical period in Greece, when a shift took place from language as rhetoric to language as logic. After learning the rules at school, individuals have two sets of experiences in their minds. The first is the experience of expressing language intuitively and freely and constructing one's own language variation perception on the basis of selected observations. The second is the experience of projecting rules onto language and language variation and accounting for these and of talking about these uninhibitedly.

These two experiences tend to be combined into new, personalised beliefs about language that can be quite durable and inflexible. Unlike the non-linguist, the linguist takes the next step of continuing to learn more about the rules and critically reviewing these while looking at actual language use.

8.3   Beliefs about language variation

8.3.1 Common beliefs

Several linguists have tried to summarise ideas that are deeply rooted in lay people's minds. Niedzielski and Preston (2000) defined a number of such general beliefs. First of all, many non-linguists believe that some languages are primitive. Dialects, for instance, are often considered to be simplified forms of the norm language, because they deviate from that norm. There also exists a belief about the distinction between correct language and other types of language, the latter being referred to as 'incorrect' or even something like 'sloppy' or 'lazy'. Furthermore, languages are often thought to reflect the ethnic/racial background of speakers. Another well-known assumption is that mother-tongue speakers are authorities and that there is no necessity for a science of language. Language, finally, is often said to be deteriorating; change and variation are generally regarded as detrimental. Many more of such beliefs exist.

8.3.2 The validity of beliefs

Some of the persistent beliefs of non-linguists are easily proven wrong. The inferiority of some languages in particular can be countered by the observation that research has shown that seemingly 'bad' language forms can in fact be as linguistically systematic as any other language form. This was revealed for African American Vernacular English (AAVE) (Bender 2000; Labov 1969), which is often considered to be 'bad English'. Such research often also shows that languages that deviate from the norm sometimes preserve old forms or distinctions more than the norm language. Language discrimination on the basis of the quality of someone's language is therefore not usually warranted on the basis of linguistic grounds and usually reflects some ideology.

KEY CONCEPTS

Linguistic appropriation

'Linguistic appropriation' refers to a kind of theft or piracy when people borrow words from other varieties (Friedrich and Diniz de Figueiredo 2016; Hill 2008). To demonstrate this, Hill (2008) gave the term 'no problemo', which is mock (and incorrect) Spanish. The idea is that speakers do not do this because they do not have a word or expression in their own language but are 'stealing' some of the rights of the users of the correct form (in this case *no problema*). Macías et al. (2018) and Hill (2008) associated this phenomenon with scorn and even racism.

Change, furthermore, is not necessarily an indication of language deterioration or the decline of richness in language. Distinctions and old forms disappear but new distinctions and forms also arise. Urban languages in particular are adding new ways of expression (see 3.4.3). It is true that unique languages are dying and that new languages are usually adjusted or are mixed forms of existing languages, so in that respect there is decline, but this is not a decline in the linguistic expressiveness or richness of language.

Language proficiency is sometimes claimed to be going down with each generation. This is unlikely. Through education and globalisation, more and more people are becoming proficient speakers of language varieties that are considered 'correct' and are gaining proficiency in an international lingua franca. This means that more and more people are speaking languages 'well' and that people are speaking more foreign languages than before. One's ability to express oneself in one's native tongue is then complemented with an ability to express oneself in another language and even to mix languages.

The perceived detrimental effects of change may be due to the fact that change in the past was more likely to go unnoticed. The high visibility of change and variation – because of modern media, television, and increased travel opportunities – contributes to people's concerns that more changes are taking place than before and that there is a decline of older norms.

8.3.3 The persistence of beliefs

It is difficult to change a non-linguist's mind, as the assumptions they make are usually also very important to them. The use of solid argumentation or of information is in itself not necessarily a priority to many language users. Tamasi (2003) indicated that even if linguistic information is presented to those expressing their opinion, the opinion it contradicts will still be given. Jackendoff (2003a) pointed out that 'people feel entitled to enter the conversation in the absence of expertise, and even to demean the experts in the interest of making a point' (4). Jackendoff added that beliefs are deep-rooted and that there is a lack of willingness to be overruled by facts and arguments.

Halliday suggested that much of the ideas about language are due to people not remembering the rules taught in class and reconstructing them into new ones. He also suggested that there is a refusal to project what one has learned on actual language use in daily communication (Halliday 1977).

Language myths

Within societies, certain persistent beliefs may take on the shape of myths, like the myth of women and men in Japan speaking wholly different languages and the common suggestion that all languages in India are derived from Sanskrit. Bloomfield (1944) gave two other examples of language myths, namely that Finns and Hungarians can understand each other's language and that there are remote places in England where original sixteenth century Elizabethan English is still spoken. Another example of a language myth is that in the city of Haarlem in the Netherlands (which is close to the capital city of Amsterdam) Standard Dutch is spoken the best. Although Haarlem lies in the area where the Dutch standard language historically sprang from, there are no reasons to believe that in this city Standard Dutch is spoken to a greater extent than in any nearby city in the area. This myth is sometimes assumed to come from a comment on certain qualities of the local speech in this city by the Frisian dialectologist Winkler (1874). The relative anonymity of this city and lack of knowledge of the way people speak there are likely to contribute to the persistence of this myth. Similar myths exist all over the world, and the causes of these myths vary.

Organised puritanism and protectionism

There are non-linguists (and a few language experts) who are firm and principled believers when it comes to the specific usage rules of their native language. This language puritanism can take on very serious forms and lead to such believers forming organisations that aim to fight the presumed deterioration of their native language. In Germany, for instance, an organisation called *Verein Deutsche Sprache* ('German Language Association'; founded in 1997) exists. Similar associations exist in other European countries, such as *De Stichting Taalverdediging* ('The Language Defence Foundation'; founded in 2001) in the Dutch-speaking area and the French *Défense de la langue française* ('Defence of the French Language'; founded in 1958). In Flanders, the Northern part of Belgium, the *Taal Aktie Komitee* ('Language Action Committee'; founded in 1972) was originally concerned about the language border between Dutch and French, which cuts across the country. Such organisations tend to receive no official support. Some of them are associated with fervent nationalist and (far) right-wing sentiments. Some of their arguments are easily refutable on linguistic, logical, etymological, or historical grounds as well as grounds of perspective and nuance. However, what they stand for is often supported by large groups of people in societies.

More moderate and official organisations also exist, each of which was initially formed for specific reasons. In the Netherlands, for example, the 'German threat' was widely felt at one point and was the main ground for the founding of the *Genootschap Onze Taal* ('Society for Our Language'; founded in 1931). In England, there is the 'Queen's English Society', which was founded in 1972 and calls itself 'by nature a prescriptive organisation' (QES 2016), and is partly a reaction to linguistic influences from abroad, stating that 'we refuse as a nation to adopt the word "sidewalk" where there is already a perfectly good word – pavement – nicely settled in our language' (QES 2016). In some cases, such as is the case with the Dutch *Genootschap Onze Taal*, prescriptivism has gradually been replaced by language counselling and explanation (advice and descriptivism), and their membership numbers have gone up. The *Genootschap Onze Taal* claims to have 29,000 members (Onze Taal 2016). The Queen's English Society has 1,000 members, according to their website (QES 2016). Some such organisations are known to be more prescriptive in their approach than others. A particularly strict language policy is known to exist in France, with the French Academy (*Académie française*; founded in 1635) at the forefront, which is an influential and highly prestigious organisation. Such organisations affect policy through education and, ultimately, the way ordinary speakers view language variation.

> **FOCUS ON...**
>
> **Threat to functions**
>
> Rather than (or in addition to) threatening the shape of a language, a 'guest' language may affect the places where the 'host' language is used. In business contexts, English may have penetrated as a guest language and may be used side by side with the host language, that is, the native tongue of most people working at the company. If the company operates in an international context and increasingly employs more international personnel, then English may slowly become the dominant language in such companies. The host language then loses its function as a business language and could thus become reduced to the language of the home (Van Hoorde 1998), but this process does not affect the linguistic shape of the host language.

8.4 Perceptual dialectology

8.4.1 Lay analyses of language variation

Yet another difference between sociolinguists and non-sociolinguists is that the latter tend to use anecdotal observation to gather information and mostly orally communicate their observations and views. These communications can be researched through the academic field of Folk Linguistics, which according to Preston (2008) 'seeks to discover what nonlinguists know about language and to derive from that knowledge evidence of their underlying folk theory of language' (1). Folk Linguistics thus studies evaluative reactions to language and language use (what is correct, beautiful, ugly, etc.). The linguist tries to find patterns in these beliefs.

Within that broad field of Folk Linguistics, the approach called Perceptual Dialectology is often applied, which approach was put forward by Preston (1999a). It is the specific study of the individual's own account of their beliefs about language varieties and their speakers. This approach offers lay explanations of language beliefs, not just demonstrations of such beliefs. Perceptual Dialectology investigates what ordinary people believe about the distribution of language varieties in their own speech community and adjacent and nearby speech communities and how they have arrived at and implement those beliefs. General folk reactions to language variation and change have been a common aspect of sociolinguistic investigations, and it has traditionally been common to ask ordinary users about how they would evaluate a language or a typical speaker. Perceptually dialectological approaches are relatively underexplored.

8.4.2 Research

Research into lay beliefs about language variation was in the past treated as part of traditional dialectology. The named research is known for its idiosyncratic self-made methodologies. Dutch dialectologist Toon Weijnen asked participants in neighbouring Dutch villages to indicate which of the people in the surrounding villages spoke like them. He also asked each participant to describe local dialect differences. Weijnen (1946, 1947) mapped these perceived dialect similarities, and arrows were used to show the similarities (hence the name *Pijltjesmethode*, 'Arrows Method'). Dialect divisions in the Itoigawa area (North/central Japan) were established by Sibata (1959), who had participants indicate where they thought dialect boundaries lay. The Flemish dialectologist Grootaers was active in Japan (Grootaers 1964) and had ordinary speakers draw dialect boundaries on maps. Inoue (1972) investigated boundaries in Northern Japan in a similar way. Perceived to be situated in the realm of Dialectology, such investigations were generally not followed by a string of similar research by other linguists.

More recently, more research has been done, in various places across the globe. Various perceptual dialectological studies are described in Preston (1999b), amongst others a study in Japan by Long (1999). Other examples of more recent research are investigations in Turkey (Demirci and Kleiner 1999), Mali (Long and Yim 2002), Hungary (Kontra 2002), and, for instance, Korea (Long and Yim 2002). Several studies have had non-linguists from a certain area draw perceived lines between dialects. Evans (2011) researched perceptions in Washington State (United States) in this way, Dinkin (2009) investigated New York State (United States), Bucholtz et al. (2007) investigated the state of California (United States), and Inoue (1996) researched Britain. Tamasi (2003) did an extensive investigation into beliefs that inhabitants of two different locations in the United States (North Georgia and Central New Jersey) held. The participants evaluated not only linguistic traits but also social traits (e.g. intelligence, trustworthiness, and social pleasantness of speakers). They were also asked to describe characteristics of the local language varieties.

Investigations reveal not only all kinds of notions about dialect boundaries and the way people speak in certain areas but also characteristics and strong prejudices of the people in the areas in question. This demonstrates the strong connection that is generally felt to exist between language and characteristics of people. Some of these studies found that people's perceptions are strongly affected by administrative divisions, which demonstrates how political divisions may affect language variation in addition to being an indirect reflection thereof. Ranges of mountains and other natural boundaries, such as rivers, also affected perceptions of boundaries, so it turned out. Another interesting finding that resurfaces in investigations is the power of language ideology (awareness of language standards and norms).

8.5   Criticism

8.5.1 Mixed appreciation of lay beliefs

A negative appreciation of folk views was expressed by German linguist Vossler (1925), who wrote that aesthetic judgements about languages should not be taken seriously by linguists and instead should be considered *Laiengerede* ('folk tattle', 'laymen talk') (49). The later plea by Hoenigswald (1966) in favour of paying attention to non-linguists and their views met with little interest. Three reasons underlying criticism towards investigating lay beliefs are described here.

1. How distinctions are processed

Niedzielski and Preston (2000) said that the non-linguist is less able than the linguist to bring linguistic phenomena to their own awareness. Silverstein (2003) also indicated that lay judges are less aware than expert judges; linguists will distinguish between phenomena that non-linguists do not distinguish between. As a result, it is difficult for a linguist to tease out the right information from the non-linguist. Silverstein (2003) explained in some detail a number of other awareness issues. For example, he suggested that non-linguists can only have knowledge about elements that refer to something tangible and understandable. So, they can talk about politeness forms, for instance, but not differences between the production of vowels. Another issue he mentioned was that non-linguists are less skilled at commenting on interrupted constructions, such as 'is reading' in, for instance, 'He is as a matter of fact busy reading' as they do not necessarily perceive detached elements as being one construction. Cuonz (2010) agreed with these criticisms and, in addition, believed that non-linguists tend not to mention things they consider to be normal and tend to focus on what is deviant, which does not lead to very balanced or objective statements. Non-linguists might hear different phenomena, such as the English word 'either' being pronounced in two different ways, namely /iːðə/ or /aɪðə/, but they will not express this distinction if the two phenomena are in their opinion equal in degree of acceptance. They may, finally, not give all the information they are able to express and apply their own degree of detail, based on what they consider relevant or interesting. A linguist may, for example, distinguish between various degrees to which a vowel beginning is different from its ending, which few non-linguists will do with the same precision and detail.

The outcome of judgements by non-linguists are faulty, so it is claimed. These judgements are not scientific or systematic and therefore incomplete and biased. In this view, lay descriptions are limited, imprecise, broad, and simple. Linguists value consistent and reliable data the most, while folklinguistic data are often inconsistent. Linguists tend to prefer to register distinctions in their own mother tongue rather than train non-linguists to register these distinctions. In other words; they are themselves good judges of their own mother tongue and folk judgements are therefore perceived not to be required.

2. Terminological knowledge of lay judges

In addition to making less reliable, less consistent, and less relevant distinctions, non-linguists do not have the proper and extensive linguistic terminology at hand to be able to express these distinctions clearly and factually. In a famous reaction to a presentation by Hoenigswald in 1963 (for details, see Niedzielski and Preston (2000)), Labov indicated that his research on the island of Martha's Vineyard showed that non-linguists do not have sufficient vocabulary to express themselves and be useful as language informants. Silverstein (2003) repeated this criticism and said that non-linguists do not have enough descriptive tools to describe their own language.

Because lay terminology deviates from that of linguists, Hoenigswald (1966) suggested we make an inventory of the terminology used by non-linguists – such as 'sound', 'synonym', 'regional', 'normal', and 'speech' – as these correlate with certain linguists' terminology. Lay terminology should then be translated to expert terms.

3. Reliability of data

The relevance of the data is another potential issue. Social psychological research, such as the one by Lambert et al. (1960), who systematically tested attitudes towards French and English in Canada, tends to look for deeper attitudes by systematically testing the reactions of selected respondent groups to several sets of recorded speech in controlled experiments. These researchers are less interested in an individual's reaction to a single language item. That reaction could well be different in other circumstances. Some folklinguistic data indeed suffer from a lack of experimental control and a small sample size.

8.5.2 Countering the criticism

The criticism expressed is to some degree justified, but it does not take away the fact that the lay beliefs in question are important and worthy of study. These beliefs of non-linguists affect their actual language use, which means that understanding them is part of understanding language variation and change. Speakers may avoid using a certain language form simply because of some trivial stereotype surrounding the form in question, its prototypical speakers, or its association with a certain language variety or style. Having non-linguists freely give their views will reveal such stereotypes. If two or more non-linguists independently from each other present a certain argument, mention a certain feature of speakers of a variety, or put forward a certain example to support their analysis of a certain language construction, then that in itself is worthy of being taken seriously.

A convincing strength of the study of lay beliefs is that findings are often strikingly systematic. Tamasi (2003) concluded that people view language variation through a large number of categories that stem from a complex network of information, especially regional, social, linguistic, and personal information. All of these bits of information form one cohesive interlinked system that underlies linguistic perceptions by non-linguists and that often agrees with how linguists view things.

The criticism that participants will formulate their own categories of distinction and relevance may be viewed positively rather than critically, because participants put forward categories that they deem relevant. A weakness of some sociolinguistic research is, in fact, that participants need to express their views through categories the researcher has come up with. They are not usually asked whether these categories are of importance to them or whether they had other categories in mind. Rather than giving the participants choices on a scale from 'beautiful' to 'ugly' or another scale, which presumes such dimensions are relevant to them, an object may be described by self-chosen adjectives and descriptive phrases (however unclear and imprecise). These findings may be interpreted and categorised by researchers, and these data can serve as the start of more systematic research in which such relevant categories are presented.

8.6   Conclusion

The analyses of language variation by non-sociolinguists are interesting in that they show very clear patterns. Finding out how non-linguists view language usage is important to understand their language choices better. Some beliefs are not in accordance with the patterns that linguists and sociolinguists have laid bare. Such findings on beliefs may explain why individuals use or avoid certain language usages, and combined many such belief systems may show consistent patterns of lay beliefs. They may also show how a common distinction made by linguists (for instance, between two dialects) may be becoming less relevant according to ordinary language users.

This chapter has revealed the obvious criticism towards the study of non-linguists' analyses and descriptions. The named criticism may be the reason for the underexposure of such analyses and descriptions in sociolinguistic research. Possibly as a result, the field of Perceptual Dialectology in particular has been underexposed within Sociolinguistics and seems dependent on a relatively small group of researchers. However, the data that research in these fields has generated have turned out to be insightful and usable for further research, amongst others because they may help to construct relevant categories for further research.

STUDY QUESTIONS

1. Can you give some examples of constructions in your native language that are subject to much debate? Why are they debated?
2. To what degree do you consider yourself an objective judge of language usage, unaffected by imposed (by school and parents) prejudices as to good and bad language use?
3. Do you think that there are good reasons not to take lay perceptions and beliefs seriously?

FURTHER READING

The first chapter in Preston and Niedzielski (2009) summarises the principles of Perceptual Dialectology and Folk Linguistics very clearly. Paveau (2007) provides an easy to read introduction to lay perceptions and to Folk Linguistics in general. The volume by Tieken-Boon van Ostade and Percy (2017) describes a range of contemporary and historical situations across the globe in which the workings of prescriptivism are demonstrated.

What Say You?

Attitudes About Language

9.1 Introduction

Language is one of the main determinants of opinions about the other. A 'wrong' accent or even word could lead to acceptance or rejection of the people producing them. Language attitudes could also lead to different inter- pretations of observations. Language could, for instance, instantly determine the interpretation of a certain dress sense: 'geeky' becomes 'retro' if the wearer has the right accent. During interaction, people readily form impressions of others on the basis of language use. Because of predictable patterns of language use (like lexicon, pronunciation, or grammar) by speakers who share certain characteristics (like geography, ethnicity, or gender), linguistic forms become indexical of the social identities of speakers (Silverstein 2003). In addition to these group associations, more personalised traits are derived from language use, such as personality and intelligence traits (Fuertes et al. 2012). These asso- ciations are often predictable and patterned (Giles and Billings 2004).

This chapter discusses the social psychology of language use. This field studies attitudes about varieties of language, about speakers of these varieties, about language variation, and about the way in which speakers interact with each other. The specific use of certain common terms in the field will be dis- cussed first. After that, ways to measure attitudes will be explained and some examples are given of research into language attitudes in the world. The origins of language attitudes will be discussed next; when people have something to say about a language, what is this based on?

9.2 Attitudes and beliefs

9.2.1 The definition of 'attitude'

'Attitude' has been a dominant theme in Social Psychology in the last century. This phenomenon has been researched extensively, but according to Eagly and Chaiken (2005) and Gawronski (2007) many of the ways in which attitudes are formed and how they change remain unanswered nevertheless. What we do know is that they are formed largely through experience in addition to being based on the qualities of the evaluated object.

In Social Psychology, the distinction is made between attitudes that are deep and stable and those that are less deep and stable. The latter type are referred to as 'beliefs'. In the social psychological literature, a layered pattern of deep and less deep feelings and experiences (which lead to evaluative behaviour) is often laid out. Here, we will stick to the following two workable definitions of 'attitude'. The first one is by Hogg and Vaughan (2005): 'a relatively enduring organization of beliefs, feelings, and behavioral tendencies towards socially significant objects, groups, events or symbols' (150). The second is by Eagly and Chaiken (1993): 'a psychological tendency that is expressed by evaluating a particular entity with some degree of favor or disfavor' (1). These definitions include the mental state of the judge, the object (language use, in our case) that causes this state, as well as the suggestion that this state leads to an evaluative reaction (approval or rejection, amongst others), which may be expressed or not.

9.2.2 'Attitude' versus 'belief'

In Sociolinguistics, the term 'attitude' is often used in a less precise way than in Social Psychology. Beliefs, attitudes, and related phenomena like values and ideals, are often simply referred to as 'attitudes'. Not all authors make distinctions very strictly and are instead using the term 'attitude' to just reflect both the mental state and the behaviour (and they use ambiguous phrases like 'a negative attitude'). In the literature on Sociolinguistics, the distinction between belief and attitude is often nevertheless maintained. The idea is that an attitude lies very deep and is not simply visible in a person's reaction to, for instance, a speech fragment. This reaction is the result of a belief, which lies much more on the surface and is subject to change more. Whether this belief is expressive of a stable attitude is not certain. Research tries to look for attitudes by collecting beliefs of many people and seeing whether they are somehow patterned.

9.3 Language attitude research

9.3.1 Measuring attitudes

The ways to measure language attitudes are usually divided into three categories (McKenzie 2010, 2006; Garrett 2005; Ryan et al. 1982): the so-called Societal Treatment Approach, the Direct Approach, and the Indirect Approach. The Societal Treatment Approach is generally qualitative and involves studying speaker behaviour. Attitudes are inferred from observed behaviour or through the analysis of available documents, like letters and websites. The relationship between attitude and behaviour remains tentative, but the strength of this approach is that it bases itself on a naturalistic behavioural expression of beliefs and attitudes, not an induced one.

The Direct Approach has a greater degree of researcher obtrusiveness and participant awareness. Participants could be interviewed about what they consider to be their attitudes. Polls, surveys, and other written response tools are typically used as well. The downside of this approach is that participants may express what they consider to be socially desirable. Subtle techniques that hide the purpose of an investigation are typical of the so-called Indirect Approach, which tries to circumvent such self-conscious behaviour by participants. This approach is associated with the so-called Matched Guise technique, whereby a perfectly bilingual speaker reads out the same text in two languages and participants evaluate the speaker of the two readings without being aware that it is the same speaker. Any different assessment of the personality characteristics of the speaker can then be assumed to be due to differences in language and reflective of language attitudes. The most famous Matched Guise investigation was by Canadian Psychologist Lambert and his colleagues, who compared evaluative reactions to French and English in Canada through this technique (Lambert et al. 1960).

9.3.2 Previous research

Attitudes are a standard component of many sociolinguistic studies. In some of these studies, attitudes are the main focus while in others attitudes are tested in combination with other aspects, so that attitudes can be correlated with all kinds of social and linguistic outcomes.

Here are a number of attitude studies from all over the world: attitudes amongst South African school children towards various languages they hear every day (Dyers 2004); villagers' attitudes as a factor in determining the nature of a speech community in a village in the Anhui province, China (Fu 2011); attitudes towards English loanwords in Indonesian (Hassall et al. 2008), in the languages of the Nordic countries in Europe (Thoegersen 2004), and in Chinese (Cai 2011); attitudes of native speakers of various international Englishes regarding characteristics of speakers of their own and other major varieties of English (Bayard et al. 2001); attitudes of Mexicans towards (learning) English (Despagne 2010); attitudes towards neighbouring languages within the Nordic area (Braunmüller 1990); attitudes in Germany towards accented German (Eichinger et al. 2009); attitudes amongst Arabic/French bilinguals in Morocco (Bentahila 1983); attitudes of Xhosa-speaking students in South Africa in the context of language learning and teaching (Aziakpono and Bekker 2010); attitudes towards the Wuhan dialect (China) and towards Mandarin by young Wuhan students (Li 2007); attitudes to codeswitching and codemixing in India (Bhatia and Ritchie 2013); attitudes that show multilingual awareness in a Japanese context (Maher et al. 2010); attitudes towards linguistic landscape (see 17.6) in an Anglo-Hispanic context (Dailey et al. 2005); ongoing changes in language attitudes in Valencia, Spain (Ferrer 2010); attitudes towards speakers of regional French (Paltridge and Giles 1984); the perception of Lithuanian adolescents of their peers' linguistic identity (Čekuolytė 2014); and, finally, attitudes towards Arabic in relation to national identity (Suleiman 2003).

This long and randomly ordered list is a mere selection of the many studies available from various parts of the world. The Direct Approach is applied in most of these cases. This list gives an impression of the perceived importance of language attitudes in describing or explaining various aspects of language use: language learning success, language discrimination, codeswitching, use of loanwords, the formation of speech communities, and, for instance, national identity.

KEY CONCEPTS

Linguistic Relativism

In addition to being the source of attitudes, language may in turn influence thought. The theory called **Linguistic Relativism** proposes that the way a language is structured affects the ways in which speakers of that language conceptualise the world around them. Linguistic relativism is nowadays popularly associated with the works of American anthropologist and linguist Edward Sapir (1884–1939) and the American linguist and engineer Benjamin Lee Whorf (1897–1941). A famous example (Whorf 1956 [1940]) came from Hopi, the language as spoken by the native American Hopi tribe in Northeast Arizona, in the United States. The Hopi language distinguishes between drinking water in a container and water appearing in a natural body of water, whereas in most languages these two would both simply be referred to as 'water'. Similarly, the Kapayo, an indigenous people of the Brazilian Amazon, express the concept of an individual's body as *me on nhin*, which translates as 'someone's flesh'. This way, no distinction is made between human and non-human bodies (Turner 1995), which reflects the way bodies of humans and animals are viewed in this society.

9.4   The origins of language attitudes

9.4.1 Language ideology

Language ideologies are defined by Silverstein (1979) as 'sets of beliefs about language articulated by users as a rationalization or justification of perceived language structure and use' (193). Research into language ideologies uses language attitudes and perceptions to see how they help people make sense of the society around them. Giles et al. (1979) presumed such ideologies and suggested that the standard language is often considered more pleasing to listen to because it is the cultural norm. This is called the Imposed Norm Hypothesis. Parents, teachers, and, for instance, the media present a certain language as the most desired language one could speak. Language ideologies perpetuate the view that there is a proper way of using language and 'other' ways. Individuals to various degrees inevitably internalise this ideology.

Bourdieu (1991) used the existing philosophical term 'habitus' to refer to behaviour regarding language use in particular. He acknowledged the prestige continuum in predominantly monolingual countries, which goes from the norm language (high status) to varieties that deviate from it (low status). Bourdieu referred to socialised (i.e., imposed by society) norms that are the guide for individuals' behaviour and thinking. He considered it not a result of free will but shaped by events in societies and indicated that these norms condition our perceptions (Bourdieu 1984). The grammarians, so Bourdieu (1991) said, are the 'body of jurists' while teachers are 'the agents of regulation and imposition' (45).

Whether language is close to the norm or not may be a factor in the perception of people's lives' successes and failures. In research, patterns can be discerned in the evaluation of the personal attributes of speakers with various degrees of closeness to the language norm. A common pattern is illustrated by Šimičić and Sujoldžić (2004) in Croatia. They found that speakers of Standard Croatian and of Štokavian, a dialect that is close to standard Croatian, were associated with competence (albeit not necessarily with a nice personality).

FOCUS ON...

Language norms and power

Part of the ideology that is so widely carried and passed on is the awareness that language use and power go together. Language use is not merely reflective of power relations, it may also affect such relations. Coulmas (2011) even suggested that there is a risk of exclusion and expulsion if one doesn't meet the language norm. Rosaldo (1984) observed that the Ilongot of the Philippines are a society that takes linguistic abilities very seriously and said that in this society 'true verbal art has social force' (140). The social force may even have political and professional consequences. Nilesh and Roy (2016), for instance, explained how the word choice and style of the Indian politician Narendra Modi, in which Hindi is interspersed with English, reflected his power and endeared him to his audience. In fact, they considered this language use critical in his 2014 electoral victory to become India's Prime Minister.

Effect of language policies

Language policies may affect attitudes quite directly. Galan (2011) described the directives given to Japanese school children over the years regarding how to view the norm language and dialects. While for previous generations dialects were presented in these directives as language forms that need to be corrected, the directives from 2009 were less condemning of dialects and simply instructed children to speak the norm language as much as possible. Sibata (1958) indicated that the dialect eradication and extermination policy in Japan had led to a dialect inferiority complex by dialect speakers, and Inoue (2011) said that dialects in present-day Japan were predominantly a 'form of amusement' (117) to many. In France, the country where Bourdieu was from, the French Academy (*Académie française*) has tried to achieve a similar effect on the way dialects are often viewed by ordinary language users.

A successful language ideology is likely to lead to a positive attitude to a certain language use. Studies into language attitudes in monolingual societies more often than not show a positive inclination of ordinary users towards the official language (Giles 1970; Šimičić and Sujoldžić 2004). Research by Tamasi (2003) showed that this approach may be shared by those associated with speaking the norm language and those that are not associated with that language. The Dutch linguist Kloeke (1951) even considered the love people have for the imposed language norm to be unconditional. As an illustration, proud Russians who love Russian unconditionally are known to replace the phrase 'the Russian language' simply with *velikij i moguchij*, 'great and mighty'. This demonstrates the enormous effects that policy can have on people's feelings towards a national language or some other language norm and towards varieties that deviate from it.

FOCUS ON...

The national language as an official part of culture

Languages are in many cases explicitly mentioned in the constitution and presented as a matter of national importance and as part of national identity. In the constitution of the Republic of Estonia (from 1992), there is a preamble in which 'the preservation of the Estonian nation, language and culture through the ages' is guaranteed (Riigikantselei 2012). Similar statements were made in the Lithuanian and Latvian constitutions. This way, a national language is associated with culture preservation, a unique heritage, and national unity.

9.4.2 Inherent qualities

Giles and Niedzielski (1998) observed that very specific linguistic features of a language variety may influence the attitudes towards that variety. The Inherent Value Hypothesis ties in with this idea and suggests that actual language features are what make certain language varieties be perceived as more pleasing to the ear. This would mean that norm languages are intrinsically more pleasing and that their widely perceived beauty is not an imposed idea.

This hypothesis has been tested. Giles et al. (1979) found that speakers of Welsh with little to no knowledge of French could not distinguish on aesthetic and prestige dimensions between varieties of French as spoken in Quebec, Canada. They could not distinguish between more standard or less standard varieties and did not attribute more prestige or more favourable personality characteristics to the speech of the European-style French speakers (the variety with the highest prestige) than those of the Canadian-French speakers (whose

French had less prestige at the time of the investigation). Giles et al. (1979) suggested that these results supported the Imposed Norm Hypothesis and not the Inherent Value Hypothesis, which two hypotheses they presented as opposites. Giles et al. (1974) had British undergraduates judge different varieties of modern Greek and came to similar conclusions.

FOCUS ON...

Intrinsic beauty as a guideline

An instruction for radio presenters in Japan in the 1930s talked about *mimi no kotoba*, a 'language of the ears', which sounds beautiful and is easy to listen to (Shioda 2011).

Pronunciation qualities

Pronunciation in particular, and suprasegmentals more so than segmentals, tend to be put forward as arguments in these and other investigations. Bourdieu (1991) attached great symbolic power to pronunciation as a characterising feature of language and referred to language as 'a body technique ..., especially phonetic' (86). Cuonz (2010) asked French-speaking Swiss participants about the beauty or ugliness of Swiss and Standard German and found that very specific pronunciation qualities (most notably suprasegmental qualities, like intonation) were used to support the argument that Swiss German was the most beautiful of the two. An observation from the United Arab Emirates by Piller (2011) also showed the importance of pronunciation. She described how certain women in this region were repelled by their husbands' 'unromantic' Emirati accents (117).

Other criteria

Characteristics other than pronunciation may nevertheless play a role too. If listeners are under the impression that a language variety contains many (difficult) words and expressions as well as a complicated and expressive grammar, then they may consider that language to be superior to other language varieties. Suggestions that certain languages are linguistically richer and structurally more systematic or even more logical than others are usually made within a language ideological framework. Some languages are more codified than others and dictionaries and grammar books usually revolve around these languages, and this may give rise to the idea that the norm language is actually richer and more elaborate than languages without dictionaries and grammar books. Milroy (2001) indicated that deviations from the prescribed norms may lead to ugliness evaluations. These deviations are more visible because of the existence of a norm that is written down and taught.

Some may claim that a language is superior if it makes certain distinctions that other languages do not. For instance, Hindi as spoken in the North Indian city of Delhi typically distinguishes two numbers in first-person pronouns:

me (singular) versus *ham* (plural). In parts of the North Indian state of Uttar Pradesh, there is a popular tendency to use *ham* for both singular and plural. Such differences in the degree of distinction can usually be found in both urban and rural languages and both norm languages and languages that deviate from the norm. In England, for instance, it is common for some non-standard speakers to distinguish between singular and plural second-person pronouns; 'you' versus 'youse', while the norm language only accepts the use of 'you' for both singular and plural.

Borrowings too may have a strong attitudinal effect. Part of the perceived intrinsic beauty of a language is typically the degree to which borrowed items are felt to be part of this language. The adoption of foreign words can go through various stages and take on various degrees of obtrusiveness. In Czech, for instance, phonological and orthographic adaptation has taken place for older borrowings (like *volejbal* and *kameraman*; 'volleyball' and 'cameraman') while later borrowings are more likely to be pronounced and written with a higher fidelity to the English original. An example is the word *baseball*, which is written as the original English word and pronounced close to the original (/'bɛjzbol/ or /'bɛjzboːl/). This shows how words may gradually lose their status of intruder (Duběda et al. 2013). Beauty judgements on the basis of borrowing depend on the recency and nature of the borrowing.

Objections to attitudinal effects of inherent qualities

A simple argument against the Inherent Value Hypothesis is that there are sounds in certain languages that are prestigious and considered beautiful despite being 'ugly'. The German-speaking and French-speaking Swiss in the investigation by Cuonz (2010) referred to the aesthetically displeasing guttural sound that is typical of Dutch. Within the Netherlands, however, this guttural pronunciation (usually of the letter 'g') is generally considered less marked (and more beautiful) than the voiced velar versions, which may to foreigners be more pleasing to the ear. This shows that an irregular and hash-sounding sound can gain the status of being beautiful. Another example is that of postvocalic 'r' ('r' at the ends of syllables, after a vowel) in all kinds of Englishes and also in a language like Mandarin Chinese. The absence of this sound (which is usually an approximant or retroflex sound) has a high status in some accents but low status in other accents (standard British English lacks this sound while standard American English has postvocalic 'r'). Beijing Chinese is known for its prominent postvocalic 'r', which is in fact imitated by many newcomers in the city and has a certain status. One pronunciation phenomenon is thus subject to several different attitudes, apparently, and different degrees of 'ugliness', which means that culturally independent inherent beauty is unlikely, or at least that cultural norms may overrule aesthetic perceptions.

9.4.3 Aesthetic associations

Trudgill and Giles (1978) added the Social Connotations Hypothesis to the discussion, thus including the lifestyle and environmental setting of speakers as determinants of attitudes. This hypothesis states that attitudes are shaped by the way people look at the lives of speakers of a language variety or the region where the dialect is spoken. People who live in nice houses in nice (preferably rural and idyllic) areas then speak more beautifully than those who live in ugly houses in an unattractive place (especially less developed city neighbourhoods). The Social Connotations Hypothesis was tested in the Netherlands by Van Bezooijen (1994), who found that knowledge of the living conditions and lives of speakers indeed affects opinions of their languages.

The perceived attractiveness of languages may also lie in cultural and other associations. Like, for instance, French, Italian is often presented as a beautiful language. Macaro (2003), however, tried to defuse the common notion that Italian is an intrinsically beautiful language by emphasising that this language does not sound like the birds singing on a sunny day or the wind in the trees but that its association with beautiful things is what makes it so beautiful, not its aesthetic qualities.

9.4.4 Socio-cultural associations

Widespread stereotypical characteristics of large groups of people exist and these may affect attitudes towards their languages. Certain peoples (in certain countries or regions) are stereotypically fiery, others are stereotypically unexpressive and a little dry, some peoples are stereotypically slow and lazy, while others are stereotypically loose and carefree. A quick internet search for 'emotional countries' or 'national stereotypes' will provide you with some of these characterisations about large groups of speakers. These stereotypes can be very persistent and may affect how the languages of these people are evaluated.

As an illustration, Ladegaard (1998) had Danish participants evaluate characteristics of several varieties of English and found that the connotations regarding speakers were often in accordance with common stereotypes on Englishes (Australians sound laid-back, Cockney speakers sound broad, for instance). Considerable effects of the international status of varieties (of English) as a source of language attitudes were also found by Bayard et al. (2001).

9.4.5 Experiences with individual speakers

Personal experiences can explain individual differences in opinions towards language varieties (Schwarz and Bohner 2001). Experiences with one individual may affect the attitude towards another speaker with the same or a similar accent. Examples of this are experiences with friends and relatives speaking a certain language variety, or a variety being spoken by people in the area where one lives or where one grew up. Famous individual speakers may also be part of this experience, like politicians, newsreaders or game show hosts. The famous Polish linguist Jan Miodek plays an important role in Poland, for instance. For a long time, he presented a television programme on the Polish language. In Poland, this particular speaker has a high status and his opinion on language is highly valued. The way he speaks is also highly valued and acts as a model.

9.4.6 Intelligibility

Intelligibility is yet another factor correlating with language attitudes; if one understands a language well, then that affects the appreciation of that language positively, and the willingness to understand a language is also affected by attitudes. An interesting example of this relationship can be found in research by Wolff (1959), who investigated mutual intelligibility between the closely related Nigerian languages Kalabari and Nembe. The results showed that Nembe speakers claimed to understand Kalabari, while speakers of Kalabari judged Nembe to be less intelligible. Wolff considered this asymmetry in mutual intelligibility to be linked to asymmetry in language attitudes. He even suggested a reduced effort to understand a language that is not liked.

Schüppert et al. (2015) investigated the link between language attitudes and spoken word recognition of Swedish and Danish respondents (who evaluated each other's languages). They found that the correlation between understanding another language and positive attitudes towards that language is very low and in fact only loosely linked. It may be that this turns out to be different in tests that study different varieties of the same language; Boets and De Schutter (1977) and Van Bezooijen (1994) found a link between the intelligibility of dialects of Dutch and their appreciation. The most intelligible dialects were judged most positively.

An individual's speaking style should not be ignored in this discussion. It may be that an unclear enunciation of sounds affects intelligibility, even if the language spoken is an understandable one.

9.4.7 Exposure

Jackendoff (1994, 1992) pointed out that a complex piece of music may require a number of hearings before one can understand the implications of its events. As these implications are worked out by the listener, appreciation increases. Pinker and Jackendoff (2005) compared the rhythmic properties of language and music and the parallel between the linguistic and musical experience of sounds. Indeed, to the average Western European the traditional music of the Middle East or China does not conform to patterns of music that they are familiar with. McDermott et al. (2016) also concluded from their study of music perceptions of a Bolivian tribe that exposure to specific types of music leads to the nature of appreciation of musical sounds and that this sound appreciation is culturally determined and not innate. This is likely to be true for language as well. The appreciation of language will depend on one's familiarity with it, which in turn depends on one's exposure to it.

9.4.8 Linguistic outlook

Tamasi (2003) found that it is an individual's own relationship with their dialect that affects reactions towards the speech of others. This investigation showed that people's own dialect is judged differently from other people's dialects. Some speakers suffer from 'linguistic insecurity' in that they feel that others will consider the way they speak ugly, or inferior in some other way. They may even agree with the people who think so. Macaulay (1975) discussed this phenomenon of 'linguistic self-hatred', specifically in urban settings. Labov (1966) laid bare an explicit hostility expressed by respondents towards New York speech, which is a nationally and internationally well-known variety that clearly deviates from the norm in the United States. He even described New York as 'a great sink of negative prestige' (499) when it comes to the language spoken there. Preston (n.d.) found that speakers from Michigan (a state that is stereotypically associated with neutral General American speech) are linguistically relatively secure in that they tend to give high 'good English' ratings to speech from their own state.

It is by no means a rule that speakers of city or other dialects that deviate from the standard language view their own language negatively. In fact, the respondents in research done in Slovenia by Lundberg (2007) showed that the participants of some dialects tended to refer to their own dialect as the most beautiful language variety in the country. These examples show the special relationship people have with their own variety and how they will treat it as a point of reference. They also show that in addition to positively appreciating the norm language speakers can appreciate deviations from that norm positively as well. Sloos and Garcia (2015) referred to this phenomenon of the attitudinal impact of one's own variety as 'own variety bias'.

KEY CONCEPTS

'Them' and 'us'

Linguistic security or insecurity ties in with the place where one was born but also one's social group. Tajfel put forward social identity as a person's sense of who one is, based on membership of one or more groups. These groups, so Tajfel (1974) claimed, are an important source of self-esteem and of belonging to the social world. Tajfel proposed that we tend to divide the world into 'them' and 'us' and exaggerate the differences between groups and the similarities of things within a group.

The appreciation by speakers themselves of a language may change over long or short periods of time. Devonish (2015) found that the appreciation of Jamaican Creole is with every generation gaining prestige in Jamaica, and he explained how the self-assurance of Jamaicans regarding their own language and culture was growing through internationally well-known symbols such as Rastafari and the Jamaican icon Bob Marley (JLU 2005). The status of various languages in South Africa has also been subject to considerable change since the abolition of apartheid in 1994.

9.5 Conclusion

Attitudes can be patterned and predictable. The present chapter has shown the multitude of reasons behind attitudes. The assumption is that these motivations behind an attitude also affect our usage of language. Research into this is challenging. It is difficult to determine with a high degree of certainty which motivations are behind an attitude, as these forces will operate subconsciously to a high degree and they will operate in formation.

We may choose to speak in a certain way because we have always been told to do so or because we think that the usage is beautiful, logical, or perhaps linguistically rich and expressive. We may refrain from speaking in a certain way to avoid certain associations that this may evoke. We are aware of the possibility that others make these associations in their mind as well. However, the interpretation of grounds for the existence of language attitudes in those producing and those receiving language may be different.

STUDY QUESTIONS

1. Name a language attitude that you have always had and explain how the origins of language attitudes mentioned in this chapter can explain this attitude.
2. Could a society do without a language ideology? What would be the outcome of such a situation?

FURTHER READING

Using a wide range of examples from recent research and from various languages and cultures, Peter Garrett (2010) gives a state of the art overview of the field of language attitudes. Ingrid Piller (2016) explores a topic related to language attitudes, namely language as a means of discrimination and exclusion. The editor's introduction to Bourdieu (1991) provides a readable insight into Bourdieu's work (which is generally very hard to read).

The Language of a Lifetime

Life Trajectories and Age as Sociolinguistic Variables

10

10.1 Introduction

Age is associated with different ways to use language. Some of the characteristics of 'old' and 'young' speech are a choice by speakers, some are very deeply engrained in the social systems they live in, while other aspects are socially less meaningful because they are physiological. Right when you're born, your language starts to develop in all kinds of ways. At each stage in your life, your language may be recognised as being typical of a certain age group. As a result, all kinds of norms and expectations exist about the language of people a certain age.

This chapter first describes the beginnings of language in individuals and how the skill of how to use a language in various social circumstances is part of one's command of language. After that, different ways to view and determine someone's age are discussed. Then, sensitivity to language norms of people with different ages is explained. The chapter ends with examples of research into the effects of age on language and the methodological challenges that this social factor entails.

10.2 Developing one's language

10.2.1 Acquiring language

Labov (1994) put forward the premise that at some level individuals preserve their speech patterns throughout their lives after their language has been established. This is supported by the so-called 'Critical Period' for language learning. The Critical Period Hypothesis refers to a time window during which language acquisition takes place naturally and effortlessly. The best known proponent of this theory is Lenneberg (1967), who noted that around the age of two the hemispheres of the brain start to become functionally specialised and each controls different areas of human activity. By puberty, the process is completed. During this so-called lateralisation, one of the hemispheres begins to control the functions of language and the other ceases its involvement in language. After lateralisation, language acquisition becomes difficult and less successful. The assumption is that many aspects of the language system increasingly become less sensitive to change and even immutable. After the Critical Period, native-like acquisition becomes harder or even impossible, even if one is immersed in a native-speaking community permanently after this period.

Much theoretical research has been published on the Critical Period and it has also been researched empirically. The existence of a Critical Period itself is widely accepted, partly because it is confirmed through what we see and hear in the language production of younger and older people around us every day. However, disagreement exists on the exact age window when this period is 'active', on its final stage and the abruptness of the ending of this stage, and on which aspects of language are affected and in which way (pronunciation, word knowledge, grammar, prosody, etc.). Researchers are generally hesitant to commit to putting exact ages on critical periods of language acquisition in individuals. Individual variation is known to be considerable and testing this period reliably over large groups of people is methodologically challenging. A few general statements can nevertheless be made.

The onset of the Critical Period is the first time a child starts to pick up language naturally. By an individual's early teens, natural language acquisition increasingly becomes more stagnant. Until their early teens, they can acquire their first language relatively effortlessly. After this period, it becomes harder to acquire a language as a first language (and you will, as they say, 'have an accent' or 'sound foreign'). Learning language after the Critical Period is associated with second language acquisition, which is discussed further in Chapter 12.

10.2.2 Acquiring sociolinguistic competence

It is important to distinguish between general language skills and sociolinguistic skills. A necessary aspect of the acquisition of language is the development of sociolinguistic awareness, that is, awareness of the social meaning of language. One learns to recognise this meaning and apply it in one's own speech as one is acquiring one's native tongue. At a surprisingly early age, children are aware of all kinds of social differences that speech will reveal, and they are able to produce speech with such social distinctions. The development of this 'sociolinguistic competence' is not restricted to age as strictly as general language competence is. The former is continuously fine-tuned after the Critical Period, and one becomes more skilled at it after this period. One can change subtle word choices, formality levels, and certain pronunciation and intonation habits, in order to make one's language more socially befitting.

FOCUS ON...

Sociolinguistic competence versus choice

Some people are highly willing to adjust their speech to changing social circumstances, while others seem more or less untouched by the speech around them or are not interested in adjusting their speech to the social setting. Likely factors that determine whether one adjusts one's speech to circumstances are: one's social (in)security, mood, interest in other people, and degree of ability to adjust one's language. In addition, there are specific social circumstances, one's social mobility, one's social awareness, and, for instance, the nature and strength of the ideologies of one's family (see 5.2).

10.3   Four types of ages

10.3.1 Age based on time: chronological age

The most obvious approach to age is looking at one's date of birth and counting the time until the present. The ensuing age is called 'chronological age'. Chronological age is convenient for methodological purposes and is used much in research. Although it is a practical method to deal with age, from a sociolinguistic point of view this is not the most relevant information about a person's development over time. As an illustration, at some points in one's life, one tends to change more than at other points. Milroy et al. (1994) presented a study in Tyneside, an area in the North of England, in which 5- and 10-year-olds showed a different pronunciation pattern. Obviously, differences between 55- and 60-year-olds will be much harder to pinpoint. This demonstrates that a difference of five years between speakers can have various degrees of relevance when it comes to language use.

Eckert (1997) distinguished between four main stages in an individual's life: childhood (including pre-adolescence), adolescence (including early adolescence), adulthood (divided into early adulthood and middle age), and old age. The way for a researcher to determine which of these stages a person is in is not simply to ask for someone's age. Some people enter a certain life-stage before others do, and their bodies will often tell them when this is while the society in which someone lives may also have ideas about the stage one is in. This way, a composite of social and biological criteria is additionally used to determine age. To distinguish between different ways to determine age, one may thus make a distinction between biological and social age, in addition to chronological age. These two are discussed here.

10.3.2 Age as a result of bodily development: biological age

'Biological age' refers to stages of physical maturity that are noticeable in the development of bodies, which sometimes mature more quickly and with more far-reaching effects than at other times. Puberty is a good example of a biological change that affects individuals and their language and that starts at a different chronological age for different people. Biological age brings physical defects and less activity. These changes affect your position in society and, as a result, your language choices and the way your language is perceived.

There are relatively few biologically determined absolute language changes between age groups. The ones that exist have to do with the fact that young children have not yet mastered their first language completely, which leads to them speaking absolutely differently from adults. A non-absolute effect of bodily change on language use is that younger people tend to have a higher voice pitch than older people. Creakiness in the voice and generally a looser speech tract are also features that may come with old age and can't always be suppressed.

FOCUS ON...

Creak

A creaky voice is when there is a very slow and often irregular vibration of the vocal folds. Creak occurs every now and again in any individual's voice. Some people have a naturally creaky voice, and the likelihood of your voice becoming creaky increases with age (and is affected by lifestyle). Some creak is sociolinguistically meaningful, while other creak is not. In some European countries, creak is known to denote poshness. In the educated version of Standard British English, creak is said to denote disparagement (Crystal 1995). Creaky voices of women have furthermore been classified as an indication of mimicking a masculine or authoritative style (Warner 2015), while Yuasa (2010) attributed a woman's creaky voice to educatedness, nonaggressiveness, and an orientation on an urban lifestyle. This perceptually salient voice quality is also said to have associations with the less competent, less trustworthy, and less educated (Anderson et al. 2014). Some people, however, speak with a creaky voice because that is just what their voice is like, and they can't fully control it. Their voice may then be unwillingly and inadvertently associated with such qualities. Older speakers in particular may sometimes sound posh and conservative in cultures where these associations are current, simply because their voice is creaking.

10.3.3 Age based on experiences: social age

Close interaction as an experience

Throughout your life, you meet people, and each of these may somehow influence your language. The older you get, the more people you will have met and the more your language has potentially been affected by social encounters; in other words, your 'social age' changes. An individual is influenced by different people at different points in their life. In most cases, you are influenced most by those emotionally close to you. At an early age, individual language change is dependent on the speed and manner in which one acquires one's mother tongue, mainly under the influence of parents. After that, friends and close-nit networks usually start influencing your language (Chambers 2009). This pattern exists in many parts in the world. People may also be sensitive to other role models and their language and imitate them a little by perhaps taking over words, expressions, and sounds.

The specifics of this influence of people around us can partly be explained culturally. Al-Wer (2002b) explained how in Middle Eastern societies adolescents generally start to form personalised networks away from their families at a later stage than adolescents do in Western societies. In fact, peer-group formation and independent socialisation is often postponed until their teen years. This means that parent influence on language is likely to be relatively strong in such cultures. Research into Western societies has suggested that younger speakers are less pressured to speak the way their parents and teachers want them to but are instead subjected more to group/peer pressure (friends, mainly). Their language is thus shaped by these friends relatively much and early (Cheshire and Milroy 1993).

The experiences of generations

Eckert (1997) and Coupland (1997) explained how age and ageing are experienced not only individually but also as part of a generation. An individual's language is part of the language of a generation that shares certain experiences in certain decades in history.

Institutionalised experiences

Any life is filled with momentous and often officialised experiences that may change the way one thinks and talks. Language is affected by such experiences: education initiation, marriage, becoming a student, having your first child, losing one or both of your parents, being charged with a crime, graduating, retiring from work, and, for instance, being given citizenship or permanent residence to a country. The society or smaller community in which you live may even acknowledge these experiences and attach certain rights and obligations to them as well as ceremonies and rituals. Eckert (1997) emphasised the role of these 'institutional age limits and landmarks' (159). Institutions, like schools and companies, can play a role in shaping individuals' attitudes towards their local community, network, or community of practice – and towards themselves as a participant in them. Religious and other influential communities and institutions may also contribute to the intensity of life experiences by acknowledging age-related changes through initiation rituals, like Bar Mitzvah, Baptism, Ablution, or perhaps Paganing. People may come out of these rites an attitudinally different person, and this may affect language choices.

High-impact experiences

Less institutionalised experiences may also seriously impact your belief system and language behaviour, like being in an accident, getting your first serious job, moving to another city, coming out of the closet as a homosexual, becoming famous, being promoted, changing from playing soccer to playing golf, medical trauma, a trip around the world, study abroad, your first sexual experience, winning the lottery, and a sudden change in wealth. All of these experiences may make you revalue things, including your language.

EXAMPLE

Coming of age ceremonies

One important social age change that is often celebrated is one's coming of age. The rituals that go with this are usually associated with sexual maturity or religious responsibility. Such celebrations are typically performed at early adolescence. Children in Apache communities (a native people living in the Southwestern United States) are introduced to adulthood through a four-day ritual that includes prayer and life lessons. In some Latin American countries, girls are thrown a large party, called *Quinceañera* (Spanish for '15 years old') or *Baile de Debutantes* (Portuguese for 'debutants' dance'). Western Christian tradition often celebrates and confirms coming of age through the Sacrament of Confirmation. These celebrations often distinguish very strongly between men and women, which means that the ages of men and women are viewed and experienced differently from a social age point of view. After these ceremonies, these new adults may be expected to behave like grown women and men, including linguistically.

10.3.4 Age according to cultural perceptions: cultural age

Each culture has its own way of determining age and attaching value to it. The age that depends on culture is called 'cultural age'. Cheshire (2005) explained how the chronological approach to age (someone's age in years) may not work in certain African societies, where people may not know their age. Van Eeden (1991) referred to the clerk of a tribal community in this region assigning age on the basis of physical attributes. Cheshire (2005), in addition, stated that some communities attach more importance to rituals than actual age, and in this light she mentioned the age-related categorisation of Xhosa men (southern Africa) on the basis of initiation rituals. In Thai, this variation in importance attached to age also poses a challenge if one wants to investigate age, because many personal pronouns in that language depend on relative rather than absolute age of interlocutors (Intachakra 2001), in addition to social and contextual factors, which necessitates determining age relative to others rather than just the actual speaker age.

A sociolinguist can determine age in individuals and groups but in some of these groups age is considered more important than in others. In some cultures, older people have a higher status than in other cultures. Hiroshi et al. (2000) found differences in the status effect of age between Japanese people under the age of 20 and adolescents in that age from the United States of America. In general, the status-related appreciation of older people, or the elderly, seems different in Asia compared to the West, with the former attaching more status to it, in addition to respect. This has an effect on the status of the language of speakers with different ages and their position as linguistic role models. Researchers should therefore try to avoid automatically attaching as much importance to age as their own culture dictates.

FOCUS ON...

Prestige of age

In many cultures, being old has intrinsic status and is associated with wisdom; hence, the Swahili sayings *Kuishi kwingi ni kuona mengi* ('To live long is to see much') and *Mpofuka ukongweni, hapotewi na njia* ('He who becomes blind in his old age does not lose his way'). This affects the prestige of the speech of people who sound old. Gibbs (1964) explained how in patrilineal societies in East Africa older people are automatically associated with leading positions. The Indian saying *Ye bal mɛne dhuup me safed nahi kiye hɛ̃* translates as 'I have not greyed these hair in the sun', which implies that grey hair shows knowledge and experience. In Hindi and Punjabi, as a final example, the elderly are referred to as *Sayaanaa*, meaning 'wise man'.

An added challenge was explained by Hockett (1950), who pointed out that age groups are not 'hermetically sealed' (453) from one another, because in by far most cultures there is always some interaction between age groups. Methodologically, the researcher needs to make sure that younger speakers 'speak young' and that older speakers 'speak old' when describing these speakers' age-typical language. Catching those types of natural, less monitored styles is hard.

10.4   Age and language norms

10.4.1 Susceptibility to norms

The variation in the way individuals at different points in their lives are influenced by people around them often comes down to a move away from or towards a norm language. The degree to which an individual adjusts their language to social circumstances depends partly on life stage. In their early lives, children will adjust to the norms as imposed by their parents, and they will do so relatively naturally, subconsciously, and uncritically.

After childhood, children will be more aware of a broader language norm and consciously develop their own style relative to that broader norm language. Labov (2001b) discussed a trend that is common in Western societies, namely adolescents being relatively free of responsibilities and thus not sensing the pressures from the linguistic marketplace too much and being less likely to adjust to a language norm while instead focussing on the language of their peers. Bigham (2012) described a prototypical Western emerging adult: aged 18–25, not married, in higher education, highly mobile, and with a large social network (which includes many superficial contacts). This group is in a stage of socioeconomic instability, identity exploration, and self-focus. They feel that they are classless and that life is full of possibilities, and they feel neither like a child or an adult; they feel like they're in between these two stages in their lives. The sensitivity to social adjustment may be large at this stage in one's life. This may even lead to the need to speak non-standard language, that is, to highlight difference between oneself and others, especially those in charge.

During adulthood, there is often an adaptation to broader language norms, as one becomes more public and more subject to the rules of mainstream society. Chambers (2009) explained the effects of adulthood on language and referred to the term 'linguistic retrenchment' (195), which is a move away from conscious deviations from the norm language as a result of greater responsibilities in society and one's home environment. Settled in one's tastes and opinions, the individual will feel less need to define themselves socially and will be more likely to adjust to a broad norm.

Older people, finally, are less influenced by language norms again (Downes 1998) and might just choose the language use that comes most naturally. This may be the language they spoke when they were young.

10.4.2 Age grading

The adjustment to language norms regarding how people a certain age are supposed to speak can be seen through the phenomenon called 'age grading', which emphasises adjustment to like-minded groups one belongs to. The original (anthropological) definition of this phenomenon by Hockett (1950) addressed the regular tendency for individuals to interact most frequently with community members of their own or of a similar age. Since then, sociolinguists have refined the use of this term, but inconsistency in its application remains, according to Evans Wagner (2012). A common and workable definition is that it refers to the phenomenon of speech being typical of different stages in an individual's life. The backdrop of this phenomenon is a stable community in which a norm language, a language ideology, is overtly present and in which repeated patterns of behaviour in the various age groups exist. In these settings, especially Western ones, the individual tends to respond to the pressures of language ideology and in particular linguistically marks their transition to, for instance, adulthood with more norm-based speech patterns than at earlier age periods.

Distinguishing 'age-graded' variation from variation due to 'generational' language variation is difficult. A difference between a younger and older speaker may be due to individuals at various points in their lives adjusting to norms regarding how people a certain age typically speak (age-graded variation) or this difference may be due to the fact that in past times individuals spoke differently, as reflected in today's language of older speakers (generational variation). Generational variation means that with each generation in a certain culture or community a certain variant is used more. A variant is age-graded when all speakers of a community use more tokens of a certain variant at a certain stage in their lives and a lower number at another stage.

10.5   Research into age and language

10.5.1 Dealing with age in investigations

Applying age categories on the basis of criteria other than chronological age in empirical research is far from easy, as you would need to interview people about things like their medical state, experiences, and cultural perceptions and design methods of determining their biological, social and cultural ages. Eckert (1997) asserted that within speech communities age cohorts can be defined 'etically' or 'emically' (155). The etic approach groups individuals into equal age spans such as decades, while the emic method takes shared experiences and attitudes – such as they arise in childhood, adolescence, and adulthood – as the grouping criterion. A common approach is to form age groups on the basis of the four main stages in life (see 10.3.1) by pinpointing ages at which groups are highly likely to be in the middle of one of the defined periods. Keeping large distinctions (in years) between age groups is safest in this case.

10.5.2 Examples of age-related research

1. Research into early sociolinguistic awareness

Awareness of social variation may start at a very early age. This was tested by Rosenthal (1977), who found considerable sociolinguistic awareness in a set of American school children regarding American English varieties that were stereotypically associated with either the black race or the white race. The investigation showed how the pre-schoolers (3- and 5-year-olds) in the experiment recognised the two types of accents when they heard them through a recording and held strong stereotypes as to the two groups of speakers these accents represented. This turned out to be true even for the 3-year-olds. Much more recently, Barbu et al. (2013) investigated both the awareness of sociolinguistic variation in French children (aged 4–6) and their production of certain sociolinguistically relevant variants. The researchers found that the ability to evaluate different sociolinguistic forms emerged at an early age and that this group of children was aware of the social value of certain language variants.

2. Research into age-graded variation

Nguyen et al. (2013) investigated Twitter communication in the Netherlands by people with various ages and looked at both topic choice and language use. They found that younger Dutch Twitter users were more likely to use text speak, talk about themselves (and use the pronoun *ik*, 'I'), use words that were all capitalised, and suggest phonetic lengthening by repeating vowels, like writing *'niiiiiiice'* (the Dutch tweeters often used English loans like this) instead of *'nice'*. The classic happy face emoticon and *ha ha* ('ha ha') were also used often by the younger users. Older tweeters were more likely to tweet Dutch politeness phrases that translate as 'good morning' and 'take care'. Their style was generally filled with more complex language, with longer tweets, longer words, and the use of a higher number of prepositions. Links and hashtags were also used more by the older group. The researchers suggested that this reflects a stronger desire to share information and what the researchers call 'impression management' (446). Nguyen et al. (2013) found that the language use of younger Tweeters was strikingly likely to change in a short period of time. This suggests that within groups of younger people, subgroups could be formed, whereas the age categories for older people (after the age of around 30) could be larger.

3. Real-time versus apparent-time research

There are two main approaches to researching age as a social variable in language variation; the 'apparent-time' approach and the 'real-time' approach (Milroy and Gordon 2003). If we take Labov's basic premise as a starting point, namely that one's basic language after it has been settled in the brain does not change seriously, then an 80-year-old, whose language acquisition was completed more or less in their mid-teens, speaks the language from about 60 or 70 years ago and gives us the opportunity to hear language from the past in today's speech. This approach is called the apparent-time approach. With this method, we can find out how one generation's language use has developed into a new generation's (slightly different) language use.

Real-time research, by contrast, looks at language data made in the past and compares these with modern language data. An example of a real-time approach is a 'trend study', which investigates language from similar speakers at specific points in time, like Van de Velde (1996) did in Flanders and the Netherlands. He researched the pronunciation of newsreaders from various decades. Another approach is investigating the same speakers (rather than similar speakers) over several decades, like Sankoff (2004) did, which is called a 'panel study'. The real-time approach with similar speakers from different time periods can be used to reveal subtle language change, or norm change, while studying the same speakers during their lifetimes is geared more towards revealing and explaining individual language change and may be interesting for finding out more about age-graded change. Interviewing the actual speakers is part of that type of investigation. It should be clear that research data like Sankoff's are extremely hard to get (she used data from a long-running documentary on television). Examples of real-time and apparent-time studies are given in Section 17.4.2.

10.6 Conclusion

Eckert (1997) stated that 'age is a person's place at a given time in relation to the social order: a stage, a condition, a place in history' (151) and drew considerable attention to a sociolinguistic variable that is often incorrectly considered to be uncomplicated and straightforward.

People with different ages produce different language. The question is whether this is due to biological factors, because they are adjusting their language to the way their age peers speak or to some other (perhaps culture-specific) model, because of the stage they are at in their lives, or maybe because they simply speak the language they naturally picked up when they were young.

Obviously, it is a mixture of these. The language of people with different ages can be revealed by looking at contemporary and past speech. Such research can show how fast change across generations can go and how subtle yet noticeable such change can be.

Researchers generally choose chronological age as their default method of dividing their groups up into age group, knowing that any other means of age categorisation is difficulty to apply. However, this approach, while being practical and efficient, overlooks the stages that people naturally go through and the life-changing events in people's lives that affect their language and it ignores cultural perceptions of age. In addition, the individual's sensitivity towards age-related norms as well as their sociolinguistic competence should ideally be part of investigations. A final challenge is to not misinterpret age-related changes that are due to an individual's tendency to adjust their language to a different stage in their life. Despite many complications of categorising people on the basis of age, results from such investigations have yielded clear effects of age on language use.

STUDY QUESTIONS

1. How important is age to you and the culture you are from? Is it a relevant factor from a sociolinguistic point of view?
2. After reading this chapter, try to describe your age from a sociolinguistic point of view, that is, according to the various ways of determining age.
3. Can you give an example of how a certain experience has permanently affected your language use?

FURTHER READING

Nussbaum and Coupland (2004) explain the social process of aging by presenting research on communication and aging (mainly from the United Kingdom and the United States) from the two decades preceding the book. It includes an interesting chapter by Coupland on age in social and sociolinguistic theory. The 200th edition of the International Journal of the Sociology of Language (2009) is about age grading and contains articles from various parts of the world. Penelope Eckert (1997), finally, wrote an important paper on age as a sociolinguistic variable. This paper has served as an inspiration for subsequent discussions on this topic.

The Language of Women and Men

Gender and Sexuality as Sociolinguistic Variables

11.1 Introduction

Although no one has explicitly instructed them to do so, male and female birds sing differently (Dunn 2014). Such differences are deeply engrained in the species. For humans too, the biological distinction between female and male is one of the most essential and visible that we know. The roles of the two sexes in the procreational system are fixed. Most societies emphasise this distinction and will raise and treat the members of the sexes in accordance with existing expectations as to how men and women are supposed to behave. Individuals' life trajectories are partly predetermined through these expectations and our language is affected by these assigned and perceived roles. Unlike birds, humans tend to be conscious of their natural inclinations and of the roles assigned to them. They play with these tendencies and roles, emphasise them, suppress them, ignore them, or go against them. Language acts as an important tool in these efforts.

This chapter discusses fixed, assigned, and chosen gender roles and how they affect the language of individuals. The problems that arise when drawing a distinction between the two sexes are explained first, and this is followed by the issue of absolute differences between the way men and women speak. The next topics are gender-based distinctions that are built in in languages themselves and sexism in language. Research findings from two major research traditions are presented next, namely those from the Anglo-Western and Arabic regions. This is followed by an overview of reasons often mentioned to explain differences between the way men and women speak. Next, speech patterns in non-heterosexual circles are touched upon, namely the language of members of the various groups of the LGBT (lesbian, gay, bisexual, and transsexual) community. The chapter ends with a critical discussion of research in the field of gender and language.

11.2 Distinguishing between two sexes

11.2.1 Practical, methodological, and principled issues

Strictly biologically speaking, the difference between men and women is worded as a 'sex' difference. However, that word is used less frequently in the Social Sciences nowadays and it has largely been replaced by the denotation 'gender'. The latter term places emphasis on social and cultural identity, rather than absolute differences between the bodies of two types of people. The idea is that the differences between people are a social characteristic influenced not predominantly by an individual's chromosomes but by their tendency to follow certain prescribed patterns regarding how they should behave. There are minor effects on speech because of the way bodies are built (most notably pitch), but no biological differences between men and women predictably make their language style different from each other (see 5.2.1). This makes the biological difference as expressed so explicitly by 'sex' sociolinguistically less relevant.

Another reason for not emphasising a biological distinction is that in some societies this binary distinction is more fluid. Third and even fourth and fifth genders are known. Third genders in particular are not as peripheral as some who are from sexually binary societies may think. The so-called hijras of India, Pakistan and Bangladesh have been legalised as an official gender identity, for instance. Estimates of their numbers vary strongly, with modest estimates starting at 50,000 (Nanda 1999; Bray 2005). Third genders are also found in Southern Mexico, Northern Albania, Africa, Asia-Pacific, and the Caribbean, amongst other places.

A final issue affecting choices to distinguish between the two sexes is that people, especially in libertarian Western industrialised societies, may for various reasons (mostly of a principled nature) feel that being one of the two biological sexes is irrelevant. In Germany and Australia, individuals not wishing to state membership of one of the two genders have even been reported, as well as official acknowledgement hereof by the government (Dow 2010; Agius 2013).

When distinguishing between men and women and how they communicate, it should be borne in mind that there are strong differences in the degree to which gender actually seems to influence language use. In English/Welsh bilingual communities in Northern Wales, the roles assigned to men and women have been shown to be relatively unpronounced (Gal 1978; Morris 2014) and the same is true for communities in the tip of Northern Europe (Aikio et al. 2015). So, before embarking on gender-induced variation, researchers might ask themselves how relevant it is.

While, ideally, the degree to which speakers abide by roles as present in society is taken as a methodological point of departure, in actual fact participants in investigations are commonly asked to state their biological gender. Practical reasons underlie this choice. The fact that this approach tends to yield very clear results between the two genders also contributes to this choice. The named distinction is very practical, despite its imprecision and its political incorrectness to some.

FOCUS ON...

Gender as a cultural marker

A way to view the difference between men and women is to consider men and women as members of two culturally different groups. Communication between the sexes then becomes equivalent to intercultural communication. Deborah Tannen (1990) is the most well-known proponent of this approach.

11.2.2 Absolute differences in language use

There are many claims that in certain languages men and women apply different forms in a systematic way. Japanese is often mentioned in the context of such sex-exclusive differentiation. Ide and Yoshida (1999) explained how there is a clear male/female distinction in the use of certain particles in this language. Horii (1992) also identified specific terms as being 'women's language'. Heinrich (2015) explained how such and other rather clear differences between the ways Japanese women and men tend to speak have led to much speculation about the existence of a male and a female way of speaking Japanese, and that this speculation is often rather overzealous. Inoue (2006), in fact, talked about how, growing up, people might never actually encounter female speech in their daily lives.

A more convincing example of such a system of gender exclusivity in language use is the language of the Karaya community in Brazil (Fortune 1998). Fortune and Fortune (1975) even indicated that the differences are salient to such a degree that they appear in every second or third word of running speech. The most clearly audible difference, so they explained, is the seemingly absolute correspondence between /k/ in the women's dialect and /∅/ (i.e., not pronounced) in the men's dialect: women in the named investigation pronounced the word 'fish' as starting with a /k/ while men systematically left out this phoneme (resulting in 'fish' being pronounced as either /kətora/ or /ətora/). Absolute differences also exist between men and women in some sign language communities, but this is usually because the two sexes led separate lives in several ways and developed their own signs (LeMaster 1997). Despite quite a few examples from all over the world, so Dunn (2014) concluded, categorical dialect differences determined by gender are rare.

11.3 Linguistic differences

11.3.1 Differences in language itself

Sex differences are not merely visible in language use but distinctions between the sexes are in various ways also built in in languages themselves. Language commonly directly indexes biological gender: a word can be semantically male or female and, accordingly, refer to either males or females. Possessive pronouns like 'his' or 'her' directly reveal the biological gender of someone referred to. Such absolute differences are the outcome of societies making distinctions and are more often than not ideological leftovers from some past. Sex distinctions even exist in the way whole cities are viewed. The Russian city of St. Petersburg is typically seen as feminine, while Moscow is viewed as more masculine. The Russian words for St. Petersburg and Moscow are of masculine and feminine gender, respectively (Gritsai et al. 2000; Lilly 2004).

EXAMPLE

Georgian

Georgian is interesting, as it is in some ways a highly gender-neutral language. Not only are there no articles showing the gender of a noun, nouns are gender-neutral, and whether one is a man or a woman waiting tables is, for instance, not expressed in the job title: *mimtani* is someone, male or female, waiting tables.

11.3.2 Sexism

Most commonly, sexism reflects more negatively on women than on men. Some examples from the European Mediterranean will demonstrate this. Cenni (2015) pointed out some asymmetries in Italian and Spanish. In Italian, the noun *pescivendolo* means 'male fish seller', but while its feminine counterpart, *pescivendola*, also refers to 'seller of fish' (who is of the female sex), it also has the connotation of 'chatterbox'. In both Italian and Spanish, furthermore, linguistic gender bias exists in dictionaries. Cirillo (2002), in fact, claimed that sexist principles rule all aspects of Italian dictionary making. This, so Cirillo claimed, is evident in, amongst others, the selection of entries, number of synonyms, the ordering of definitions, and in the selection of examples. The sex-biased representation of women in the 21st and 22nd editions of the Dictionary of the Spanish Academy was revealed by Vargas et al. (1998).

The tendency of some words slowly developing a negative meaning or association is called 'semantic derogation'. In English, for one, sexist connotations are part and parcel of quite a few words. If the words 'wizard' and 'witch' are considered counterparts, then the sexism lies in the fact that the male equivalent has much more positive connotations. The same is true for 'bachelor' and 'spinster'. While wizards are smart and a 'computer wizard' is typically a man who is admired for his technical skills, a witch is typically an unappealing woman, either in appearance or personality. It also works the other way around. The pejorative words 'nerd' and 'geek' both mostly refer to clumsy and unattractive boys.

Derogation is common in other respects as well. In Persian, attitudes towards women and men are shown in proverbs in which animals are metaphorically related to people. The metaphorical meanings of the female version tend to connote worse qualities than their male equivalents do. Estaji and Nakhavali (2011) gave the example of a proverb translating as 'a woman's love and affection is like a donkey's tail'. They found only four Persian proverbs containing such derogation towards males, while countless examples could be found of proverbs derogatory to women. Such proverbs with metaphors and comparisons in which characteristics are assigned to the sexes are common in languages across the globe.

FOCUS ON...

Order of the genders

When both men and women are mentioned separately in a phrase, then one of them needs to come first, obviously. In many languages, women are mentioned first in announcements. French, Arabic, and German, amongst many other languages, address groups of men and women as 'ladies and gentlemen'. When it comes to calling children, then the order sometimes seems less strict: both 'girls and boys' and 'boys and girls' seem very common across various languages. This order may or may not be sociolinguistically relevant.

Unsuccessful efforts to reverse sexism

Fighting these types of sex biases in language and communication is difficult because they are firmly cemented into the language and because they often reflect persistent attitudes in society. Nevertheless, efforts have been made to reverse situations. Some of these have proven more successful than others. An example of an unsuccessful suggested change occurred in the Netherlands, where the academic title *doctoranda* was introduced as a female alternative to the existing male-based *doctorandus* title, but it never caught on and was hardly used. Nowadays, the not so gender-neutral international term *Master* has replaced both. In Russia, female professional terminology to replace male profession names was proposed. An example was the phrase 'The doctor came', which was originally *Vrach prishel*, with a masculine gender verb. The female alternative that was constructed was *Vrach prishla*, with a verb belonging to the female gender. This added possibility, however, never caught on. Another example is the word 'author' (*avtor*), which is by certain groups of enthusiasts given a female equivalent (*avtorka*). This female form, however, is highly marked and not in fact known to all native speakers. In Macedonia, female equivalents of certain names of professional positions were invented, like *ministerka* for *minister* ('minister'), *direktorka* for *direktor* ('director'), and *profesorka* for *profesor* ('professor'). The female equivalents are accepted and are used, but Petkovska (2014) demonstrated that amongst ordinary users, the possibility of using the female forms remains unknown.

Successful efforts to reverse sexism

Other changes have been more successful, probably because attitudes in society have changed. A notable one, seen in several languages, is the use of a single male or female form to refer to both men and women. In English, 'secretary' (a word traditionally referring to women) is sometimes used to refer to both male and female office managers and assistants, and 'manager' has lost much of its male-exclusive association. Few complaints are heard about the male etymologies of the academic titles 'Bachelor of Arts' and 'Master of Arts' as these titles have more or less lost their male connotations. Another successful method is the creation of a neutral term; the word 'police officer' has, for instance, successfully replaced 'policeman' and 'policewoman' in many Englishes. Furthermore, in Kenyan English the words 'headmaster' and 'headmistress' are often replaced by the gender-neutral 'heady'.

The same gender neutralisation is true for the previously mentioned 'computer wizard', which could nowadays also refer to women, and the words 'nerd' and 'geek', with their male connotations, could refer to girls nowadays. While in the past 'gay' referred mainly to male homosexuals and carried pejorative connotations, it is now a more sex-independent generic term to refer to homosexuals of either sex and it has shed some (not all) of its pejorative connotations. In many countries, the language thus gradually neutralises and naturally adapts to the changes in society. It is safe to say that forcing the issue through language change itself is difficult if society is not ready yet.

11.4   Research into gender

11.4.1 The Anglo-Western tradition

Much Sociolinguistic research into gender is available. The most well-known investigations are from the Anglophone areas. Holmes (1998) summarised some common generalisations about men and women and their language that research in the Anglo-Western area has yielded. One generalisation is that women show and are more sensitive to emotion in language and are relatively less focussed on content while men focus more on the information than the way it is communicated or the emotion that goes with it. Men provide less encouragement to their interlocutor in discourse while women tend to use minimal support tools like 'mm' and 'uh-huh' more. Women show more concern for their partner's positive face needs (need for approval) and they value and express solidarity more. Women use hedges (language that is careful and tentative), tag questions, and modifying terms like 'sort of' and 'as you know' more, making them stereotypically come across as either uncertain, hesitant, helpful, and/or more precise and nuanced. Women interrupt less and men speak more. Men, finally, pay relatively much attention to maintaining and increasing power, while women focus more on maintaining and increasing solidarity (Holmes 1998: 468–472).

11.4.2 Gender research outside the Anglo-Western area

It has been acknowledged that Anglo-Western research should not too eagerly be used to generalise. The extensive tradition of gender studies in the Anglo-West has not been countered by similar waves of interest outside these areas. Each area or country developed its own tradition (to highly varying degrees) in studying gender, and those that took up this topic applied their own angle – for political and cultural motivations, in addition to academic ones. In East Africa, so Musau (2004) indicated, language varieties tend to be researched as a source of testing linguistic theories, not theories of how gender interacts with other social variables and shapes language. As a result, sociolinguistic and gender research from this area is scarce (Barasa 2015). Another example is the post-Soviet region, where gender research arose and led to a fair number of publications but only as late as the 1990s, as Kirilina and Tomskaya (2005) indicated. This late start was due to such research being prohibited by law until the 1990s. After that time, it was still not embraced wholeheartedly, and Russia is currently making a very slow start on this topic. In some other cultures too, this topic was ignored because of political circumstances or simply because it was so closely entwined with a factor like politeness, and was only mentioned haphazardly as an independent factor. Furthermore, gender research often touches on sexuality, including homosexuality, and the phenomenon of one of the sexes showing behavioural patterns that are stereotypically associated with another gender. Researchers from cultures where men and women are subjected to strict behavioural rules while homosexuality is ignored, denied, or even persecuted will feel hesitant to research this theme and publish on it. Feminism is another theme associated with gender research and that forms a negative association in some people's minds, and this is true in certain cultures more than it is in others.

Existing theories from the Anglophone world often serve as an important model of comparison in other areas, even if these theories ill-fit the local situation. Li (2014) demonstrated the approach that is often taken to tackle this and described a typical Chinese article on gender: it starts with a summary of studies abroad, then explains sexism in the language studied, and, finally, moves on to giving some analyses of research results into gender differences (most of which involve English).

11.4.3 Comparing two research traditions

To demonstrate the workings of gender and to give an idea of available research, investigations from two regions will be discussed here. First, some samples of mainstream theories and some important research findings from the Anglo-Western area will be given. After this, a non-Western area where gender research is taking flight at the moment is described, namely the Arab region. These descriptions and the subsequent mutual comparison will show how two traditions may be mutually supportive in creating a broader understanding of the issue. The focus here is on the relationship between biological gender and the tendency to adopt the prestige language. Both traditions have paid much attention to this issue.

11.4.4 Gender research in the Anglophone area

Norm sensitivity

One of the most well-known and popularised findings in Anglo-Western sociolinguistic research has been that women are more inclined to meet the language norm than men are and thus do what is prescribed. This early generalisation was made on the basis of research into the pronunciation of all kinds of Englishes across the globe, and it quickly popularised in sociolinguistic circles in general. Trudgill (1974a) and Horvath (1985), for instance, found that women were less inclined than men to use the less standard /ɪn/ form instead of the /ɪŋ/ in English words ending in '-ing'. In other words, women were less likely to say 'walkin' than the more socially acceptable 'walking'. Trudgill did his research in Norwich, England, and Horvath's speakers were from Sydney, Australia. Shopen (1978) also reported that (Australian) women used the standard /ŋ/ variant more than men did. In the same vein, in Detroit, a city in the United States, Wolfram (1969) found that women tended less towards various alternatives to the most accepted realisation of a certain sound; the women were less likely to pronounce the 'th' sound in a word like 'nothing' as a 't' or 'f' rather than pressing the tongue against the upper teeth, which is the norm. Milroy and Milroy (1978) also investigated this sound, in Belfast (Northern Ireland), and found a similar pattern.

In investigations like the ones described here, variables like class and age appeared to correlate strongly with gender. Lower-class and middle-class women in particular were found to be more inclined to use more prestige forms, so Paulston and Tucker (2003) concluded from existing research. Across classes, the relative differences between the sexes are generally maintained, so findings showed. Barbieri (2007) examined the effect of sex and speaker age on the use of 'be like', 'go', 'be all', and 'say' in modern, spoken American English, which are used to quote oneself ('I went "yes",' meaning 'I said "yes",' for example). She found sex differences to be more visible for those under 40, with age negatively correlating with the use of 'be like' for women.

FOCUS ON...

Speech tract use style

Thompson (2003) referred to the ways specific classes are associated with different uses of the mouth when speaking and how this affects perceptions of stereotypically male and female speech. He explained this through the common distinction in French made between the pinched mouth (*la bouche*) and a large, open mouth (*la gueule*). He indicated that it is common for members of the working class to draw a strong opposition between these two, with *la bouche* being associated with the bourgeoisie and femininity and *la gueule* with the popular and the masculine. Thompson explained how the middle-/upper-class style acts as a 'negation ... of their sexual identity' (18). For male working-class speakers to adopt these 'higher' speech styles, it would mean not only giving up their class but also their masculinity.

Appeal of progressive speech

Another tendency that is often found is that of women leading change and actually embracing new sub-standard forms more eagerly than men. This tendency seemingly contradicts the idea that women are more conservative by following the standard more. Batterham (2000) found evidence of this in the pronunciation of certain vowels by men and women in Auckland (New Zealand) and in Utah and Texas in the United States, respectively. The women adopted innovative vowels more than the men did, possibly below the level of consciousness. Tagliamonte (1998), in addition, investigated the use of non-standard 'were' in negative tags ('I was getting fed up, weren't I?' rather than 'I was getting fed up, wasn't I?'). She found that her male speakers in the Northeastern English city of York were less likely than the women to use 'weren't' in places where 'wasn't' would be the norm. She concluded that the contrasting behaviour of the men and the women revealed that the women were leading linguistic change. The famous Northern Cities Shift, which vowel change is said to be taking place in the northern states of the United States, has been reported in a string of investigations (Labov et al. 2006; Labov 1994). These investigations revealed a conservative role for the men and a leading one for the women. Evans (2004), as an illustration, revealed how sex was a significant social factor, with women leading in the raising (pronouncing something higher in the mouth; with a smaller aperture of the speech tract) of the vowel /æ/.

There is no rule that says that women lead language change. Fox (2015) demonstrated that young urban males with a Bangladeshi background were forerunners of change in a neighbourhood in London, England. They were in fact speakers of the traditional variety associated with London (called 'Cockney') and were leading innovations of the vowels in words like 'price' and 'face'. Ethnicity and ethnic identity affects these results of course. Results like these suggest that a broader look at the issue is needed, both culturally and linguistically.

11.4.5 Gender research in the Arab region

Norm sensitivity

One region outside the Anglo-Western region where gender research has flourished to such an extent that broader research tendencies are visible, is the Arab region. Pronunciation research on various vowels and consonants in particular has revealed that women tended less towards the traditional standard realisation than did the men (Haeri 1987). Research (Haeri 1995; Bakir 1986) has shown that men tended towards greater usage of /q/ (which is a consonant that is pronounced very deeply in the mouth) whereas women tended towards /ʔ/ (which is pronounced even deeper in the mouth); the /q/ realisation is associated with standard speech, whereas the consonant /ʔ/ is typical of an urban pronunciation. Features other than gender appeared to be part of the correlation. Haeri (1995) observed that when men and women have high educational levels, the women use features of Standard Arabic – that is, the norm – significantly less than the men did. This study also found that young, educated, middle-class women used more foreign lexical items than men did. Education in this study seemed relevant and the same was true for sensitivity to prestige.

One explanation of women's lesser use of the standard is that women sometimes have less access to education and the professional world and thus use Standard Arabic (which is a simplified and modernised version of Classical Arabic, the language of the Holy Quran) less often. Bassiouney (2015), however, challenged this common conclusion in variationist studies on the Arab world. When women have a choice between the prestigious urban variety, a rural variety, and Standard Arabic, they are more prone to choose the urban variety as a means of asserting their identity. Al-Wer (2002a) revealed another possibility, namely that education acts indirectly, as it often leads to a widening of the individual's network and mobility and results in a higher use of urban variables.

Appeal of progressive speech

In addition to the prestige urban dialect, there is of course the codified and explicitly accepted standard variety, Standard Arabic, as a pronunciation model. Urbanisation has led to a distinction between prestige and standard dialects. Ibrahim (1986) differentiated between standard and prestige to highlight the role of urban speech among educated speakers. Standard, literary Arabic has high prestige and it is a supra-national regional standard, but nationally (for the various countries in Northern Africa and the Middle East, where Arabic is spoken) it is not the common spoken standard (Chambers 2009). It is not the native tongue of speakers, generally, but its pronunciation does act as a model (Chambers 2009).

A string of studies in Northern Africa has shown that in urban areas a localised vernacular is most prestigious. This prestige depends on a number of social, geographical, and political factors. It is usually the dialect from one of the largest cities within the country. Cairene Arabic in Egypt is a good example of a prestigious city dialect (Bassiouney 2015), and so is the dialect from Casablanca, the largest city in Morocco (Hachimi 2007) and that of Tripoli, the capital of Libya (Pereira 2007). Certain types of women in particular seem drawn to these urban dialects.

It should be noted that not all Arabic research has pointed in the same direction. Abu-Haidar (1987) found women in the Iraqi capital of Baghdad using a greater percentage of Standard Arabic forms than the men. Walters (2003) and Mejdell (2006) also found a tendency among educated women to use many standard variants in formal speech, in Tunisia and Egypt, respectively.

11.4.6 Overall trends

It might be concluded that in the Arab region the norm language ideology is partly in agreement with the Anglo-Western model while emerging city dialects are serious contenders for the position of prestige dialect and that these exert influence on (certain types of) women more than on men. The prestige of city dialects seems more covert in the Anglo-Western world, as shown by the fact that the media would not necessarily broadcast in it. In the Arab region, the urban varieties are commonly used more in the broadcast media. The contribution of the Arabic research lies in the description of situations where there is more than one contender for the prestige language position and brings home the fact that the widespread assumption that standard and prestige are the same quality is culture-determined and that this affects the way men and women speak.

FOCUS ON...

Cultural differences

Generalisations about the way men and women talk cannot easily be made because cultural differences tend to have a particularly strong effect on male and female relationships and, as a result, the way men and women talk. Within cultures, more cultural distinctions need to be reckoned with even. As an illustration, Satyanath (2015) explained how much of Indian gender research has drawn from patrilineal communities (in which power is inter-generationally passed on through men) and that the gender-related findings are highly deviant from those of less patrilineal societies. This aspect of societies may explain how people apply language to express identity. In the South Indian region of Kerala, which region is a mix of patrilineal and matrilineal communities (in which power is passed on through women), the behaviour of Nair women (an Indian group of castes) is different from the rest of the women from other groups, as well as that of Nair men (Satyanath 2015). The Nair caste is known for its matrilineal practices and behaves differently from the patrilineal castes that surround them.

11.5 Explanations for difference

11.5.1 Access and societal role

Two facts are key in determining language use by men and women, according to Romaine (2003), namely 'access' and 'role' (109); the degree to which men and women have access to the prestige language and the role that the sexes play in their community. The assumption is that men often have more access to the language norm because they are a more prominent part of the professional sphere, where this language is more common. As for societal role, research in countries where more than one type of prestigious language exists reveals how high levels of education, progressiveness, and urbanness lead to more sensitivity to modern prestige language use, and this may be due to women who these features appeal to playing a different role in society than less educated, progressive, and urban female speakers. Women who do meet these requirements are more likely to hold positions in which they are surrounded by norm awareness.

11.5.2 (Socio-)linguistic and perceptual skills

A well-known explanation of the difference between the way men and women speak is that of ability. Differences like superior verbal qualities (extensive grammar and vocabulary) and sociolinguistic ability (knowing how to use the right language in the right social context) are often assigned to women. Also, the more fine-grained observational skills and sensitivity of women are sometimes claimed to lead to the use of very specific qualifications in language use like 'divine', 'adorable', and 'charming' (Lakoff 1975). It should be noted that these may also be part of choice rather than skill; a difference in attaching importance to such distinctions and acting upon them linguistically.

11.5.3 Applying language as a symbol

Eckert (2000) referred to the possibly greater willingness of women to apply language – as well as other features, like clothes – as a symbolic resource to identify or dissociate with a social group and feel more powerful that way. The same could apply to men. Haeri (1995) suggested that the Arab-speaking men in her research used heavier pharyngealisation than women in order to sound tough and manly. Women could be claimed to associate the prestige forms with male language as men more often function in circles where the prestige language is needed to be powerful (Bakir 1986). Something similar is demonstrated by Cao (1985), who showed that two variants of a certain dental/alveolar consonant in the dialect of the Chinese city of Beijing were for long assumed to be free variants but turned out to serve symbolic functions. They turned out to index femininity (in addition to age difference and the coming of puberty).

11.5.4 Sensitivity to prestige

Women are sometimes said to act upon prestige more than men. An important interpretation of Western studies in particular is that lower-middle-class women sometimes tend to use more prestige forms than their social stature would suggest. A typical explanation is that this is done to compensate for their socially insecure position (Lakoff 1975; Paulston and Tucker 2003). The tendency of men showing a preference for change from below and women being more interested in prestige forms is often explained through the idea of overt and covert prestige (Labov 1963; Trudgill 1972). Covert prestige refers to the tacit prestige of non-standard forms, and overt prestige is the visible and overtly expressed prestige that is associated with the prescribed language norm. So, people are to various degrees aware of assigning prestige to certain speech forms.

This phenomenon of norm sensitivity coincides with economic and social factors, according to James and Drakich (1993), so that some are more sensitive to prestige than others because of their socioeconomic background. In some communities, variables associated with upper-middle-class women tend to become prestigious norms associated with refinement and become models for ambitious women from the lower social strata.

> ### KEY CONCEPTS
>
> **Change from above and below**
>
> Change can also be subject to degrees of awareness. 'Change from above' refers to change taking place in a speech community with speakers being aware of it. 'Change from below' refers to language change that is taking place below the level of consciousness of people. It is important not to confuse these two types of changes with change coming from a higher or lower social class.

11.5.5 Politeness and power

Politeness is often also used to explain gender differences. The alleged female sensitivity to face (see 5.4.2) is often put forward in this context. Women in this view are more polite than men. Some studies argue that the social status of women determines their degree of politeness; less power leads to more concern for verbal or other ways to display politeness. Deuchar (1989) suggested that people with less power tend to monitor face more carefully than people who do have that power. However, in some societies, women have been found to act more assertively while men adhered more to a subservient and stereotypically polite role with less power; for instance, Kharraki (2001) found that in Morocco men sometimes tended to apply more solidarity devices while women appealed more to hierarchical rank.

11.6 Non-heterosexual speech patterns

11.6.1 Sexual orientation and language

In each society, there are prototypical ways to communicate that are by default associated with men and women that are sexually attracted to the other gender. However, other sexual preferences are common as well, and this may affect language use. Members of the so-called 'lesbian, gay, bisexual, and transgender' ('LGBT') community may deviate strongly from the patterns mentioned so far. Men and women from the LGBT community are known to actively play with identity. Prototypically male and female behaviours are often used by members of this community as a model to either follow or reject.

11.6.2 Some research findings and tendencies

Very few generalisations will apply when it comes to the speech of the members of the LGBT community, because research comes mainly from the West and is often focussed on English. Also, as is the case for heterosexuals, within the LGBT community there are large differences in the degree to which sexual identity or male or female identity are foregrounded by individuals (Zwicky 1997). The speech in these investigations is often described in comparison to women's speech, and it frames these speakers as being deviant and as being mere imitators of speech. Based on several studies into pronunciation characteristics, however, Munson and Babel (2007) found that gay, lesbian and bisexual speech is not necessarily an imitation of a gender. A final complicating issue is that too many subgroups exist to draw any conclusions (Podesva et al. 2001).

A brief overview of some studies is given here to provide a general idea of findings in the field. Much more research is needed; especially into non-Western LGBT communities.

Western LGBT communities

Smyth et al. (2003) found that pitch range (in Canadian English) weakly correlates with judgements of sexual orientation. Speakers recorded different types of reading tasks, and their sexual orientation was rated by listeners. Pitch did not correlate with sexual orientation and did not differ between straight and gay talkers. Podesva et al. (2001) also looked at (American English) pronunciation and found some pronunciation features that distinguished the gay males in their research (into radio interviews), namely regarding the duration of certain vowels and, for instance, speakers' pitch. Slang is associated with both male and female gay speech, so Jacobs (1996) concluded on the basis of a study of the literature. Gay females have been found to speak with a lower pitch, so Van Borsel et al. (2013) demonstrated in their research into Dutch. It has been claimed, furthermore, that this group uses a mixture of stereotypical male and female speech (Queen 1997).

Transgenders are people whose gender identity is not in accordance with the biological gender that was determined at birth. They often go through intense medical and other procedures and transitions, including surgery, hormone treatment, and speech therapy. This is an important added factor when describing their speech patterns. A drop in voice pitch and certain acoustic correlates of the voice were found by Zimman (2012) in the (American English) speech of male transgenders who had undergone these transitions. Such changes may be sociolinguistically relevant, especially when it comes to how speakers are perceived.

Non-binary communities

As indicated, there are communities in which binary distinctions between male and female are less pertinent. The Bakla (Philippines) are an example of this. Sexual identity is closely related to gender identity for this group, meaning that stereotypical female behaviour is common amongst them, including linguistically. They are known to use Spanish and English loans and they borrow sounds from these two languages (Manalansan 1997). Quite a different case are the Hijras, who would not categorise themselves as either male or female. They are not necessarily homosexually oriented. As part of their ambiguous gender identity, they are known to combine masculine and feminine language uses.

A group that has been studied in some detail are the kathoey, who are male-to-female transgenders in Thailand. Kathoey are a marginalised community, yet they occupy a notable space in Thai society. They are recognised as a third gender. Analyses by Saisuwan (2014) revealed that kathoey systematically lengthen the final syllables of information units and combine this rhythmic pattern with a specific phrase-final intonational contour. Luksaneeyanawin (1998) associated this tendency with grammatical and attitudinal meaning, including emphasis. Saisuwan (2014) associated it with humour and with the adoption of stances. These stances, so she indicated, contribute to the construction of kathoey gender identity.

11.7 Research waves

11.7.1 Problematic methods

This chapter could continue mentioning research findings from different geographical, social, and other strata. Many tendencies seem generalisable across men and women while other results seem highly specific for subsets of men or women, for certain subgroups of the LGBT community, or for a region or culture. This chapter started with the suggestion that separating the men from the women to draw conclusions is problematic. Let us continue in that vein and first explain why this biological approach, and even a more group-based social gender approach, often leaves many questions unanswered. Four issues are described here that underlie the fact that generalisations across groups are highly tentative. These are followed by examples of research that has tried to tackle or circumvent the existing issues.

1. Persistence of generalisations

The traditional method of grouping and correlating social and linguistic factors has been criticised, amongst others because it yields contradicting findings and leads to very general, even crude generalisations. Superficially describing groups is highly insightful but at the same time ignores all kinds of inter-speaker, intra-speaker, and circumstantial variation and instead leads researchers and their readers to draw (often sweeping) generalisations on the basis of what group members have in common. The generalisations about the differences in the language of women and men have appeared to be particularly enduring and memorable. There are quite a few lecturers who keep telling students that women simply speak language more correctly and use a more varied vocabulary and that this comes down to vanity and carefulness, while men don't care about those things and are often not even able to speak as correctly as women. Things are obviously more nuanced than that, but research indicating differences between the two genders tends to popularise in this way and lead to stereotypes.

Complaints from the research field have been heard about this. Sadiqi (2003) considered it not helpful to look at the category of Moroccan women as one entity in view of diversity within Moroccan society. Bassiouney (2015) extended this argument: 'If it is an oversimplification to speak about "Moroccan women", then it is also too simple to speak about "North African women" without acknowledging the diversity in their situations and positions' (126). Indeed, it is risky to generalise about more than half the world's population on the basis of small-scale research in very specific places and under very specific circumstances and often without asking participants about their motivations to speak the way they do.

2. Underexplored correlation with other factors

Gender does not usually account for variation within a community and interacts particularly strongly with other speaker aspects. In these descriptions of Arabic and Anglo-Western research and of the language of the LGBT communities, several of such deceptive correlations were mentioned, like education, urbanness, strength of association with gender roles, and sexuality. Age could be added to this list, as it is often applied towards power; with age of North African women comes a certain degree of power (Bassiouney 2015), for instance. Eckert (2003) even recommended that gender always be studied in relation to age. There is also the development of gender constructions over time in groups and individuals (Sankoff and Blondeau 2007), and **lifespan changes** between men and women may be highly different. Cameron (2005) addressed this theme and demonstrated that gender is indeed constructed in different ways depending on the period in an individual's lifespan.

When such gender-related variables are nevertheless used in investigations, then this is often limited to a small number, chosen by the researcher. Cameron (1997) confirmed that variables are often arbitrarily combined and correlations are applied to suggest certain causal connections.

3. Underexplored effect of functions and social context

Even if interactions of speaker characteristics with biological gender are established, that still ignores intra-speaker and inter-speaker variation motivated by specific communicative circumstances. Language choices are known to be highly socially contextualised. Averages about men and women do not tell us how each of them would act in each situation. Speakers adhere to different strategies in following the norm or not in, for instance, requests, orders, or apologies. Each individual's relationship with assertiveness and hesitance is unique as is their handling of politeness issues. Ochs (1992) described how the difference between the use of final particles *ze* (associated with male speech) and *wa* (associated with female speech) by Japanese speakers was mostly depending on the degree of assertiveness of speakers, not their femininity or masculinity or their biological gender. In other words, these particles do not index a typical man or typical woman. According to Ochs, they are indexes of two types of affective intensity, 'coarse' versus 'gentle', and this line of argumentation strongly reduces the role of gender.

An example that Meyerhoff (2011) put forward is the different functions tags (e.g., 'isn't it?' and 'aren't you?') have in the speech of men and women. These have a strictly linguistic function (their literal meaning; a request for information), but they are mostly known for their interactional purpose. They are often associated with certain functions: urge interlocutors to continue talking and, for instance, ask for a reaction. Certain professional or social situations are more likely to evoke a certain function, and the mutual relationship of interlocutors is also a determining factor. Although women are likely to use more tag questions in general (which habit is popularly associated with insecurity and/or good manners), looking at the specific circumstances more closely might reveal a systematicity in the use of certain tags in certain contexts. In specific circumstances, men and women may be identical in their usage, while in other situations one of the sexes may avoid using a certain type. Increasing the focus on what language users do with language, how they are agents of language use in certain situations, is likely to provide answers.

4. Underexplored role of identity

Identities are constantly renegotiated and reshaped (Romaine 2003), and people do so to varying degrees. Munson and Babel (2007) reviewed the literature on perceptual language cues of sexual orientation address and found considerable variation in the degree to which speakers represent their sexual orientation through their speech. Not each speaker is managing their identity equally consciously and actively. This aspect is usually not taken into consideration in research.

11.7.2 Examples of new approaches

Hazen (2014) exemplified the renewed ways to view gender by suggesting that a research question posed in 1970 would be something along the lines of 'How do women speak differently from men?' while the same issue would in 2010 be defined as 'How does this speaker in this local context construct gender through language?' (17). Along with this renewed approach come new theoretical and methodological foci in research, alongside the established ones. Schoenthal (1998) suggested that in studies of women's and men's communicative behaviour a more interactional approach, which makes use of discourse analysis, could be used more. Other qualitative approaches may also be used, especially those that test the motivations and self-perceptions of speakers, which can be done through interviews. Observations of the same speakers in various circumstances are another clue provider.

According to Ball (2010), a study by Kowal et al. (1998) on interruptions in German media interviews responded to methodological criticism by giving extensive definitions, using large samples, and avoiding experimental situations. This study showed that not gender as such is of utmost relevance, but the role of the person one speaks to. Another example of an investigation that digs a little deeper beyond the straightforward categories is the one by Páramo (2002), who investigated Spanish speaker strategies and showed how girls and boys are supportive of each other's utterances and are constantly constructing the face of both themselves and the other. Biemans (2000), finally, used an extensive questionnaire to establish degree of stereotypical 'womanness' and 'manness' of participants and correlated this with voice quality choices and behaviour in communication between and amongst the sexes.

11.8 Conclusion

Across cultures, women and men are generally assigned different roles and these are generally felt to affect language use. Research on gender and language is done across the world but the motivations and approaches are wildly different, as are the interpretations. When we compare two research traditions, namely that of the Anglophone world and that of Northern Africa, we see that results from these two areas can support each other. In particular, the Northern African distinction between the appeal of two types of prestigious language is interesting for research into more monolingual areas, while the Northern African research tradition can take the extensive data and theories from the Anglophone research tradition as a model to adjust and to build on.

A binary distinction between people on the basis of biological gender yields many relevant generalisations, yet it fails to answer certain very fundamental questions. The motivations for individuals to apply gender symbolically in particular may be researched in different ways. Qualitative approaches are able to provide answers as to the factors that may lead to more powerful effects than biological gender generates at the moment.

STUDY QUESTIONS

1. Have you noticed any changes in the way men and women speak during your lifetime?
2. Do you know of any sexism in your own language?
3. Do the North African and Anglo-Western findings on the way women and men speak mostly contradict each other or do they mainly show common trends? Please explain.
4. To what degree do you think it is acceptable and advisable to take biological gender as a point of departure in research, after reading this chapter?

FURTHER READING

Romaine (2001) pays a relatively high amount of attention to gender in her introduction to Sociolinguistics and draws from a high number of cultures around the world. The volume edited by Coates and Pichler (2011) includes an overview of gender research linked to the waves of feminism. The edited volume by Milani (2015) covers a wide range of cultures. The journal *Gender and Language* (published by Equinox Publishers in Sheffield) publishes articles on gender and language in a wide range of cultures. The edited volume by Livia and Hall (1997) contains a range of chapters on the language within the LGBT community, and the very readable book by Cameron and Kulick (2003) also comes recommended for this purpose.

Second Language Sociolinguistics

12

Language Learner Choices

12.1 Introduction

People all over the world commonly acquire one or more second languages in addition to their mother tongue(s). 'Second language', or 'L2', in this chapter refers to a language acquired not as a first, native language ('L1') but after the Critical Period (see 10.2.1). This acquisition could be the result of active and conscious learning in a classroom or subconscious acquisition through exposure and use.

Researchers in 'second language acquisition' ('SLA') have become aware that socio-cultural context is a relevant aspect of the space in which second language acquisition takes place and look to sociolinguists to provide more explanations of the individual variation in the success with which people acquire a second language. Sociolinguists, in turn, are finding research in SLA interesting because it is nowadays an integral part of a global society whose participants are becoming more geographically and culturally mobile and who naturally acquire and use bits of one or more second languages in daily life. Sociolinguists see much use of second languages happening outside the classroom and consider this to be part of the larger language variation situation.

This chapter will address, first of all, the changed realities of SLA in and outside the traditional classroom as well as the changed image of the second language user in a mobilising and globalising world. It then looks at the aspects of SLA that are sociolinguistically relevant. After this, the question is asked whether new situations call for new language acquisition targets in addition to the native speaker norm.

12.2 The second language learner

12.2.1 Traditional language learning

Traditionally, SLA is associated mostly with schoolchildren sitting down in a classroom and studying rules. The method used is the Grammar-Translation Method (Davies and Pearse 2000). During the classes, the rules of the language are taught by contrasting them with those of the students' native tongue. Tricks are taught to master the usage of the right grammar and vocabulary in accordance with the rules. Exercises involving gap-filling (filling in missing words), translation, puzzles, and other linguistic problem-solving are the main activity. Typical homework involves memorisation of vocabulary from a book. An important academic goal is understanding the mutual sameness of languages at certain linguistic levels and understanding the culture of the native speaker. A practical goal is to communicate with native and non-native speakers. The target language is the language native speakers speak. The students know that they may never use the language in daily social communication. Many of them are acquiring a second language as a so-called foreign language, which means that the language is not spoken in the learner's immediate environment. Other learners as well as native speakers are encountered on holidays and in professional environments mainly.

12.2.2 Modern-day language acquisition

Language acquisition is becoming more diverse. The acquisition of the second language increasingly takes place outside the classroom, in combination with in-class learning. The opportunities for those who start learning a second language at school to use that language in real life have widened at a fast pace, and these opportunities help the in-class acquisition process. There is also an increasing group of speakers who move to another country, start out acquiring the language naturalistically, and at a later stage take courses and become learners in a classroom setting again.

Communication with permanent or temporary residents who have various language and cultural backgrounds is now not so exceptional anymore. Technological change has also brought languages and cultures in closer contact with each other. Increasing numbers of individuals can participate in communication online and use their second language not for academic or professional goals but for real, down-to-earth, informal daily information exchange. This exchange is nowadays more likely to take place amongst speakers with diverse backgrounds. This all makes the language acquisition process more individualistic and based on personal needs. To summarise the change, Tarone (1998) compared the traditional second language learner to a solver of jigsaw puzzles, who struggles to fit all the grammatical and lexical pieces into the puzzle. The modern learner, so Tarone explained, is a dancer who learns to dance by dancing with different partners, who all react differently to their moves as a learner.

Parallel to these changes, didactic methods have evolved. The traditional classroom approach of combining grammar and translation is still the most common basis of second language teaching, but new methods have arisen. In many parts in the world, a didactic move has occurred towards more communicative teaching methods focussing on real-life spoken and written communication (Edisherashvili 2014). These approaches emerged in the West in the 1970s, have spread globally, and have remained popular since (Davies and Pearse 2000). Rather than focussing only on understanding the grammar and learning vocabulary, situations in which the language is used have been introduced in the classroom through such methods. This has contributed to the spoken communicative skills of new generations of second language speakers in the places where these communicative methods have been popular (Edisherashvili 2014).

A more recent didactic approach is currently settling that incorporates the realisation that acquiring a second language is culturally bound in all kinds of ways. It is a social event and the acquisition and the real-life usage take place simultaneously and in a diversifying world. This view has led to the addition of social and cultural dimensions to teaching, such as teaching about multiculturalism, globalisation of certain languages, language contact, and hierarchical relations between different ethnolinguistic groups (Dornyei 2003), all as part of second-language classes. Learning from other learners' native tongues or gaining general insights into language by discussing and analysing language together is another modern-day aspect of language acquisition. These didactic changes in combination with the previously mentioned social changes have made second language acquisition interesting for sociolinguists. The type of acquisition that takes place outside the classroom in particular is relevant.

FOCUS ON...

Subtitling and dubbing and English language proficiency

Part of a person's language acquisition experience takes place not inside the classroom or in the public sphere but in front of the television. Some countries dub programmes (voices replacing the spoken foreign language) while other countries tend towards subtitling. This choice between two systems may affect second language proficiency, especially when it comes to English (because of the enormous television programme and film output from the United States, mainly). This is hard to prove, though, because many other aspects are involved, like the didactic system in a country as well as the linguistic difference between the native tongue of television viewers and the subtitled or dubbed language. A likely effect of subtitling is more familiarity with the second language in question, which may lead to more willingness to use it and naturally acquire it.

12.3   Sociolinguistic aspects of second language acquisition

12.3.1 Sociolinguistic competence

L2 language users must learn to adjust their speech to social situations and expectations. This skill is called sociolinguistic competence (see 10.2.2), and it is needed in one's native tongue but also in one's second language. The norms of the target language culture are usually taken as a model. As an illustration, Schmidt (1986) discussed certain words in Arabic that are strongly associated with learnedness and for that reason cannot be colloquialised through pronunciation. Furthermore, there is the complicated system of address forms in Arabic and the rules of discourse as part of the sociolinguistic build-up of the language. There are also subtleties, like intonation and word choice, that have a strong rhetorical effect. Politeness is often determined by these subtleties as is the correctness of a speaker's register choice (the degree of formality).

Some research has been done on this topic. Mougeon et al. (2010) studied the sociolinguistic competence of immersion students in Canada by looking at whether they acquired spoken Canadian French patterns well enough to engage in a variety of interaction types. Sax (2000), furthermore, studied the acquisition of stylistic variation regarding the pronunciation of the letter 'l' in third-person pronouns in French by American learners. These investigations showed various degrees of sociolinguistic competence by learners and a considerable learner awareness of such a competence so as to make communication as smooth as possible.

12.3.2 Identity

Another sociolinguistic aspect of second language acquisition and usage is that it involves identity motivations (Cook 2009). Like native speakers, second language users systematically use variable features to highlight or mark certain aspects of their identities. In fact, so Geeslin and Long (2014) indicated, one's own identity is developed and projected in the second language to convey social information. Adamson and Regan (1991) investigated variation in the pronunciation of the final consonant of English words ending in 'ing' (like the word 'working') and found that male Southeast Asian immigrants to the United States were more likely to use the informal variant (/ɪn/, rather than /ɪŋ/), which suggests that they sought to identify themselves as informal, perhaps masculine.

Several researchers have acknowledged that second language users participate in multiple (and shifting) identities and that this may be used to explain patterns in their language use. Actual or imagined cultural identities are part and parcel of this process, and an individual could draw from different traditions in a situation in which identities are not fixed. Hall (1992) and Norton (2000) discussed these cultural mixes and complicated cross-overs that are nowadays so highly common. As an illustration, long-term Slovak and Czech immigrants in Edinburgh were found to form blended identities that reflect values from both home and local cultures but remain distinct from both, so Elliott and Hall-Lew (2015) found. Many L2 users nowadays play with both their first and second language(s) and they do so systematically and with clear identity goals.

It should be noted that not all L2 users are equally capable of creatively playing with their second language or inclined to do so. Dewaele (2004) found that degree of extraversion of the speaker and the related likelihood of them communicating with native speakers influence whether speakers choose to adopt a certain substandard to shape their identity. Dewaele described extraverts as prepared to take risks and use informal variants. Young (1991) and Bayley (1994) also mentioned extraversion as a possible factor in their studies of Chinese speakers of L2 English. Introverted and extraverted behaviour may be based in culture; Saville-Troike (1984) observed that the patterns of behaviour and interaction of South American, Middle Eastern, and European children were much more conducive to language acquisition than those of Asian learners.

12.3.3 Power

As is the case for the use of one's native tongue, a second language can be used as a power tool. First of all, there is the actual ability to speak a certain second language, and secondly there is one's degree of proficiency. Both factors contribute to an L2 speaker's power.

English is often referred to in this context. Speaking English leads to a certain degree of power, simply because of the enormous amount of information and number of potential interlocutors it provides access to. It also symbolises an international outlook. The idea exists that insufficient linguistic competence in English has a negative effect on one's success in, for instance, business communication (Maclean 2008) and ultimately even one's career (Cook 2009). Wright (2004) considered English the language of power and said that those not learning it will be disempowered and be a new linguistic minority. Being a monolingual native speaker in a country where a second language – English or another one – is growing in dominance leads to reduced power.

FOCUS ON...

A second language as a linguistic threat

The right to speak a certain language in all contexts can, according to Suzuki (2000), be associated with basic human rights (and this author even associated it with spiritual freedom). Language rights, which are, according to Tsuda (1990), 'the rights to use one's own language freely' (236) are often said to be undermined by the dominant presence of a second language in a country. Tsuda spoke about the hegemony of English in Japan and considered it a language rights problem. If the dominance of such an external language in a certain country grows, then the role of the native language and the language rights of speakers of the indigenous language(s) become one of concern.

12.3.4 Social connotations

Widespread connotations surround language varieties, and these are also active for those who use these languages as a second language. People choosing to acquire a certain second language need to know about the connotations that certain variants of these languages naturally have (Williams 1994). Certain types of Spanish, Portuguese, English, Arabic, or German in particular come with such connotations. British English is, for example, considered the more conservative choice of English while American English sounds more international to many (Van der Haagen 1998). Similar widespread connotations are active for varieties of Arabic (Bassiouney 2015). Schmidt (1986), as an illustration, explained that everyone involved in teaching Arabic must recognise that the way native speakers of Arabic usually speak is neither purely colloquial nor purely classical Arabic. Instead, an intermediate variety is usually used in public discourse. So, certain styles and registers come with certain connotations.

With language choice, certain expectations are activated regarding communication style and all kinds of values. In intra-Asian communication, for example, Japanese and Chinese often play important roles. With these languages comes a certain decision-making and confrontation-avoidance style that would not work if a meeting was done in English (Tanaka and Sugiyama 2011). This style is partly built in in the language already, like certain fixed politeness phrases and a lower amount of available face-threatening language (see 5.4.2).

12.3.5 Norm language

When trying to improve sociolinguistic competence or when choosing which language variety to speak, the underlying assumption is that what native speakers do or say is the guiding principle. Their language is the norm language to the average L2 user. In the average classroom, the adherence to such a norm is usually quite explicit; acquiring Chinese requires acquiring Mandarin Chinese like typical speakers of the standard variety in China speak it, acquiring French means acquiring French like those Frenchmen who typically speak the standard variety in France.

FOCUS ON...

Language ownership

The 'ownership' and cultural associations of some languages remain firmly in their country of origin. Examples of such languages are Swedish and Russian, which are associated with Sweden and Russia and the respective stereotypical cultures of these countries. This is different for English, whose association with the cultures of the United Kingdom and the United States is dwindling, according to Graddol (2006). Instead, this language is in a way not the exclusive property of native speakers from these two countries anymore but of all L1 speakers and also of the many people who speak it as an L2. Spanish and Portuguese, two other languages of former colonisers, are in a similar position, although their cultural associations are more strongly regionally grounded (South America and the Iberian Peninsula).

12.4   Challenging the native norm

12.4.1 Separating language and culture

It is impossible to disconnect the cultural backgound of speakers in discourse from their language use. There are all kinds of understandings, routines, and practices in second language communication coming from the interlocutors. The cultures of interlocutors, irrespective of whether one of them is a native speaker of the language used, may be similar or deviant. In either case, the question is where to draw the communicative norms from. For instance, if someone from Norway has acquired English well but is applying Norwegian politeness forms when communicating in English, does that speaker then qualify as a less successful one? Aukrust and Snow (1998) found that the shared dispositions of Norwegians generally involved equality and belonging to the local community while those of United States families were civic values such as democracy, freedom of choice, individualism, and equal opportunities. When Norwegians and Americans communicate with each other in English, then only the Americans will be expressing their values in their native language. The requirement for L2 users to adopt not only the linguistic mannerisms but also the values of the culture would mean that the Norwegians would need to change values and habits when using a second language. Singh et al. (1988) recommended that greater emphasis be placed on such aspects of intercultural communication and that this type of communication may be seen as an accomplishment of both parties in which the perspectives of both interlocutors are relevant rather than only those of the native speaker.

'Language socialisation' refers to the process of becoming a member of a certain society while learning to use the language of that society (Ochs and Schieffelin 2012). These two processes are considered to be reciprocal. Having to acquire the culture together with the language makes the acquisition process harder for those whose culture is far removed from the culture associated with the language to be acquired. Acculturation Theory (Schumann 1978) suggests that cultural distance between learner and target language determines the learner's success; the smaller the distance, the more successful the acquisition. The culture aspect, therefore, creates a hindrance to many L2 users. The traditional approach of considering the native speaker and their culture as the ideal model to imitate becomes even more questionable if a language has more non-native speakers than native speakers and if the chances of meeting a native speaker are thus relatively small.

An important question is whether L2 users' language choices will be and should be interpreted as those of native speakers. The assumption seems to be that listeners, both native and non-native, will in their interpretation apply native norms. This is not necessarily the case. It is likely that generally speakers who are obviously L2 users will be approached with fewer assumptions and expectations in this respect; their communicative imperfection and vagueness may be forgiven.

> **FOCUS ON...**
>
> **A second language as a cultural threat**
>
> According to De Koning (2009), English is 'the uncontested language of work and socializing' (61) in upper-middle class circles in some Arab countries, making Standard Arabic in a country like Egypt an option rather than necessity for some. This leads to a certain alienation of the Egyptian elite from their own culture and language, according to Mehrez (2010).

12.4.2 Reviewing the native/non-native distinction

Another factor that weakens the native-speaker model is the questionable dividing line that is usually drawn between first and second language acquisition. The drawback of this categorical approach is not only that it gives a special, almost mythical status to native speakerdom and alienates the classroom situation from reality. This divide is nowadays also not always so realistic. Some examples will demonstrate this.

There is, first of all, the very common situation in which children start acquiring a second language at some point within their Critical Period (see 10.2.1) and reach an uncertain degree of nativeness. This is very common in Kenya, for instance, where starting English at primary school is very common. Although these children will reach a native-like level, the lack of input in the first six years and the limited communication in English from the age of six onwards may leave their mark. Another example is a diplomat's child who attends international schools from primary school age onwards and speaks English with their peers but not with their parents. Does that make the child a native speaker of English at some point? In immigrant communities, all kinds of variants to these situations exist, from obvious non-nativeness to a native-like acquisition but with a non-native-sounding accent or a limited proficiency. If a person's native-like proficiency is not really distinguishable from native proficiency by listeners, should that person then be qualified as a second-language user (and be treated as such)? If speakers themselves feel that they are not native speakers (like many of the previously mentioned English-speaking Kenyans would), should they be overruled by sociolinguists and be categorised as native speakers anyway? What is the status of immigrant accents; how non-native are they if they are acquired as a native tongue? There is also the issue of individuals adopting a different sociolect of a language at a later point in life, oftentimes only to be used in specific social contexts; does that make them L2 users?

All of these examples demonstrate that the division between first and second language acquisition should be viewed critically. Although in most classrooms across the globe the distinction between native and second language proficiency is clear, exceptions to that rule are many. This division underlies the norms that are applied on the basis of which L2 users are officially (by teachers) and unofficially (in daily discourse) viewed as doing well or not so well, although the linguistic difference between native and non-native speakers is in many ways continuous and not absolute.

FOCUS ON...

Misconceptions about language acquisition

A well-known folk claim was put forward by Jackendoff (2003b), namely that acquiring more than one language is confusing for children. Jackendoff reminded us that becoming a native speaker in more than one language, with separate grammars, is a very common thing in the world and the confusion between languages is generally minor. Multilingual children have even been found to be cognitively enriched because of the interplay between the two languages, so he indicated.

12.4.3 New proficiency targets

So, the dividing line between native and non-native is not so obvious in many cases, or at least not so relevant. A revised approach to the concept of target language proficiency seems in order, especially for language acquisition that is aimed at intercultural communication. One way to view the language learner's target language is by considering the degree to which an L2 sufficiently fulfils certain desired sociolinguistic and practical functions rather than measuring the degree to which it deviates from a native norm. Different social contexts call for different standards of language acquisition. Various, personalised degrees and manners of proficiency would be the outcome if targets were applied this way. Two are described here. In both cases, learners could achieve a perfect command.

1. The 'incomplete' L2

A common scenario is that a language learner chooses not to apply their second language in its full richness. High-speed communication involving short, quick, unfinished, and abbreviated utterances is nowadays a rule in certain contexts. In these contexts, a highly limited command is satisfactory. Speakers who live in a multilingual environment switch languages on a moment to moment basis but may not have a high-level proficiency of all the languages they switch between. They may go to a shop and buy food, negotiate the rent with their landlord, and, for instance, talk to people with different cultural backgrounds. For each context, they may need a certain command of a certain language to achieve their specific goals (social or practical). If these goals are achieved, then one could conclude that they have perfectly acquired the language needed for that specific communicative context. This target could be applied in language acquired outside the classroom.

2. The 'incorrect-sounding' L2

Another possible target is the second language that contains many features of the native tongue of the speaker. This is reminiscent to the phenomenon of the 'nativised language' as discussed in Section 6.3.5. Many speakers feel no desire to sound like native speakers and instead prefer to speak with a recognisable non-native accent. Non-native speech with a slight accent may even have advantages, so research by Hendriks et al. (2016) showed. Slightly accented Dutch speakers in this investigation were evaluated as more likeable than native English speakers, even. A requirement of such a foreign-sounding target could be that the accent is not strong to such a degree that it becomes distracting to listeners.

FOCUS ON...

Incorrect versus low-quality

The low status of deviations from what is generally considered correct is not necessarily based on linguistic qualities. Labov's research (Labov 1969) convincingly demonstrated that certain aspects of African American Vernacular English were in fact linguistically perfectly systematic. This finding even triggered suggestions to use this type of English as the language of instruction (Simpkins and Simpkins 1981).

A high proficiency level is achieved when speakers can successfully express the content and symbolic messages they wish to communicate. Inevitably, they sound like non-native speakers and therefore the interpretation with what they say and how they say it will be interpreted with a degree of flexibility and not be compared to the language of a native speaker with all its cultural and other connotations. This target may be considered in classroom teaching as an alternative to the native norm. In reality, this is already the unwritten norm in many a classroom.

12.5   Conclusion

This chapter has shown that while Sociolinguistics tends to focus on people's native tongue, the sociolinguistics of the second language shows much agreement with that of the first language. In addition to many intersecting themes, there is also the question of the hard and fast dividing line between first and second language acquisition, which is hard to draw in contexts in which people speak several languages, acquire only bits and pieces of languages, and switch between languages. People's second language use may consist of various combinations of (bits of) languages in all kinds of culturally mixed situations. The theories of superdiversity (see 2.3.3 and 4.4) and indexicality (see 5.3.3) remind us that the language use of non-native speakers deserves more weight and should be incorporated in a larger sociolinguistic framework.

The traditional language acquisition situation, with children or young adults sitting in a classroom and performing a range of practical and analytical tasks to try and master the second language and become like a native speaker is as common as ever. However, in addition to this setting a more naturalistic setting is becoming part of many people's daily lives. New types of L2 users and their targets now need to be reckoned with as a reality, in addition to the existing ones.

STUDY QUESTIONS

1. Argue for and against a native-speaker model in language learning and teaching.
2. Is there such as thing as an international sociolinguistic competence? Do speakers give up their own models of sociolinguistic competence when communicating in an international context?

FURTHER READING

Geeslin and Long (2014) present the most complete work on the social aspects of second language acquisition. Taking a very intercultural approach, Chapter 5 of Saville-Troike (2012) provides an overview of macro- and micro-social factors that are relevant in second-language acquisition.

PART 3
PROCESSING SOCIOLINGUISTICS

The following four chapters give you some necessary tools to initiate and carry out a sociolinguistic investigation and process the findings. First, steps are described to go from general observations of language use around you to transforming these to an actual research design (Chapter 13). The next chapter in this part gives you the sections of a typical sociolinguistic research report (Chapter 14). The following two chapters specifically accommodate readers with a lack of statistical (Chapter 15) and phonetic (Chapter 16) knowledge. After reading Part 3, you will be aware of what a sociolinguistic research project entails. You will be better able to select and perform one of the methodologies as laid out in the final part of this book, Part 4.

Ready, Set, Research!

13

Steps towards a Sociolinguistic Research Project

13.1 Introduction

You now know about language variation and how it is embedded socially in all kinds of ways. The next step is that you explore the field in a more hands-on way and carry out a research project into the social structure of language variation. Sociolinguistics is amongst the more practical fields within Linguistics, and few sociolinguists sit down and read books to find out the truth about how language works in societies. Instead, most go out and observe communication; on television, on the Internet, in the supermarket, during family gatherings, at work, in the streets, and so on. Another scenario is entering a speech community as a participant. One could also arrange a more controlled experimental setting and generate speech.

Through five preparatory steps, the current chapter presents a way into kick-starting an investigation. If you have only a vague idea or no idea at all about what you'd like to research, then starting at Step 1 is advisable, which teaches you to scan for topics. Step 2 is to ascertain whether the variation that you've found is worth investigating. If you've got a topic, then Step 3 will help you organise that topic into researchable parts. Step 4 gives some basic instructions on how to formulate research questions. Step 5, finally, helps you commit to a specific methodology.

13.2 Step 1: Scan

13.2.1 Discovering language variation

To find a relevant research topic, you need to find language variation. Variation is usually socially relevant if people are talking about it or noticing it, but variation that is more subtle and often goes unnoticed may be equally interesting for research. In word choices that people make or subtle variation in the way to pronounce a certain sound there may be an indication of a language change or a changing norm. In Section 13.4.4, some examples are given of this from various languages. Here are three basic ways to go about finding language variation.

a) Observation

As a sociolinguist, you always need to be on the look-out for language variation around you. You need to notice how one person expresses something in one way while another person seemingly expresses the same thing in a different way. You also need to notice how the same person expresses the same thing in different ways.

Language is everywhere, so finding language use 'in the wild' should be no problem. Busy places are usually suitable for such observations, like parties, places of worship, waiting rooms, social gatherings, workplaces, and shops. Examples of other sources of language variation are social media, television, radio, road signs, books, websites, and magazines. You will have some sort of idea of what type of people are in certain places or which people produce certain language. If you, for instance, stand on a train platform at the end of a workday, then you know that a relatively high percentage of those around you are from the destination of the train they are waiting for. In places of worship, many people are religious. Certain types of people are drawn to certain online communities. This way, each social space attracts a certain type of people, and these people may produce language in a certain way.

Language that is already available because it is written down is easy to find. Road signs and restaurant menus are in town centres, written digital communication can be found online, the language of ordinary people is in all kinds of corpora (see 17.2.2). In phrasebooks, vocabulary books, encyclopedias, and in literature, examples can be found of riddles, proverbs, and ritual language, in which much cultural information is hidden.

While observing or browsing, make mental or written notes on those who produce language and on any type of language variation or usage that is striking. Do not record people, unless you are observing language as produced on television, radio, or online. The data are typically unsystematic and intuitive. The outcome are certain language items, where they can be found, and some first impression of how they are socially distributed (who produce them and under which circumstances).

(b) Ad hoc interviewing

Besides this eaves-dropping and this looking around, you may also ask people you know challenging questions like 'Can you give an example of things in the language that people do differently today compared to 30 years ago?', 'How do you think this letter in this word should be pronounced?', or even 'What annoys you about the way people use language these days?'. Usually, this approach reveals all kinds of ideas that people have about language variation

FOCUS ON...

Popular music as a source

Language variation in pop songs makes for an interesting source of sociolinguistic data. Lyrics are often pronounced in all kinds of mixed accents, which are very different from the way the singers speak in their daily lives. Examples are Hong Kong singers using various ways to pronounce Cantonese in their music and both native English and non-Anglophone singers using a mix of Englishes when they sing. These singers are ostensibly making up their own accents. It seems to be a kind of cosplay, that is, performance art, almost, where they put on an act of being someone else. Are there linguistic patterns? What motivates them to put on this act?

today and in the past. They will probably be able to give you explicit ideas about which type of people (old, educated, foreign, male, rural, etc.) tend to say or write things in a certain way. With the information one person gives you, you can continue to the next person and gradually discover whether it is interesting to find some sort of system in the production of certain language features by certain people.

(c) Finding discourse on language

Comments about language are sometimes just thrown in your lap. In newspapers, letters to the editor often contain comments about language. In other media – such as television, blogs, and social media – such discourse about language use also turns up. Maybe you know of a specific magazine or site about language and language use. Family gatherings are also good sources for encountering spontaneous discussions about the state of a language. These discussions may inspire you to find a relevant topic.

KEY CONCEPTS

Discourse and reflexivity

Discourse refers, amongst others, to the exchange of information. It could refer to two people having a discussion and trying to understand each other or in a more general way to discussions taking place in a society or in certain circles regarding a topic. When the topic is language, then these discussions may affect how we all think about what is right and wrong in language. This function of language, as a tool to talk about language, is called 'reflexivity'. Language is used to evaluate, judge and correct one's own language conduct and that of others (Leppänen et al. 2015).

13.2.2 Other approaches

If you wish to research language other than the one you know best, then you could of course read about such a language or, better yet, get in touch with a native speaker. Reading articles in peer-reviewed open-access journals will also give you instant information. Doing an Internet search for a topic while adding 'pdf' to your search may help you find such articles, while your university or college may give you access to journals that are not open access.

Besides Wikipedia (www.wikipedia.com), there are language-related websites that you may find interesting for inspiration, like the one by Ethnologue (www.ethnologue.com), which gives you information on language variation in the world. The English Proficiency Index web page (www.ef.com/epi/), which shows estimates of people's English proficiency in countries across the world, may be useful. The United Nations web page on the so-called Human Development Index (http://hdr.undp.org/en/content/human-development-index-hdi), which shows the socioeconomic development of countries across the world, may also be interesting. The website YouTube (www.youtube.com) is probably one of the easiest possible sources of inspiration, giving you instant access to language by ordinary people. Many other such websites can ignite ideas to research something from a sociolinguistic angle.

13.3   Step 2: Checking with experts

It is possible that your observations are not original, relevant, or correct. It is advisable to contact a teacher or other expert and tell them about your basic observations. You can also consult the literature. You may be lucky and find a journal article that gives you an introduction into the phenomenon that you are interested in and informs you as to its relevance amongst other topics. Experts and the literature may confirm your first findings and help you zoom in on relevant things to investigate. They may tell you whether what you find interesting has already been researched and whether research is still necessary. They may also help you find a theoretical framework.

13.4   Step 3: Organise the research topic

13.4.1 Variables and their values

After your very general exploration of language, you should have an idea as to which language items are subject to variation and worth investigating. These are called 'variables', because they can take on more than one form. These forms are called 'values'. In other words, variables are the sources that vary (e.g., word order) while values are the shapes that the sources take on (e.g., one word order versus another word order). In the language examples and the discourse that you have encountered, all kinds of variables and values will have been mentioned, and you need to formalise these. Non-numerical values are also referred to as 'variants'.

In more qualitative research, variables and values are determined while the research is taking place (observing or interviewing speakers, for instance). This type of research may also place less importance on variables and simply describe communication in general. Nevertheless, it is always advisable to think in terms of variables and values, because this makes the investigation more tangible to readers.

13.4.2 Sociolinguistic variables

Linguistic variables that are often used in the field are broadly interpreted. First, there is the variation typically associated with Linguistics, namely in word choice and grammar. Furthermore, there is variation in pronunciation: vowels and consonants as well as prosodic features like intonation and stress patterns. Finally, there is variation in the more general field of communication amongst people, which aspect can be interpreted very widely: politeness markers, style, formality, discourse markers, interruptions, greetings, and many more ways to communicate meaning as well as emotion. The variation could also be in the field of Pragmatics, which is the study of the varying meanings of words in particular situations. An English word like 'nice' could mean opposite things, depending on the social situation, for instance.

Any variation that it is not linguistic but correlates with – and may cause – language variation can be considered suitable for correlating with linguistic variables. These non-linguistic variables are those present in the social, psychosocial, psychological, historical, political, or societal space. Characteristics of speakers – like age, status, gender, geographical origin – are the most typical ones. Besides these, broader variables are commonly tested: type of communicative setting (e.g., an interview setting or a school setting), broadly defined groups of people in society (like ethnic groups), time period, cultural variation, and language policy features. All of these could be interpreted as variables with certain values (for instance, prescriptive versus lenient language policy, Anglo-Western versus non-Anglo-Western culture, or modern versus postmodern time period).

13.4.3 An example of values and variables

Let's look at an example and see how this works in practice. If you observe young girls saying 'I was like' all the time to simultaneously quote their own speech and express their emotions ('I was like "Oh my gosh, no way!", you know'), then you have language-related variables and values and non-linguistic variables and values. The most obvious non-linguistic variables are gender and age. Age-wise there is the value 'young', which means that you can also form a group that is 'old'. Gender-wise, you have been given 'girls', and these can be contrasted with the value 'boys'. So, now you have at least four groups to research: 'young women', 'old women', 'young men', and 'old men'. The linguistic variable in this example is 'self-quoting'. You can self-quote by saying 'I was like', followed by what your thoughts, feelings or actual sentence were. But you can also say 'I said', 'I went', 'I felt', or perhaps 'I thought'. These are all values. After some consideration, you will have a list of variables and values like the one below. Note that values can be of a categorical nature or a numerical nature; this is explained in Section 15.4.1.

Variables	Values
Self-quoting techniques	'to be' + 'like'
	'to go'
	'to feel'
	'to say'
	'to think'
	Other
Person referred to	Speaker (e.g., 'I was like')
	Other person (e.g., 'he was like')
Emotion in the quote	Strong
	Weak
Age of speaker	10–20
	30–40
Gender of speaker	Female
	Male
Masculinity of the speaker	High masculinity (value 3)
	Intermediate masculinity (value 2)
	Low masculinity (value 1)
Gender of addressee	Female
	Male
	Male and female
Social context	Talk to members of own age group
	Talk to members of different age group

13.4.4 Sociolinguistic variables from around the world

Below are some examples from various languages in the world. They will give you some idea of the type of sociolinguistic variation that you may encounter as well as the possible variables. It is likely that one or more of these examples will remind you of something similar in the speaker(s), language(s), or setting(s) that you wish to investigate.

Plural formation

In certain communities where Scottish Gaelic is spoken many younger speakers do not know how to form plurals correctly. Less proficient speakers tend to form a plural by using a simplified method, namely to simply add *an* in those cases where a word is plural, because they only know that one method of plural formation in Gaelic. The main variables here are speaker age and plural formation method.

Consonant pronunciation

The pronunciation of 'r' at the ends of syllables in Mandarin Chinese is associated with the prestige city dialect from Beijing. Newcomers often adopt this very prominent so-called postvocalic 'r' ('r' after a vowel). Other newcomers do not adopt it. There may be differences amongst the newcomers; maybe those who adopt the Beijing 'r' are more ambitious, or perhaps there is an age or gender effect. Possible variables are degree of ambition, whether the speaker is a Beijing native, and the pronunciation of this 'r'.

Pronunciation simplification

In Italian, *va bene* ('okay') can be reduced to something that is spelled like '*vabbe*' in informal written communication, because the pronunciation is often simplified. Ease of articulation motivates this adapted pronunciation. This phenomenon, reduction, actually takes place in all languages, probably. In Japanese, progressive verb endings like *the-iru* may be reduced to something that could be written as '*teru*'. In German, you can say the words *haben sie* ('have you') as '*hammse*' when you speak quickly and informally. It may be that some people do this more than others and/or it may depend on the social context. Possible variables in an investigation addressing this phenomenon are degree/type of reduction, degree of formality, speech rate, speaker status, social context, and gender.

Word choice

In Colloquial Singaporean English, a set of short words is commonly used, like *lah*, *ah*, and *lor*. These so-called discourse facilitators, which have various meanings and functions, have an ethnolinguistic origin that is not English. The awareness of this origin amongst speakers of this language varies considerably. The speakers who speak the language in question also have mixed ethnic and linguistic origins. The variables in an investigation into the distribution of these discourse facilitators could be speaker ethnicity, degree of awareness of the ethnolinguistic origin of the discourse facilitator, origin of the facilitator, and, of course, type of facilitator (its function).

Word order

In Dutch, you can say the past participle form 'have had' as *hebben gehad* (lit. 'have had') or *gehad hebben* (lit. 'had have'). There is some possible regional variation, but this difference in word order does not seem to be overly socially marked to some, while others may frown upon one of the variants. Investigating this would entail the variables regional/social origin of speaker, regional/social origin of judges, awareness of this variation, and word order in the past participle.

Intonation

The Georgian word *argi* means 'good', unless it is pronounced with a rising intonation, in which case it means 'really?' So, with a change in intonation the meaning changes, not just the mood. The variables in an investigation into this phenomenon could be intended meaning of the utterance, type of intonation pattern, interpretation by listeners, and, perhaps, listener characteristics.

'Incorrect' pronunciation

Sometimes, an 'incorrect' pronunciation changes into 'correct', and speakers forget the correct version. This has happened for the sound combination /ph/ in Hindi, which has been replaced by /f/. The word 'flower' in Hindi used to be pronounced as /phul/ but now it is homophonous with English 'fool', and knowledge of the original form is dwindling. Something similar is happening in Dutch. The stress in the word *normaliter*, 'normally', is more often than not placed on the *li* syllable although the strict norm is that the stress is on *ma*. Another Dutch example is the French-sounding pronunciation of the

French-looking word *notoir*, which does not in fact have a French pronunciation in Dutch according to the strict norm. The incorrect realisations of these and other words seem to be developing into the most widely accepted correct forms, very gradually. The variables in an investigation into this topic are knowledge of the rules, educational level of speakers, and, of course, the various ways to pronounce these words.

Less obvious variables

Some things are not generally described in books on language use or grammar, yet they are sociolinguistically very powerful, relevant, and researchable. A source of pronunciation variation, for instance, are 'vocalisations', which are sounds that you can produce to affect the meaning of your speech, like 'shhh' or sounds like 'tss' and 'pff'. So-called 'paralanguage' is another way to express meaning, and this includes creak in your voice (see 10.3.2) or sighing as well as grunting and snickering. Besides spoken language or language-related sounds, body language may be studied. How body movements communicate social information is often referred to as 'kinesics'. So-called 'proxemics' can also be studied. This is the study of physical distance in communication. American speakers, according to Eller (2016), on average keep approximately a 24 inch (61 centimetre) zone between them, while Japanese abide by a larger zone and Middle Easterners abide by a smaller one. Deviating from this distance may be meaningful. Silences (see 5.4.3) are another powerful sign in communication, and their length, frequency, and position in discourse may be analysed.

KEY CONCEPTS

Hexis

Bourdieu (1991) did not draw a strong dividing line between body-language variables and other language variables and discussed the concept of 'bodily hexis', which can be described as a durable, consistent and unchanging organisation of one's body that leads to certain mannerisms. It reveals itself not only in pronunciation and word choice, but also in the way one stands, walks, eats, and laughs. It is associated with a certain way of thinking and feeling.

13.5   Step 4: Write up research questions

When all of the variables are lined up, then you need to put into words what you want to know about how they interact. This should be worded through one or more research questions. In these questions, you mention the variables without being too suggestive of how they hang together. Rather than 'Do older people use X more than younger people do?', you say 'What is the effect of age on the use of X?' Another example may be a more general one, which doesn't look for strict correlations: 'How are the speech communities in this larger community organised?'

A research question needs to be unambiguous, relevant, practicable, and clear. Preferably, it builds on questions posed by previous researchers while being new and unique. A well-designed research question is embedded in a research tradition, contributes to the existing knowledge in the specific field, is realistic, and it is related to the methodology. In other words, it should come as no surprise to the reader after reading the literature section, it should be answerable and not too broad or philosophical or general, and the methodology that follows in your report should be able to answer your research questions.

13.6   Step 5: Decide on a specific methodology

If you have a research issue and some sort of preference as to which direction you want your research to go, then you are ready to start choosing from all the methodologies that are available. These are described in Chapters 17 to 20, and the conditions for each type of methodology are in the overview here. These investigations vary from mainly quantitative variationist studies on the basis of categorised variables to mainly explorative qualitative studies in which variables and variants are treated more loosely and which focus on the nature of language use in certain settings. By going from left to right in the table, you can systematically select the methodology that fits your situation.

Research approach			Research methodology
Available language (Chapter 17)	Modern language	Written language	Corpus Analysis; Linguistic Landscape
		Spoken language	Corpus Analysis; Linguistic Geography; Time Study (apparent-time)
	Historical language		Historical Sociolinguistics; Corpus Analysis; Time Study (real-time)
Elicited language (Chapter 18)	Researcher records	Less spontaneous language	Intergenerational Proficiency Description; Sociolinguistic Interview; Conversation Analysis; Discourse Analysis
		More spontaneous language	Rapid Anonymous Survey; Intergenerational Proficiency Description; Conversation Analysis; Discourse Analysis
	Participants record		Intergeneration Proficiency Description; Conversation Analysis; Discourse Analysis
Naturally occurring communication (Chapter 19)	Written communication		Computer-Mediated Communication
	Spoken communication	Researcher interacts with speakers	Ethnographic Fieldwork; Computer-Mediated Communication
		No researcher interaction with speakers	Computer-Mediated Communication; Street Use Survey; Classroom Observation
Attitudes (Chapter 20)	Participants listen to fragments		Language Evaluation Test; Matched Guise Test; Identification Task
	Participants answer questions		Questionnaire; Interview; Folk Linguistics
	Participants perform other tasks		Folk Linguistics

It should be noted that despite the neat categorisation of the studies into four types (left-hand column), specific methodologies may fall into more than one category or another category. Conversation Analysis, for instance, might depend on available language or the researcher may need to record it themselves. Furthermore, the above overview is not a fixed blueprint for how the methodologies of the various approaches should be executed. Methodologies are often combined, and certain data types can be investigated using more than one methodology. The overview already shows how certain methodologies fit more than one research approach. In the coming four chapters, these methodologies will be explained, and the degree to which there is flexibility in applying them will become clearer. For each one, a sample investigation will be given to serve as inspiration.

13.7 Conclusion

The first step towards a research project is to switch on to finding researchable and relevant language variation by keeping your ears and eyes open. This means registering language variation around you by reading, listening, and observing. Another approach is scrolling through documents or other sources. After that, find experts to tell you whether you've found a good topic to research or not. After these two steps, you need to determine and organise variables and values and decide whether they will be treated strictly (as labels for correlations) or loosely (as points of interest). The fourth step is to design and formulate a relevant research question. After that, you can start to think about a general and specific research approach to tackle the issue that you have decided to investigate further.

FURTHER READING

Meyerhoff et al. (2015) provide extensive instructions, tips, and exercises on a variety of sociolinguistic research methods (especially Chapters 5 to 9) and how to start an investigation (Chapter 1). This book also helps you combine quantitative and qualitative research approaches. In Mallinson et al. (2013), a range of authors give very useful insights into how they do research and how they deal with the practical issues that arise when doing research. This book brings home the realities of doing fieldwork.

Write about Research

14

Introducing the Sociolinguistic Research Report

14.1 Introduction

A sociolinguistic research report describes all aspects of your research. It describes why you've done what you've done, how you've done it, and how your research findings and those of others complement each other. Typically, such reports consist of an Introduction, Methodology, Results, and Conclusion chapter. This is called the IMRC structure. It is useful as a basis for any investigation, but much variation exists in the degree to which the many components are relevant and will appear in a research description.

This chapter describes each of the four chapters of a research report that is based on systematically collected sociolinguistic data. After that, it briefly refers to certain components that come before and after these chapters. The words and phrases in italics in the text constitute possible components of the research report.

14.2 Chapter 1: Introduction

The purpose of the Introduction chapter is to justify your study and to demonstrate that it is important and necessary. You summarise earlier research, identify what has not yet been studied, and you explain in general terms what you are going to do. After reading the first chapter, the reader knows what to expect: what research you did, why you did it, and which questions you've answered. The chapter should start very generally and end generally as well. Here are the most important sections and the subcomponents within these sections.

1. Overview

Start the Introduction chapter broadly and begin by mentioning the general *field of research* and what we all know to be true. You may need to *explain/define the field* briefly as well and explain the *relevance of the field*. Perhaps the field of study is relevant to people's lives or maybe there's an ongoing debate in the field. Mention the *main issues* being discussed nowadays by experts and mention the *most important literature* (without elaborating. You then introduce the *specific area of study* that your research is part of. Give a bird's eye view of the most pertinent *literature and findings in the specific area of study*. Do not elaborate, just give some major findings and tendencies without giving details. In general terms, explain *how your findings might contribute to what we know*.

If you will be trying to contribute to knowledge on a certain *theoretical framework*, then mention this here too. Do not elaborate. The theoretical background makes clear which theory has triggered your study. Theories tend to have names (e.g., 'politeness theory' or 'indexicality theory'), and these need to be mentioned along with the researcher who invented the theory. Previous literature itself is not the theoretical framework. If there's no theoretical background, then don't suggest that there is.

Briefly mention the *methodology* that you will be applying and the *variables* that will be in the methodological model. Indicate *how your research fits in the specific area of study* when it comes to the theoretical and/or methodological approach.

FOCUS ON...

Exploring a field

To familiarise yourself with a field, find a handful of recent articles in reliable peer-reviewed journals in which the current state of affairs in the field is described. These descriptions are often more critical and state-of-the-art than those in general introductory texts.

---

2. Literature review

Present the *previous literature* and the theories involved. This section is a relatively long one. Mention the *issues* that experts keep running into, like theoretical or methodological discussions, on-going and recurring debates, and schools of thought. You have already mentioned these briefly when explaining the research field, but here you can elaborate on the current situation in the field. Include studies that support your approach and those that do not.

The literature review is usually thematic, and within that thematic approach, chronology or importance can be the guiding principle. You can mention approaches or schools of thought, for instance, and start with the oldest or most dominant one. For each issue you address, start by giving *assumptions and findings* that are general and not controversial. Then, present *results that support and contradict mainstream assumptions*. Explain in clear terms the nature/source of any discrepancy: methodology, wrong generalisations, type of argumentations, incorrect conclusions, cultural bias, etc.

Focus on findings and conclusions. Only discuss methodologies of existing research if these are somehow exceptional or relevant (especially if the method in an article is very weak or very original or remarkable).

FOCUS ON...

Quoting

In the literature overview, keep quotes to a minimum, and only quote if the message itself or the language used to communicate it are in some way remarkable.

Now, mention the *research gap(s)*; your main motivation to do your research. These are issues not yet addressed by previous researchers or questions not yet answered. Indicate which one(s) you will be focussing on specifically. Indicate in general terms *how your research intends to fill the gap*.

3. Research questions

Some authors briefly make a *statement of purpose* before giving the specific research questions. They might, for instance, say something like 'The aim of the present report is to better understand the identity effects of lexical choices.' The theoretical framework might be part of this statement: 'This research contributes to the discussion on the behavioural factors determining politeness.'

The *research questions*, which come next, indicate through which questions your research will be helping to fill a knowledge gap or help to solve a practical or theoretical issue. First, mention the *main research* theme, and then break this down into two or three *detailed research questions*.

The *tool/method to answer the research questions* could then be mentioned. This consists of one sentence describing what you did (methodologically) to answer the research questions (like a survey or ethnographic study). This is a preview of the methodology and should not give any details. A possible next item is the *statement of value*: how will your investigation contribute to theory or something more practical? In the Conclusion chapter, you can expend more sentences on the value of your research but here you can mention it already. Finally, you could give a few motivated *hypotheses*, unless they are too obvious or redundant. Make sure to base the hypotheses on the literature, not your own intuitions and opinions.

14.3   Chapter 2: Method

The Method chapter gives a detailed description of the practical research steps that you've taken. This enables others to replicate the research or assess its quality, and it gives you the opportunity to explain the reasons behind methodological choices. The style in the Method chapter is dry and highly non-redundant: methodological facts and steps are mentioned as well as the reasons behind them. Most Method chapters include tables, itemised lists, and other overviews, and these might even take up the bulk of the chapter.

In a *research overview*, briefly indicate the kind of research you did: where, with which participants, which research tool, etc. This is for the reader to see the whole picture before details are given. Mention the *variables* and state whether they are dependent or independent (see 15.4.2). Indicate which *values/variants* each variable took (see 13.4.1). Give *definitions* of variables and values/variants if these definitions are subject to debate. Explain why you are abiding by a certain definition and not another.

Mention the *sample*. This is an overview of listeners, informants, or, for example, speakers that you have used in your research. The way you selected the sample, that is, the *sampling technique*, could also be given. Remind the reader of the larger group that the sample represents, that is, the *population*. If possible, use a table and systematically include relevant features of the people in the sample (age and gender, for instance). Explain on the basis of which *criteria* they were selected. Indicate to what degree they met the criteria and *how they were found*. Rather than using the word 'sample' in the heading, it is often clearer if you mention the nature of the people involved, based on what they actually did: 'Speakers', 'Listeners', and so on. *Instructions* refer to the information given to the participants before they participated, and these may be mentioned next.

KEY CONCEPTS

Participants in research

A 'participant' is a generic term for someone who generally participated in an investigation. A 'speaker', obviously, is someone who lends their voice as speaker, while 'listeners' listen in listening experiments. 'Informants' are people who collect data from within a community and report back to the researcher. A 'subject' is someone who is the subject of investigation. A 'respondent' answers questions in a questionnaire and an 'interviewee' answers questions in an interview.

Mention the written or spoken corpus or other type of source to be analysed and call this *material*; the type of data you are dealing with or the source you are extracting data from. Any *research tools* used to generate data (surveys, questionnaires, listening tests, acoustic measurements, transcriptions, computer models, for instance) should also be mentioned. Explain *how a tool works*, if this is relevant and not obvious. Acoustic measurements and computer programmes may need some explaining or a reference to a source explaining them. When you give such an explanation, start with a general overview, then zoom in on principal parts and then explain how they function. If participants listened to recordings, then *recording details* need to be described: length, source, type of accent, quality of recording, and so on. If these recordings brought about (i.e., stimulated) responses in an Identification Task (see 20.4), then they can be referred to as 'stimuli'.

A chronological overview of the steps taken to complete the methodology is given next and this is called the *procedure*. It is important to explain the motivations for each detailed step; which methodological challenges did you encounter and which steps did you take to solve or bypass these issues? End by mentioning the *statistical treatment*. This refers to the statistical tests you may have done. If necessary, succinctly explain the workings of the statistical tests you did.

14.4 Chapter 3: Results

The Results chapter describes the findings that the methodology has generated. Tables and graphs may appear here and sometimes they take up more space than the text will. First, briefly reiterate the *purpose* of the study and the *method* with which you generated data. This should not take up more than two sentences. Then, present what is the bulk of the Results chapter, namely the actual *findings* of the investigation(s) you've done. Help the reader understand the findings. Explain phonetic and other technical terminology, if necessary. Use long table and graph titles, if necessary, which include the number of speakers or tokens used. Give information on how to read the table if it is complicated. For each finding, stick to the following order: *announce the data* and what they show, then *present the data* (table/graph, usually) and then mention the *main tendencies*. Do not repeat all the findings literally, and leave out insignificant details. A good basis for ordering data presentations is to do so thematically rather than in the order in which they were collected. Another good system is the order in which research questions have been posed, and a presentation based on variables is also logical.

FOCUS ON...

Naming tables and graphs

The numbering system for a table and a graph (a graph is anything that's not a table, and a graph is the same as a figure) is different. Tables and graphs are numbered separately, and there might be a Table 3.2 and a Figure 3.2 in the same chapter. The numbering of tables and graphs is as follows: the first number is the chapter number, and the second number (after a dot) is the chronological number of the table or graph in that chapter. So, the third graph in Chapter 3 is called 'Figure 3.3' or 'Graph 3.3' and the first table in Chapter 4 is called 'Table 4.1'. Table captions go over the table and figure/graph captions go underneath the figure/graph.

After giving the main tendencies of each of the findings, you could very briefly *comment* on remarkable tendencies (if there are any), or you could *explain* remarkable tendencies. If there is a striking (dis)agreement between your specific data and data on the same or a similar topic in existing research or with data you presented earlier in the Results chapter, then single these out and *compare* your specific results with those other data and point out the striking similarities/differences. If there are no remarkable findings, then do not add comments. Comments and comparisons in the Results chapter, if presented, should never be long, because the Conclusion chapter is where elaborate comments are made. So, the Results chapter is not the place for speculation and all kinds of analytical thoughts, only for pointing out things that will be discussed in the next chapter.

14.5 Chapter 4: Conclusion

This final chapter of your research report summarises the main research findings and how they fit into the existing literature. It also gives the researcher the opportunity to present thoughts that occurred whilst doing the research. This chapter is likely to contain the sentences with the most complex constructions, because you need to express views and attitudes in a very nuanced way and make all kinds of logical and intuitive connections between theories, methodologies, research data, and your own thoughts. This chapter should start and end with general comments.

Start with an *introduction*. In one or a few short sentences, introduce the study; say what you have tried to do and in which way. Then, briefly *summarise the main results*, focussing only on the findings that are relevant to your research questions and leaving out any analyses or discussion. So, cherry-pick the most striking results and build the summary around them. Make sure that every time you refer to a result you include a reference to the section, graph or table where the reader can find the specific result (so, include the section numbers). Mention specific results (including the data) only if they are relevant or if a specific finding is striking. Your results may be presented in a different order than in the Results chapter and the results may here be combined in various ways. This reshuffling may be very enlightening to you and the reader. Your research findings should come to life here, as all kinds of connections and patterns surface (hopefully).

Succinctly *answer the research questions*. The answer to a research question could be based on various results (raked together from various tables and graphs). Do not mention specific findings (no numbers), just the general tendencies and (if you've used statistics) whether some difference or correlation was 'significant' or merely 'considerable'. The *original hypotheses* can now also be mentioned; did you hypothesise well, and how come?

A *comparison with other research* is the next component; contrast your data with existing data generated by others. Explain why your findings are different from existing ones or why they are not (are there methodological grounds or is there some other explanation?). This component should be full of detailed data-mentioning and reference-mentioning, and it may be longer than other components of the Conclusion. It is particularly challenging because you need to distinguish explicitly between facts, findings, and opinions (yours and of others). You need to be clear on who said, found, thought, or concluded what.

Mention the *limitations* of your research and advise the reader on *future research*. If your research stirs the way theory is viewed in the field or if it in some other way affects future methodologies or how the subject matter is viewed, then indicate this here (and call it *implications*). There may also be *practical applications*. Maybe you've designed or redesigned a teaching model or phonetic transcription system – explain how people can use this in the future or why it will improve their professional and/or personal lives.

The final component of the paper is what many call a *discussion*. This is an inspired piece of writing in which everything comes together and which reveals how your views have changed on the basis of the findings. What is surprising, what isn't? If possible, include the theory that the research might be based on in this discussion. This piece of writing may be added if you have anything left to say after the implications, or it may be merged with these implications.

14.6 After finishing the writing

14.6.1 Before the main text

After you've done all the research and written all the chapters, some components of the final research report need to be added before the main text. The ones to consider are; a *Table of Contents*, a *List of tables/graphs and abbreviations*, a *Preamble*, and an *Abstract*. These are all discussed on the companion website, at www.macmillanihe.com/companion/smakman.

14.6.2 After the main text

After the main text comes the *Bibliography*. Hints and tips on referencing are also on the companion website. After that, you could add an *Appendix*. In the Appendix, you put background data, raw (i.e., unanalysed) data, and generally information that is not easy to read because of size and detail, like surveys or questionnaires you've used, acoustic measurement results, statistical output, and lists of words or items that you refer to in the text. In the Method and Results chapters, you need to refer to the Appendix where necessary. The Appendix may be relatively long and you can use (very) small print. Making raw data available online is very common these days.

14.7 Conclusion

Each research report is unique. It is up to the researcher to decide which of the smaller components mentioned in this chapter end up in the actual report. Research reports that do not describe systematically collected data may have deviant shapes and degrees of detail but do follow the system of introducing the topic and the research steps, presenting the findings, and discussing the findings. Reports based on ethnographic observation or conversation analysis, for instance, are particularly liberal in their approach.

FURTHER READING

The companion website (www.macmillanihe.com/companion/smakman) contains an overview of all the parts printed in italics in this chapter. If relevant, then an example of typical language used in the various parts is given. Furthermore, Weissberg and Buker (1990) is recommended as a very user-friendly guide to structuring the parts of a research reports and using the academic English to go with these parts.

Crunching Numbers

Introducing Statistics

15.1 Introduction

Language students are usually more interested in the clearly visible workings of language than seeing language as a set of data that can be transformed into numbers. However, approaching language this way is very insightful and helps you to see all kinds of tendencies more objectively and draw reliable conclusions rather than intuitive ones. Statistics prevents you from claiming that a certain tendency is 'striking' or a number is 'high'. It teaches you how to make firm and unambiguous statements on certain patterns.

This chapter explains, first of all, some basic statistical terminology. After that, it discusses how you can analyse your data. It will explain how you can describe data by summarising them numerically and visually (descriptive statistics) and by doing some numerical tests (inferential statistics). The steps to enter data in SPSS and activate the tools described in this chapter are on the companion website, at www.macmillanihe.com/companion/smakman.

15.2 Qualitative versus quantitative research

Qualitative studies describe language use without predetermined types and numbers of variables and variants. Studying networks is often qualitatively done, and interviewing and observing people producing language generally also falls into the category of qualitative research. The interest in qualitative approaches is particularly pertinent in a globalising and diversifying world in which old categories are increasingly subject to change and variation. Qualitative research projects tend to have few assumptions regarding the interaction amongst variables and all kinds of conditions. Patterns are described in-depth and can often be used to single out relevant variables for quantitative research.

This chapter focuses specifically on quantitative methods. Quantitative research usually does work with predetermined social and linguistic categories for analysis. Medium-sized data and large-sized data can be distinguished.

Medium-sized data are usually data from experiments and tests or perhaps a small corpus. Large-sized data could be many hundreds or thousands of items over enormous corpora. Nowadays, big data can be accessed more easily than before because language corpora are constantly being built, old paper corpora are being digitised, and search engines are developed.

Many topics can be researched in both ways, and researchers often look at topics with one of these approaches as their leading one, with the other one as the supportive approach. Applying both qualitative and quantitative methods within one larger investigation is called a mixed-methods approach.

15.3 SPSS

In this chapter, we will focus on SPSS, which is a very commonly used statistical package that will enable you to perform the most common statistics tests in Sociolinguistics. Free trial versions of SPSS are available online and your university may have a licence for a more permanent one. Earlier versions usually have only slightly different buttons and visualisations. A fun and convenient way to run the tests is to find instruction clips on the Internet. If you search for 'SPSS tutorial' or something like 'T-test in SPSS' on websites such as www.youtube.com, then you can find all types of tutorials by statistical enthusiasts explaining how to enter data in this programme and do the tests explained here.

15.4 Terminology

15.4.1 Categorical variables and continuous variables

Variables can be categorical (like 'place of articulation' or 'biological gender'). This means that the values of the variable are categories, like 'bilabial' or 'male'. If the values of a variable are of a numerical type, then the variable is usually of the continuous type. For instance, participants can be high in masculinity and be assigned a number from 1 to 5 on a scale from 'not very masculine' (i.e., '1') to 'very masculine' (i.e., '5'). NB: So-called 'ranked variables' refer to the position a value takes relative to others; 'highest', 'middle', and 'lowest'.

15.4.2 Independent variables and dependent variables

The values of a 'dependent variable' depend on other variables. An example of a dependent variable is 'perceived formality', which might vary under all kinds of conditions. The values of an 'independent variable' cannot be changed by all kinds of influences. Age is an example of an independent variable. Sociolinguistic research often tries to see what the effect is of independent variables on dependent variables; for instance, the effect of age on how formal a language variety is perceived to be.

FOCUS ON...

Likert scales

Likert scales are named after their likely inventor, the American sociologist and psychologist Rensis Likert, who first used this scaling system in 1932 to measure attitudes. The use of Likert scales is still strongly associated with attitude research. The idea is that a certain quality (for instance 'ugly') is assigned a number, while the opposite quality ('beautiful') is assigned the opposite number. Five-point and seven-point Likert scales are quite common. Researchers should bear in mind that the choice of scale size may sometimes lead to statistically significant different results between groups of participants, as Dawes (2008) showed. When using scales with extreme qualifications at either end, like 'beautiful'/'ugly' and 'correct'/'incorrect', then be aware of the risk of putting all the positives on one side and all the negatives on the other. Participants are sometimes lazy and if they see that you've put the positives on one side and the negatives on the other then they may decide to copy the scores from one scale to the next.

15.4.3 Sample and population

Statistical inference refers to using a fact about a smaller group (a so-called 'sample') to estimate whether this is also true for the larger group that that sample is part of (the 'population'). If you have a good sample – that is, large enough and a good representation of the larger group – then it is likely that what is true for the sample is also true for the larger group. The sample should be random. This means that each member of the population should have an equal chance of being part of the sample during the selection procedure. This could be achieved by blindly picking each member of the sample. So, if your sample consists of students, then any student will do, irrespective of which subject they are reading or in which year of their studies they are, and irrespective of their gender. The population is denoted as 'N' and it may consist of subpopulations (for instance, women and men), and each of these can be denoted as (non-capitalised) 'n'.

15.4.4 Mean, mode, and standard deviation

Researchers are interested in central tendencies in their data: which value or set of comparable values is common and frequent, and how much agreement is there about whether this value or set of values is in fact central. There are a number of terms that give an idea as to the centrality of certain values.

The 'mean' is, simply, the mathematical average and represents a kind of benchmark value. It may, however, be that none of the values is equal to the mean, so in that respect the mean is theoretical. The 'mode' refers to the most commonly occurring value. The mode consists of a value that actually occurs. The mean and the mode could be close to each other but are not necessarily the same.

The 'standard deviation' shows the amount of variation within a set of values; how close the values are to each other. If an average of 3 consists of the values 3, 3, and 3, then the standard deviation is 0, because none of the values deviate from the mean. A high standard deviation means that values are more spread out (for instance, 2, 3, and 4), yet they may have the same mean. This is important because while a mean is interesting in itself, the standard deviation tells us whether there was internal agreement. For instance, if three people judge the beauty of a speech fragment, then it is important to know if they all strongly agreed or not.

15.4.5 Significance

The word 'significance' is a central point of interest in statistics and has a specific use in statistical discourse. Statisticians like to divide results binarily: a result is meaningful or it is not. Results that are meaningful are (on the basis of a consensus amongst statisticians) referred to in texts as 'significant'. The word 'significant' therefore means 'statistically significant'. Please note that the word 'insignificant' means 'unimportant' and is not the same as 'not significant'.

Significance is expressed in so-called 'p-values', where 'p' stands for 'probability'. Make sure the letter 'p' is italicised in your texts, so as to remind the reader that it is not just an ordinary 'p'. The lower the p-value, the more meaningful a result (a difference between two or three groups or the correlation between two sets of results, for instance). It has been decided that p-values below a certain number are referred to as 'significant', and above that number they are 'not significant'. These are called significance levels.

Significance levels

SPSS will at some point give you a p-value, and you need to check whether this value is below one of three significance levels. There are three significance levels: 0.05, 0.01, and 0.001. The three values refer to a 5 per cent, 1 per cent, or 0.1 per cent chance that a correlation or a difference is a coincidence. The first one is the most common one and is often set as a default in SPSS. A p-value of 0.02 is considered to be significant at the 0.05 level (because it is lower than 0.05) but not according to the other two levels (it is higher than 0.01 and 0.001). If your p-value is 0.02, then you can simply say the difference or correlation is 'significant at the 0.05 level'. If the p-value is 0.003, then you say that the difference or correlation is 'significant at the 0.01 level'.

You need to report the p-value and then indicate whether a result was significant (for instance, '$p < 0.05$', meaning the p-value was lower than 0.05) or not ('$p > 0.05$'). Note that it is a convention to leave out the '0' before the dot in the data presentation: you can write '$p = .11$' rather than '$p = 0.11$', and you can also write '$p < .05$' rather than '$p < 0.05$'.

15.4.6 Two-tailed versus one-tailed

When you conduct a statistical test in which you want to know about significance, then you are given a p-value in the output that will say (possibly between parentheses) 'two-tailed' or 'one-tailed'. In this context, 'tailed' refers to the two ends of a bell curve in which the peak represents the most frequently occurring value. Left and right of that value are the two 'tails', which represent values that are less common. The right-hand tail contains the higher values and the left-hand tail represents the lower values. A two-tailed analysis takes the values of both tails into consideration, rather than one. If you need to choose between the two, then choose 'two-tailed'; this is usually the default setting.

15.4.7 Descriptive statistics versus inferential statistics

You can present your data applying several levels of analytical depth. The most superficial data presentation are the raw data, which refers to the unanalysed, literal results, like all the scores all participants gave in an investigation. Very few data sets are suitable to be presented like that. A deeper level is to give an overview of certain numerical tendencies, like the means and added-up values per group or visualised data in a graph. This is called 'descriptive statistics'. The deepest level of analysis is a numerical interpretation of the data, in which you not only give means and trends but mutually compare these means and trends, and in which you do not just give strings of data but compare them to each other mathematically. This is called 'inferential statistics'. These comparisons usually contain a statement as to whether a result is significant.

In the next sections, we will distinguish between the latter two levels; descriptive and inferential statistics. The descriptive tools and tests described are the most basic and common analytical techniques in Sociolinguistics.

15.5 Descriptive statistics

15.5.1 Numerical descriptives

Once you've entered your data in SPSS, you can do some straightforward descriptive statistics. All kinds of summarised information can be generated that is already very informative in itself. SPSS distinguishes between the following descriptive tools: Explore, Descriptives, Frequencies, and Crosstabs. Each gives you its own perspective on the data.

1. Explore

The Explore function in SPSS produces summary statistics and basic graphic displays. This function is useful for general data screening, like finding values that strongly deviate from the others. Unusual, perhaps extreme values will be visible, as will possible gaps in the data or other oddities. For instance, the number of missing data is indicated, which is hopefully in line with the missing number(s) that you are aware of. If unexpected numbers and graph shapes show, then you should check for mistakes in your data. Perhaps you've entered them incorrectly. The output tables that Explore generates speak for themselves, and you will recognise the many values if you've labelled them well when entering data in SPSS.

2. Descriptives

The Descriptives procedure displays a summary for several continuous variables (not categorical ones) and provides an overall look at your numerical data. One table with the basic information you ask for appears. The variables in this summary may be ordered alphabetically or perhaps in ascending or descending order (depending on your settings).

3. Frequencies

The Frequencies procedure gives you what Descriptives gives you and more. It provides basic numbers added up, including categorical data. It is a good way to start viewing the trends in your data. You can order the categories by their frequencies or arrange the distinct values in ascending or descending order. In the output tables, you will find the information you've asked for and more. You can select the information you need and put it in a table or overview of your own, or mention it in the text of your report. Frequency tables may generate long lists with numbers of raw data, and these may also function as a check that your data have been entered well. This function also makes it easier to decide which inferential statistical test to do.

4. Crosstabs

If you are comparing two variables, then SPSS can produce simple two-way tables for you, called Crosstabs, that are immediately very insightful. You need to specify a row and a column.

15.5.2 Visual descriptives

Besides giving averages and frequencies in the text, you can visualise them. The advantage is that certain tendencies become instantly apparent. There are many ways to visualise your data. Some very common ones in Sociolinguistics are presented here.

1. Bar chart

Bar charts show numerical data by displaying rectangular bars against a numbered scale. A clear image of values per bar arises because they stand side by side. The bars in a bar chart usually show categorical variables. The bar chart shows the frequency of a value, or it could show averages. It could, for instance, compare the percentages of people from three different age categories tending to speak at a certain rate of words per minute. This would be a so-called simple bar chart, with distinct bars next to each other. There are two other types of bar charts: 'clustered' and 'stacked'. The difference is the amount of information in them, particularly the number of categorical variables. In the clustered bar chart, you can put more than one categorical variable and distinguish the bars belonging to each variable with a different colour or pattern. In a stacked bar chart, this information is put on top of each other, to see how they add up. They might add up to 100 per cent or to a certain number. Below are the types of bar charts, with the two types of stacked charts.

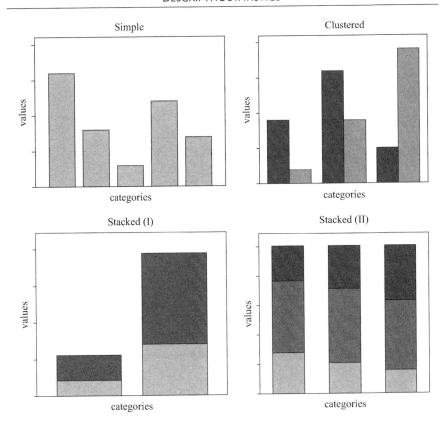

2. Pie chart

A pie chart looks like a pie, and the size of each slice represents how much it is part of the total pie. Pie charts work best when your data consist of several large sets. Too many variables, unfortunately, divide the pie into small pie pieces, and that makes it difficult to see the whole picture. Each piece of the pie can be visually contrasted from the others with a certain colour or pattern. It should be noted that pie charts are not very popular, probably because giving this information in a table or bar chart is often equally clear. Here is an example of a pie chart.

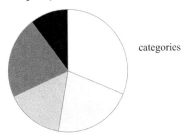

3. Line chart

A line chart is mostly associated with developments over time. On the horizontal axis, time units are placed, and the values can be seen for the various points in time through a line. Line charts can also be used to compare changes over a period of time for more than one group. These uses are in the examples here.

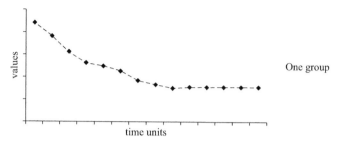

One group

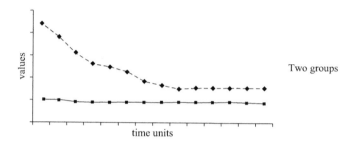

Two groups

4. Boxplot

A boxplot looks like a box with a vertical line coming out of it at the bottom and one at the top. Only the vertical dimension of boxplots is relevant. The boxplot will show the median (the value in the middle of the list of values) of a set of values. In addition, it gives insight into how close the various values are to that median; a smaller box means that more of the values were close to the median, a larger one means that the values were more spread out. The vertical lines shooting out of the box represent the set of values that are further removed from the median. Boxplots also show whether some individual values (called 'outliers') differed from the median very strongly; these extreme values are indicated as separate dots or asterisks, usually. Below is an example of a boxplot.

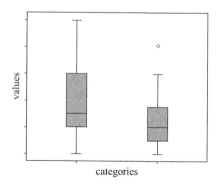

categories

5. Scatterplot

A scatterplot is used to visualise or scan relationships between two numerical variables that somehow depend on each other. They show individual values in a two-dimensional overview. The x-axis is used to display one variable and the y-axis is used to display the other. Sometimes, the variables don't follow any pattern and have no relationship, and a scatterplot will show this instantly. Possible correlations will also show clearly. Here is an example of a scatterplot.

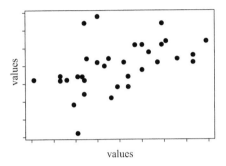

6. Table

If these visualisations don't present themselves naturally, then it is wise to consider the most basic type of visualisation, namely the traditional table. Although presented as the last visualisation type here, the table is the most quintessential data representation tool in Sociolinguistics. Data are presented objectively and not through artwork in which colours and shapes often emphasise certain effects or correlations. A table simply and straightforwardly organises values and variables and shows them in labelled rows and bars. Most people make tables in their text processor, but SPSS also has the option to make tables. Below is an example of a table.

Listener	Score
A	
B	
C	

15.6   Inferential statistics

15.6.1 Chi-square Test

If you have data of two groups of categorical variables, then you can compare them by doing a so-called Chi-square Test, also called χ^2 Test or Test for Independence. For instance, you could ask a group of people if they think

Swiss German, Austrian German, or German German is the most pleasing to the ear. It might be that half of the respondents choose German from Germany while a quarter chose Austrian German and another quarter chose Swiss German as being most pleasing to the ear. If you want to know whether perhaps the men and women within this larger group had comparable preferences or significantly different ones, then a Chi-square test will give you the answer.

15.6.2 T-tests

If you want to compare the values from two sets of continuous variables, then you can do a T-test. There are two types of T-tests that are particularly useful in sociolinguistic research, namely the Independent Samples T-test and the Matched Samples T-test.

You should use an Independent Samples T-test when you are comparing two different (i.e., independent) groups. Usually, you collect information from two sets of people on a single occasion. If you had two different groups of people judge a set of speech fragments on a 5-point scale from 'ugly' (= 1) to 'beautiful' (= 5) (so each fragment was judged separately through this scale), then you can do an Independent Samples T-test to determine whether the average judgements by the two groups of the set of fragments were significantly different or not.

A Matched Samples T-test, which is often also called Repeated Measures T-test, can be used if you want to know whether a measurement at one point in time is significantly different from another measurement of the same or comparable item at a later point in time. A common situation is if participants do something (like judge the beauty of a speech fragment, as in the example just given) and are asked to do the same thing at a later point in time. In between these two measuring points, some form of manipulation is typically introduced. For instance, they could judge a sound fragment of a certain dialect before and after meeting a speaker of this dialect for the first time. The effect of this experience is then tested through a Matched Samples T-test.

15.6.3 Analysis of Variance

While T-tests describe the differences between the means from two sets of continuous variables, an Analysis of Variance, which is usually referred to as ANOVA, compares the means for more than two groups of such variables. So, rather than judging the beauty of two fragments, as in the example above, participants may be judging the beauty of three fragments. After performing an ANOVA, you know whether there is an overall significant difference between the means tested. To find out between which groups the significant difference exists, if there is such a difference, you need to do a so-called Post-hoc Test.

15.6.4 Correlation

Correlations measure whether two (continuous or ranked) variables are related. A correlation coefficient will be calculated, called Pearson's Correlation Coefficient, which shows whether the relatedness is significant. A significant correlation coefficient means that two variables are indeed related. A correlation coefficient runs from value '–1' (a perfectly negative relationship) to '+1' (a perfectly positive relationship). The value '0' means that there is no relatedness between the variables whatsoever.

For instance, you want to know whether two speaker characteristics, namely 'height of income' and 'degree to which one speaks the norm language' are related. If there is a positive correlation, then that means that if speakers have a high income that they are more likely to speak the norm language than speakers with a lower income are. A negative correlation would mean that the higher one's income is, the less likely it is that one speaks the norm language.

15.6.5 Factor Analysis

Sometimes, several possible factors could explain a result and are mutually related or referring to a similar quality. To test whether in fact they can be merged as being one and the same more general factor, you can do a Factor Analysis. Some of these factors may have a similar effect on your results, which means that they could in fact be treated as one and the same. A Factor Analysis attempts to identify such combinations of related factors. A Factor Analysis is often used to reduce the data set, as a reduced number of factors is the outcome.

Maybe, for instance, level of education and income have a similar effect on how participants in an experiment judge speech samples (so, participants with a high income and participants who are highly educated judge the fragments similarly). These two could be reduced to a factor that you, the researcher, could perhaps call 'social development', just because they seem to behave similarly. A Factor Analysis tells you whether that should be done for certain combinations of (two or more) factors. A Factor Analysis is only possible for continuous variables, not categorical ones.

15.7   Conclusion

This chapter gave you a first glance of the possibilities of dealing with data systematically. Asking for help when doing statistics is advisable, because every research project is unique. You may be able to do the tests in this chapter, but extra tests or adjusted tests may in addition be necessary.

Statistical analyses build on the premise that high numbers of occurrences are the main way to prove something. However, a good sociolinguist also pays attention to detail and even looks for meaningful exceptions. One slip of the tongue or one occurrence of a certain word or sound may often be as telling as a statistically reliable quantitative analysis. Researchers should keep their eyes and ears open and see to it that such meaningful exceptions do not get lost in a statistical analysis.

The three tables that follow contain the choices that you may make in your data analysis and presentation. These overviews help you to choose an analysis technique and a way to write down or visualise your data and/or analyses in your research report (Tables 15.1, 15.2 and 15.3).

Table 15.1   What are the goals of the statistical techniques, and which questions do they answer?

Technique	Goal	Question answered
Explore	Screen data	Are my data basically okay, or did I make mistakes? Were there anomalies?
Descriptives	Summarise data	How are my data structured?
Frequencies	View trends in the data	Do the trends point to a certain statistical test?
Crosstabs	Display two variables in a table	Do two sets of values seem related?
Chi-Square	Determine if there are differences between groups	Are the make-ups of two groups comparable?
T-test	Determine significance of two mean group differences	Are differences between two means significant?
ANOVA	Determine significance of three or more mean group differences	Are differences between three or more means significant?
Correlation	Determine the relationship between two variables	How strongly and in which way (positively or negatively) are two variables related?
Factor Analysis	Determine the number of relevant factors	Can certain factors be merged into a new factor?

Table 15.2   Which variables fit in inferential tests?

Test	Variables	
	Independent	Dependent
Chi-Square	1 categorical	1 categorical
T-test	1 categorical	1 continuous
ANOVA	1 or more categorical	1 continuous
Correlation	1 ranked or continuous	1 continuous
Factor Analysis	1 or more continuous	1 or more continuous

Table 15.3   Which techniques of data presentation go with the type of data?

Visualisation	Displays
Bar chart	Values per categorical variable next to each other and/or on top of each other
Pie chart	Relative sizes of subgroups in a larger group
Line chart	Tendencies over time or continuous data
Boxplot	How close values are to the most central value
Scatterplot	Two variables whose values depend on each other
Table	Most types of numerical data

FURTHER READING

The companion website (www.macmillanihe.com/companion/smakman) presents the practical steps that are necessary to enter your data into SPSS and do the calculations as introduced in the current chapter. Chapters 11 to 15 of Meyerhoff et al. (2015) demonstrate the use of statistical analysis in Sociolinguistics through practical examples and exercises. Rumsey (2010) gives an extensive overview of statistics for beginners. This text is known for its accessible style and elaborate explanations.

The Sounds of Language

16

Introducing Sociophonetics

16.1 Introduction

Phonetics is the study of the production and perception of speech. Sociophonetics is the specifically sociolinguistic approach to Phonetics. In Sociolinguistics, pronunciation receives relatively much attention because language choices are often hidden in subtle pronunciation differences. Unlike Grammar, Phonetics is not a regular part of secondary or tertiary education, and for that reason it is explained in this chapter. (For those with not enough knowledge of grammatical terminology, there is a Glossary of grammatical terms on the companion website, at www.macmillanihe.com/companion/smakman.) Another reason is that Sociolinguistics approaches Phonetics in its own specific way.

This chapter contains the most basic phonetic terminological canon that is needed to explore pronunciation in a sociolinguistic context. The so-called International Phonetic Alphabet (IPA) is taken as the model of description and this alphabet is therefore described first. An explanation will be given of the most important terminology as it appears in the IPA, along with some additional relevant terminology. The second part of this chapter contains a guide to describing speech sounds.

16.2 Aspects of speech

16.2.1 The International Phonetic Alphabet

Spelling is at most a static and crude method of representing speech sounds, while some spelling systems bear no relationship to pronunciation at all. Because of this, a system of representing language has been invented that is based purely on actual pronunciation and that reflects pronunciation realities more closely than spelling does. This system is called the International Phonetic Alphabet (IPA). IPA enables us to describe the sounds of any variety of language and any style in an understandable and relatively precise manner. In the IPA overview below, you will see that the symbols used are often in accordance with Latin orthography, so to those who know this system the IPA transcription system is easy to learn.

THE INTERNATIONAL PHONETIC ALPHABET (revised to 2015)

CONSONANTS (PULMONIC)   © 2015 IPA

	Bilabial	Labiodental	Dental	Alveolar	Postalveolar	Retroflex	Palatal	Velar	Uvular	Pharyngeal	Glottal
Plosive	p b			t d		ʈ ɖ	c ɟ	k g	q ɢ		ʔ
Nasal	m	ɱ		n		ɳ	ɲ	ŋ	N		
Trill	ʙ			r					R		
Tap or Flap		ⱱ		ɾ		ɽ					
Fricative	ɸ β	f v	θ ð	s z	ʃ ʒ	ʂ ʐ	ç ʝ	x ɣ	χ ʁ	ħ ʕ	h ɦ
Lateral fricative				ɬ ɮ							
Approximant		ʋ		ɹ		ɻ	j	ɰ			
Lateral approximant				l		ɭ	ʎ	L			

Symbols to the right in a cell are voiced, to the left are voiceless. Shaded areas denote articulations judged impossible.

CONSONANTS (NON-PULMONIC)

Clicks	Voiced implosives	Ejectives
ʘ Bilabial	ɓ Bilabial	' Examples:
ǀ Dental	ɗ Dental/alveolar	p' Bilabial
ǃ (Post)alveolar	ʄ Palatal	t' Dental/alveolar
ǂ Palatoalveolar	ɠ Velar	k' Velar
ǁ Alveolar lateral	ʛ Uvular	s' Alveolar fricative

OTHER SYMBOLS

ʍ Voiceless labial-velar fricative
w Voiced labial-velar approximant
ɥ Voiced labial-palatal approximant
ʜ Voiceless epiglottal fricative
ʢ Voiced epiglottal fricative
ʡ Epiglottal plosive

ɕ ʑ Alveolo-palatal fricatives
ɺ Voiced alveolar lateral flap
ɧ Simultaneous ʃ and x

Affricates and double articulations can be represented by two symbols joined by a tie bar if necessary.

t͡s k͡p

VOWELS

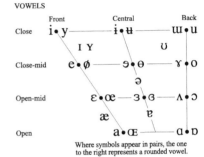

Where symbols appear in pairs, the one to the right represents a rounded vowel.

SUPRASEGMENTALS

ˈ	Primary stress	ˌfoʊnəˈtɪʃən
ˌ	Secondary stress	
ː	Long	eː
ˑ	Half-long	eˑ
˘	Extra-short	ĕ
ǀ	Minor (foot) group	
ǁ	Major (intonation) group	
.	Syllable break	ɹi.ækt
‿	Linking (absence of a break)	

TONES AND WORD ACCENTS

	LEVEL			CONTOUR	
e̋ or	˥	Extra high	ě or	˩˥	Rising
é	˦	High	ê	˥˩	Falling
ē	˧	Mid	e᷄	˧˥	High rising
è	˨	Low	e᷅	˩˧	Low rising
ȅ	˩	Extra low	e᷈	˧˩˧	Rising-falling
↓	Downstep		↗	Global rise	
↑	Upstep		↘	Global fall	

DIACRITICS Some diacritics may be placed above a symbol with a descender, e.g. ŋ̊

	Voiceless	n̥ d̥		Breathy voiced	b̤ a̤		Dental	t̪ d̪
	Voiced	s̬ t̬		Creaky voiced	b̰ a̰		Apical	t̺ d̺
ʰ	Aspirated	tʰ dʰ		Linguolabial	t̼ d̼		Laminal	t̻ d̻
	More rounded	ɔ̹	ʷ	Labialized	tʷ dʷ	~	Nasalized	ẽ
	Less rounded	ɔ̜	ʲ	Palatalized	tʲ dʲ	ⁿ	Nasal release	dⁿ
	Advanced	u̟	ˠ	Velarized	tˠ dˠ	ˡ	Lateral release	dˡ
	Retracted	e̠	ˤ	Pharyngealized	tˤ dˤ	̚	No audible release	d̚
¨	Centralized	ë	~	Velarized or pharyngealized	ɫ			
ˣ	Mid-centralized	e̽		Raised	e̝ (ɹ̝ = voiced alveolar fricative)			
	Syllabic	n̩		Lowered	e̞ (β̞ = voiced bilabial approximant)			
	Non-syllabic	e̯		Advanced Tongue Root	e̘			
˞	Rhoticity	ɚ a˞		Retracted Tongue Root	e̙			

The sections in this chapter will go through the most important terminology in this overview in a step by step manner, so it is advisable to keep the IPA overview ready when going through the text. If a term in the text below is bolded the first time it is used, then that means that you can also find it in the actual chart. Phonetic symbols and terminology in principle do not take a specific language as its basis or point of departure. However, for practical reasons, the examples given will be in the language used in this book, English, and they will work for British and American English.

16.2.2 Entities of description

Languages use **vowels** and **consonants**, both of which are generally produced by shaping the speech tract while exhaling. The difference between vowels and consonants is the nature of that shaping. To produce a consonant, the air must be obstructed in some audible way whereas during the production of vowels the air flows freely through the mouth. To form distinct vowels, the shape of the tongue and mouth is adjusted. Certain languages have one or more **non-pulmonic consonants**, which are produced in the speech tract without such an outgoing airstream. The most famous consonants in this category are probably **clicks**, which occur in some languages in southern and central Africa. It should be noted that articulatorily the distinction between vowels and consonants is somewhat fluid. The consonants /w/ and /j/, for instance, are quite vowel-like, strictly speaking.

Phonemes versus allophones

The vowels and consonants shown in the IPA overview are 'phonemes'. A phoneme is a sound entity as it exists in the mind of a language user. Linguists use this assumption as a basis of analysis. Phonemes may have different phonetic realisations, but in the mind of the listener these will be categorised as instantiations of the same phoneme. For instance, a 't' may come out with a strong puff of air (which is called **aspiration**) or without such a puff (like the ones in 'tea' and 'sting', which are, respectively, pronounced with and without aspiration), but a language user will still categorise them as a 't'. The various ways in which the same phoneme may be pronounced are called its 'allophones'. When writing down (i.e., 'transcribing') sounds, phonemes need to be placed between slashes ('/.../') while allophones need to be placed between square brackets ('[...]'). You can use an online IPA keyboard to generate phonemes and **diacritics** (the latter are explained below) through http://ipa.typeit.org/full/ or by searching for an online IPA keyboard.

   Usually, a phoneme is systematically pronounced as a certain allophone because of a rule. The rule in the 'tea' and 'sting' examples is that in many Englishes at the beginning of the syllable the /t/ will be produced with aspiration unless it is preceded by an /s/ in the same syllable. Allophones themselves may be subject to a sociolinguistic rule, namely that some speakers pronounce their syllable-initial /t/'s in a more strongly aspirated manner than others do. It is important to distinguish between such sociolinguistic variation (dependent on individual speakers' choices and habits) and variation that comes from a phonetic rule for a certain language variety.

Consonants

The manner of airflow obstruction to produce consonants is used to classify phonemes into several categories. In the note underneath the **consonants (pulmonic)** table in the IPA overview, there is a reference to 'voice'. Indeed, a main distinction is between **voiced** and **voiceless** consonants, which refers to whether the vocal cords (also called 'vocal folds') are used during their production ('voiced') or not ('voiceless'). Vowels tend to be voiced by nature, unless you whisper them or if their voice disappears due to, for instance, a high speech rate. Consonants can be either.

Besides being either voiced or voiceless, consonants may also be subdivided as either 'fortis' or 'lenis'. Fortis (often also called 'tense') means 'strong' in Latin, and lenis (also called 'lax') means 'weak'. Strictly speaking, these words denote the energy (force of airflow obstruction) with which sounds are produced, but these two labels are not usually applied literally. They serve as tools to be able to discuss phonemes across languages. Fortis sounds often have a lenis equivalent. Besides /s, z/, other examples of such pairs of sounds are /t, d/ and /f, v/; these pairs are placed next to each other in the IPA overview. The fortis/lenis and voiceless/voiced qualities often coincide, with lenis consonants being voiced and fortis consonants being voiceless.

As explained, consonants are produced through an obstruction of the outgoing airstream. This obstruction takes place in a certain place in the vocal tract (see the top horizontal bar in the 'consonants (pulmonic)' table) and in a certain manner (see the left-hand side vertical bar in the same table). The picture below shows the various places of articulation in the mouth and throat.

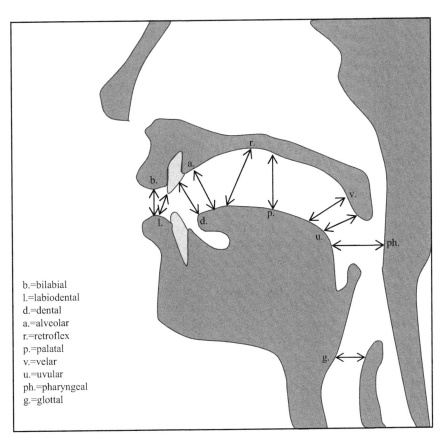

b.=bilabial
l.=labiodental
d.=dental
a.=alveolar
r.=retroflex
p.=palatal
v.=velar
u.=uvular
ph.=pharyngeal
g.=glottal

When producing consonants, you will feel that some lower part in your mouth (tongue, lower teeth, lower lips) will touch some upper part of your mouth (upper teeth, palate, velum, alveolar ridge, upper lips). In the IPA overview, you can see that the indicated places of articulation go from the front of the mouth (lips; left in the chart) to the back of the speech tract (throat; right in the chart). The most important places of articulation are **bilabial** (the two lips touching), **labiodental** (lower lip against the upper teeth), **dental** (tongue against the upper teeth), 'interdental' (tongue between the upper and lower teeth), **alveolar** (tongue touching the alveolar ridge, which is the bump in between the upper teeth and the hard palate), **retroflex** (the end of your tongue bent backwards and/or pushed behind the alveolar ridge), **palatal** (tongue touching the hard palate), **velar** (tongue against the velum), and **uvular** (deeper in the mouth than velar). **Pharyngeal** and **glottal** pronunciations are even deeper in the throat, namely by using the pharynx and even glottis (the latter is the space between the vocal cords).

All kinds of combinations of places of articulation exist, such as **palatoalveolar** (which might occur in texts as 'palatal/alveolar' or 'alveopalatal') or **dental/alveolar**. This means that the place of articulation is between two places of articulation or – more likely – in both places of articulation at the same time.

As for manner of articulation, there are five basic ways consonants are pronounced. A consonant can be a **plosive** (also called 'stop'), which means that the airstream is completely obstructed during its production. Furthermore, a consonant can be a **nasal** (the air passes through the nose only), a **trill** (with a vibrating tongue), a **fricative** (there is a partial obstruction, a narrowing, that causes friction), or an **approximant** (very weak or hardly any obstruction). Ways to indicate combinations of sounds also exist, and the most well-known one of these is the **affricate**, which term refers to a plosive that is directly followed by a fricative, as in the first consonant cluster in 'cheat'.

Consonants with manners of articulation involving considerable obstruction are called 'obstruents' (plosives, affricates, and fricatives) and are typically voiceless. 'Sonorant' refers to the manner of articulation that lets the air come out more freely (like with vowels, nasals, and approximants), and consonants with this quality are often voiced (and they can be sung, unlike most obstruents). The phonemes in the 'liquids' category are also sonorants – the two best known liquids are the first sound in the words 'light' and 'right'.

When people speak, phonemes may merge with surrounding sounds (this is called 'assimilation') or even disappear ('deletion'). This is normal rather than lazy, although it is true that these phenomena occur less in formal, careful speech. Sounds that assimilate become a little bit like each other. One sound may predominantly adjust to the other, or vice versa. Deletion can take place in very fast speech. A reason to delete a sound is that it is redundant in the sense that the hearer will know which sound is deleted and will not misinterpret the utterance.

Vowels

With a bit of imagination, the vowel diagram as shown in the IPA overview can be looked at as a cross-section of an actual mouth, with the top left-hand

---

FOCUS ON...

The importance of /r/

Certain phonemes seem to be sociolinguistically more interesting than others. This may be due to the wide range of possible ways to pronounce them and the perceptual salience of these ways. The phonemes /n/ and /f/ do not tend to have much allophonic variation, for instance, while /l/ and /r/ are subject to considerable variation in the ways they can be pronounced. The phoneme /r/ in particular has almost extreme variation in its possible realisations. In many languages, this phoneme can take on many shapes, especially at the ends of syllables, and the various realisations can be strongly marked. In Brazilian Portuguese, for instance, the retroflex /r/ is qualified as *caipira*, 'redneck'. Leite (2004) found that the university students in her research regarded this /r/ realisation as ugly. Retroflex /r/ in the Netherlands is highly marked as well, and it carries both connotations of poshness and of broadness (Sebregts 2014; Smakman 2006). Something similar is the case in the United States. Among older European-American speakers in Charleston, South Carolina, the absence of postvocalic /r/ carries connotations of high-status groups (Wolfram 2004a), but in New York City it is associated with low-status groups, even by speakers themselves (Labov 1966).

---

corner showing the speech tract in the front of the mouth and the right-hand side bottom part showing the deepest place in the mouth where vowels can be produced.

Although vowels are more difficult to fathom articulatorily than consonants are, they are usually described using fewer features than is the case for consonants. They are commonly categorised on the basis of two main dimensions: part of the tongue involved in their production (called the **Front/Back** dimension) and height of the tongue (the **Open/Close** dimension). The idea is that vowels are qualified on the basis of the place where a certain part of the tongue is closest to the upper part of the speech tract. This could be the back of the tongue, the front of the tongue, or the bit in between. This is the Front/Back dimension. The openness of the mouth in general, as controlled by the tongue and the lower jaw, determines the height of the vowel, as expressed in the Open/Close dimension. An important but less frequently used vowel feature is whether the lips are 'spread' or the opposite of spread, **rounded**, during its production.

FOCUS ON...

Number of vowels in languages

The number of vowels in various languages varies. The Australian Aboriginal language Warlpiri has only three basic vowels (O'Shannessy 2005) while the East African language Nuer has fourteen (Needham 1972).

In the centre of the vowel diagram lies the easiest and perhaps even most frequent vowel of all, 'schwa' (/ə/). It is the sound produced in unstressed syllables, as in the first sound in the word 'above' (/əbʌv/). It is produced with the least change to the shape of the vowel tract. Sociolinguistically, this phoneme is very important, as it could constitute a sociolinguistic choice in many cases. In certain phonetic contexts or specific words in many languages it is associated with relaxed and informal speech.

Vowels can be short or long, and they can be 'monophthongs' or 'diphthongs'. A monophthong is a vowel that doesn't change shape during its production, like the vowels in 'pet' (/pet/) and 'sleet' (/sliːt/). A diphthong consists of a combination of two vowels, like the one in 'by' (/baɪ/). The IPA overview takes the short monophthong as its basis of description, but most languages have a set of diphthongs and semi-diphthongs (the latter are articulatorily between diphthongs and monophthongs) at their disposal in their basic vowel inventory in addition to short monophthongs.

Mixed categories

The lists of types of vowels and consonants is by no means exhaustive, as other types exist as well (like 'sibilant' for consonants). These are often derived from existing categories, combinations of other manners of articulation, highly language-specific features, or very rare. There are also sounds that in some ways qualify as a consonant, while they also resemble vowels. The first sounds in the word 'hope' and 'yoke' are good examples of this and so is any approximant. From an articulatory point of view it is not necessary to strongly distinguish between vowels and consonants, because in some cases variation might consist of a consonant being pronounced in a more vowel-like manner, or vice versa. Vowels and consonants do have strict positions within syllables, so the first sound in 'yolk' is a consonant because it occurs at the beginning of the syllable and not in the position where the vowel is. Nevertheless, this sound is vowel-like in nature, some might say.

KEY CONCEPTS

Rhoticity

If you narrow your vocal tract when pronouncing schwa, then the sound may become subject to **rhoticity**, especially at the end of an open syllable. This is a sociolinguistically and phonetically salient feature in some languages, like Beijing Mandarin and most varieties of American English. 'Rhotic speakers' pronounce approximant /r/ at the end of syllables, while 'non-rhotic speakers' do not. In fact, it is more complicated than that, as 'rhotic' could refer to the presence of the consonant in question but also to the addition of an /r/-like quality of the preceding vowel. It may be that this vowel quality constitutes the actual rhoticity.

Diacritics

To describe allophones (or phonemes that are not in the standard list of vowels and consonants), diacritics can be used. These are ways to indicate, for instance, that while a certain phoneme is pronounced with the tongue against the alveolar ridge, the tongue also touches the teeth during production (you can then add the '**dental**' symbol). Whether a certain sound is aspirated can also be expressed through a diacritic. Diacritical descriptions sometimes speak for themselves; **palatalized**, for instance, means that during the production of a consonant part of the tongue is moved close to the hard palate. You can also use diacritics for vowels; for instance, to express that a vowel is produced with the tongue slightly higher than expected (add the '**raised**' symbol to the transcription).

For each language, a limited set of diacritics is relevant, so don't worry about having to categorise every sound by considering all diacritics. An over-use of diacritics in fact leads to less understandable text, and it may be useful to explain your usage of a diacritic in a footnote or in the text. Always bear in mind that no two sounds are ever the same, and that trying to capture all subtle pronunciation variations in transcription is not possible. Try to focus on repeated tendencies in individuals' speech rather than attaching too much importance to one-off pronunciations in running speech.

Suprasegmentals

Above the 'segmental' level of individual vowels and consonants, there is the level of **suprasegmentals**. This refers to elements that cross phoneme and syllable boundaries, like **intonation** (the tone of your voice going up and down) and **stress** (placing emphasis on syllables by making them a little louder and/or higher in pitch). These features, which are sometimes called 'prosodic' features, are notoriously difficult to grasp and note down. The IPA overview does not distinguish between segmental and suprasegmental features very strictly and categorises certain features, like vowel length, as suprasegmental. This is not a mistake but because certain features are difficult to categorise as either applying to individual phonemes or to higher levels like the syllable or sets of words. The **tones** in the bottom right corner of the IPA overview are mostly relevant for the study of tonal languages, like Cantonese Chinese.

16.2.3 The syllable as a relevant entity

Not every sound can appear in every part of a syllable, and certain sounds cannot appear next to each other in speech. This systematic organisation of speech sounds is called 'Phonology', which has very obvious connections with Phonetics. Phonology operates at the level of sound units and is interested in how these units behave. The position of a phoneme in the syllable is a very important determinant of the nature of that phoneme. It is important to recognise a phoneme quality that is due to position in the syllable and not qualify this quality as the result of a sociolinguistic choice or the result of phonetic context. The 'tea'/'sting' example mentioned earlier demonstrates this; the difference between the two does not constitute an act of identity but simply the speaker applying a pronunciation rule.

Phonology studies the sound systems of languages. Each language uses a select set of sounds, and these can be put into phonological units. Phonologists try to draw general conclusions about the nature of the sound system of a specific language and they try and draw conclusions about sound systems of languages of the world. Sounds can be contrastive in certain positions but not in others. The relevance for sociophonetic research is then that allophonic variation is also typically conditioned by syllable structure.

16.3   Determining the quality of vowels and consonants

16.3.1 Preliminary considerations

To prepare for a description of sounds, you are advised to find an overview of sounds of the particular variety you are studying (if such an overview exists). Learn about that variety – its consonants and vowels but also its stress patterns and intonation structure. Knowing its sociolinguistics is also good; when are certain phonemes produced in a certain way, in which social contexts? Which speakers typically pronounce things that way? Maybe it is a tone language, which means that you need to know about the meanings of its tones. Although your expectations regarding the way certain sounds are pronounced may hinder objectivity to a degree when describing sounds, experience has shown that in the end the more you know about a variety, the easier it is to analyse it.

To be able to write about the pronunciation of the language you are studying, you need to make sure that the description you obtain is IPA-based. Codified languages in the world usually have an IPA-based overview of sounds. If you encounter other ways of sound representation, perhaps because the sound description is very old or because only a non-expert has ever tried their hand at such a description, then your challenge is to find a way to translate these idiosyncratic descriptions into IPA-compatible terminology.

16.3.2 Transcribing individual variation

When you have your description of the canonised language (the language as it is supposed to be pronounced according to the norm, or the most common way to pronounce it) then you, as a sociolinguist, will want to describe variation in the way individuals deviate from this way of pronouncing things. In other words, the description you find will give you a rough indication, but usually no one speaker abides by the system, and instead most choose to speak differently or speak differently because of their social background or because of the social and communicative setting they are in.

You need to view the way phonemes are produced by individuals as variants and compare them with the canonised description or the pronunciation of other speakers. For instance, you may say that a certain speaker's /t/s are relatively strongly aspirated in a certain word compared to the same word as pronounced by another person or the model. Or you would like to state that a certain speaker pronounces a certain vowel in a very open way compared to another speaker or compared to the norm. To be able to make those statements, you first need to determine the quality of vowels and consonants in a reliable way. The reliability of the descriptions of sounds leans on three important principles, namely number of tokens, degree of narrowness of the phonetic context, and the measuring technique. These three are described next.

1. Number of tokens

The reliability of vowel and consonant descriptions goes up with the number of tokens measured. If you want to find out what a certain phoneme by a certain speaker typically sounds like, then picking one token is not very reliable, as the same person might pronounce that phoneme differently at another time. Five or ten tokens is generally considered to be enough to draw conclusions as to what a certain phoneme by a certain speaker typically sounds like. Ten is better than five, of course. In a read text, with the speaker paying much attention to pronunciation, five may be enough, but in spontaneous speech you may not want to rely on such a low number. It may be that three or eight is your maximum because there are no more tokens available, and that's fine, providing you state the reason for the deviant number of tokens used. Five or ten could be considered the target number, and in your methodology you can write down that in certain cases this target was not met because there were not enough tokens or not enough of the right quality.

2. Phonetic context

If you are studying a certain pronunciation phenomenon, like vowel diphthongisation, vowel length, consonant devoicing, consonant deletion, or perhaps vowel reduction, then this is usually that phoneme within a certain phonetic context. This context may be very strict (for instance, 'followed by /p/ or /t/ in syllables receiving sentence stress') or more lenient (for instance, 'followed by a voiceless consonant').

If you want to determine whether a certain phoneme in a certain speaker's speech is typically pronounced in a certain way, then you need to find a context that is stable for all the investigated tokens of this vowel that this person produces. Another requirement is that you pick a phonetic context that does not affect the natural quality of the phoneme too much. For instance, a voiced sound next to a voiceless sound may suffer from devoicing (i.e., a loss of voice), not because the speaker tends to devoice sounds that are basically voiced but because of the voiceless nature of that neighbouring sound. Furthermore, a voiced consonant between two vowels (which are almost always voiced) will be more strongly voiced than the same consonant followed by a silence. The same principle is true for vowels. A vowel before a liquid in the same syllable is likely to diphthongise less than the same vowel in an open syllable, because that's the effect that liquids tend to have on preceding vowels. You therefore need to make sure that the sounds (or the silence) surrounding the vowel you want to investigate is not the reason for variation in the tokens.

There are a few rules that will help you with this. For vowels, a rule (Van Nierop et al. 1973; Adank 2003) is that they can be mutually compared if they are preceded by /h/ and followed by /t/. This very specific context is not likely to recur frequently in spontaneous speech, so you may need to be more lenient and accept other contexts. A more lenient context for vowels is when they occur in closed syllables and are followed by an obstruent. Be warned that vowels before liquids often tend to change shape quite seriously, and to a lesser degree this is also true for vowels before nasals, especially in closed syllables. Make sure that you compare vowels that receive a similar degree of stress (main word stress, preferably), and if possible do not compare vowels in open and closed syllables.

For consonants, place in the syllable is an important feature to keep stable as well as the quality of adjacent sounds. An important thing to bear in mind with consonants is that they are sensitive to the place and manner of articulation as well as the voice of surrounding sounds. If you are testing for speakers' tendencies to produce certain consonants in a certain way, then in choosing the tokens to study you need to make sure that the surrounding sounds are not the cause of the tendency for the speaker to pronounce the consonant in that particular way.

Selecting tokens is quite a challenge, because you are usually dealing with various degrees of sound quality, the many considerations described above, and you are depending on the availability of tokens in the actual speech you are studying. The following steps might help.

1. First, write down 20 words in which a sound occurs that has a pronunciation that you'd like to study. Presumably, you have observed variation in pronunciation, with some people pronouncing a phoneme one way and others in another way. Now, write down 20 words (in the speech of one or more speakers or just imagined words) that demonstrate the phenomenon (tendency of certain speakers pronouncing something a certain way) you'd like to study. Do not think about phonetic context yet.

2. Categorise each of the 20 occurrences of the phoneme on the basis of the type of context they occur in: for example, 'in an open syllable' or 'before a voiced obstruent'. It may also be more narrow: 'before /l/ in a closed syllable receiving word stress'.

3. If a certain context occurs very often in speakers' speech, while it is a good context according to the rules described previously, then select that context as the only context under investigation. The more narrowly defined the context, the better.

4. If the context is very broadly defined, then you need to narrow it as much as possible. If in the group of 20 random tokens there are several recurring more specific contexts, then select the best one and the second-best one. Take the best one as the preferred choice and only choose tokens of the second-best context if you cannot find tokens that are in the preferred context.

3. Measuring technique

Articulatory Phonetics largely relies on the perception abilities of humans to come to a description of sounds. The field also uses the physical properties of sounds to come to measurements with acoustic software as an extra aid towards a description. These aural and acoustic approaches to sound description are described here.

(a) Phonemes can be transcribed in several ways. The least preferred way is for you to listen by yourself and describe the place and manner of the phoneme tokens you are investigating. A more reliable method is to have someone else help you.

(b) One way to work together is for both of you to listen to a number of tokens together and discuss what the characteristics of the tokens are. After some practice rounds, you could do the remaining tokens yourself.

(c) In addition to this so-called 'semi-consensus transcription', you could also transcribe all the tokens together, through a 'consensus transcription', which makes the transcription more reliable.

(d) Another method is to transcribe all the tokens separately, compare notes, and then reconsider the ones that you disagree on.

(e) You could, finally, also decide to transcribe independently and then calculate statistically whether the two transcriptions are mutually similar enough (you need to calculate a so-called 'Cronbach's Alpha' for that; see the companion website at www.macmillanihe.com/companion/smakman). This is the most acceptable method.

In addition to transcribing by ear, there is a more technical method of determining the qualities of phonemes, namely acoustic description. The programme *Praat* is used for acoustic descriptions by researchers from all over the world. It can be downloaded for free through www.fon.hum.uva.nl/praat/. *Praat* (which means 'talk' in Dutch) can provide all kinds of information about vowels and consonants relatively objectively. The workings of *Praat* are explained in detail on the *Praat* web page, and on that page beginner's manuals are also available. Finding a tutorial on the Internet on how to measure something in *Praat* step by step is also very efficient.

For consonants, the main usage of *Praat* is to determine whether voice is used during their production. Aspiration can also be seen in the visualisations the programme generates. Duration, rhoticity, and nasalisation of consonants may also be detected through *Praat*. This programme is, however, used most often to measure vowels. The likely frontness and backness of vowel realisations can be measured, as it has been determined that these correlate strongly with two values of vowels (the so-called first formant and second formant, also called 'F1' and 'F2') that *Praat* is able to generate. *Praat* can generate a value for F1 and F2 and these can be plotted in a two-dimensional diagram and roughly show the degree to which vowels can be considered front or back and open or closed. This is under the common premise of a high F1 denoting a high degree of openness and a high F2 denoting a high degree of frontness. The programme can also measure vowel length and diphthongisation. Intonation patterns can also be generated, but these are often difficult to read, categorise, and mutually compare.

16.4 Conclusion

This chapter has provided some basic phonetic background. This information will help you analyse the speech sounds that you hear around you every day. From the sounds that you hear around you or that come to you through certain media, you need to create categories on the basis of clear criteria, and these can systematically be correlated with social and situational factors. In addition to helping you to get started on an investigation in which pronunciation is the main linguistic variable, the information in this chapter is also necessary to be able to read some important publications on Sociolinguistics, as these often mention pronunciation.

Bear in mind that pronunciation is more than simply a set of speaker choices regarding individual sounds or intonation patterns. Each sound is part of a larger system of pronunciation variation within the speech of individuals, and while individual sounds can have a certain symbolic effect it is in the end the system as a whole that has such an effect. Bourdieu (1991) emphasised that while individual sounds are often studied in isolation, and subsequently compared with equivalents in other people's speech, they are a mere part of a larger pronunciation style in which all individual articulation features (phonemes but also intonation and other aspects) should be studied as an 'indivisible totality' (86).

FURTHER READING

Hardcastle et al. (2013) contains an extensive description of basic and advanced Phonetics. The introduction into Phonetics by Ladefoged (2003) offers many useful suggestions for collecting and analysing your own data. The volume by Di Paolo and Yaeger-Dror (2010) discusses Phonetics from a sociolinguistic perspective and can be used as a manual to collect and process data.

PART 4
DOING SOCIOLINGUISTICS

Now that you know the history and theory of Sociolinguistics and the practical ramifications of doing actual research, you are ready to decide on a methodology. The final four chapters of this book contain 20 different methodologies for you to choose from. Methodologies are given to investigate language that is already available (Chapter 17), language that needs to be elicited (Chapter 18), naturally occurring communication (Chapter 19), and, finally, language attitudes (Chapter 20). Use Chapter 13 to determine which methodology fits your personal research interests most. The idea behind each methodology in the chapters here is described as well as its practical workings. For each methodology, a ready-made suggested investigation is given that you can start on straight away.

Language out There

Investigating Available Language

17.1 Introduction

The most ideal language to investigate is the one that appears in conversations instigated by speakers themselves. Without external mediation or stimulation, this language is based on speakers choosing to speak at a certain time, in a certain way, about a certain topic, and for a certain length of time. This is true for written language as well, which is most natural if writers make their own choices on the language they put on paper. Ideally, the researcher walks around with a microphone, camera, and notepad and registers people in their most uninhibited moments of social interaction, without these speakers and writers knowing that they are being observed. The outcome would be the language of negotiation and apology as well as the language of feelings like joy, anger, and grief. It would include the language used in diaries and even the language used in the bedroom. The ethical and practical issues involved need little clarification. You cannot slip into funeral services and bedrooms or open people's diaries and personal letters. Stalking with a microphone is also frowned upon. You may therefore need to look for language of the type described here that is already available.

The current chapter looks at sources containing language that is already available and that to various degrees meets the requirements of spontaneity. The following methodologies will be explained: Corpus Analysis, Linguistic Geography, Time Study, Historical Sociolinguistics, and Linguistic Landscape research.

17.2 Corpus Analysis

17.2.1 The idea behind it

A language corpus is a systematically collected, naturally occurring set of texts. The language it contains may originally have been written but it may also consist of transcribed spoken language. An important goal of corpus research is gaining insight into the absolute and relative frequency of certain language items. The larger the corpus (more speakers, more words, etc.), the better. The more you know about those producing the language, the better.

Corpus Analysis is a precise and arduous task in which statistical analysis tends to play a role. The outcome can be highly reliable. Biber et al. (1998) summarised the main features of corpus research: it analyses the actual patterns in natural texts, uses many texts, makes use of computer programmes for the analysis (search engines), and it relies on both quantitative and qualitative research techniques. The latter comment in particular is relevant, because while corpora may offer text and social group descriptions that are measurable the findings must nevertheless still be interpreted. Knowing that a certain social group uses a certain item quite often is in itself not a finished research product.

17.2.2 How it works

Friginal and Hardy (2014) gave tips on the practical side of collecting and analysing a corpus for sociolinguistic study. Most of all, the researcher needs to find a corpus the language use patterns in which could logically answer their research questions. To find out whether men and women have different written styles, letters (by female and male authors) to the editor in newspaper archives may be used, for instance. If you want to know about politeness words, then a corpus in which speakers are debating and negotiating is useful. Furthermore, the corpus you use needs to be representative of the population whose language you would like to make generalisations about (letters to the editor might generally be by highly educated people, so generalisations can only be made for such a subgroup of people). Some corpora are available online while universities also provide access to all kinds of corpora. Making your own corpus is another possibility, but this is very time-consuming.

FOCUS ON...

Corpora

For the Russian language, there is the National Russian Corpus (NRS), which contains a spoken corpus with recordings of public and spontaneous spoken Russian and the transcripts of Russian movies. Sociological parameters are available for creating sub-corpora. There is a dialectal sub-corpus in this corpus. In the Netherlands, there is the *Corpus Gesproken Nederlands* (CGN) ('Corpus of Spoken Dutch'), which contains many hours of informal chatting by Dutchmen. For Colloquial Singaporese English, there is the Grammar of Spoken Singapore English Corpus (GSSEC) and for Scottish Gaelic there is the Digital Archive of Scottish Gaelic (DASG). Information on such corpora is usually available online; for instance, www.ruscorpora.ru/en/search-spoken.html for NRS, http://lands.let.ru.nl/cgn/ for CGN, and www.dasg.ac.uk/en for DASG. Some of these sites give direct access. If this online access is not there, then access needs to be requested.

17.2.3 The data

Once the corpus has been found/created, it needs to be analysed; the researcher needs to find ways to count numbers of words and grammatical constructions. Computer programmes are available for this, as suggested by Friginal and Hardy (2014). In addition to counting occurrences, alternatives to these occurrences need to be found in some cases. If, for instance, the use of a conservative word is the research topic, then modern versions of this language item need to be found so as to reveal the relative usage of the conservative and modern forms.

If the corpus is large, then statistical correlation between social factors and linguistic ones is possible, and in the interpretation thereof the researcher can make relatively strong generalisations. The data are typically group data and give little information about individual language choices.

17.2.4 Sample investigation: The language of male and female journalists

Motivation

Journalists are often at the forefront of language change. While they tend to use the norm language, they are also known to play with language, coin words, and use interesting metaphors – all in a very free and creative way. Their language is read by large groups of people and inevitably serves as inspiration for readers. Oftentimes, the use of modern language forms rather than more conservative ones is associated with one of the genders more than with the other, and this may show in the language of female and male journalists. The Corpus Analysis investigation described here aims to reveal whether one of the genders uses certain modern language forms more than the other gender does.

Research steps

a. Select 10 common words or phrases that are considered very modern and that at the same time have one dominant conservative equivalent. So, if you asked people what the conservative equivalent is of each of the modern words or phrases that you selected, then most people would give the same word. The use of certain foreign loanwords might be a good suggestion as might words that are derived from popular youth culture. They need to be words that journalists use in articles.

b. Find a corpus of newspaper articles. A good corpus might be all editions of a certain newspaper from last year or perhaps all Saturday editions of that year. Make sure that the newspaper employs many male and female journalists (not predominantly men). It is also advisable to opt for a newspaper that is not overly conservative.

c. Do a search for the set of 10 modern words/phrases and their conservative equivalents.

Data treatment

Each token your corpus search yields can be entered into SPSS and labelled as 'conservative' or 'modern' and on the basis of the gender of the user of the token. You can run Frequencies to get an overview of the overall preference for modern and conservative forms by men and women. These can be transformed into percentages for the men and the women. These data can be presented in a table or bar chart (women and men compared). A Chi-square Test will tell you whether any difference between the preferences of men and women towards modern forms is significant. The various uses of the modern and conservative equivalents in context by women and men can also be studied, and this can be done by selecting a number of tokens of each and describing their contexts (like topic and type of article) in detail.

Theoretical angles

The main theoretical angle is gender. Your results can add to the existing body of research on whether women or men are more likely to tend towards modern, progressive language (see 11.4.4 and 11.4.5). Try and find out if the more progressive forms have a different meaning or different connotations and connect this with theory on stereotypically male and female behaviour.

17.3 Linguistic Geography

17.3.1 The idea behind it

The principles behind Linguistic Geography are described in Section 3.3.3. An important motivation is describing characteristics of language varieties; usually small ones, especially those that run the risk of disappearing or becoming like surrounding languages due to language contact. Another interest of this methodology is determining the dividing lines between neighbouring dialects.

17.3.2 How it works

This method involves finding speakers from a certain area who meet the characteristics of dialect speakers. If people themselves claim to be dialect speakers, then that is a reasonably reliable indication, and finding people who according to friends, neighbours, and family are true speakers of a dialect is another approach. On the basis of a selection of linguistic variables, the language of these speakers is described. Geographical patterns in the use of certain sounds or words (or perhaps constructions, phrases, or sayings) are mapped to see if speakers in certain areas show similar patterns and can on the basis of such agreement be classified as speaking the same dialect. In addition to finding dividing lines between dialects, linguistic distance can be established; if two neighbouring dialects are different in many ways or if the pronunciation of a sound is radically different although it is geographically close, then this implies a large linguistic distance in a small geographical space.

FOCUS ON...

Dialect border criteria

Borders between dialects are not necessarily purely linguistic or influenced by geographical features. Other factors that form dialect borders are the perception of dialects by people living in a certain area, economic and political differences, religion, culture, and ethnicity of speakers (Watt and Llamas 2014).

17.3.3 The data

All kinds of ways to visualise the data can be applied. Indicating on a map in which places which variants were produced most will instantly give a good visualisation of the nature of differences amongst dialects. As for linguistic distance, one could draw lines between linguistic items that are linguistically different and make the lines between linguistically very different items thicker than those between items that are linguistically close. This is what Nerbonne and Heeringa (1997) did, and their map with thick and less thick lines shows clear dialect differences on the basis of linguistic grounds.

17.3.4 Sample investigation: Perceived dialect proximity

Motivation

Geographical and linguistic distance do not always coincide. Linguistic variants that are considerably different might exist geographically close to each other, while variants that are linguistically close might be geographically very far apart. The study here gives you more insight into this phenomenon. Expert knowledge (dialectologists), knowledge that stereotypical speakers of the variety in question have, and information in dialect dictionaries are all helpful for this investigation.

Research steps

a. Within a region, select three dialects (dialect 'a', 'b', and 'c') that do not border on each other but do have a high degree of mutual intelligibility. They should be at more or less the same geographical distance from each other.

b. Choose 5 items for which there is more than one word in the region, or a strongly different pronunciation, and that are probably different in at least two of the three dialects. Usually, words related to traditional skills and trades are suitable for this, like farming tools and household objects, but also trees, fruit, meals, or perhaps types of weather.

c. For each word – for instance, a certain animal – establish the variants that occur in each of the three places. So, if the animal in question is referred to in more or less the same way in two of the dialects (or has more or less the same base but is only pronounced slightly differently) but quite different in the third dialect (a completely new word), then there are two variants. A strongly deviant pronunciation of a word with the same base could also be categorised as a different variant. There could also be three or more variants, of course. Make sure to write down carefully which criteria you used to determine whether variants were 'the same' (or 'similar') or 'different'.

Data treatment

In coding the variants, one of the areas can for practical reasons function as the benchmark from which other variants deviate, and the occurrences of the most frequent variant in that area can thus be coded '1'. The deviant variant can be coded '2', and if there is a third variant then that can be coded '3', etc. On a self-designed map with the three dialect areas on it, indicate which five variants occurred most frequently in which area by putting such codes of variants in each area. So, if in area 'b' the most common variant was '3', then put that number on the map in that area. Do this for all variables.

The map itself can be presented. In a table or other overview, you can indicate the number of dominant variants that dialect area 'a' and 'b' share, the number of dominant variants that area 'b' and 'c' share, and the number of dominant variants that areas 'a' and 'c' share. The two dialects that share the most features are linguistically closest to each other when it comes to these five variables. Statistics is not useful because the agreement between the number of shared dialect words between the various areas speaks for itself. A deeper analysis and description of the various connotations and meanings of the variants in the areas breathes more life into the data. Maybe the sources and people you consulted gave you some interesting information hereon. These can be described in a convincing text with examples.

Theoretical angles

These results give us insight into the workings of the dialect continuum as well as into the difference between geographical and linguistic distance. They can also be used as the basis of drawing isoglosses between dialects (see 3.3.3), which can be compared to the isoglosses on older dialect maps. That way, possible changes in these borders over time can be established. These data contribute to discussions on dialect levelling (see 6.3.4), which refers to dialects starting to sound mutually alike more as a result of speakers adjusting to those who speak slightly differently. Dialects may also be becoming more mutually different, which may be based in identity needs of speakers.

17.4   Time Study

17.4.1   The idea behind it

Sociolinguists try to complement existing historical/theoretical descriptions of language change with language use data over the past few generations of speakers. They investigate how subsequent generations of similar individuals will use language differently, and they generate information on how social factors are important in explaining differences between the ways people talk now and in the past.

17.4.2 How it works

There are basically two ways to describe contemporary change, namely through a so-called real-time or an apparent-time approach (see 10.5.2). Real-time research is based on a comparison of contemporary and historical data, while apparent-time research is based on a comparison of speech from older and younger speakers in the present.

Real-time

Real-time research usually comes down to describing the language of similar groups of individuals at various points in time, with fixed intervals of 10, 20, or more years between the periods studied. Real-time descriptions can be based on, for instance, recordings that are available of radio and television programmes from today and the past. The investigation by the Belgian researcher Van de Velde (1996) is a good example of this approach. He described a set of pronunciation characteristics of newsreaders in the Dutch-language area (the Netherlands and Flanders). These newsreaders obviously had the same profession, they were all men, and probably spoke in accordance with the language norm. Because of this mutual sameness in all kinds of ways, the changes between the speakers from the various periods studied (1935–1993, with 15-year intervals) were deemed to reflect contemporary language use change.

Typically, real-time research takes much time and effort. The researcher needs to systematically collect specific linguistic data from archives, which is highly time-consuming, and the researcher needs to make sure that the various recordings or transcriptions actually reflect similar types of speakers in similar circumstances.

EXAMPLE

Panel study

An example of a real-time study is a panel study, which comes down to interviewing people and re-interviewing them later. An exceptional example of this type of study is the investigation by Sankoff (2004), who studied the language in the British television series called 'The Up Series', in which children from various social layers in British society were interviewed at the age of seven and every seven years after that. The programme started in 1964. These interviews are still taking place because many speakers are still both alive and willing to participate every seven years.

Apparent-time

Apparent-time research is based on the assumption that the way older people speak today resembles the way they spoke when they were young. A 60-year-old speaker represents an older speech norm while a 20-year-old speaker represent a modern speech norm, for instance. The idea is that the speech of the speakers whose speech you want to describe is available or is recorded by you. An apparent-time description is usually easier than a real-time description but may also be less reliable because it is based on the tentative assumption that individuals do not change their speech dramatically during their lifetime (see 10.2.1). This type of research should focus on certain aspects of language that are known to be persistent in individuals, like word usage and grammar, rather than subtle pronunciation variation. Those robust language features will have been acquired in the speaker's youth and stood the test of time and resisted all kinds of influences.

17.4.3 The data

The data for studies into language change over three or so generations of speakers are usually systematic descriptions of occurrences of specific language items, like the change of a certain set of phonemes over time or certain words whose frequency or meaning seems to be changing. A set number of variants of a language variable per speaker is studied, and this way comparisons between speakers from different time periods (or representing such periods) are enabled.

17.4.4 Sample investigation: Pronunciation norm change

Motivation

Determining language norms can be done by investigating the language of people who are considered to speak the norm language. To gain insight into the nature and rate of change in a language norm, recordings of such authoritative speakers could be used from various points in time. Below, a Time Study (real-time) is layed out that requires you to collect speech recordings from various points in time and describe a specific language variable.

Research steps

a. Define a prototypical speaker who is linguistically authoritative and of whom recordings are probably available from several periods of time (see item c below). Choose either males or females. These speakers could be female television presenters, for instance, or male politicians.

b. After selecting the speaker type, find out how many speakers are available that meet the criteria and how much speech is available in the various time periods you wish to study for the type of speaker you've defined. Make sure the available speech for the various speakers is produced under similar circumstances; for instance, during an interview or during a live news broadcast.

c. Make an overview with five available speakers from today, five from 30 years ago, and five from 60 years ago. For each of these periods, you need to have several minutes of speech per speaker. The speaker selection could be done randomly from the available group.

d. Select a pronunciation variable for investigation. This could be a specific word, syllable, sound, or sound cluster whose pronunciation you think may have changed over time. It needs to be a pronunciation variable that is highly frequent.

e. Define the variants of the variable, that is, the possible ways to pronounce it. So, the variable could be 'pronunciation of /r/ at the end of a syllable', and the variants could be 'clearly pronounced', 'weakly pronounced', and 'not pronounced'. Place and manner of articulation could also be taken into consideration. It is possible that the number of variants per period will be different.

f. For each speaker, find ten occurrences of the variable studied, preferably all in a similar phonetic context (see 16.3.2). Because it is a frequent language item, you can select clearly pronounced tokens. If all are pronounced clearly, then choose the first ten that you encounter.

g. For each occurrence of the variable, determine which of the variants is produced.

Data treatment

Statistical treatment is not advisable, as the number of variants per period will be different (there might be four ways to realise the variable in one period and only two in another period). You can rely on the tendencies that a line diagram will show. This diagram could contain frequencies of the various variants (vertical dimension in the chart) of the variable at the various points in time (horizontal dimension). The variants across the speaker group in each time period can be added up. A table or (clustered) bar chart is also convenient for these data.

Theoretical angles

Because you've selected speakers who are supposed to speak 'good' language, language ideology (see 9.4.1) is your broader theoretical angle. The rate, nature, and breadth of variation and the change in the norm is the more specific angle. Do those who speak 'good' language speak the same language nowadays as similar speakers did in the past? Does that language change within one or two generations of speakers or is it more conservative?

17.5   Historical Sociolinguistics

17.5.1 The idea behind it

Historical Sociolinguistics describes the relationship between language and society from a historical perspective. It tends to go further back in time than Time Studies (see 17.4). It tries to answer questions like 'When did people start using a certain grammatical construction?', 'Which words did the various status groups in societies use in the past?' or 'How and due to which social circumstances has a certain language item changed meaning over the ages?' It can, amongst others, reveal which discussions of 'good' and 'bad' language are recent and which ones have been going on for a while. As the name suggests, this type of research is interested in language as it was used in the past, although inevitably comparisons with contemporary language use are made. Research can go back as far as the Middle Ages, depending on the availability of sources.

17.5.2 How it works

Historical Sociolinguistics relies mostly on whatever unsystematic language data or observations are available in online or other corpora. The language typically researched comes from letters (to newspaper editors or between individuals), disclosed diaries, wills, newspaper articles, and, for instance, literature. These sources also contain interesting comments about language. More systematic data come from dictionaries, grammar books, and usage guides, which list all kinds of language rules in societies very explicitly.

When researchers are interested in studying actual language use (in letters, etc.), then they need to make an overview of occurrences of language items and who delivered them, and find out as much as possible about the socio-historical circumstances in which each item was produced. As much information as possible about the speakers needs to be found, most notably any facts or suggestions regarding their personalia (age, gender, social status, profession, regional/language background, etc.). Furthermore, the most probable date or period when the language was produced is important and the place where it was produced. Any details on specific circumstances under which language items occurred could be relevant. Depending on the research question, researchers may need to look for linguistic alternatives. To determine whether a certain word choice is made relatively often, they need to determine how often the alternative to the word is used. The same person could produce a very modern word on one occasion but an old-fashioned synonym on other occasions.

If the descriptions in dictionaries, grammar books, and usage guides are the object of study, then a straightforward description of what these sources say can be applied. Descriptions of language rules across the decades are then given. These may reveal a changing language norm. Comments about language, both by important and less important people, may also give such information on past norms.

FOCUS ON...

Literature

Literature does not necessarily need to be written down to be used as data. Oral literature is common in many societies across the world, like in native American societies, where storytelling is common (Eller 2016). Research into oral literature of the past requires you to interview those that have a good memory of it.

17.5.3 The data

In the sources with actual language use, the researcher needs to scan for the specific language features that they are after: examples of politeness, examples of double negatives, examples of the use of synonyms of a certain word, the use of a certain grammatical construction, expressions of attitudes towards speaking in a certain way, uses of foreign words, and, for instance, different ways to address different interlocutors. After collecting the data, the researcher has a list of occurrences of language items, when they occurred, under which circumstances, and the characteristics of speakers.

Their data may also be selected words or grammatical descriptions in older and newer versions of dictionaries, grammar books, and usage guides. These data can be analysed to reveal changes over time, and they could possibly be put in tables. Comments about language can be summarised in a convincing piece of text on language attitudes over the years in which examples of such comments are given.

17.5.4 Sample investigation: Changing language norms

Motivation

Ideas as to what is correct or not vary across time. Some things that were in the past considered incorrect are today considered acceptable and vice versa. Two ways of saying something may exist side by side for short or long periods of time. The Historical Sociolinguistics investigation described below will lay bare changes in norms across time. This proposed investigation applies a quantitative approach to address a historical topic.

Research steps

a. Determine five grammatical or other constructions that are often used, on television and in newspapers, and that have two realisations; a modern one and a conservative one. Some people tend to use one version, while others tend to use the other.

b. You will be comparing two time periods: today and 150 years ago. Get access to 150-year-old editions of a newspaper that is still published nowadays. Libraries, online and regular ones, are usually the bearers of the archives of newspapers, and newspapers themselves often publish back copies in historical archives that they themselves maintain. Some newspapers have archives dating back well more than 150 years, so you may decide to go back further in time. Or you may need to choose a shorter period, like 50 or 100 years.

c. Choose a month; all the editions in this month will be your data base. This selection should yield more or less the same number of editions, but if not, then delete a few editions from the month with more editions, so that the number of editions per month (for instance, March 2017 and March 1867) is the same. If older editions contain much fewer words, then you can decide to only look at the first few articles of the newer editions. More such practical considerations to make the data from the same month in two years that are studied comparable may be necessary. Make sure to mention your considerations and selection methods in your methodology.

d. For all (close to 50) newspaper editions (2 years, about 4 weeks, 6 editions per week), count the number of times the modern and conservative variant of all five variables is used.

e. Collect as much information as possible on the total number of words in each newspaper.

Data treatment

A simple visualisation of the data in a table is most convenient. You can show the degree to which each of the variants was used (both in absolute numbers and in percentages of total numbers of occurrences, and even relative to the total number of words in editions) for each of the five grammatical variables in each of the two months studied. The data (with or without statistics) give a general impression of the shifting of norms. If you wanted to do statistics, then a T-test for independent groups would be the correct test to compare the two months.

Theoretical angles

The nature of variation and the rate of change in language norms is a useful theoretical backdrop of this investigation. The assumption is that the journalists using the language in question considered what they wrote is correct and acceptable. Any changes between the two months under investigation represent a likely change in a language norm. You will be able to show how a norm can go from narrow to less narrow or vice versa. All kinds of other findings, like changes in the meanings and usages of words, may typically present themselves, and these can be included in the report. Finally, you could discuss how and why certain constructions are subject to variation and to continuous debate while others are not.

17.6 Researching Linguistic Landscapes

17.6.1 The idea behind it

Linguistic Landscape refers to language use in the public space. Commercial and official signs are the main topic of investigation: the language that you encounter on shop signs, public road signs, billboards, shop windows, price tags, public government communication, public notices, etc. Labels and graffiti can also be studied as well as mobile signs like protest signs, pamphlets, flyers, stamps, tickets, bills, banknotes, restaurant menus, and even t-shirts, according to Kasanga (2014). Basically, any language that you encounter when you walk out into the streets or into a government building is part of the linguistic landscape (Androutsopoulos 2014).

Linguistics Landscapes are usually studied in the theoretical framework of Semiotics and researchers look at syntax, semantics, and pragmatics, mainly. Language choice is another important focus (which language(s) is/are used). Research interests also go out to the material, visual, and spatial properties of the object containing the language – how it is designed and placed relative to other objects with language. Various signs interact with each other, so to speak, and affect each other's meaning and general effect.

Researchers often get in touch with those who design and those who encounter the signs. Understanding both the interpretation of publically visible language and the motivation of those who produce it helps to deepen the understanding of the signs and notices. Malinowski (2009) found a degree of unawareness amongst shopkeepers of the nature and effect of their signs. Indeed, the researcher may have to ask object designers to think hard about their motivations to choose a certain language on a sign or to use a certain design.

FOCUS ON...

Minority language in public signs

Public signs are not necessarily in a national language only. The use of written Sámi in public signs only started a few decades ago in the bilingual municipality of Enontekiö (northern Finland). A similar situation exists in the central Russian city of Khanty-Mansiysk, where written representations of the Ob-Ugric language have only been (a small) part of urban public space for a short period. These language choices often reflect the position of a culture and a language in a society.

17.6.2 How it works

Garvin (2010) suggested a number of steps in the data collection for Linguistic Landscape research. The first two steps are the selection of the research site(s) and taking photographs of the signs under investigation. At this stage, codes need to be given to the signs. Examples of coding criteria are: number of languages in a sign, type of sign (advertisement, warning, etc.), branch (commercial, government, etc.), relation between what is said in the two languages on a sign, the dominance of each language in the sign (if more than one language is used), and domain (work-related, education-related, etc.) where the sign was positioned.

Then, the ethnographic part can start by selecting and contacting participants (shop owners, customers) and doing individual interviews (perhaps while walking along with random people in the streets or acting as a customer). Thirdly, the field notes need to be transcribed and analysed. Finally, follow-up meetings with participants could take place, to obtain a deeper understanding motivations and experiences. They could be shown the photographs you took and answer general interview-like questions and/or fill in Likert scales (see 15.4.2) for each of the signs that you want their perception or evaluation of.

FOCUS ON...

Font size

Font size may be motivated by symbolic reasons but it may also be practical. Some Asian writing symbols display no individual letters but whole syllables and therefore take up less space than the Latin alphabet. This may be a (purely practical) reason to give a bigger size to the often complicated symbols.

17.6.3 The data

The data are both qualitative and quantitative. The qualitative data are the interview data (how did passers-by or customers perceive a certain sign and what were the motivations of designers) and any relevant anecdotes and details that you wrote down. The quantitative data consist of possible Likert scales the interviewees filled in and perhaps the codes given to the various signs. The mutual relationship of signs can be described qualitatively and even anecdotally.

17.6.4 Sample investigation: Signs in a bilingual community

Motivation

In areas where two languages exist side by side in the public space, the makers of signs, labels, and other means to show information are faced with the choice to use both or one of the languages. This choice may be based on all kinds of motivations. It may be below the level of consciousness and affected by the maker's command of the languages. There may also be conscious motivations behind this language choice; the maker of the information may be expressing something, may be trying to achieve a certain effect, or perhaps they are trying to reach a certain group of readers. For the investigation described below, you will go out and search for publically displayed information and find out what the motivation is of the maker of the information display and how this matches with the effect on the people seeing the information. Language choice in particular is a focus.

Research steps

a. Start walking around in a street where two languages are used regularly in public displays of information. Choose one type of display, like shop signs. Take a photograph of the first 20 instances of the selected public display in which only one language is used exclusively. Do this for both languages, so that in the end you have 40 photographs. Do the same for the first 20 displays in which both languages are used.

b. Make an overview of the nature of each of the displays: its size, type of information, and any other feature that is relevant.

c. For each of the three groups of signs (two monolingual groups, one multilingual group), select a photograph, making sure that the three photographs are as similar as possible (size, font, function, type of information, type of shop).

d. Find the maker(s) of each of the three selected signs; the person(s) who decided on the language use. If you cannot find them, then select another picture and try and find the maker(s) of that sign.

e. Interview the makers on the reasons for the language choices in the signs, including font type, size and other characteristics that have an effect on the presentation of information and that may possibly have a symbolic function. Show them a selection of pictures from each of the three groups, or show all of them, and ask them why they think the language choice is the way it is. Ask them if they see a tendency and ask them to elaborate on motivations of sign makers. Ask them if there was a symbolic reason for the language choice in their own sign.

f. Go to the place where the three selected signs are and interview five passers-by or customers on their evaluation of the sign in question. Ask them about how the sign comes across: the practical and symbolic function of the information, mostly. At the beginning of the interview, do not state what your research is about. In the last part of the interview, ask the participants explicitly what they think of the language choice.

Data treatment

Describe the three selected signs in detail and give more general physical descriptions of the signs in each group of signs. For each of the three signs, make notes on what the sign maker and the sign viewers said. In a table or overview, write down which arguments, criteria, or comments were repeatedly given by the senders and receivers. Then, write a convincing text on all of your findings. In your analyses, focus as much as you can on language choice.

Theoretical angles

A broad semiotic approach is advisable (see 6.2), in which various aspects mentioned above are used to describe language-choice situations. Your findings are interesting in themselves as they reveal successful and less successful communication. There is an intended message and an interpretation. These can be compared, along with the characteristics of the factors used by the sender and receiver of language. Culture is an inevitable aspect of an investigation into language choice. The results can be compared with existing research that focuses on matches and mismatches between sender and receiver and the role of culture and language choice in these matches and mismatches.

Speak to Me

18

Investigating Elicited Language

18.1 Introduction

The drawbacks of language that is already available, as described in Chapter 17, is that you have no control over which language items occur in it, like which grammatical constructions, words, intonation patterns, or speech sounds. You also cannot control the degree of formality of the language produced. Sometimes, you want to know something linguistically specific rather than find out what naturally comes out if people open their mouths. In that case, you need to prompt people to produce language in such a way that the linguistic variables that you wish to study will certainly or probably be available in the language data.

This chapter describes how to urge people to speak and how to subsequently organise and study the ensuing language. A selection of elicitation techniques is presented whereby speakers are to varying degrees aware of being recorded. The following techniques are described: Intergenerational Proficiency Description, the Sociolinguistic Interview, Conversation Analysis, Discourse Analysis, and Rapid Anonymous Survey.

18.2 Intergenerational Proficiency Description

18.2.1 The idea behind it

Minority languages are relevant objects of study because of their authenticity and cultural importance. The same goes for all kinds of other smaller languages, like dialects in countries with a dominant norm language. Sadly, many of these languages are viewed in a context of decay. From generation to generation, many minority languages are spoken less well and by fewer people, and many dialects are becoming less distinct and more like surrounding dialects and/or like a dominant norm language. This declining proficiency can be made visible through an Intergeneration Proficiency Description.

KEY CONCEPTS

Authentication

Language can be used as a tool to connect speakers with authenticity. In other words, it has the ability to authenticate or be used as an authenticating index (Bucholtz 2003). Minority languages and dialects in particular are often used in this way; as a symbolic tool to sound like someone who knows a certain subculture well or someone who really knows about life in a certain area as led by a recognisable and non-mainstream group of people.

18.2.2 How it works

This type of research has some ethnographic features, because the researcher may need to become part of the community under investigation to a degree. Typically, the researcher finds a contact who is part of the community, who speaks the local language well (preferably as a native speaker), who is willing to offer a great deal of help, and who has some knowledge of the formal aspects of the language studied. This informant introduces the researcher to other speakers. If no knowledgeable informant is available, then the researcher will need the help of experts or of a speaker with no specific formal knowledge of the language.

With the informant, certain language-inducing situations need to be designed – like language tests to gauge knowledge of formal language features and situations where only native speakers speak to each other and are recorded – as well as interviews with speakers about the language and its functions in the community. Speakers from several generations need to participate.

Many practicalities depend on whether the speakers studied speak or understand the language of the researcher and what the researcher understands and speaks. Translation of tasks may be necessary as well as translation of the language produced by participants. Another challenge is deciding who talks to whom, if free speech is collected; the native informant could talk to all but the researcher may want speakers to speak to those they are close to or who are their own age. The presence during interviews of the researcher is another issue. Usually, the social and practical limitations of the local situation are the main guideline for all these choices.

18.2.3 The data

The researcher collects data reflecting the proficiency of speakers of the language as well as their views; the results of the language tests by people of different ages, the spontaneous speech, and interview answers. The language test results can be placed in tables and graphs, with the various results of speakers of different ages put side by side to show whether the language has degenerated intergenerationally. It helps if a calculation system is designed to translate the success of each speaker in a score going from 1 to 10. The spontaneous speech is supportive material to test actual usage and can be described systematically (richness of lexicon and grammar and authenticity of pronunciation, most notably). The interview answers can be used to describe the social conditions in the community that cause the language to slowly disappear or develop a new position in the local or regional society or amongst certain groups. Collectively, these data show the rate and manner of decline and the reasons why the situation is taking place.

18.2.4 Sample investigation: Rate of intergenerational language shift

Motivation

The Intergenerational Proficiency Description described below aims to, first, gain insight into the rate of disappearance of a language/dialect. It then establishes the most important linguistic constructions that are subject to shift.

Research steps

a. Find a community in which the existence and vitality of a certain language (or dialect) is under more pressure with each new generation.

b. Find 35 people in the community with varying ages. Three main age groups should be represented: young, middle, old. You need to decide what the ages in the groups are. All participants must have lived in the community or very near it all their lives.

c. Have pairs of participants within each age group (e.g., 60 to 69 years old or 30 to 39 years old) chat about a topic that is not language-related. They can read out questions from a paper and interview each other. Record the chatting and make sure that not much attention is drawn to the recording device. Two recording devices is usually better than one, so that you know who's talking.

d. Find someone who is known in the community as a good speaker of the language studied and who is not participating as a speaker in your research. Let this person listen to a few minutes of the speech of each speaker and grade it on a scale from 1 (bad rendition of the language studied) to 5 (perfect example of the language studied). Let this person do this separately for pronunciation and other linguistic aspects.

e. Have this expert informant draw up a list of examples of language items for each of the participants: examples of good and less good language items.

f. Interview all participants and the selected informant about their ideas about the language shift: what is the nature of the shift, what are the motivations for it, and is there a role for the language in the future?

Data treatment

In a line diagram, in which individual or grouped speakers are on the horizontal axis and degree of command of the language studied (according to the expert informant) is on the vertical axis, you can create a clear overview of the likely age group that has accelerated the shift. In your report, use the language examples by the informant in your description of the linguistic nature of the shift across the various groups and individuals. Use the interviews to determine the social mechanisms behind the shift.

Theoretical angles

Language ideology (see 9.4.1), especially regarding a standard or dominant language, is an important angle, and so is identity (see 5.3.1). Language revitalisation (see 3.5.4) is another theme that could be at the centre of this investigation. The data fit into a language shift paradigm as described in 3.5.1 and 3.5.2.

18.3   The Sociolinguistic Interview

18.3.1 The idea behind it

The term 'Sociolinguistic Interview' refers to systematically eliciting speech in various social contexts, not to interviewing people about their opinions (this more general interpretation of 'interview' is described in Section 20.6). William Labov laid the foundations of the Sociolinguistic Interview in the early 1970s and improved the technique in the decades after that (Labov 1972a, 1984, 2001a).

The main goals behind this technique are to find patterns of stylistic variation (the same person speaking with different styles) and to elicit the interviewee's so-called vernacular, which refers to their most casual style. Labov (1972d) considered this vernacular to be the 'most regular in its structure' (112), making it a central object of interest to sociolinguists. The assumption is that speech that receives much monitoring by the speaker is closer to a broader norm in a society and is furthest removed from the vernacular.

An important aim in conducting the Sociolinguistic Interview is to control attention paid to speech and thus overcome the so-called Observer's Paradox (Labov 1972d), which states that in order to 'obtain the data most important for linguistic theory, we have to observe how people speak when they are not being observed' (113). When people know they are being observed, they often stop producing their most natural language, and instead they intuitively start speaking more 'neatly'.

18.3.2 How it works

The focus is usually on a specific linguistic item (for instance, a phoneme in a certain context). A requirement is that it is a very frequent item.

The Sociolinguistic Interview controls style by eliciting the type of language that goes from casual to formal. These styles require different degrees of attention paid to speech (different degrees of awareness). Four methods of eliciting speech are part of a full Sociolinguistic Interview:

1. In a regular interview (on a random topic, except language), casual speech is elicited, which is assumed to be close to the vernacular of the speaker, especially if the interviewer asks personal questions, like questions about childhood experiences.
2. After that comes the reading passage, which induces a less casual style.
3. Then the speaker reads out a word list, in which a slightly formal style will be used.
4. The most formal style is assumed to occur when the speaker under investigation reads a list of minimal pairs, which are pairs of words that differ in only one phoneme, like in 'seal'/'zeal' and 'gut'/ 'got'.

The number of participants in the Sociolinguistic Interview depends on the research aim. Studies could range in number of participants from a few dozen to well over a hundred per community studied (Wolfram and Fasold 1974). A full Sociolinguistic Interview is an arduous task and may take up to two hours. You could decide to adjust your research focus and only do two or three of the parts of a Sociolinguistic Interview or otherwise adjust the approach to meet your personal research requirements and time limitations.

18.3.3 The data

You will have the realisations (variants) of the variable(s) under investigation in various styles. In addition, you will have information about the speakers, which could be made part of the analysis although this aspect is not usually the central focus.

18.3.4 Sample investigation: Vernacular use and attention paid to speech

Motivation

A common assumption is that people speak their most natural language, their vernacular, when they are at their most relaxed. If they don't pay attention, then a more spontaneous language may come out, like someone's original local dialect. The Sociolinguistic Interview methodology described below is built on this assumption and tries to see if it is true. It is not a full version of a Sociolinguistic Interview.

Research steps

a. Select a place where both a broader norm language and a more local language are spoken amongst people.

b. Find a pronunciation variable that typically has a certain realisation (variant) in the local language and a different one in the norm language. This should be a highly common and frequent variable. Pay attention to phonetic/ phonological context (see 16.3.2).

c. Make a list of 20 words in which the variable in question occurs, and add some so-called distracter words. These distracter words are added to make the purpose of the investigation less obvious and to avoid certain repetitive reading styles and rhythms.

d. Find or write a text in which the variable occurs at least 20 times.

e. Construct questions for a regular interview in which the phenomenon does not occur in the questions but is likely to be part of the answers.

f. Find 10 speakers who were born and raised in the area and regularly speak the local language. Try to stick to a limited age range. Do not tell them what the research is about.

g. Ask each speaker to answer the questions in the interview. If feasible, make sure that the item under investigation is produced at least 20 times. Record the speakers.

h. After the interview, let them read the text and then the word lists, and record them while doing so.

i. Determine which types of pronunciation realisations (variants) the speakers produced for the variable that you selected. Create three variants: 'local', 'norm', and 'between local and norm'. You need to decide on the criteria that determine which variant is produced.

Data treatment

For each of the 10 speakers, you now have 20 tokens of the variable under investigation for each of the three types of speech: interview, text and word list. This means that you have 600 variants. Enter these into SPSS. A Frequencies test will tell you how each linguistic variant ('local', 'between local and norm' or 'norm') is distributed across each degree of attention paid to speech. This information can be put in stacked bar charts, with a bar for each degree of attention paid to speech (word list, text, and interview). From the bars, which all add up to 100 per cent, it is clear which variant was used most during each of the three degrees of attention paid to speech. An ANOVA with repeated measures can be done to see whether the linguistic variable significantly tends towards the local variant or not under different degrees of attention paid to speech.

Theoretical angles

The effect of attention paid to speech is the main theme. An assumption is that a move towards the vernacular automatically also means a move towards the local language, but this may not be true. This investigation will show the strength of this hypothesis in this particular speech community.

18.4 Conversation Analysis

18.4.1 The idea behind it

Conversation Analysis is a method of researching the structure of conversations and their coherence (Crystal 1995). In daily social interaction, people often go through certain fixed conversational steps. Interlocutors are assumed to have some knowledge of them; when to start talking, when to end, how to be polite, etc. A set of turn-taking actions is part of this. Besides everyday conversations between ordinary people, conversations between a doctor and a patient are interesting, as is the language in the court room and a conversation between a teacher and pupil – that is, conversations involving a certain hierarchical relationship.

18.4.2 How it works

Unless recordings of conversations are already available, the researcher tries to generate conversations between two people. The researcher can ask people to talk to each other on a certain topic while an audio-recording device is active (and the researcher is not in the room). They could solve a problem, for instance. Interactions are often video-taped.

18.4.3 The data

The researcher writes out the conversation and indicates which of the interlocutors talks when (the actual times; to be measured with a digital clock) and any other relevant details. In the transcripts and recordings, the researcher tries to look for recurring interaction patterns, like interruptions, word choice, a rising intonation at certain points in the interaction, codeswitches, silences, or loudness of voice. Non-verbal cues like gestures are also researchable.

18.4.4 Sample investigation: Codeswitching in a multilingual context

Motivation

Within highly multilingual communities, codeswitching is often a common habit. People switch between the various languages that they have at their disposal and they might be convinced that the switches are meaningless. Indeed, this switching could be a habit but there could also be stylistic or other motivations. The Conversation Analysis described below can lay bare the patterns and motivations of switching.

Research steps

a. Find two bilingual speakers in a bilingual community who tend to codeswitch regularly.

b. Record these speakers while they chat with each other (during 30 minutes) about a random topic that is not related to language. Record them on two separate devices. Tell them to act and talk naturally. Don't tell them that you are interested in their language use. Tell them you are interested in what they say about the topic at hand.

c.   Write out the recording, indicating exactly when each speaker speaks. Indicate when each speaker switches languages and look for patterns as to the moment when they switch: technique of switching (after a silence or when a certain word category is used, for instance), discussion topic when switching, or any other pattern. Determine intonation patterns, silences, and other cues as well, if they seem to correlate with the switches.

d.   On the basis of the patterns, define meaningful categories of switches. This is difficult, and it is advisable to listen to the recording with someone else and together draw up types of switches and the criteria to define the types. Do not define more than a handful of types.

e.   Select one switch from each of the switch-type categories formed, present them to the speakers (on paper or through a fragment in the actual recording) and ask them why they think they switched. Was it just out of habit or was there a reason?

Data treatment

Make an overview of the categories you've distinguished and present the reasons why the speakers thought they switched. Using examples of switches, write a convincing text in which you describe the features involved in codeswitches and the motivations to codeswitch of these two speakers.

Theoretical angles

Accommodation Theory may be used to explain the results, and so may other theories as described in Chapter 5 that describe the social motivations of language choices. Audience Design (see 5.4.5), for instance, is a potential angle. Myers-Scotton (1998) is an important source (see 3.6.2) for theory about codeswitching and styleswitching.

FOCUS ON...

Self-recording

Spontaneous speech can also be elicited by having pairs of people agree to record themselves while talking to each other. They could use their own recording devices and decide themselves when to record their conversations. They give their recording to the researcher. If all goes well, then speech that closely resembles natural speech is in the recording. The nature, length, and quality of the recordings will vary. These conversations will lend themselves well for Discourse Analysis and Conversation Analysis.

18.5   Discourse Analysis

18.5.1 The idea behind it

Communication amongst people from different cultures and with different personalities often leads to misunderstanding because cues are misinterpreted. Discourse research tries to describe these cues systematically to find patterns. The field is often associated with the American linguist John Gumperz, who was motivated by his interest in cross-cultural miscommunication (Gumperz 1982). Discourse Analysis is interested in how interactants create meaning through social interaction and how social actors themselves develop meaning in **speech events**. The assumption is that people do not express everything literally and that much of the communication is not in the literal meaning of words or sentences. The interactants rely on all kinds of knowledge they have and assumptions they hold in hypothesising what the other person means, which is particularly challenging if the two interactants are from different cultural backgrounds. Step by step, the interactants make sense of the conversation and construct meaning while talking. Researchers try to describe how meaning is expressed and interpreted and how this influences the conversation.

Unlike Conversation Analysis, Discourse Analysis looks at sets of sentences – not just individual sentences. According to Crystal (1995), a very general interpretation of 'discourse' is that it consists of 'behavioural units' (106), referring to a set of utterances that together form a speech event, like a conversation or a joke. Discourse Analysis tries to establish rules regarding how units of information are patterned. Researchers try and see if a sentence is well-formed in a discourse sense in the same way one can say that a sentence is grammatically well-formed.

18.5.2 How it works

The field of Discourse Analysis prefers naturally occurring speech. Typical aspects of the analysis are pronunciation (especially prosody), register, gestures, semantics, grammar, word choice, syntax, rhetorical devices, and style. Cues to show (dis)agreement or (mis)understanding can be highly subconscious and subtle and also highly culture-specific and highly dependent on the personality of individuals.

18.5.3 The data

Audio- and video-recordings and/or transcripts of audio-recordings are the outcome of a Discourse Analysis. The researcher needs to find speech units and their intended and interpreted meaning and use a range of linguistic and social variables to do that. With that knowledge, the researcher determines what went wrong in a conversation or what determined its success.

18.5.4 Sample investigation: Communication in a hierarchical relationship

Motivation

This sample investigation looks into the communication between two people in a hierarchical relationship. The one lower in the relationship needs to explain something to the one higher in the hierarchy. The reason for the explanation is for the latter to do the former a favour, like write a reference letter, talk to another high-placed person, cure an illness, speak on behalf of the one lower in the hierarchy, or lend some money. The steps below are relatively difficult, so you could consider finding an existing recording (perhaps from a 'reality TV' programme) and do only part of the investigation.

Research steps

a. Find someone who intends to see a person in a higher hierarchical position to explain something and ask for a favour and who is prepared to share this with you, the researcher. The one who receives the information and request also needs to agree to being recorded.

b. The conversation between the two people then needs to be audio-recorded. The person lower in the hierarchy also needs to make mental notes of any hand or other gestures and facial expressions of the interlocutor and of themselves and when they occurred, if possible.

c. Afterwards, the recording can be analysed by describing the various stages, like the stage in which the two people do not understand each other and the stage when one of the interlocutors started to understand something the other interlocutor explained or requested.

d. Interview the interlocutors afterwards. Ask both for an account of the conversation and about crucial moments in the conversation. Ask them about the speed and successes of the discourse. Ask them about their analysis of possible misunderstandings and about the solution, and in doing so feel free to show them the transcript of the discussion. Ask them if they remember certain facial expressions or hand gestures. Ask them how they interpreted these.

Data treatment

The discussion needs to be written out in full, including silences. In the transcript, indicate the moments of misunderstandings in the discussion and which linguistic techniques coincided with information being successful or less successful. Use the interview(s) to analyse the misunderstandings and the moments when there was mutual understanding. Make sure to use linguistic cues as support rather than basing your analysis on content mainly.

Theoretical angles

The data coming from this Discourse Analysis mainly have a practical angle and can be used to improve communication between two interlocutors in a hierarchical relationship. Theoretically speaking, the data generated here can be used to analyse how people communicate who have an unequal power relation; in this case one of one-sided dependence. If the interlocutors are seen to represent two subcultures, then theories on intercultural communication (see 4.4) can be the theoretical backdrop, as explained in Gumperz and Hymes (1972) and Paulston et al. (2012)

FOCUS ON...

Finding participants

Finding people for interviews or any other tests that you wish to do can be done through the 'friend-of-a-friend technique'. The resultant selection of participants is known as 'snowball sampling'. The motivation of participants is high in these cases, as they know they are helping a friend.

18.6   Rapid Anonymous Survey

18.6.1 The idea behind it

As was indicated above, spontaneous, unmonitored language is the main type of language that sociolinguists are interested in. The researcher must control the social/communicative setting systematically. The idea behind the Rapid Anonymous Survey is to elicit such speech. This technique elicits short utterances only. A very specific linguistic variable is the topic of investigation, and the assumption is that it is reflective of certain characteristics of the speaker and/or the social/communicative setting itself.

18.6.2 How it works

Labov (1966) did the most well-known of Rapid Anonymous Surveys and this investigation, performed in New York City, still stands as exemplary (see 7.4.8 and 18.6.2). He asked people working in department stores where a certain product was in the stores, knowing that the answer was 'fourth floor'. He then asked for a repetition of the answer ('Excuse me?'). This way, he could determine what the effect of attention paid to speech was on the pronunciation of coda /r/ in these two words. The investigation involved class of speakers.

So, the Rapid Anonymous Survey elicits short spoken utterances as a reaction to a question or request. The researcher asks a question and knows the literal answer the participant will give. The idea is that contact with the participant is quick and minimally intrusive. Speakers are unaware that their speech is the subject of investigation and they will remain anonymous. The speech will be natural, because speakers don't know they're being observed. Speaker characteristics are assessed or estimated by the investigator. The speech is uttered in the public space. Speakers are posed the question and the researcher writes down the relevant part(s) of the answer. Many minor and easy adjustments could be invented to customise the investigation to a specific research question, like using two different intonation patterns in the question and asking questions with a different accent.

The selection of participants can be done through so-called 'intercept sampling' or 'opportunistic sampling', that is, select any individual who the interviewer comes across, as explained by Cooper and Emory (1995). The researcher could also be on the lookout for certain speaker characteristics. In his research in New York, Labov (1966) estimated speakers' social status on the basis of type of department store in New York where they worked. This principle may be tricky to apply these days as social layerings have become less predictable in many societies. People's gender, by contrast, can usually be determined without a problem, and people's ages can be guessed.

The practical challenges of this type of investigation are considerable. It is not considered completely ethical by some people, for instance. Also, writing down people's answers inconspicuously after receiving the answer or recording people can be awkward and so can asking several people the same question in the same place.

18.6.3 The data

After the data have been obtained, the researcher will have some precise or estimated speaker characteristics and the linguistic choices the speakers made. The linguistic variable under investigation usually has a small number of variants, and if no recordings have been made then the decision on these variants is ready immediately after the observation by the researcher. If you enter the data into SPSS, then Crosstabs will give you an overview of the findings and a Chi-Square Test will reveal whether there is a difference between groups of participants in the tendency to choose certain variants. If you have defined more than two groups of participants and there is a significant difference, then a post-hoc test will tell you between which two groups this significant difference exists.

18.6.4 Sample investigation: Adjusting to an interlocutor

Motivation

People are known to adjust their speech to their interlocutor in all kinds of ways. Whether the person they talk to speaks with a formal style or not may affect such adjustments. The Rapid Anonymous Survey here describes a way to test this.

Research steps

a. Choose an informal and a more formal way of getting the attention of strangers in order to ask them a question.

b. Go to a public place where people are walking but are not in a rush. Ask 100 random people for attention in the formal way, and then ask them for the time. Do this with intervals over a longer period of time (say, 10 or 20 a day on 5 to 10 days) and leave sufficient time between each individual approach, so as to avoid marked behaviour in the public place. For each 'interview', write down what the response reaction was: a certain greeting or other type of reaction or no reaction at all. Write down the gender and estimated age category of the respondent and any other factor that you deem may affect the nature of the response.

c. Using the same procedures (same place, similar time, you wearing similar clothes and behaving similarly, etc.), greet 100 people in the more informal way, and again keep track of the responses.

Data treatment

Categorise the reactions (certain reactions that are slightly different could be put into the same category) and enter the variants into SPSS. Relevant labels in SPSS are the formality of the initial greeting by you (formal/informal), the categorised reply reaction, and the age category and gender of the person you approached. Run Frequencies to determine which replies were induced by each of the two types of greetings. You can do this for the whole group. After that, you can split up the group into men and women and into age categories and do the same, to see if men and women and people with different ages had different reaction tendencies. All of these results can be put in tables indicating the frequencies of each of the reaction categories you have formulated for each of the participant groups. A Chi-square Test can tell you whether the formal or informal greeting induced significantly different reaction greetings. Two other Chi-square Tests can tell you what the effect of age and sex on the response greeting was. Other participant characteristics can also be tested this way.

Theoretical angles

The effect of age, gender, and other respondent characteristics as well as that of register will become clear, and this will show you whether certain types of people react differently to register. Accommodation Theory (see 5.4.4) and gender theories (see Chapter 11) may be used as a theoretical framework. Age effects can be compared to age-related theories: generational differences may exist and you may find age-grading effects (see 10.4.2).

While You Were Speaking

Investigating Naturally Occurring Communication

19

19.1 Introduction

Within certain practical and ethical boundaries, naturally occurring language, as described in Section 17.1, can be found by observing it while it is being produced. You can also immerse yourself in it by becoming a participant in communication. The specific circumstances in which language is produced then also become an interesting research concern, besides the language itself, and these circumstances could become part of the argument a researcher wants to make about language use under certain circumstances and in certain places. Indeed, language production that is studied while it is taking place tends to be observed from a broader communicative perspective rather than merely the linguistic. Culture, specific communicative settings, and interpersonal relationships in particular are important factors in such research.

The research techniques described in this chapter are Ethnographic Fieldwork, Computer-Mediated Communication, Street Use Survey, and Classroom Observation. While doing one of these investigations, you will find that as a researcher you will need to be the one to determine what is important and what is worth researching and that your intuitions, assessments, and experiences are important guidelines for determining the methodology. You will also find that the methodology develops while doing the research. The descriptions here, therefore, give options rather than tell you exactly what to do.

19.2 Ethnographic Fieldwork

19.2.1 The idea behind it

Ethnography refers to the study of people in a cultural context. Ethnographic Fieldwork is a useful way to learn more about, what Levon (2013) called, the 'social lives' (69) of members within a community. It is inspired by the works of Dell Hymes (see 4.4). According to Blommaert (2007), ethnography as a theory leans on two important principles. First, all social events, of which language is one, are connected to other events (amongst others, historically, spatially, and temporally) and have many meanings (this principle is often referred to as the 'ecology' of language). The second principle is that knowledge of these social actions is by default subjective. Ethnography tries not only to objectively describe what goes on, who is involved in the social events, and what the characteristics are of the participants (age, sex, etc.) but it also tries to lay bare how the participants themselves interpret these events. Besides these subjective interpretations by the participants, the researcher also needs to place the social events in a structured and independent social reality (Cameron et al. 1992).

Ethnographic Fieldwork uses these principles and focuses on communication of people in certain cultures. An ethnic group is a category of people who identify with each other based on similarities, such as common ancestry and experiences. In addition to the study of minority cultures, modern-day communities of practice, speech communities, and social networks can also be investigated using ethnographic principles. One could use these techniques to investigate communication in a sports club, student fraternity, or perhaps in a company.

19.2.2 How it works

Ethnographic Fieldwork involves participation in the daily activities of a speech community as well as observation, preferably over a longer period of time. It takes sensitivity, a social attitude, patience, and understanding to find and successfully penetrate a speech community as a participant. Once in the community, the researcher needs to decide to which degree they will want to participate in social actions; become an unintrusive insider or assume the role of bystander who is observing and investigating with the speech community being aware of this. Inside the community, the researcher collects data on how people communicate, with a focus on language choice, relationships, and circumstances. Interview data are also collected to find out how community members view communicative patterns.

Levon (2013) gave some practical preparatory tips for those wishing to do such fieldwork. The researcher, most of all, needs to study the speech community in detail, including any seemingly meaningless detail that is striking. In order to go from an 'etic' (i.e., an outsider's) viewpoint to an 'emic' viewpoint (a more intimate insider's perspective), one needs to be guided by the local practicalities when doing the fieldwork. The researcher needs to abide by the existing rules of conduct and may need to give up a well-laid-out research plan. It should be clear that this type of investigation is demanding. Blommaert and Jie (2011) stressed the fact that ethnographic investigations can be intensive, frustrating, and time-consuming, especially during the actual fieldwork itself. Chaos is intrinsic to this technique of data collecting.

19.2.3 The data

The goal is a description of systematic patterns of communication: linguistic interaction (what actually takes place when two or more people communicate), the motivations for the various language choices speakers make, and the non-linguistic context that determines the language used (the social and cultural beliefs and practices of the members of a speech community). The main research objects are the context that induces certain language choices and these language choices themselves

Blommaert and Jie (2011) indicated that a complex situation is described and that no efforts need be made to simplify things into neat tables and graphs in the data presentation. Levon (2013) recommended that researchers write engaging ethnographic descriptions with personality characteristics and other idiosyncrasies of participants as well as details on the circumstances in which an interview was done. Blommaert and Jie (2011) also stressed the importance of details and anecdotes.

19.2.4 Sample investigation: Communication in an old people's home

Motivation

When elderly people move to an old people's home, then their old networks are disturbed and they are thrown into a new one, with similarly old people but each with a different background, and they need to start building a new network again. Communication is part of this effort; with other elderly people, with old friends, with caretakers, and with visiting family. In your culture, there may be special homes for the elderly with a certain cultural background, like a home for certain types of immigrants. The suggested investigation given here focuses on the shaping of new networks and general communicative patterns in such a culturally distinct home.

Research steps

a. Find an old people's home where elderly whose cultural background is different from yours live together. Ask management if you can act as a volunteer and participate in the daily lives of the elderly and do research. Both the elderly and the staff should be aware that you are a researcher. Make sure that the people in the home are there for physical reasons, not for mental reasons. Make sure that staff with various cultural backgrounds are socially accepted in the environment you wish to enter.

b. Try to blend in as much as possible, participate in the community, possibly by doing all kinds of chores and having many chats with the inhabitants of the home. Ask them about their social lives now and in the past; past and new friends and groups of friends. The inhabitants' cultural, regional and social background and the language use that is typical thereof are important factors. Gender is another factor.

c. Make notes of the situation in a broad sense; make recordings of conversations if people allow you to do that, write down anecdotes, describe the social relations in the home (including power relations), describe gestures that the participants in the home make sometimes. Facial expressions may also be part of the description. Generally, any detail that seems a relevant factor in shaping that communication should be part of your notes. Focus specifically on the nature and coming to existence of groups within the home and of special bonds between certain individuals.

Data treatment

You now need to combine all your notes on language use, gestures, and all kinds of social circumstances with the many anecdotes on relationships and networks that you have heard. All of these observations combined will give you a good idea of how the communication by the elderly with the various types of interlocutors they communicate with goes and how this is associated with networks. In an extensive report, which includes many examples, you need to create a picture of what this communication is like and how social network formation is visible in communication. Present language as the basic descriptive object (such as words, phrases, and pronunciation).

Theoretical framework

It is common to do an ethnographic study by describing a communication situation in a very broad and extensive way and leave it at that. A specific research question or theoretical framework is not necessary in that case. The switching between types of language (one's old dialect versus the norm language, mainly) with different interlocutors might nevertheless be placed in a perspective of codeswitching or style-shifting (see 3.6). The difference between caretaker and the elderly may be placed in a paradigm of power relations by comparing it with the communication in doctor/patient and teacher/pupil relationships.

19.3 Computer-Mediated Communication

19.3.1 The idea behind it

Computer-Mediated Communication, which is often abbreviated as CMC, refers to the language used in interpersonal written communication via digital media, such as texting and email. Social networking platforms, blogs, and gaming platforms are other sources of language data. This branch of Sociolinguistics, referred to by Danesi (2016) as 'e-sociolinguistics' (xi), has ethnographic features, because not only are linguistic data studied, all kinds of circumstantial data are taken into consideration as well, and the researcher may sometimes even participate in communication – with various degrees of anonymity (Friedrich and Diniz de Figueiredo 2016). Another approach is a quantitative one, in which systematically collected facts about language and the circumstances in which it was produced are used.

Thurlow and Mroczek (2011) put forward some important sociolinguistic fields that CMC research could be interested in: language differences between writers, identity, interpersonal communication, and, for instance, codeswitching.

FOCUS ON...

Arabizi/Arabish

In digital communication, playing with spelling sometimes leads to new systems of writing things down. In the United Arab Emirates, texting and chatting in Latin-transliterated Arabic (called 'Arabizi' or 'Arabish') is common, even if the device is Arabic-script enabled (Yaghan 2008).

19.3.2 How it works

CMC research sounds like fun because it often involves enthusiastic people's online messages. Besides being fun, it is also particularly challenging. Data need to be collected systematically, first of all, and a few sentences from some Facebook friends will not be enough. Instead, you need much data to draw reliable conclusions. The degree of access to onscreen data (like logfiles or the option to download web forum pages in HTML) varies. Hundt et al. (2007) provided hints to mine for large-scale data by means of Web Crawlers and Application Program Interfaces (API) or customised scripts.

Androutsopoulos (2014) provided more general instructions for collecting data that are part of CMC. On-screen data can be collected (the written text on the screen) as well as user-based data (information about users). One type of onscreen data mining is online observation, which refers to the act of 'virtually being there' while the online communication is developing on the medium you are studying (e.g., a discussion). Information on users can be obtained through interviews and consulting information users post online. Systematic observation is the general approach as is collecting information such as group memberships, pace of communication, common topics, and other such non-linguistic information that will help you analyse communication and language practices.

Androutsopoulos (2014) explained three approaches, namely to 'revisit', 'roam around' and 'try out' (78). Revisiting comes down to visiting the online space regularly and documenting everything relevant that is going on as well as the changes between the moments when one views the space. Roaming around refers to exploring the digital space in question; documenting information on profiles and, for instance, threads. Trying out, finally, refers to exploring all the options that users have within the online space, that is, all the resources of participation, such as search facilities, statistics, user lists, and tags. Systematically taking and documenting screenshots is a useful method of capturing data. Herring (2004) provided some other useful methods to select data, amongst others random sampling (for instance, every tenth message), applying time criteria (sample at regular intervals), or selection of authors by individual/group characteristics.

Once you have collected your language and (possibly) the circumstances under which it was produced, there may be the opportunity to interview the authors about motivations to use certain language. This can be done through a questionnaire or survey, but another method is to ask an online community to discuss your topic and hand you the actual discussion threads.

Challenges

Ethical and practical issues and issues of quantitative representability arise when doing CMC research. The researcher needs access to people's communication, and although some of it is public, describing it affects the authors personally if they do not choose to be investigated. If you tell people you are monitoring their communication, then these people may feel aware of being researched during the discourse with others, and this may affect the naturalness of their language. Methodologically, the problem arises that it is not always clear to which message participants are reacting. The number of participants itself and who is communicating with whom is also not always clear. Another issue is the enormous potential variation in the number of words (amount of language) used by each participant as well as the irregularity (time-wise) of communicating online. Finally, there is the issue of identity of the authors. In online platforms, users often take on another identity or write anonymously.

19.3.3 The data

The data that a researcher ends up with consist of as much information as possible about the circumstances surrounding each bit of communication collected: (likely) author, (likely) time of writing, (likely) audience, (likely) participants in the conversation, type of CMC (e.g., blog), speech act type (e.g., request, announcement), typical users, and any other information that may be used to explain language choices. The researcher needs a carefully administrated set of language utterances, screenshots, and interview data. The researcher will need to put forward a convincing argument that a certain pattern is taking place and support it with the various types of data and convincing examples. Another data analysis approach is the quantitative one, where automatically or manually generated data on language variables and all kinds of circumstances are systematically analysed.

19.3.4 Sample investigation: Politeness strategies by gamers

Motivation

Communication on the internet is interesting because the number of participants and their identities are unclear. The traditional assumption that everyone is who they say they are is distorted. In gaming environments, this distortion of reality is even worse. The participants are often from various countries and cultures and might be using their second language, which intensifies the blurriness. The investigation below tries to find patterns in such blurriness by revealing how politeness strategies are applied in online international gaming environments.

Research steps

a. Gain access to in-game text chats of a game in which an international audience of participants is active. A requirement is that communication between players takes place to organise the games, like requests (for player action, for information, or to join a group) or comments about a player's playing style. In certain games, the exchange of all kinds of credit and help needs to be negotiated.

b. In the discourse between gamers, look for politeness strategies that are applied. Presumably, no one will simply say 'Make me a member now' to the Administrator. Instead, they need to request this and requests require politeness. Sometimes, players will discuss playing style and become agitated and then politeness in communication starts playing a role, too. Look for discourse in which such politeness is reasonably required and see whether politeness is actually applied. You could focus on one such type of situation, like a conflict/disagreement, a request, the reply to a request, or giving thanks after a request has been fulfilled. Most probably, you will not have enough information on players' real identity to take that into consideration as a factor. Instead you look at common communication patterns that the discussions share. The assumption is that all participants, irrespective of their background, adjust to a common consensus on how politeness works on an international platform like theirs, and in this respect all players are equal.

c. Collect 100 samples of instances where politeness could optionally be applied. Note down the techniques (word choices, mainly) that players use to be polite or whether they leave out politeness strategies altogether. These should be from a variety of players and not a small set.

Data treatment

The 100 samples can be categorised and put in lists and tables to form a picture of politeness forms in international online discourse. It is advisable to do this categorisation together with another researcher. Write a lively story, including many anecdotes and including the most common politeness techniques that you have found through your categorisation. Make sure to note down and explain the instances of a lack of politeness strategy too.

Theoretical angles

Politeness Theory (see 5.4.2) is the most obvious theoretical angle you can apply. This theory presumes that interlocutors know each other, so you'll need to emphasise that in your investigation mutual relations are quite different. Codeswitching and styleswitching may be of interest too (see 3.6); maybe a certain style or language or the use of emojis or emoticons are associated with politeness, irony, or another stance. Intercultural communication is another possible angle (Paulston et al. 2012).

19.4   Street Use Survey

19.4.1   The idea behind it

The current linguistic state of affairs (the languages generally used) in a certain place can be mapped out through a Street Use Survey. Such a survey applies observation as a tool to determine the language in a particular neighbourhood or town (Altuna and Basurto 2013), focussing on places where language is produced, the individuals producing the language, and times when it is produced. If collected well, then the data reflect the common use of language in a certain geographical and social space. Determining which languages are used (i.e., language choices of individuals) and whether there is some sort of pattern of usage (by certain people, at certain times, aimed at certain interlocutors) are the aims. Such surveys, based on relatively loose yet systematic observations, can be done every year and then trends of usage will arise.

19.4.2 How it works

The researcher should select places where a broad range of people regularly come and a time of day or day in a week when these people tend to be in the designated streets. Busy streets are generally good places. Within a limited space (a few streets, not the same spot) and within a predetermined time-frame, the researcher collects data about conversations taking place. The researcher inconspicuously walks towards a conversation taking place, eaves-drops, walks away, writes down the language or languages used and any other relevant information, and then moves on to the next eaves-dropping opportunity. Many such sessions should take place over a period of time, possibly by more than one researcher. Every observation session should replicate the previous one methodologically as much as possible.

The researcher works with a custom-made form and simply ticks boxes. On the form, they can indicate, for instance, which language varieties are used as well as estimated characteristics of the speakers (estimated age, gender, estimated ethnicity). Pairs of researchers could work together; one listens and passes on the information to the other.

19.4.3 The data

The number of conversations in the limited time frame can be compared to the total size of the population. A mathematical design to deal with data in this way was developed by Yurramendi and Altuna (2009). This model is based on estimates: the average quantity of personal relations (through the average size of an individual's network), the number of interlocutors in conversations occurring in the street (through the town's population figure), and the likely number of speakers of certain languages (through the percentage of people that know a certain language in a city/neighbourhood). A simpler method for calculating the desired sample for the street survey research is by looking at the population of a town and the percentage of multilinguals. You will need to find sources that give you this information explicitly or make a good estimate on the basis of population data such as ethnic and linguistic background of speakers.

19.4.4 Sample investigation: Dialect vitality

Motivation

In many areas/countries where a codified and/or official language is quite dominant, the use of all kinds of dialects that are linguistically related to that official language still function as an important communication tool. Across generations, dialect knowledge often becomes less, but in informal communication it is often surprisingly persistent and is often even used as a strong identity marker across generations. To test the degree to which a dialect, in some shape or form, is still alive, the Street Use Survey as described here can be used.

Research steps

a. Select a village in an area where a certain dialect is known to be used by locals. This needs to be a village that does not attract too many tourists or workers from other regions. Another requirement is that the researcher needs to be able to distinguish between a more widely intelligible standardised version of a language and a more locally understandable dialect.

b. This survey will take place in shops. Go to shops where a general audience would go (not a very specific age group or type of people), where you can hear people talking at the counter while you browse around inconspicuously, where the people behind the counter speak both the dialect and a more standardised form of the language, and where the person behind the counter is roughly between a certain age range of about 15 years (for instance, between 30 and 45). Select four of those shops (which must be no more than a few minutes apart).

c. Choose two hours on a certain weekday (not during holidays) and do the research on five such days (for instance, between 10 and 12 on five consecutive Tuesdays).

d. During those two hours on each of these days, visit each of the shops and write down the language use in five conversations that you hear at the counter between the person behind the counter and the customer (for instance, 'light dialect', 'strong dialect', or 'no dialect'). Note down the approximate age of the customer and the language used in the conversation, including whether there is codeswitching, whether the conversation starts in one language and ends in the other, or some other circumstances or features that you deem relevant.

Data treatment

The information you have can be put in tables in which degree and manner of dialect use can be compared with speaker characteristics (especially age). You do not need to distinguish between the times when the observations were made.

In the table, you present the four shops and the language choices you observed as well as the approximate age of the speakers or other details that you deem relevant. After that, all the information on language use from the various shops can be merged. Statistical analysis of the effects of age (Chi Square test) is possible, but bear in mind that a general description of language use across people with different ages is the main issue.

Theoretical angles

Dialect vitality (see 3.5.4) is a theoretical issue in this investigation. This investigation can be used to contextualise language shift and language revitalisation research by providing information about actual usage. Dialect knowledge may be dwindling but the use of a modified form in daily life may be persistent nevertheless. The data can be used in a framework of language shift (see 3.5.1 and 3.5.2) and identity formation/retention (see 5.3.1). Maybe younger speakers use the dialect more but differently (weak accent, more codeswitching, etc.).

19.5   Classroom Observation

19.5.1 The idea behind it

The language in the classroom is interesting for several sociolinguistic reasons. First, there is the way teachers and students communicate, including how they take turns. The mutual relationship between the interactants in the classroom is in fact established and played out through language use, and the status and social habits of the interactants play an important part in this. Secondly, there is the actual language used by pupils and teachers – which variety do they use and do they styleswitch?

19.5.2 How it works

Studying the language and communication of the classroom can best be done semi-ethnographically; through observations and interviews and with no hard and fast research question. So, the researcher needs to enter the classroom and act as an observer and/or semi-participant. Recordings can be made, separate interviews with individual pupils and teachers may be done, and language and interactions can be analysed in some detail. The greatest challenges in the data collection will be the consent of schools, teachers, and parents as well as full cooperation of the pupils. For a teacher and their pupils, the classroom setting is their safe domain and place of confidentiality and trust, in which critical observation and evaluation takes place. The moment a researcher enters the room, the atmosphere changes, and as a consequence the language and communication may change. With time, and with a good attitude of the researcher, the language and communication may 'normalise', become natural.

19.5.3 The data

Interviews, observation notes, and audio-recordings will come out of this research. Video-recordings may be too intrusive but are an option, too. The interviews and observations can be analysed qualitatively while the language use can be analysed more systematically. Language variables and variants may end up in tables.

19.5.4 Sample investigation: The social/academic correlates of classroom communication

Motivation

In classrooms, there are pupils with different social backgrounds, intellectual dispositions, and different communicative styles. It is said that language use correlates with social success (see 6.3.4 and 7.3.1). The Classroom Observation methodology below describes the way these factors hang together and allows you to hypothesise on the effects of communication on the future social success of the pupils.

Research steps

a. Try to gain regular access to a classroom at a primary school and permission to observe and audio-record a number of lessons. Ideally, there are clear social differences amongst pupils in the classroom that you will be studying.

b. Find out as much as you can about the social background of the pupils and about their academic results.

c. While recording, make notes helping you to indicate who is speaking as well as any observations about miscommunication and possible hand or other gestures.

d. Afterwards, write out selected speech, until you have at least a few sentences by each pupil interacting with the teacher. Inevitably, some students will talk more than others. Do not forget to write down which students are and are not communicating.

e. For each pupil, count the number of words they produced each time they talked, and write down the number of times each pupil initiated a discussion or made a comment that was not provoked but that was relevant to the content discussed, and note down the number of times each pupil asked a question. Make notes on language choices (words and pronunciation but also style and/or register).

f. Note down any other relevant observations, like inappropriate language, emotional language, pupil participation in activities, pupils communicating amongst each other, fights, compliments, overenthusiasm, quietness, bullying, and voice raising.

g. Interview the teacher about the language use of the pupils.

h. Go back to the class every time your newly found trends need further observation; slowly focus on what your findings tell you is worth investigating (like a certain set of interesting pupils), bearing in mind that you want to know what the correlation is between communication style and social and academic background.

Data treatment

The data can be put in tables and overviews. The language findings need to be split up into two groups; students with a relatively high social background and those with a relatively low one. Within these groups, students who are relative smart need to be studied separately from those who are not doing so well academically. No statistical analysis is necessary, as the data are not systematic. The numerical findings as well as the type of utterances (questions, etc.) per group can be reported. Through these data and through examples of actual speech, demonstrate the differences in the language use of various students and make clear whether this is related to social and academic distinction. The pupils' school successes may be used as additional proof for the tendencies that you will be describing. Your research report is an argumentative essay with all the data combined and includes many examples of individual striking observations.

Theoretical angles

(Verbal) Deficit Theory or Difference Theory (see 6.3.3) could be the theoretical basis of the investigation. If social differences are interpreted as cultural differences, then the data can be viewed in the context of intercultural communication (Paulston et al. 2012). The relationship between perceived academic qualities (by the teacher) and language is another issue, although this is a sensitive issue and difficult to measure.

20 Don't Get Me Started

Investigating Attitudes

20.1   Introduction

In Section 9.3.1, three ways to find language attitudes were presented: looking at speaker behaviour, asking them directly for their attitudes, and discover their attitudes about language while they think they are expressing their opinion about something else. The current chapter presents specific methodologies to find language attitudes to go with these three approaches. Statistical analysis is intrinsic to most methods.

This chapter discusses the following methodological approaches to measure how people perceive and evaluate language varieties and language variation: Language Evaluation Test, Matched Guise Test, Identification Task, Questionnaire, Interview, and Folk Linguistics.

20.2   Language Evaluation Test

20.2.1 The idea behind it

A Language Evaluation Test generates reactions to language varieties. The basic principle is that participants are given a language stimulus (usually a recording or set of recordings) and then express their opinion; either through a Likert scale (like a 5-point scale going from 'ugly-sounding' to 'beautiful'; see 15.4.1) or interview-like questions.

20.2.2 How it works

Usually, a Language Evaluation Test involves varieties of the same language, like dialects of German or accents of United States English. A common approach is to do a test involving stimuli (i.e., speech fragments) of different language varieties. This could be spontaneous speech or a read text. Fragments could be less than a minute, and listeners fill in one or more Likert scales for each fragment. For each fragment, a specific question could in addition be asked ('Which dialect is this?' or 'How beautiful is this dialect?', for instance). Nowadays, these tests are mostly done through an online tool.

FOCUS ON...

Challenges

A drawback of using stimuli is that the various speakers in the recordings have different voices and styles and such subtle features will also be evaluated by participants. Another drawback is that, if free speech is used, listeners will also judge the contents. A final challenge in this type of test is that when presented with a number of scales to be used to evaluate one single fragment, listeners will use different bits of the recording to fill in each scale, not all of the language cues in the fragment. A way to bypass this problem is not making the response possibilities available until the fragment is played completely.

20.2.3 The data

Unless participants were allowed to formulate their own answers, the most common output of a Language Evaluation Test are evaluation scores that need to be correlated with participant characteristics (age, education, native tongue, regional origin, gender, etc.).

20.2.4 Sample investigation: Language connotations

Motivation

Certain styles of speaking, or certain accents, are associated with certain stereotypes: smart, dumb, rich, poor, and so on. This Language Evaluation Test lays bare such ideas and connotations.

Research steps

a. Record three speakers – of the same gender and with similar voices – with the following three accents: an accent resembling the norm language, an accent that is slightly removed from the norm language, and, finally, an accent that is obviously deviant from the norm language.

b. Create sound files of language (about a neutral topic, not related to language) for each speaker of about 30 seconds.

c. Design an online test in which you have participants evaluate the fragments. In the test, ask participants to indicate through Likert scales to what degree they would evaluate the personality and other characteristics of the speaker, like intelligence, kindness, sense of humour, wealth, educational level, and physical attractiveness ('1' means 'does not apply', '5' means 'applies to this person perfectly').

d. For each fragment, add a Likert scale going from 'Exactly like the norm language' (=1) to 'Deviates strongly from the norm language' (= 5).

e. Finally, design questions to find out relevant listener personalia: age, gender, own language/accent, regional origin, profession, educational level, and other relevant features.

f. Make an online test.

g. Find at least 100 people to take the test.

Data treatment

The numerical data can be entered into SPSS. Run Frequencies over the three types to determine which qualities are assigned to each of the fragments and to which degree. The results can be presented in a table. Then, do a Correlations test on the scores for the 'exactly like the norm language' scale with all the other scales. This shows you directly which speaker characteristics are associated with speaking in accordance with the language norm. Furthermore, a Factor Analysis will reveal whether certain Likert scales on personality characteristics can be combined into new, more general qualities.

Theoretical angles

Norm language ideology (see 6.3.1) is a relevant issue. In particular, the correlation between characteristics of the judges (age, etc.) and the way the language norm and speakers who deviate from it are evaluated is interesting. The origins of language attitudes (see 9.4), in particular prejudices towards languages (see 9.4.4), are also interesting angles.

20.3 Matched Guise Test

20.3.1 The idea behind it

When people judge language, they are automatically also judging the way a speaker uses their voice. To eliminate the effect of voice-related characteristics and obtain a pure evaluation of language, the Matched Guise Test was designed. The test was introduced by a group of Canadian psychologists, headed by William Lambert (Lambert et al. 1960). They developed the test to discover people's attitudes towards ethnic, social, or geographical language varieties and to different languages spoken in bilingual communities.

20.3.2 How it works

The word 'guise' means 'appearance' or 'assumed appearance'; the listener judges what appear to be two speakers while they are in fact one and the same speaker. The assumption is that when speaking different languages individuals exhibit more or less the same voice qualities. Finding the right speaker for such a test is difficult.

Participants listen to a recording of each of the presumed speakers. For each rendition, they are asked questions about non-linguistic characteristics of the speaker, like looks, intelligence, and sense of humour. The idea is that if the same person is given different qualifications when they speak different languages that this is a reflection of attitudes to the language.

20.3.3   The data

With the Matched Guise Test, attitudes towards languages as well as all kinds of regional and social varieties of languages can be deduced in a reliable way. The data will usually be Likert-scale results. The scale results of the two languages judged can be compared.

20.3.4 Sample investigation: Connotations of two languages

Motivation

Languages carry connotations. People who speak a language are judged partly on the basis of these connotations. The Matched Guise Test described below lays bare the effect of the language one speaks on how one is evaluated.

Research steps

a.   Find someone who has two native tongues or two languages that sound equally native.

b.   Have this speaker talk about a certain topic (but not language) in the two languages, and record the two versions. The content of both versions should be more or less the same.

c.   Find a homogenous group of 20 people (similar age and background) who are native speakers of one of the languages in the recordings. Let these people judge the personality of the guise who speaks their language. In an online test, give the listeners Likert scales with several personality characteristics to judge the personalities of the guises on the basis of the recordings. Then find a homogenous group of 20 people who speak the other language as a native tongue and have them judge the other guise. Both groups should live in a bilingual area where both languages are used and they should be able to speak both languages, but only one as a native tongue.

Data treatment

The data can be entered in SPSS. Run Frequencies and put the results in a table or bar chart: separately for the two guises. A Factor Analysis can show whether certain personality characteristics correlate strongly and can be clustered into a more general factor. An Independent Samples T-test for each Likert scale can reveal whether the difference between the two groups for that scale was significant or not.

Theoretical angle

Differences between the way the same speaker was judged when speaking the two languages are interesting in themselves, especially if the two groups that judged the two guises are similar in their make-up (age, etc.). A Chi Square test will tell you this. That means the differences in the outcome are due to ideas about languages. Language attitudes may be discussed in your research report as well; where do they originate from (see 9.4)?

20.4   Identification Task

20.4.1 The idea behind it

While the Matched Guise Test answers the question in what way language affects how social information is perceived, an Identification Task tries to reveal the way in which social information affects how language is perceived (Drager 2014). Such a task typically comes down to testing the listener's ability to distinguish between sounds or other types of subtle language cues. The focus is on how identification ability (identifying cues correctly) correlates with listener characteristics. An important assumption behind many of such tests is that pronunciation is a major distinguishing feature between varieties of the same language and that individuals base their evaluations of language varieties on specific (marked) pronunciation cues rather than on every speech sound to the same degree. Another tenet is that some differences exist between languages that listeners can't actually hear, while other differences are instantly noticed.

20.4.2 How it works

Most commonly, an Identification Task tests the phonetic level of language; for instance, whether listeners can hear the difference between two sounds (the place/manner of articulation or degree or presence of voice, perhaps). Listeners may be presented with two tokens (words, usually) that are the same except for the pronunciation of one of the phonemes; for instance, the English vowels in the words 'set' and 'sat' or the first consonant in the words 'light' and 'right'; so-called minimal pairs. The task is to indicate which word is said. They may also be given the task in a discriminatory form and be asked to indicate whether the pairs of words they hear are identical or different. Drager (2014) mentioned another way for listeners to express the degree to which they can express distinctions between sounds, namely in a so-called 'coach task', in which the target sounds appear in two different words in a text, and, depending on which phoneme is heard, the meaning of the text changes. Examples are the sentences 'It is in the back' and 'It is in the bag'. The participant could be asked to explain the meaning of the sentence and inadvertently reveal which sound they hear. This is useful when non-native listeners are participating.

The effect of differences between the voices and speech style (if more than one speaker is used) will be relatively small compared to a test involving stretches of speech because speakers will not produce full sentences. Another advantage of this test type is that it is very specific and the researcher knows exactly which linguistic stimulus the listener reacts to.

20.4.3 The data

The data are often categorical and/or numerical although they don't have to be. The difference between articulatory distance between variants and perceived distance between them becomes clear in such tests. After the test, the researcher has a large matrix of judgements (Likert-scale results or yes/no results) that need to be correlated with the participant features (gender, native tongue, age, etc.). A typical result may be that place of articulation is only by older male listeners considered a criterion to determine beauty.

20.4.4 Sample investigation: Interpreting intonation patterns

Motivation

Amongst the functions of intonation is expressing mood. This function causes misinterpretation when those who produce an intonation pattern to express one thing are perceived to express something else. Through an Identification Task, the perceived meaning of intonation patterns can be demonstrated. The sample Identification Task given here combines recognition of a phonetic difference with an assessment of meaning.

Research steps

a. Choose a language to study. Determine what the intonation patterns are of this language variety. Learn about the various moods they express. Usually, there are descriptions of intonation patterns and the moods they express in the literature.

b. Create sound files in which a person (native speaker) says one word or one short phrase with the various intonation patterns. In English, for instance, five ways of saying 'yes' could be recorded; to express a firm statement (fall intonation pattern), to express surprise (rise/fall intonation pattern), etc. This part of the investigation is very challenging and requires some practice with the speaker. You may even need an expert to help you record the right renditions of the intonation patterns. Maybe recordings can be found online.

c. Design an online listening test in which you present the fragments and give the participants the opportunity to write down the mood expressed in each fragment. Let the listeners freely write down which associations each intonation evokes: 'This person sounds confused', and so on. At least 100 participants (native speakers of the language in question) may participate.

Data treatment

Try and find patterns in the opinions. For each fragment, list all the qualifications and combine some of the ones that seem to be referring to a similar quality (for instance, 'gloomy' and 'dejected') and give a more general name to these groups of qualities (for instance, 'unhappy'). Compare the tendencies that you have found in your investigation with those that you found in the literature. In what way do they agree or overlap and in what way do your data provide new meanings of intonation patterns? In what way are the descriptions in the literature of the meanings of intonation patterns in accordance with actual perceptions of these patterns?

Theoretical angles

The findings provide information on the difference between theoretical or assumed language norms and real-life ones. Prescriptivism and descriptivism are relevant themes in such a comparison (see 8.2.2). In addition to the ability to identify patterns correctly, an important interest is whether listeners distinguish between certain patterns or not. Two patterns may be interpreted similarly.

20.5 Questionnaire

20.5.1 The idea behind it

If you want the opinion of members of a larger group of people on several related issues, then you can do a questionnaire, which is a list of questions. The idea is that the results of a sample of participants tells you something about a larger population.

KEY CONCEPTS

Questionnaires, surveys, and polls

Although the words 'questionnaire' and 'survey' are often used interchangeably, a survey is, strictly speaking, a much broader tool for gathering data. It could involve a questionnaire but in combination with other data collection methods, like observations of behaviour. The word 'poll' is also used to denote a large-scale investigation to extract opinions. A poll focuses specifically on a single question or a very small set, and the response options may be very limited (such as 'yes' versus 'no').

20.5.2 How it works

Making a questionnaire is easy, but the potential pitfalls are numerous. The phrasing of questions is an important one. Researchers need to be aware that the way questions are posed gives the participants information on the researcher's approach to the topic of the survey. If the researcher offers certain response categories then that means that they are preselecting what they consider to be relevant and not necessarily what is relevant to participants.

A good approach to questionnaires are interview-like questions combined with Likert scales. If you do that, then it is advisable to offer the Likert scales last. That way, the participants first give their own intuitions and present their own criteria or qualifications and are later on reminded of other criteria. Such interview-like questions need to be phrased neutrally and not overly positively/negatively. So, rather than asking 'Which aspect accentuates the beauty of Russian?' you should ask 'Name some features of Russian that you consider to affect your opinion of this language' or 'Explain your opinion about Russian'. In total, a questionnaire should not take longer than 10 minutes or so to fill in. Nowadays, online questionnaires are most common.

20.5.3 The data

Simply running Frequencies and presenting the frequencies of each response category in a table for each question suffices. The interview-like questions can be analysed differently. The answers can be scanned to find similar arguments used by the respondents and these can be grouped together. Individual participants may produce one or more qualifications, arguments, or criteria, or they may produce none. The percentage of respondents who spontaneously referred to a certain quality or criterion may be reported as a result. It is advisable to do this categorisation of written answers together with someone else. You could, in addition, form groups of respondents with certain characteristics and compare their results. Maybe older participants gave different responses.

20.5.4 Sample investigation: The role in society of the norm language

Motivation

Most countries have one or more official or standard languages, and in classrooms one of them is usually used as the language of instruction. The children may or may not use the language of instruction outside the school and at home. Their parents may or may not feel that these children should. Here, a questionnaire is described to find out more about how parents view the use outside the classroom of the norm language.

Research steps

a. Determine which country you would like to do your study in. The most obvious choice is your own country.

b. Design an online questionnaire.

c. Find 100 parents who can fill in the form in detail.

d. Ask the respondents for relevant information about their background: profession, age, and so on.

e. Present them with interview-like questions: how important the norm language is to them and to the next generation of speakers, whether they think that schools should pay more attention to dialects and other less acknowledged languages, and, for instance, whether they try and speak the norm language with their children or not (and why).

f. The second part could contain Likert scale questions going from 'unimportant' to 'important' or from 'always' to 'never'. Ask the parents about the degree to which they attach importance to the use of the norm language, whether they speak the norm language in daily life, whether their children do, and so on. The Likert scale questions should not overlap with the interview-like questions.

Data treatment

Study the interview-like questions and make an overview of the most common arguments put forward by the participants. Make categories of responses on the basis of the raw responses. Add up categories and indicate how often a certain category was put forward across respondents. Make a table or bar chart containing the results of the response categories. The results of the Likert scales can be presented in tables and charts. Run Frequencies in SPSS to get an overview of the Likert-scale results. The Likert scales can be correlated; there may, for instance, be a correlation between a person's own command of the language and the importance attached to one's children using the language outside the classroom.

Theoretical angles

The added up and visualised findings are interesting in themselves. In addition, they can be compared with whatever information you can find on language policy and the official government stance towards the use of the norm language in education in the country or community you are studying. The effect of language policy can be discussed.

20.6   Interview

20.6.1 The idea behind it

Asking people directly for their attitudes and asking them for elaboration is the most straightforward technique of eliciting attitudes. The advantage is the depth and quality of answers. You sit down with someone and ask questions, and you ask for explanations where necessary. At the end of the interview, the researcher should have answers to all their questions plus some extra issues to think about. The interviewee should in some way be very knowledgeable when it comes to the topic of the interview.

20.6.2 How it works

The questions need to be open and open-minded and give interviewees the opportunity to elaborate. You should ask all of the questions on your list, but in addition you should give the interviewee the opportunity to present new views and explore new angles. It is important to ask follow-up questions, even if they are not in your list of questions. The researcher needs to decide on the amount of time and space they give to interviewees to elaborate on less than central issues.

20.6.3 The data

Afterwards, the researcher needs to write out the interview and scan for patterns and striking results. If more than one interviewee was asked the same questions, then the interviews could be mutually compared. Van Meurs et al. (2015) found that isolating aspects of answers and then categorising these into larger groups, across interviews, was very helpful in finding patterns in the responses of more than one interviewee.

20.6.4 Sample investigation: The definition of a speech community and its language

Motivation

Speech communities are an elusive phenomenon. A speech community is based on similarities in the way people speak (like word choice and pronunciation) and the way they talk about language (express norms and expectations). They are recognisable by the restrictions that the members place on each other (Xu 2015). The interviews described here try to determine the linguistic ways in which the community reveals itself. It involves interviewees with specific experience-based knowledge.

Research steps

a. Find five people that you assess to be members of a speech community. Make sure they know each other.

b. You need to find out the characteristics of people in the speech communities under investigation and of the way they speak. In individual interviews, find out how they would describe their own language and that of each of their four fellow community members. Ask the participants to indicate which people speak like them and who doesn't and let them give examples of differences. When asking them to describe language, let them give examples (pronunciation, intonation, grammar, and word choice, mainly).

c. Ask the participants to indicate non-linguistic features that distinguish them from other speech communities.

d. Stop each interview after about half an hour.

Data treatment

Write out the interviews. On the basis of language examples given by interviewees, try to describe the most characteristic (perceived) features of the language in the community. Furthermore, describe how/whether this language is perceived to be different from that of other speech communities and to what degree and in which way it distinguishes the speakers as a community. The most interesting thing to find out is whether language or other means are mainly used for distinction.

Theoretical angles

The angle that requires further analysis here is that of identity (see 5.3.1) and linguistic identity in particular. Theories on speech communities can also help you put the findings in perspective, like the one by Xu (2015). Linguistic and non-linguistic characteristics are part of the larger analysis.

20.7 Folk Linguistics

20.7.1 The idea behind it

Chapter 8 presents an extensive description of ways to deal with evaluative reactions to language and language use (Folk Linguistics) and lay beliefs about language varieties and their speakers (Perceptual Dialectology). The chapter showed that despite a certain degree of unpredictability and unreliability of data generated by non-linguists, if enough are collected then they often reveal clear patterns. These data put expert views and findings into a different perspective, and they explain language choices.

20.7.2 How it works

Few long-standing traditions can be discerned in methodologies to capture patterns in non-linguists' approaches to language. Methodologies often have in common that participants are given considerable freedom to express their perceptions and evaluations.

FOCUS ON...

Directly reporting societal treatment

Some ideas about how language is treated in society are readily available. In social media, in newspapers, in magazines, in blogs, and on websites, people spontaneously express their ideas about certain language issues. Researchers could venture to systematically find and describe such discourse, which comes down to much patient browsing and scanning.

20.7.3 The data

The data consist of descriptions worded by the participants and possibly also non-verbal ways of expressing their views, like circles drawn around an area on a map. It is up to the researcher to 'translate' the expressions of the participants into standardised terminology. Carefully interpreting the oftentimes less than nuanced expressions is advisable. It is best to do this with someone else.

20.7.4 Sample investigation: Perceived dialect boundaries

Motivation

The way traditional maps delineate dialects does not always agree with the way actual speakers of these dialects view boundaries. The region near a historical boundary as found on such maps is an interesting place to collect people's views on the dialect boundaries. Investigating this by directly asking these speakers falls in the category of Perceptual Dialectology and in the broader field of Folk Linguistics.

Research steps

a. Find two dialects whose dividing line is subject to some debate.

b. Find 25 people who live on one side of the traditional border between the dialects (which is visible on a historical dialect map, possibly) and another 25 who live on the other side. These people should all live very close to each other.

c. Give each participant a map with the area on it, including an indication of towns, cities, villages, and important landmarks like rivers, forests, and mountain ranges.

d. Ask the participants to draw a line between the two dialects and ask them to write down everything they know about what separates those dialects. They should feel free to indicate that there is no dividing line.

e. Then ask the participants in a more systematic way what distinguishes both dialects (if there is a distinction, in their view) by giving them themes to think about in addition to language difference, such as history, natural dividing lines, religion, politics, and ethnicity.

Data treatment

Copy all the lines that the participants drew onto a new map, to see to what degree they agreed with each other. Find any patterns in agreement amongst the lines and compare these patterns with the conventional lines as they are available on dialect maps. Then, find patterns in the linguistic and non-linguistic arguments the participants used. Make an overview of the most popular criteria used and also of the type of criteria (linguistic or not). In your report, provide a picture of a map revealing all the lines drawn by participants or some other graphic way of revealing where they coincide. Provide many telling details that individual participants came up with.

Theoretical angles

Theories on lay perceptions of language variation are the main theoretical angles for these data (see Chapters 8 and 9). The discussion as to whether lay perceptions are of importance in determining dialect borders is also an interesting angle. The criteria to define language borders (see 3.3.3) are relevant, too.

References

Abdulaziz, Mohamed H., and Ken Osinde. 1997. "Sheng and English. Development of mixed codes among the urban youth in Kenya." *International Journal of the Sociology of Language* 125:43–63.

Abu-Haidar, Farida. 1987. "The Treatment of the Reflex of /q/ and /k/ in the Muslim Dialect of Baghdad." *Zeitschrift für Arabische Linguistik* 17:41–57.

Adamson, H. Douglas, and Vera Regan. 1991. "The Acquisition of Community Speech Norms by Asian Immigrants Learning English as a Second Language." *Studies in Second Language Acquisition* 13:1–22.

Adank, Patti. 2003. "Vowel Normalization. A Perceptual-Acoustic Study of Dutch Vowels." Ph.D., Department of Linguistics, Nijmegen University.

Agius, Silvan. 2013. "Third gender: A step toward ending intersex discrimination." *Der Spiegel*, 22 August 2013.

Agliati, Alessia, Antonietta Vescovo, and Luigi Anolli. 2005. "Conversation patterns in Icelandic and Italian people: Similarities and differences in rhythm and accommodation." In *The Hidden Structure of Interaction: From Neurons to Culture Patterns*, edited by L. Anolli, S. Duncan Jr., M.S. Magnusson and G. Riva, 224–235. Washington, DC: IOS Press.

Ahmed, Musavir. 2014. "Language use patterns and ethnolinguistic vitality of the Shina speaking Gurezi immigrants." *International Journal of the Sociology of Language* 230:1–17.

Aikio, Ante, Laura Arola, and Niina Kunnas. 2015. "Variation in North Saami." In *Globalising Sociolinguistics. Challenging and Expanding Theory*, edited by Dick Smakman and Patrick Heinrich, 243–255. London: Routledge.

Al-Ali, Mohammed Nahar, and Heba Isam Mahmoud Arafa. 2010. "An experimental sociolinguistic study of language variation in Jordanian Arabic." *The Buckingham Journal of Language and Linguistics* 3:207–230.

Al-Wer, E. 2002a. "Education as a Speaker Variable." In *Language Contact and Language Conflict Phenomena in Arabic*, edited by A. Rouchdy. New York, NY: Routledge Curzon.

Al-Wer, E. 2002b. "Jordanian and Palestinian dialects in contact: Vowel raising in Amman." In *Language Change: The Interplay of Internal, External and Extra-Linguistic Factors*, edited by A Jones and E. Esch, 63–79. Berlin: Mouton de Gruyter.

Albirini, Abdulkafi. 2016. *Modern Arabic Sociolinguistics. Diglossia, Variation, Codeswitching, Attitudes and Identity*. London: Routledge.

Allsop, Richard. 1958. "The English language in British Guiana." *English Language Teaching* 12 (2):59–66.

Altuna, Olatz, and Asier Basurto. 2013. *A Guide to Language Use Observation. Survey Methods*. Vitoria-Gasteiz: Servicio Central de Publicaciones del Gobierno Vasco.

Amaral, Luís Isaías Centeno do. 2003. "A concordância verbal de segundapessoa do singular em Pelotas e suasimplicaçõeslinguísticas e sociais [Second Person Singular Verb Agreement in Pelotas and its Linguistic and Social Implications]" Ph.D., Instituto de Letras, Universidade Federal do Rio Grande do Sul.

Ammon, Ulrich, Norbert Dittmar, Klaus J. Mattheier, and Peter Trudgill, eds. 2004. *Sociolinguistics. An International Handbook of the Science of Language and Society.* 2nd ed. Vol. 1. Berlin/New York, NY: Walter de Gruyter.

Anderson, Benedict R.O.G. 1983. *Imagined Communities Reflections on the Origin and Spread of Nationalism.* New York, NY: Verso.

Anderson, Rindy C., Casey A. Klofstad, William J. Mayew, and Mohan Venkatachalam. 2014. "Vocal fry may undermine the success of young women in the labor market." *Plos One* 9 (5).

Androutsopoulos, Jannis. 2014. "Computer-mediated communication and linguistic landscapes." In *Research Methods in Sociolinguistics: A Practical Guide*, edited by Janet Holmes and Kirk Hazen, 74–90. Hoboken, NJ: John Wiley & Sons, Inc.

Ash, Sharon. 2002. "Social class." In *The Handbook of Language Variation and Change*, edited by Jack K. Chambers, Peter Trudgill and Nathalie Schilling-Estes, 402–422. Malden, MA: Blackwell.

Auer, Peter. 1998. *Code-Switching in Conversation.* London: Routledge.

Aukrust, V.G., and C.E. Snow. 1998. "Narratives and explanations during mealtime conversations in Norway and the U.S." *Language in Society* 27:221–246.

Awadelkarim, Abdelmagid Abdelrahman. 2013. "Language-crossing: The sociolinguistic dynamics of the language/discourse of 'Shamasha' Group (Randok) in Sudan." European Conference on Arts & Humanities 2013, 18–21 July 2013, Brighton.

Aziakpono, P., and I. Bekker. 2010. "The attitudes of isiXhosa-speaking students toward language of learning and teaching issues at Rhodes University, South Africa: General trends." *Southern African Linguistics and Applied Language Studies* 28:39–60.

Baeza Ventura, Gabriela, and Marc Zimmerman, eds. 2009. *Estudios Culturales Centroaméricanos en el Nuevo Milenio.* San Pedro, CA: Editorial Universidad de Costa Rica.

Bakir, Murtadha J. 1986. "Sex differences in the approximation to Standard Arabic: A case study." *Anthropological Linguistics* 28:3–9.

Bakir, Murtadha J. 2010. "Notes on the verbal system of Gulf Pidgin Arabic." *Journal of Pidgin and Creole Languages* 25 (2):201–228.

Ball, Martin J., ed. 2010. *The Routledge Handbook of Sociolinguistics around the World.* London: Routledge.

Banda, F. 1996. "The scope and categorization of African English. Some sociolinguistic considerations." *English World-Wide* 17:63–65.

Barasa, Sandra Nekesa. 2015. "Ala! Kumbe? "Oh my! Is it so?." Multilingualism controversies in East Africa." In *Globalising Sociolinguistics. Challenging and Expanding Theories*, edited by Dick Smakman and Patrick Heinrich, 39–53. London: Routledge.

Baratz, J.C. 1969. "Teaching reading in an urban Negro school system." In *Teaching Black Children to Read*, edited by J.C. Baratz and R.W. Shuy, 92–116. Washington, DC: Center for Applied Linguistics.

Barbieri, F. 2007. "Older men and younger women: A corpus-based study of quotative use in American English." *English World-Wide* 28:23–45.

Barbu, S., A. Nardy, J.-P. Chevrot, and J. Juhel. 2013. "Language evaluation and use during early childhood: Adhesion to social norms or integration of environmental regularities?" *Linguistics* 51 (2):381–412.

Barker, Chris. 2005. *Cultural Studies. Theory and Practice*. London: Sage.

Barrenechea, A.M. 1951. "Études sur la phonétique de l'Espagnol parlé en Argentine." *Filología* 3 (1–2):143.

Barton, David, and Karin Tusting, eds. 2005. *Beyond Communities of Practice: Language, Power and Social Context*. New York, NY: Cambridge University Press.

Bassiouney, Reem. 2009. *Arabic Sociolinguistics. Topics in Diglossia, Gender, Identity, and Politics*. Washington, DC: Georgetown University Press.

Bassiouney, Reem. 2015. *Language and Identity in Modern Egypt*. Edinburgh: Edinburgh University Press.

Bassiouney, Reem, and Mark Muehlhaeusler. 2018. "Cairo. The linguistic dynamics of a multilingual city." In *Urban Sociolinguistics around the World: The City as a Linguistic Process and Experience*, edited by Dick Smakman and Patrick Heinrich. London: Routledge.

Batterham, Margaret. 2000. "The apparent merger of the front centering diphthongs – EAR and AIR – in New Zealand English." In *New Zealand English*, edited by Allan Bell and Koenraad Kuiper, 111–145. Wellington: Victoria University Press.

Battisti, Elisa, and João Ignacio Pires Lucas. 2015. "Class in the social labyrinth of South America." In *Globalising Sociolinguistics. Challenging and Expanding Theory*, edited by Dick Smakman and Patrick Heinrich. London: Routledge.

Bauer, Robert S. 1984. "The Hong Kong Cantonese speech community." *Cahiers de linguistique. Asie orientale* 13 (1):57–90.

Baumann, Gerd, and Andre Gingrich. 2004. "Foreword." In *Grammars of Identity/Alterity: A Structural Approach*, edited by Gerd Baumann and Andre Gingrich, ix–xiv. New York, NY: Berghahn Books.

Bayard, Don, Ann Weatherall, Cynthia Gallois, and Jeffery Pittam. 2001. "Pax America. Accent attitudinal evaluations in New Zealand, Australia and America." *Journal of Sociolinguistics* 5 (1):22–49.

Bayley, Robert. 1994. "Interlanguage variation and the quantitative paradigm: Past-tense marking in Chinese-English." In *Research Methodology in Second-Language Acquisition*, edited by Elaine Tarone, Susan M. Gass and Andrew Cohen, 157–181. Hillsdale, NJ: Lawrence Erlbaum.

Beijering, Karin, Charlotte Gooskens, and Wilbert Heeringa. 2008. "Predicting intelligibility and perceived linguistic distance by means of the Levenshtein algorithm." *Linguistics in the Netherlands*, 13–24.

Bell, Allan. 1984. "Language style as audience design." *Language in Society* 13:145–204.

Bell, Allan. 2013. *The Guidebook to Sociolinguistics*. Malden, MA and Oxford: Wiley-Blackwell.

Beller, Emily, and Michael Hout. 2006. "Intergenerational social mobility. The United States in comparative perspective." *Future Child* 16 (2):19–36.

Bender, Emily. 2000. "Syntactic Variation and Linguistic Competence: The Case of AAVE Copula Absence." Ph.D dissertation, Stanford University.

Bendix, Reinhart. 1960. *Max Weber: An Intellectual Portrait*. London: Heinemann.

Bentahila, A. 1983. *Language Attitudes among Arabic-French Bilinguals in Morocco*. Clevedon: Multilingual Matters.

Benwell, Bethan, and Elizabeth Stokoe. 2006. *Discourse and Identity*. Edinburgh: Edinburgh University Press.

Bernstein, Basil. 1958. "Some sociological determinants of perception. An enquiry into sub-cultural differences." *British Journal of Sociology* 9:159–174.

Bernstein, Basil. 1959. "A public language. Some sociological implications of a linguistic form." *British Journal of Sociology* 10:311–326.

Bernstein, Basil. 1960. "Language and social class. A research note." *British Journal of Sociology* 11:271–276.

Bernstein, Basil. 1961. "Social class and linguistic development. A theory of social learning." In *Education, Economy and Society. A Reader in the Sociology of Education*, edited by A.H. Halsey, J. Floud and C.A. Anderson, 288–314. New York, NY: The Free Press of Glencoe.

Bernstein, Basil. 1964. "Elaborated and restricted codes. Their social origins and some consequences." *American Anthropologist* 66 (6):55–69.

Bernstein, Basil. 1965. "A socio-linguistic approach to social learning." In *Penguin Survey of the Social Sciences*, edited by J. Gould, 144–168. Harmondsworth/New York, NY: Penguin Books.

Bernstein, Basil. 1971. *Class, Codes and Control: Theoretical Studies Towards a Sociology of Language*. Vol. 1. London: Routledge & Kegan Paul.

Bernstein, Basil. 1972. "A socio-linguistic approach to socialization: With some references to educability." In *Directions in Sociolinguistics*, edited by J. Gumperz and D Hymes. New York, NY: Holt, Rinehart & Winston.

Bhabha, Homi K. 1994. *The Location of Culture*. London: Routledge.

Bhatia, T., and W. Ritchie. 2013. "Bilingualism and Multiculturalism in South Asia." In *Handbook of Bilingualism and Multilingualism*, edited by T. Bhatia and W. Ritchie, 843–870. Oxford: Wiley-Blackwell.

Biber, D., S. Conrad, and R. Reppen. 1998. *Corpus Linguistics. Investigating Language Structure and Use*. Cambridge, MA: Cambridge University Press.

Biemans, Monique Adriana Johanna. 2000. "Gender Variation in Voice Quality." Ph.D., Department of General Linguistics, Nijmegen University.

Bigham, Douglas S. 2012. "Emerging adulthood in sociolinguistics." *Language and Linguistics Compass* 6 (8):533–544.

Blake, R. 1997. ""All o' we is one": Race, Class and Language in a Barbados Community." Ph.D., Leland Stanford Junior University.

Blishen, Bernard R. 1971. "A socioeconomic index for occupations in Canada." In *Canadian Society: Sociological Perspectives*, edited by Bernhard R. Blishen, Frank E. Jones, Kaspar D. Naegele and John Porter, 495–407. Toronto: MacMillan.

Block, David, and Victor Corona. 2016. "Intersectionality in language and identity research." In *The Routledge Handbook of Language and Identity*, edited by Siân Preece, 505–522. London: Routledge.

Blom, Jan-Petter, and John Joseph Gumperz. 1972. "Social meaning in linguistic structures: Code switching in Northern Norway." In *Directions in Sociolinguistics*, edited by John J. Gumperz and Del Hymes, 407–434. New York, NY: Holt, Rinehart, and Winston.

Blommaert, Jan. 2007. "On scope and depth in linguistic ethnography." *Journal of Sociolinguistics* 11:682–688.

Blommaert, Jan. 2010. *The Sociolinguistics of Globalization*. Cambridge, MA: Cambridge University Press.

Blommaert, Jan, and Dong Jie. 2011. *Ethnographic Fieldwork. A Beginner's Guide*. Bristol, Buffalo, NY and Toronto: Multilingual Matters.

Blommaert, Jan, and Ben Rampton. 2011. "Language and superdiversity." *Diversities* 13 (2):1–21.

Bloomfield, Leonard F. 1944. "Secondary and tertiary responses to language." *Language* 20:45–55.

Boch, Jules. 2010. *Castes et dialectes en Tamoul.* Paris: Imprimerie nationale.

Boelens, Krine, and J. Van der Veen. 1956. *De taal van het schoolkind in Friesland [The Language of the School Child in Friesland].* Leeuwarden: Fryske Akademy.

Boets, H., and Georges De Schutter. 1977. "Verstaanbaarheid en appreciatie. Nederlandse dialecten uit België zoals inwoners van Duffel die ervaren [Intelligibility and appreciation. Dutch dialects in Belgium as experienced by inhabitants of Duffel]." *Taal en Tongval* 29:156–177.

Bortoni-Ricardo, Stella Maris. 1985. *The Urbanization of Rural Dialect Speakers: A Sociolinguistic Study in Brazil.* Cambridge, MA: Cambridge University Press.

Bourdieu, Pierre. 1984. *Distinction: A Social Critique of the Judgement of Taste.* London: Routledge.

Bourdieu, Pierre. 1991. *Language and Symbolic Power.* 7th ed. Cambridge, MA: Harvard University Press.

Boztepe, Erman. 2003. "Issues in code-switching. Competing theories and models." *Working Papers in TESOL and Applied Linguistics* 3 (2):1–27.

Brandist, Craig. 2003. "The origins of Soviet sociolinguistics." *Journal of Sociolinguistics* 7 (2):213–231.

Braunmüller, K. 1990. "Sprachkonflikte als Sprachnormenkonflikte (Am Beispiel der Interskandinavischen Semikommunikation [Language conflict as language norm conflict. Inter-Scandinavian semi-communication])." In *Language Attitudes and Language Conflict,* edited by P.H. Nelde, 29–40. Bonn: Dümmler.

Bray, Marianne. 2005. "A eunuch's tale from the slums. A glimpse into a secretive world reveals a hard life." *CNN International,* 7 October 2005. Accessed 7 March 2016. Available at: http://edition.cnn.com/2005/WORLD/asiapcf/09/07/india.eye.eunuch/.

Bright, William, ed. 1966. *Sociolinguistics. Proceedings of the UCLA Conference.* The Hague: Mouton.

Bright, William, and A.K. Ramanujan. 1964. "Sociolinguistic variation and language change." In *Proceedings of the Ninth International Congress of Linguists,* edited by H.G. Lunt. The Hague: Mouton.

Britain, David, and Peter Trudgill. 2005. "New dialect formation and contact-induced reallocation: Three case studies from the English Fens." *International Journal of English Studies* 5 (1):183–209.

Brown, Penelope, and Stephen Levinson. 1987. *Politeness: Some Universals in Language Use.* Cambridge, MA: Cambridge University Press.

Bucholtz, Mary. 2003. "Sociolinguistic nostalgia and the authentication of identity." *Journal of Sociolinguistics* 7 (3):398–416.

Bucholtz, Mary, Nancy Bermudez, Victor Fung, Lisa Edwards, and Rosalva Vargas. 2007. "Hella Nor Cal or totally So Cal?: The perceptual dialectology of California." *Journal of English Linguistics* 35 (4):325–352.

Bucholtz, Mary, and Kira Hall. 2010. "Local identity in language." In *Language and Identities,* edited by Carmen Llamas and Dominic Watt, 18–28. Edinburgh: Edinburgh University Press.

Cai, C. 2011. "Language attitude of college students under the perspective of multicultural education." *Journal of Nanchang College of Education* 26 (97):79–80.

Cameron, Deborah. 1997. "Performing gender identity: Young men's talk and the construction of heterosexual masculinity." In *Language and Masculinity,* edited by Sally Johnson and Ulrike Hanna Meinhof, 47–64. Oxford: Blackwell.

Cameron, Deborah, E. Frazer, P. Harvey M.B.H. Rampton, and K. Richardson. 1992. *Researching Language: Issues of Power and Method*. London: Routledge.

Cameron, Deborah, and Don Kulick. 2003. *Language and Sexuality*. Cambridge: Cambridge University Press.

Cameron, Richard. 2005. "Aging and gendering." *Language in Society* 34:23–61.

Cao, Zhiyun, Y. 1985. "Beijing hua yuyin li de xingbie chayi [Gender differences in the phonology of the Beijing dialect]." *Hanyu Xuexi [Chinese Studies]* 6 (31).

Čekuolytė, A. 2014. "Streetwise active and cool. How do Vilnius adolescents perceive their peers' linguistic identity." *Taikomoji kalbotyra* 6:1–28.

Cenni, Irene. 2015. "Positive politeness in the Mediterranean. Sociolinguistic notions." In *Globalising Sociolinguistics. Challenging and Expanding Theory*, edited by Dick Smakman and Patrick Heinrich. London: Routledge.

Chaer, Abdul, and Leonie Agustina. 2010. *Sosiolinguistik Perkenalan Awal [Beginner's Introduction to Sociolinguistics]*. Jakarta: Rineka Cipta.

Chambers, Jack K. 2009. *Sociolinguistic Theory. Linguistic Variation and Its Social Significance (revised edition)*. Oxford: Blackwell.

Chambers, Jack K., and Peter Trudgill. 1980. *Dialectology*. 1st ed Cambridge, MA: Cambridge University Press.

Chambers, Jack K., and Peter Trudgill. 1998. *Dialectology*. 2nd ed. Cambridge, MA: Cambridge University Press.

Chatfield, Tom. 2013. *Netymology: From Apps to Zombies. A Linguistic Celebration of the Digital World*. London: Quercus Books.

Chemodanov, Nikolai, ed. 1975. *Novoe v Lingvistike [New in Linguistics]*. Moscow: Progress.

Chen, Y. 1980. *Yuyan Yu Shenghuo [Language and Social Life]*. Shanghai: Xuelin Press.

Chen, Y. 1983. *Shehui Yuyanxue [Sociolinguistics]*. Beijing: Sanlian Press.

Cheshire, Jenny. 2005. "Age and generation-specific use of language." In *Sociolinguistics: An Introductory Handbook of the Science of Language and Society*, edited by Ulrich Ammon, N. Dittmar, K. Mattheier and Peter Trudgill, 1552–1563. Berlin: Mouton de Gruyter.

Cheshire, Jenny, and James Milroy. 1993. "Syntactic variation in non-standard dialects: Background issues." In *Real English: The Grammar of English Dialects in the British Isles*, edited by Lesley Milroy and James Milroy, 3–33. Harlow: Longman.

Cirillo, Chiara. 2002. "Sexism and Gender Issues in the Italian Language." In *Multilingualism in Italy. Past and Present*, edited by Anna Laura Lepschy and Arturo Tosi, 141–149. Cambridge: Legenda.

Clark, S. 1988. "Linguistic stratification in the non-stratified social context." In *Methods in Dialectology*, edited by A.R. Thomas, 684–699. Clevedon: Multilingual Matters.

Clyne, Michael. 1994. *Intercultural Communication at Work: Cultural Values in Discourse*. Cambridge, MA/New York, NY: Cambridge University Press.

Coates, Jennifer, and Pia Pichler, eds. 2011. *Language and Gender. A Reader*. Chichester: Wiley-Blackwell.

Coggle, Paul. 1993. *Do you Speak Estuary?* London: Bloomsbury.

Coles, Anne, and Katie Walsh. 2010. "From "Trucial State" to "Postcolonial" City? The imaginative geographies of British expatriates in Dubai." *Journal of Ethnic and Migration Studies* 36 (8):1317–1333.

Cook, Vivian. 2009. *Second Language Learning and language Teaching*. London: Hodder.

Cooper, D.R., and C.W. Emory. 1995. *Business Research Methods*. 5th ed. Chicago, IL: Irwin.

Cornips, Leonie. 1998. "Syntactic variation, parameters and social distribution." *Language Variation and Change* 10:1–21.

Cornips, Leonie, and Vincent A. De Rooij. 2013. "Selfing and othering through categories of race, place, and language among minority youths in Rotterdam, The Netherlands." In *Multilingualism and Language Diversity in Urban Areas: Acquisition, Identities, Space, Education,* edited by Peter Siemund, Ingrid Gogolin, Monika Edith Schulz and Julia Davydova, 129–164. Amsterdam: John Benjamins.

Coulmas, Florian. 2011. "Foreword." In *Language Life in Japan. Transformations and Prospects,* edited by Patrick Heinrich and Christian Galan. Abingdon: Routledge.

Coulmas, Florian. 2013. *Sociolinguistics. The Study of Speakers' Choices.* Cambridge, MA: Cambridge University Press.

Coulmas, Florian. 2016. *Guardians of Language. Twenty Voices through History.* Oxford: Oxford University Press.

Coupland, Nikolas. 1997. "Language, ageing and ageism. A project for applied linguistics?" *International Journal of Applied Linguistics* 7:26–48.

Coupland, Nikolas. 2001. "Language, situation and the relational self. Theorizing dialect shift in sociolinguistics." In *Style and Sociolinguistic Variation,* edited by John R. Rickford and Penelope Eckert, 185–210. Cambridge, MA: Cambridge University Press.

Coupland, Nikolas, ed. 2016. *Sociolinguistics. Theoretical Debates.* Cambridge, MA: Cambridge University Press.

Croucher, Stephen M., ed. 2017. *Global Perspectives on Intercultural Communication.* London: Routledge.

Crystal, David. 1995. *A Dictionary of Linguistics and Phonetics.* Oxford: Blackwell.

Culpeper, J. 2011. *Impoliteness. Using and Understanding the Language of Offence.* Cambridge, MA: Cambridge University Press.

Cuonz, Christina. 2010. "Folk Conceptualisations of German Varieties in Switzerland: A Case of Inherent Ugliness?" In *34th International LAUD Symposium: Cognitive Sociolinguistics: Language Variation in Its Structural, Conceptual and Cultural Dimensions,* 376–290. Essen: LAUD Agency Prepublication.

Currie, Haver. 1952. "Projection of sociolinguistics: The relationship of speech to social status." *Southern Speech Journal* 18:28–37.

Dai, Qingxia X. 1993. *Shehui Yuyanxue Jiaocheng [An Introduction to Sociolinguistics].* Beijing: Central University for Nationalities Press.

Dailey, R.M., Howard Giles, and L.L. Jansma. 2005. "Language attitudes in an Anglo-Hispanic context: The role of the linguistic landscape." *Language and Communication* 25:27–38.

Danesi, Marcel. 2016. *Language, Society and Media. Sociolinguistics Today.* New York, NY/Abingdon: Routledge.

Danilov, Georgy Konstantinovich. 1929. "Yazyk obshchestvennogo klassa [The language of a social class]." *Uchenye zapiski Instituta yazyka i literatury RANION [Scientific notes of the Institute of Language and Literature RANION]* 3:163–194.

Davies, P., and E. Pearse. 2000. *Success in English Teaching.* Oxford: Oxford University Press.

Dawes, John. 2008. "Do data characteristics change according to the number of scale points used? An experiment using 5-point, 7-point and 10-point scales." *International Journal of Market Research* 50 (1):61–77.

De Koning, Anouk. 2009. *Global Dreams: Class, Gender, and Public Space in Cosmopolitan Cairo.* Cairo: The American University in Cairo Press.

De Saussure, Ferdinand. 1978 [1916]. *Course in General Linguistics [Introduction by Jonathan Culler].* London/New York, NY: Fontana/Collins.

Demirci, Mahide, and Brian Kleiner. 1999. "The perception of Turkish dialects." In *Handbook of Perceptual Dialectology*, 263–282. Amsterdam/Philadelphia, PA: John Benjamins.

Despagne, Colette. 2010. "The difficulties of learning English. Perceptions and attitudes in Mexico." *Education canadienne et internationale* 39 (2):59–74.

Deuchar, Margaret. 1989. "A Pragmatic Account of Women's Use of Standard Speech." In *Women in their Speech Communities: New Perspectives on Language and Sex*, edited by Jennifer Coates and Deborah Tannen, 27–32. London: Longman.

Devonish, Hubert. 2015. "The Creole-speaking Caribbean: The architecture of language variation." In *Globalising Sociolinguistics. Challenging and Expanding Theory*, edited by Dick Smakman and Patrick Heinrich. London: Routledge.

Dewaele, J.M. 2004. "Retention or omission of the ne in advanced French interlanguage: The variable effect of extralinguistic factors." *Journal of Sociolinguistics* 8 (3):333–350.

Di Paolo, Marianna, and Malcah Yaeger-Dror, eds. 2010. *Sociophonetics: A Student's Guide*. New York, NY: Routledge.

Díaz-Campos, Manual, ed. 2011. *The Handbook of Hispanic Sociolinguistics*. Malden, MA: Wiley-Blackwell.

Dick, Howard. 2015. "Policy regimes, statistics and unintended consequences: Transitions in Indonesia's Modern Economic History." In *Promises and Predicaments: Trade Entrepreneurship in Colonial and Independent Indonesia in the 19th and 20th Centuries*, edited by Alicia Schrikker and Jeroen Touwen, 279–97. Singapore: NUS Press.

Dick, Howard, Vincent Houben, J. Thomas Lindblad, and Wie Thee Kian. 2002. *The Emergence of a National Economy: An Economic History of Indonesia, 1800–2000*. Honolulu, HI/Leiden/Sydney: University of Hawaii Press/KITLV Press/Allen & Unwin.

Dil, Anwar S., ed. 1976. *Aspects of Chinese Sociolinguistic*. Stanford, CA: Stanford University Press.

Dillard, Joey Lee. 1972. *Black English. Its History and Usage in the United States*. New York, NY: Random House.

Dinkin, Aaron J. 2009. "Dialect Geography and Phonological Change in Upstate New York." University of Pennsylvania.

Dorian, Nancy C. 1981. *Language death: The Life Cycle of a Scottish Gaelic Dialect*. Philadelphia, PA: University of Pennsylvania Press.

Dornyei, Zoltan. 2003. "Attitudes, orientations, and motivations in language learning: Advances in theory, research, and applications." In *Attitudes, Orientations, and Motivations in Language Learning*, edited by Zoltan Dornyei, 3–32. Malden, MA: Wiley-Blackwell.

Dow, Steve. 2010. "Neither man nor woman." *Sydney Morning Herald*, 27 June 2010.

Downes, William. 1998. *Language and Society*. 2nd ed. Cambridge, MA: Cambridge University Press.

Drager, Katie. 2014. "Experimental methods in sociolinguistics." In *Research Methods in Sociolinguistics. A Practical Guide*, edited by Janet Holmes and Kirk Hazen, 58–73. Chichester: Wiley Blackwell.

Drbohlav, D. 2011. "Imigrace a integrace cizinců v Česku: několik zastavení na cestě země v její migrační proměně z Davida na téměř Goliáše [Migration and integration of foreigners in the Czech Republic: Several stops to go. The transformation of migration from a David to a Goliath]." *Geografie* 4 (116):401–421.

Duběda, T., M. Havlík, L. Jílková, and V. Štěpánová. 2013. "Loanwords and foreign proper names in Czech: A phonologist's view." In *Language Use and Linguistic Structure*.

Proceedings of the Olomouc Linguistic Colloquium 2013, edited by J. Edmonds and M. Janebová, 313–321. Olomouc Univerzita Palackého.

Duchênes, Alexandre. 2008. *Ideologies Across Nations. The Construction of Linguistic Minorities at the United Nations*. Berlin: Mouton de Gruyter.

Dular, Janez. 1986. "Ohranjanje maternega jezika pri slovenski manjšini v Porabju [Native language maintenance among the Slovene minority in Porabje]." *Slavistic'na Revija [The Slavonics Journal]* 34:121–134.

Dunn, Michael. 2014. "Gender determined dialect variation." In *The Expression of Gender*, edited by G.G. Corbett, 39–68. Berlin: De Gruyter.

Dyer, Judy. 2001. "Changing dialects and identities in a Scottish-English community." *University of Pennsylvania Working Papers in Linguistics* 7 (3):43–57.

Dyers, C. 2004. "Ten years of democracy: Attitudes and identity among some South African school children." *Per Linguam* 20:22–35.

Eades, Diana. 2010. *Sociolinguistics and the Legal Process*. Bristol/Buffalo, NY/Toronto: Multilingual Matters.

Eagly, A.H., and S. Chaiken. 1993. *The Psychology of Attitudes*. San Diego, CA: Harcourt Brace Jovanovich College Publishers.

Eagly, A.H., and S. Chaiken. 2005. *Attitude Research in the 21st Century: The Current State of Knowledge*. Mahwah, NJ: Lawrence Erlbaum Associates Publishers.

Eckert, Penelope. 1997. "Age as a sociolinguistic variable." In *The Handbook of Sociolinguistics*, edited by Florian Coulmas, 151–167. Oxford: Blackwell.

Eckert, Penelope. 2000. *Linguistic Variation as Social Practice: The Linguistic Construction of Belten High*. Malden, MA: Blackwell.

Eckert, Penelope. 2003. "Language and gender in adolescence." In *The Handbook of Language and Gender*, edited by Janet Holmes and Miriam Meyerhoff, 381–400. Oxford: Blackwell.

Eckert, Penelope. 2008. "Variation and the indexical field." *Journal of Sociolinguistics* 12 (4):453–476.

Eckert, Penelope, and Sally McConnell-Ginet. 1992. "Think practically and look locally: Language and gender as community-based practice." *Annual Review of Anthropology* 21:461–490.

Edisherashvili, Natalia. 2014. *Communicative Language Teaching in Georgia. From Theory to Practice*. Utrecht: Landelijk Onderzoeksschool Taalwetenschap.

Edwards, J.R. 1977. "Students' reactions to Irish regional accents." *Language and Speech* 20 (3):280–286.

Edygarova, S. 2014. "The varieties of the modern Udmurt language." *Finnisch-Ugrische Forschungen* 6 (2):376–398.

Eelen, Gino. 2001. *A Critique of Politeness Theories*. Manchester: St. Jerome.

Eichinger, L.M., Gärting, A.K., A. Plewnia, Roessel, J., A. Rothe, S. Rudert, C. Schoel, D. Stahlberg, and G. Stickel. 2009. *Aktuelle Spracheinstellungen in Deutschland [Contemporary language attitudes in Germany]*. Mannheim: Institut für Deutsche Sprache.

Eller, Jack David. 2016. *Cultural Anthropology. Global Forces, Local Lives*. 3rd ed. London/New York, NY: Routledge.

Elliott, Anthony. 2016. *Identity Troubles. An Introduction*. London/New York, NY: Routledge.

Elliott, Anthony, and Charles Lemert. 2009. *The New Individualism. The Emotional Costs of Globalization*. 2nd ed. London: Routledge.

Elliott, Anthony, and John Urry. 2011. *Mobile Lives*. Cambridge, MA: Routledge.

Elliott, Z., and L. Hall-Lew. 2015. "Production of FACE and GOAT by Slovak and Czech immigrants in Edinburgh." In *Proceedings of the 18th International Congress of Phonetic Sciences*, edited by The Scottish Consortium for ICPhS 2015. Glasgow: University of Glasgow.

Eltouhamy, Ibrahim. 2016. "Language attitudes towards rural dialects of Arabic in Egypt." MA Degree, American University in Cairo.

Estaji, Azam, and Fakhteh Nakhavali. 2011. "Semantic Derogation in Persian Animal Proverbs." *Theory and Practice in Language Studies* 1 (9):1213–1217.

Evangelos, Afendras, and Eddie Kuo, eds. 1980. *Language and Society in Singapore*. Singapore: Singapore University Press.

Evans, Betsy E. 2004. "The role of social network in the acquisition of local dialect norms by Appalachian migrants in Ypsilanti, Michigan." *Language Variation and Change* 16:153–166.

Evans, Betsy E. 2011. "Seattletonian' to 'Faux Hick': Perceptions of English in Washington State." *American Speech* 86 (4):383–414.

Evans Wagner, Suzanne. 2012. "Age Grading in Sociolinguistic Theory." *Language and Linguistics Compass* 6 (6):371–382.

Fedorova, Kapitolina. 2018. "Elusive variables: Problems of studying social class variation in Russian." *Urban Sociolinguistics around the World: The City as a Linguistic Process and Experience*, edited by Dick Smakman and Patrick Heinrich. London: Routledge.

Ferguson, Charles. 1959. "Diglossia." *Word* 15:325–340.

Ferrer, R.C. 2010. "Changing linguistic attitudes in Valencia: The effects of language planning measures." *Journal of Sociolinguistics* 14:477–500.

Filipović, Jelena, Julijana Vučo, and Ljiljana Djurić. 2007. "Critical review of language education policies in compulsory Primary and Secondary Education in Serbia." *Current Issues in Language Planning* 8 (2):222–242.

Findlow, Sally. 2006. "Higher education and linguistic dualism in the Arab Gulf." *British Journal of the Sociology of Education* 27 (1):19–36.

Finegan, Edward. 2007. *Language: Its Structure and Use*. Boston, MA: Thomson Wadsworth.

Finlayson, Rosalie, and Sarah Slabbert. 1997. ""I'll meet you halfway with language". Code-switching within a South African urban context." In *Language Choices. Conditions, Constraints and Consequences*, edited by Martin Pütz, 381–421. Amsterdam/Philadelphia, PA: John Benjamins.

Fishman, Joshua Aaron. 1958. "Social influences on the choice of a linguistic variant." *Word* 14:47–56.

Fishman, Joshua Aaron. 1964. "Language maintenance and language shift as fields of inquiry." *Linguistics* 9:32–70.

Foley, William A. 2003. "Genre, register and language documentation in literate and preliterate communities." *Language Documentation and Description* 1:85–98.

Fortune, Gretchen. 1998. "Sex-Exclusive Differentiation in the Karaja Language of Bananal Island, Central Brazil." Ph.D., Lancaster University.

Fortune, Gretchen, and David L. Fortune. 1975. "Karajá Men's-women's speech differences with social correlates." *Arquivos De Anatomia e Antropologia* 1:111–124.

Fox, Susan. 2015. *The New Cockney: New Ethnicities and Adolescent Speech in the Traditional East End of London*. Basingstoke: Palgrave Macmillan.

Fox, Susan, and Devyani Sharma. 2018. "The language of London and Londoners." In *Urban Sociolinguistics around the World: The City as a Linguistic Process and Experience*, edited by Dick Smakman and Patrick Heinrich. London: Routledge.

Friedrich, Patricia, and Eduardo H. Diniz de Figueiredo. 2016. *The Sociolinguistics of Digital Englishes*. Abingdon: Routledge.

Friginal, Erik, and Jack A. Hardy. 2014. *Corpus-Based Sociolinguistics. A Guide for Students*. New York, NY: Routledge.

Fu, Yirong. 2011. *Yanyu shequ he yuyan bianhua yanjiu: Jiyu anhui fucun de shehui yuyanxue diaocha [Studies of the Speech Community and Language Change: A Sociolinguistic Investigation of the Fu Village in Anhui]*. Beijing: Peking University Press.

Fuertes, J.N. W. Gottdiener, H. Martin, T.C. Gilbert, and Howard Giles. 2012. "A meta-analysis of the effects of speakers' accents on interpersonal evaluations." *European Journal of Social Psychology* 42:120–133.

Fukuyama, Francis. 1992. *The End of History and the Last Man*. New York, NY: The Free Press.

Gadet, F. 1989. *Le français ordinaire*. Paris: Armand Colin.

Gal, Susan. 1978. "Peasant men can't get wives. language change and sex roles in a bilingual community." *Language in Society* 7:1–16.

Gal, Susan. 1979. *Language Shift. Social Determinants of Linguistic Change in Bilingual Austria*. San Francisco, CA: Academic Press.

Galan, Christian. 2011. "Out of this world, in this world, or both? The Japanese school at the threshold." In *Language Life in Japan. Transformations and Prospects*, edited by Patrick Heinrich and Christian Galan. London/New York, NY: Routledge.

Garcia, Ofelia, and Li Wei. 2014. *Translanguaging: Language, Bilingualism and Education*. London: Palgrave Macmillan.

Garrett, Peter. 2005. "Messung von Einstellungen [Attitude measurements]." In *Soziolinguistik. Ein internationales Handbuch zur Wissenschaft von Sprache und Gesellschaft [Sociolinguistics. An International Handbook of the Science of Language and Society]*, edited by Ulrich Ammon, N. Dittmar, K. Mattheier and Peter Trudgill, 1251–1260. Berlin/New York, NY: Walter de Gruyter.

Garrett, Peter. 2010. *Attitudes to Language*. Cambridge, MA: Cambridge University Press.

Garvin, R. 2010. "Postmodern: walking tour." In *Linguistic Landscape in the City*, edited by E. Shohamy, E. Ben-Rafael and Barni. M., 254–276. Clevedon: Multilingual Matters.

Gawronski, B. 2007. "Attitudes can be measured! But what is an attitude?" *Social Cognition* 25 (5):573–581.

Geeslin, Kimberly L., and Avizia Yim Long. 2014. *Sociolinguistics and Second Language Acquisition: Learning to Use Language in Context* New York, NY: Routledge.

Gibbs, James L., 1964. *Social Organizational Studies in American Anthropology*. Edited by Sol Taks, *Anthropology Series 12*. Washington, DC: US Information Services.

Giddens, Anthony. 1991. *Modernity and Self-identity. Self and Society in the Late Modern Age*. Cambridge, MA: Polity Press.

Giles, Howard. 1970. "Evaluative reactions to accents." *Educational Review* 22:211–227.

Giles, Howard. 1973. "Accent mobility. A model and some data." *Anthropological Linguistics* 15:87–105.

Giles, Howard, and A.C. Billings. 2004. "Assessing language attitudes: Speaker evaluation studies." In *The Handbook of Applied Linguistics*, edited by A. Davies and C. Elder, 187–209. Oxford: Blackwell.

Giles, Howard, Richard Y. Bourhis, and Ann Davies. 1979. "Prestige speech styles: The imposed norm and inherent-value hypotheses." In *Language and Society: Anthropological Issues*, edited by William Charles McCormack and Stephen Adolphe Wurm, 589–596. The Hague: Mouton.

Giles, Howard, Richard Y. Bourhis, and Donald M. Taylor. 1977. "Towards a theory of language in ethnic intergroup relations." In *Language Ethnicity and Intergroup Relations*, edited by Howard Giles, 307–348. London: Academic Press.

Giles, Howard, Richard Y. Bourhis, Peter Trudgill, and Alan Lewis. 1974. "The imposed norm hypothesis: A validation." *Quarterly Journal of Speech* 60:405–410.

Giles, Howard, Nikolas Coupland, and Justine Coupland. 1991. *Contexts of Accommodation*. New York: Cambridge University Press.

Giles, Howard, and Nancy Niedzielski. 1998. "Italian is beautiful, German is ugly." In *Language Myths*, edited by Laurie Bauer and Peter Trudgill, 85–93. London: Penguin.

Giles, Howard, and Tania Ogay. 2007. "Communication accommodation theory." In *Explaining Communication: Contemporary Theories and Exemplars*, edited by Bryan B. Whaley and Wendy Samter, 293–310. Mahwah, NJ: Lawrence Erlbaum.

Giles, Howard, and P.F. Powesland. 1975. *Speech Style and Social Evaluation*. London: Academic Press.

Giles, Howard, and Philip Smith. 1979. "Accommodation theory. Optimal levels of convergence." In *Language and Social Psychology*, edited by Howard Giles and Robert N. St. Clair, 45–65. Baltimore: Basil Blackwell.

Gluszek, Agata, and Karolina Hansen. 2013. "Language attitudes in the Americas" In *The Social Meanings of Language, Dialect and Accent. International Perspectives on Speech Styles*, edited by Howard Giles and Bernadette Watson, 26–44. New York, NY: Peter Lang.

Goddard, Cliff, and Anna Wierbicka. 2004. "Cultural scripts. What are they and what are they good for?" *Intercultural Pragmatics* 1 (2):153–166.

Goebel, Zane. 2005. "An ethnographic study of code choice in two neighbourhoods of Indonesia" *Australian Journal of Linguistics* 25:85–107.

Goeman, Ton. 2000. "Naast NORMs ook MYSFs in het veranderende dialectlandschap en het regiolect [Besides NORMs also MYSFs in the changing dialect landscape and the regiolect]." *Taal en Tongval* 52 (1):87–100.

Goffman, Erwin. 1967. *Interaction Ritual. Essays on Face to Face Behaviour*. New York, NY: Pantheon.

Gordon, J.C.B. 1981. *Verbal Deficit*. Totowa, NJ: Croom Helm Ltd.

Gould, Stephen Jay. 2000. *Wonderful Life. The Burgess Shale and the Nature of History*. New York, NY: Vintage.

Graddol, D. 2006. *English Next*. London: British Council.

Granovetter, Mark S. 1973. "The strength of weak ties." *American Journal of Sociology* 78 (6):1360–1380.

Grassi, Corrado. 2001. "Dialetto, quasi dialetto, non più dialetto. Brevi note in margine ad alcune recenti pubblicazioni [Dialect, near-dialect, no longer dialect. Short notes in the margin and some recent publications]." I confini del dialetto. Atti del convegno [Dialect boundaries. Conference proceedings], Sappada/Plodn (Belluno), 5–9 July 2000, Padua.

Greenberg, Robert D. 1996. "The Politics of Dialects Among Serbs, Croats, and Muslims in the Former Yugoslavia." *East European Politics and Societies* 10 (3):393–415.

Griffin, E. 2009. *A First Look at Communication Theory*. 7th ed. New York, NY: McGraw-Hill.

Gritsai, Olga, and Herman Van der Wusten. 2000. "Moscow and St. Petersburg, a sequence of capitals, a tale of two cities" *GeoJournal* 51 (1/2):33–45.

Grootaers, Willem A. 1964. "La discussion autours des frontieres dialectales subjectives [The discussion on subjective dialect boundaries]." *Orbis* 13:380–398.

Grosjean, F. 1982. *Life with Two Languages. An Introduction to Bilingualism*. Cambridge, MA: Harvard University Press.

Guilliéron, Jacques, and Edmond Edmont. 1902–1910. *Atlas Linguistique de la France*. Paris: H. Champion.

Guitarte, Guillermo. 1955. "El ensordecimiento del zaísmo porteño [The silencing of Buenosairean Zaísmo]." *RFE* 39:261–283.

Gumperz, John Joseph. 1958. "Dialect Differences and Social Stratification in a North Indian Village." *American Anthropologist* 60 (4):668–682.

Gumperz, John Joseph. 1967. "Language and communication." *The Annals of the American Academy of Political and Social Sciences* 373:219–231.

Gumperz, John Joseph. 1971. *Language in Social Groups. Essays by John J. Gumperz. Selected and Introduced by Anwar S. Dil*. Stanford, CA: Stanford University Press.

Gumperz, John Joseph. 1982. *Discourse Strategies*. Cambridge, MA: Cambridge University Press.

Gumperz, John Joseph, and Dell H. Hymes, eds. 1964. *The Ethnography of Communication*. New York, NY: Holt.

Gumperz, John Joseph, and Dell H. Hymes. 1972. *Directions in Sociolinguistics. The Ethnography of Communication*. New York, NY: Holt, Rinehart and Winston.

Hachimi, Atiqa. 2007. "Becoming Casablancan. Fessis in Casablanca as a case study." In *Arabic in the City. Issues in Dialect Contact and Language Variation*, edited by Catherine Miller, 97–122. London: Routledge.

Haeri, Niloofar. 1987. "Male/female differences in speech: An alternative interpretation." NWAV-XV at Stanford, Stanford, CA.

Haeri, Niloofar. 1995. "Language and gender in the Arab world: Analysis, explanation, and ideology." *Language and Gender* 2:25–45.

Hagen, A.M. (1990). Groepsportret van het Nederlands [Group portrait of the Dutch language]. *Onze Taal, 2/3*, 32–39.

Hall, Edward Twitchell. 1959. *The Silent Language*. New York, NY: Doubleday.

Hall, Edward Twitchell. 1976. *Beyond Culture*. New York, NY: Doubleday.

Hall, Stuart. 1992. "The question of cultural identity." In *Modernity and Its Futures*, edited by Susan Hall, D. Held and T. McGrew, 274–316. Cambridge, MA: Polity Press/Open University.

Halliday, Michael A.K. 1976. "Anti-languages." *American Anthropologist* 78 (3): 570–584.

Halliday, Michael A.K. 1977. "Ideas about language." In *Aims and Perspectives in Linguistics*, 32–49. Applied Linguistics Association of Australia. Occasional Papers.

Halman, Loek, Ronald F. Inglehart, Jaime Díez-Medrano, Ruud Luijkx, Alejandro Moreno, and Miguel Basáñez. 2008. *Changing Values and Beliefs in 85 Countries. Trends from the Values Surveys from 1981 to 2004*. Leiden: Brill.

Hardcastle, William J., John Laver, and Fiona E. Gibbon. 2013. *The Handbook of Phonetic Sciences*. Malden, MA: Wiley-Blackwell.

Hassall, Tim, Elisabet Titik Murtisari, Christine Donelly, and Jeff Wood. 2008. "Attitudes to Western loanwords in Indonesian." *International Journal of the Sociology of Language* 189:55–84.

Haugen, Einar 1966. "Dialect, language, nation." *American Anthropologist* 68:922–935.

Hazen, Kirk. 2014. "A historical assessment of research questions in sociolinguistics." In *Research Methods in Sociolinguistics: A Practical Guide*, edited by Janet Holmes and Kirk Hazen, 7–22. Malden, MA: Wiley Blackwell.

Heeringa, Wilbert, Febe De Wet, and Gerhard B. Van Huyssteen. 2015. "Afrikaans and Dutch as closely-related languages: A comparison to West Germanic languages and Dutch dialects." In *Stellenbosch Papers in Linguistics Plus*, edited by Christine

Anthonissen, Johan Oosthuizen, Frenette Southwood and Kate Huddlestone, 1–18. Stellenbosch: Stellenbosch University.

Heinrich, Patrick. 2010. Difficulties of establishing heritage language education in Uchinaa. In *Language life in Japan*, 34–49. Abingdon: Routledge.

Heinrich, Patrick. 2015. "The study of politeness and women's language in Japan." In *Globalising Sociolinguistics. Challenging and Expanding Theory*, edited by Dick Smakman and Patrick Heinrich. London: Routledge.

Heinrich, Patrick, and Hidenori Masiko. 2015. "Japanese sociolinguistics. A critical review and outlook." In *Contemporary Japan. Challenges for a World Economic Power in Transition*, edited by Paolo Calvetti and Marcella Mariotti, 249–266. Venice: Edizioni Ca' Foscari.

Heller, Monica. 2007. *Bilingualism: A Social Approach*. Basingstoke: Palgrave Macmillan.

Hendriks, Berna, Frank Van Meurs, and Nanette Hogervorst. 2016. "Effect of degree of accentedness in lecturers' Dutch-English pronunciation on Dutch students' attitudes and perception of comprehensibility." *Dutch Journal of Applied Linguistics* 5 (1):1–17.

Henrich, J., S. Heine, and A. Norenzayan. 2011. "The WEIRDest people in the world?" *Behavioral and Brain Sciences* 33 (33):61–135.

Hernández-Campoy, Juan Manuel. 2016. *Sociolinguistic Styles (Language in Society)*. Chichester: Wiley Blackwell.

Herring, S.C. 2004. "Computer-mediated discourse analysis. An approach to researching online communities." In *Designing for Virtual Communities in the Service of Learning*, edited by S.A. Barab, R. Kling and J.H. Gray, 338–376. Cambridge, MA: Cambridge University Press.

Hibiya, Junko. 1988. "A Quantitative Study of Tokyo Japanese." Ph.D., University of Pennsylvania.

Hill, Jane H. 2008. *The Everyday Language of White Racism*. Oxford: Wiley-Blackwell.

Hiroshi, Ota, Jake Harwood, Angie Williams, and Jiro Takai. 2000. "A cross-cultural analysis of age identity in Japan and the United States." *Journal of Multilingual and Multicultural Development* 21:33–43.

Hockett, Charles F. 1950. "Age-grading and linguistic continuity." *Language* 26:449–459.

Hockett, Charles F. 1958. *A Course in Modern Linguistics*. New York, NY: MacMillan.

Hodson, Thomas Callan. 1939. "Sociolinguistics in India." *Man in India* XIX:94.

Hoenigswald, Henry. 1966. "A proposal for the study of folk-linguistics." In *Sociolinguistics*, edited by W. Bright, 16–26. The Hague: Mouton.

Hofstede, Geert. n.d. "The Hofstede Centre." The Hofstede Centre. Accessed 1 March 2017. Available at: http://geert-hofstede.com/.

Hofstede, Geert. 1980. *Culture's Consequences: International Differences in Work-Related Values*. Beverly Hills, CA: Sage Publications.

Hofstede, Geert, Gert Jan Hofstede, and Michael Minkov. 2010. *Cultures and Organizations: Software of the Mind*. 3rd ed. New York, NY: McGraw-Hill.

Hogan-Brun, G., and M. Ramonienė. 2005. "Perspectives on language attitudes and use in Lithuania's multilingual setting." *Journal of Multilingual and Multicultural Development* 26 (5):425–441.

Hogg, M.A., N. Joyce, and D. Abrams. 1984. "Diglossia in Switzerland? A social identity analysis of speaker evaluations." *Journal of Language and Social Psychology* 3 (3):185–196.

Hogg, M.A., and G. Vaughan. 2005. *Social Psychology*. 4th ed. London: Prentice-Hall.

Holmes, Janet. 1998. "Women's talk: The question of sociolinguistic universals." In *Language and Gender. A Reader*, edited by Jennifer Coates, 461–483. Oxford: Blackwell.

Holmes, Janet. 2001. *An Introduction to Sociolinguistics*. Harlow: Pearson.

Holmes, Janet, Allan Bell, and Mary Boyce. 1991. Variation and Change in New Zealand English. A Social Dialect Investigation. Project Report to the Social Sciences Committee of the Foundation for Research, Science and Technology. Wellington: Victoria University.

Honey, John. 1985. "Acrolect and hyperlect: The redefinition of English RP." *English Studies* 3:241–257.

Horii, R. 1992. *Hataraku Josei no Kotoba [The Language of Working Women]*. Tokyo: Meiji Shoin.

Horvath, B. 1985. *Variation in Australian English: The Sociolects of Sydney*. Cambridge, MA: Cambridge University Press.

Horvath, B. 2005. "Australian English: Phonology." In *A Handbook of Varieties of English: A Multimedia Reference Tool*, edited by E.W. Schneider and B. Kortmann, 625–664. Berlin: Mouton de Gruyter.

Horvath, B., and R. Horvath. 2001. "A multilocality study of a sound change in progress: The case of /l/ vocalization in New Zealand and Australian English." *Language Variation and Change* 13:37–56.

Hu, Hsien Chin. 1944. "The Chinese concept of 'face'." *American Anthropologist* 46:45–64.

Hundt, M., N. Nesselhauf, and C. Biewer, eds. 2007. *Corpus Linguistics and the Web.* Amsterdam: Rodopi.

Hymes, Dell H. 1964. "Introduction: Toward ethnographies of communication." *American Anthropologist* 66 (6):1–34.

Ibrahim, Muhammad H. 1986. "Standard and prestige language: A problem in Arabic sociolinguistics." *Anthropological Linguistics* 28 (1):115–126.

Ide, Sachiko, and Megumi Yoshida. 1999. "Sociolinguistics: Honorifics and gender differences." In *The Handbook of Japanese Linguistics*, edited by Natsuko Tsujimura, 444–480. Oxford: Blackwell.

Inglehart, Ronald F., and Christian Welzel. 2004. "What insights can multi-country surveys provide about people and societies?" *APSA Comparative Politics Newsletter* 15 (2):14–18.

Inglehart, Ronald F., and Christian Welzel. 2005. *Modernization, Cultural Change, and Democracy: The Human Development Sequence*. Cambridge, MA: Cambridge University Press.

Inoue, Fumio. 1972. "Chiiki meisho to hôgensha ishiki [Names of districts and consciousness of dialect differences]." *Chimeigaku Kenkyu* 1:18–30.

Inoue, Fumio. 1996. "Subjective dialect division in Great Britain." *American Speech* 71 (2):142–161.

Inoue, Fumio. 2011. "Standardization and de-standardization processes in spoken Japanese." In *Language Life in Japan. Transformations and Prospects*, edited by Patrick Heinrich and Christian Galan, 109–123. London/New York, NY: Routledge.

Inoue, Miyako. 2006. *Vicarious Language. Gender and Linguistic Modernity*. Berkeley, CA: University of California Press.

Intachakra, Songthama. 2001. "Linguistic Politeness in British English and Thai: A comparative analysis of three expressive speech acts." Ph.D., Queen Mary, University of London.

Irvine, Judith T., and Susan Gal. 2000. "Language ideology and linguistic differentiation." In *Regimes of Language. Ideologies, Polities, and Identities*, edited by Paul V. Kroskrity, 35–84. Santa Fe, NM: School of American Research Press.

Jackendoff, Ray. 1992. *Languages of the Mind*. Cambridge, MA: MIT Press.

Jackendoff, Ray. 1994. *Patterns in the Mind. Language and Human Nature*. New York, NY: Basic Books.

Jackendoff, Ray. 2003a. *Foundations of Language*. Oxford: Oxford University Press.

Jackendoff, Ray. 2003b. "The structure of language: Why it matters to education." Conference on Learning and the Brain, Cambridge, MA, 5–8 November 2003.

Jacobs, Greg. 1996. "Lesbian and gay male language use: A critical review of the literature." *American Speech* 71 (1):49–71.

Jaffe, Alexandria. 2004. "Language rights and wrongs. A commentary." In *Language Rights and Language Survival*, edited by Jane Freeland and Donna Patrick. Manchester: St. Jerome Publishing.

James, D., and J. Drakich. 1993. "Understanding gender differences in amount of talk: A critical review of research." In *Gender and Conversational Interaction*, edited by Deborah Tanne, 281–312. New York, NY: Oxford University Press.

James, Paul. 2006. *Globalism, Nationalism, Tribalism*. London: Sage Publications.

Jameson, Fredric. 2011. *Representing Capital: A Commentary on Volume One*. London: Verso.

Jaworski, A. 1992. *The Power of Silence, Social and Pragmatic Perspectives*. Newbury Park, CA: Sage.

Jenkins, Jennifer. 2009. *World Englishes: A Resource Book for Students*. 2nd ed. London: Routledge.

Jespersen, Otto. 1925. *Mankind, Nation and Individual from a Linguistic Point of View*. Cambridge, MA: Harvard University Press.

JLU. 2005. *Jamaican Language Unit*. Kingston: University of the West Indies.

John, Theresa Arevgaq. 2015. "Nutemllaq Yugtun qaneryararput. Our very own way of speaking Yugtun in Alaska." In *Globalising Sociolinguistics. Challenging and Expanding Theory*, edited by Dick Smakman and Patrick Heinrich, 233–242. London: Routledge.

Jørgensen, J.N., Martha Sif Karrebæk, Lian Malai Madsen, and J.S. Møller. 2011. "Polylanguaging in Superdiversity." *Diversities* 13 (2):23–37.

Joseph, John E. 1987. *Eloquence and Power: The Rise of Language Standards and Standard Languages*. New York, NY: Blackwell.

Joseph, John E. 2004. *Language and Identity. National, Ethnic, Religious*. Basingstoke/New York, NY: Palgrave MacMillan.

Joseph, John E. 2010. "Identity." In *Language and Identities*, edited by Carmen Llamas and Dominic Watt, 9–17. Edinburgh: Edinburgh University Press.

Joseph, John E., Nigel Love, and Talbot J. Taylor. 2001. *Landmarks in Linguistic Thought II. The Western Tradition in the Twentieth Century*. London/New York, NY: Routledge.

Kachru, Braj B. 1976. "Models of English for The Third World: White man's linguistic burden or language pragmatics?" *TESOL Quarterly* 10 (2):221–239.

Kachru, Braj B. 1985. "Standards, codification and sociolinguistic realism: The English language in the outer circle." In *English in the World*, edited by R. Quirk and H.G. Widdowson, 11–30. Cambridge, MA: Cambridge University Press.

Kapteijn, M., and Harry Scholtmeijer. 1998. "Het Nederlands van jongeren in Oost Flevoland [The language of young inhabitants in East Flevoland]." *Taal en Tongval* 50 (1):63–80.

Kasanga, Luanga A. 2014. "The linguistic landscape. Mobile signs, code choice, symbolic meaning and territoriality in the discourse of protest." *International Journal of the Sociology of Language* 230:19–44.

Kharraki, Abdennour. 2001. "Moroccan sex-based linguistic difference in bargaining." *Discourse and Society* 12:615–632.

Kimura, Goro Christoph. 2011. "Language rights in Japan. What are they good for?" In *Language Life in Japan. Transformations and Prospects*, edited by Patrick Heinrich and Christian Galan. Abingdon: Routledge.

Kirilina, A., and M. Tomskaya. 2005. "Lingvisticheskie gendernye issledovaniya' [Linguistic gender studies]." *Otechestvennye zapiski [Domestic notes]* 2 (23):112–132.

Kloeke, G.G. 1951. *Gezag en Norm bij het Gebruik van Verzorgd Nederlands [Authority and Norm in the Use of Polished Dutch]*. Amsterdam: Meulenhoff.

Koch, Gertraud. 2009. "Intercultural communication and competence research through the lens of an anthropology of knowledge." *Forum Qualitative Social Research* 10 (1).

Koerner, Konrad. 1991. "Toward a history of modern sociolinguistics." *American Speech* 66 (1):57–70.

Kontra, Miklós. 2002. "Where is the 'most beautiful' and the 'ugliest' Hungarian spoken?" In *Handbook of Perceptual Dialectology*, edited by Dennis R. Preston and Daniel Long, 205–218. Amsterdam: John Benjamins.

Kontra, Miklós. 2006. "Sustainable linguicism." In *Language Variation. European Perspectives*, edited by Frans Hinskens, 97–126. Amsterdam: John Benjamins.

Kourdis, Evangelos. 2004. "A sociolinguistic study of evaluation criteria of Modern Greek dialects and regional accents." *Modern Greek Dialects and Linguistic Theory* 2 (1):198–205.

Kowal, S., H.-C. Barth, H. Egemann, G. Galusic, C. Kögel, N. Lippold, A. Pfeil, and D.C. O'Connel. 1998. "Unterbrechungen in Medieninterviews, Geschlechtstypisches Gesprächsverhalten [Interruptions in media interviews: gender-specific conversational behaviour]." In *Feministische Linguistik – Linguistische Geschlechterforschung*, edited by G. Schoenthal, 279–99. Hildesheim: Olms.

Kraus, Wolfgang. 2006. "Alltägliche Identitätsarbeit und Kollektivbezug. Das wiederentdeckte Wir in einer individualisierten Gesellschaft [Everyday identity work and collective terms. The rediscovered We in an individualised society]." In *Subjektdiskurse im gesellschaftlichen Wandel. Zur Theorie des Subjekts in der Spätmoderne*, edited by Heiner Keupp and Joachim Hohl, 143–164. Bielefeld: Transcript Verlag.

Krysin, Leonid, ed. 1974. *Russkiy Jazyk po Dannym Massovogo Obsledovaniya: Opyt Socialno-lingvisticheskogo Izucheniya [The Russian language by the data of mass examination: A sociolinguistic study]*. Moscow: Nauka.

Krysin, Leonid. 2000. "Sotsial'naya markirovannost' yazykovykh edinits [Social loading of language units]." In *Voprosy yazykoznaniya* 4:26–42.

Kurath, Hans. 1949. *A Geography of the Eastern United States*. Ann Arbor, MI: University of Michigan Press.

Kurniasih, Yacinta. 2005. "Gender, class and language preference. A case-study in Yogyakarta." Australian Linguistic Society Annual Conference 2005.

Labov, William. 1963. "The social motivation of sound change." *Word* 19:273–309.

Labov, William. 1965. "Linguistic research on nonstandard research on negro children." Paper presented to the New York Society for the Environmental Study of Education, New York, NY.

Labov, William. 1966. *The Social Stratification of English in New York*. Washington, DC: Center for Applied Linguistics.

Labov, William. 1969. "Contraction, deletion, and inherent variability of the English copula." *Language* 45:715–762.

Labov, William. 1972a. "The isolation of contextual styles." In *Sociolinguistic Patterns*, edited by William Labov, 70–109. Philadelphia, PA: University of Pennsylvania Press.

Labov, William. 1972b. *Language in the Inner City. Studies in the Black English Vernacular*. Philadelphia, PA: Pennsylvania University Press.

Labov, William. 1972c. *Sociolinguistic Patterns*. Philadelphia, PA: University of Pennsylvania Press.

Labov, William. 1972d. "Some principles of linguistic methodology." *Language in Society* 1:97–120.

Labov, William. 1984. "Field methods of the project on Linguistic Change and Variation." In *Language in Use*, edited by J. Baugh and J. Sherzer. Englewood Cliffs, NJ: Prentice Hall.

Labov, William. 1994. *Principles of Linguistic Change. Internal Factors.* Oxford: Blackwell.

Labov, William. 2001a. "The anatomy of style-shifting." In *Style and Sociolinguistic Variation*, edited by Penelope Eckert and John R. Rickford, 85–108. Cambridge, MA/New York, NY: Cambridge University Press.

Labov, William. 2001b. *Principles of Linguistic Change. Social Factors.* Oxford: Blackwell.

Labov, William, S. Ash, and C. Boberg. 2006. *Atlas of North American English.* The Hague: Mouton de Gruyter.

Ladefoged, Peter. 2003. *Phonetic Data Analysis: An Introduction to Fieldwork and Instrumental Techniques.* Oxford: Blackwell Publishing.

Ladegaard, Hans J. 1998. "National stereotypes and language attitudes: The perception of British, American and Australian language and culture in Denmark." *Language and Communication* 18:251–274.

LaGrandeur, Kevin. 2014. "What is the Difference between Posthumanism and Transhumanism?." The Institute for Ethics and Emerging Technologies. Accessed 23 February 2016. Available at: http://ieet.org/index.php/IEET/more/lagrandeur20140729.

Lakoff, Robin T. 1975. *Language and Women's Place.* New York, NY: Harper and Row.

Lakoff, Robin T., and Sachiko Ide. 2005. *Broadening the Horizon of Linguistic Politeness.* Amsterdam/Philadelphia, PA: John Benjamins Publishing Company.

Lambert, William E., R.C. Hodgson, R.C. Gardner, and S. Fillenbaum. 1960. "Evaluational reactions to spoken languages." *Journal of Abnormal and Social Psychology.* 20 (1):44–51.

Larionova, E. 2015. "Variativnost' proiznosheniya soglasnykh v zaimstvovanykh slovakh kak sotsial'naya peremennaya. [Pronunciation of consonants in loanwords as a social variable]." MA diss., University of St Petersburg.

Lawson, Robert, and Dave Sayers, eds. 2016. *Sociolinguistic Research. Application and Impact.* Abingdon: Routledge.

Le Page, Robert Broderick, and Andrée Tabouret-Keller. 1985. *Acts of Identity. Creole-Based Approaches to Language and Ethnicity.* Cambridge, MA: Cambridge University Press.

Lehtonen, J. and K. Sajavaara. 1985. "The silent Finn." In *Perspectives on Silence*, edited by Deborah Tannen and M. Saville-Troike, 193–201. Norwood, NJ: Ablex Publishing Corporation.

Leite, Candida Mara Britto. 2004. "Atitudes linguísticas: A variante retroflexa em foco." MA thesis, Campinas Unicamp.

LeMaster, Barbara. 1997. "Sex difference in Irish Sign Language." In *The Life of Language: Papers in Linguistics in Honor of William Bright*, edited by Jane H. Hill, P.J. Mistry and Lyle Campbell, 67–86. Berlin: Mouton de Gruyter.

Lenneberg, Eric Heinz. 1967. *Biological Foundations of Language.* New York, NY: Wiley.

Leppänen, Sirpa, Janus Spindler Møller, Thomas Rørbeck Nørreby, Andreas Stæhr, and Samu Kytölä. 2015. "Authenticity, normativity and social media." *Discourse, Context and Media* 8:1–5.

Levon, Erez. 2013. "Ethnographic fieldwork." In *Data Collection in Sociolinguistics: Methods and Applications*, edited by Christine Mallinson, Becky Childs and Gerard Van Herk, 69–79. New York, NY and London: Routledge.

Lewis, Richard D. 1996. *When Cultures Collide. Leading across Cultures*. London: Nicholas Brealey International.

Li, Jie. 2014. "A sociolinguistic study of language and gender in Desperate Housewives." *Theory and Practice in Language Studies* 4 (1):52–57.

Li, L.H. 2007. "On Wuhan young students' attitudes to Wuhan dialect, Mandarin and English" *Journal of Technology College Education* 6:122–125.

Lilly, Ian. 2004. "Conviviality in the prerevolutionary "Moscow Text" of Russian culture." *The Russian Review* 63 (3):427–448.

Lippi-Green, Rosina. 1994. "Accent, standard language ideology, and discriminatory pretext in the courts." *Language in Society* 23 (2):163–198.

Lippi-Green, Rosina. 2012. *English with an Accent: Language, Ideology and Discrimination in the United States*. 2nd ed. New York, NY: Routledge.

Livia, Anna, and Kira Hall, eds. 1997. *Queerly Phrased. Language, Gender and Sexuality*. New York, NY: Oxford University Press.

Livingstone, Sonia, and Peter Lunt. 2014. "Mediatization. An emerging paradigm for media and communication research?" In *Mediatization of Communication*, edited by K. Lundby, 703–723. Berlin: De Gruyter Mouton.

Locher, Miriam, A. 2004. *Power and Politeness in Action: Disagreements in Oral Communication*. Berlin: Mouton de Gruyter.

Loman, Bengt, ed. 1972. *Språk och samhälle [Language and Society]*. Lund: Liber Läromedel.

Long, Daniel. 1999. "Mapping non-linguists' evaluations of Japanese language variation." In *Handbook of Perceptual Dialectology*, edited by Dennis Preston, 199–226. Amsterdam: John Benjamins.

Long, Daniel, and Y.C. Yim. 2002. "Regional differences in the perception of Korean dialects." In *Handbook of Perceptual Dialectology*, edited by Dennis R. Preston and Daniel Long. Amsterdam: John Benjamins.

Lu, Hsun. 1960. "On 'Face' [1934]." In *Selected Works of Lu Hsün*, 129–132. Beijing: Foreign Language Press.

Luksaneeyanawin, Sudaporn. 1998. "Intonation in Thai." In *Intonation Systems. A Survey of Twenty Languages*, edited by Daniel Hirst and Albert Di Cristo, 376–394. New York, NY: Cambridge University Press.

Lundberg, Grant H. 2007. "Perceptual Dialectology and the Future of Slovene Dialects." *Slovenski jezik [Slovene Linguistic Studies]* 7:97–109.

Macaro, E. 2003. "Italian language teaching research: Living up to expectations." *Tuttitalia* 27:14–19.

Macaulay, Ronald K.S. 1975. "Negative prestige, linguistic insecurity, and linguistic self-hatred." *Lingua* 36:147–161.

Macías, Reynaldo F., Arturo Díaz, and Ameer Drane. 2018. "Notes on the language ecology of the City of Angels: Los Angeles, California, 1965–2015." In *Urban Sociolinguistics around the World: The City as a Linguistic Process and Experience*, edited by Dick Smakman and Patrick Heinrich. London: Routledge.

MacKinnon, Kenneth. 1977. *Language, Education and Social Processes in a Gaelic Community*. London: Routledge.

Maclean, D. 2008. "Beyond English. Transnational corporations and the strategic management of language in a complex multilingual business environment." *Management Decision* 44 (10):1377–1390.

Maher, John C. 1997. "Linguistic minorities and education in Japan." *Educational Review* 49 (2):115–123.

Maher, John C. 2005. "Metroethnicity, language, and the principle of cool." *International Journal of the Sociology of Language* 175/176:83–102.

Maher, John C., M. Millar, N. Sayanagi, D. Rackham, A. Nishozono-Maher, N. Usui, and L. Buckley. 2010. "Multilingual awareness in Japan: A national survey of young people's attitudes." *The Japan Journal of Multilingualism and Multiculturalism* 16:37–49.

Malinowski, D. 2009. "Authorship in the linguistic landscape. A multimodal, performative view." In *Linguistic landscape. Expanding the Scene*, edited by E. Shohamy and Durk Gorter, 107–125. New York, NY: Routledge.

Malkiel, Yakov. 1976. "From Romance philology through dialect geography to sociolinguistics." *International Journal of the Sociology of Language* 9:59–84.

Mallia, Fiona. 2012. *Il-Kultura Maltija* [Maltese Culture]. Santa Venera: Midsea Books.

Mallinson, Christine, Becky Childs, and Gerard Van Herk. 2013. *Data Collection in Sociolinguistics. Methods and Applications.* New York, NY/London: Routledge.

Manalansan, Martin F. 1997. "'Performing' the Filipino gay experiences in America: Linguistic strategies in a transnational context." In *Beyond the Lavender Lexicon: Authenticity, Imagination and Appropriation in Lesbian and Gay Language*, edited by William L. Leap. New York, NY: Gordon and Breach.

Margaret, Florey, and Aone Van Engelenhoven. 2001. "Language documentation and maintenance programs for Moluccan languages in the Netherlands." *International Journal of the Sociology of Language* 151:195–219.

Massey, Doreen B. 2005. *For Space.* London: Sage.

McKenzie, Robert. 2006. "A Quantitative Study of the Attitudes of Japanese Learners Towards Varieties of English Speech: Aspects of the Sociolinguistics of English in Japan." Ph.D. dissertation, School of Philosophy, Psychology and Language Sciences, University of Edinburgh.

McKenzie, Robert. 2010. *The Social Psychology of English as a Global Language.* Heidelberg: Springer.

McCormack, William. 1966. *A Causal Analysis of Caste Dialects.* Washington, DC: ERIC Clearinghouse.

McDavid, Raven Ioor. 1948. "Postvocalic /-r/ in South Carolina: A social analysis." *American Speech* 23:194–203.

McDermott, Josh H., Alan F. Schultz, Eduardo A. Undurraga, and Ricardo A. Godoy. 2016. "Indifference to dissonance in native Amazonians reveals cultural variation in music perception." *Nature. International Weekly Journal of Science* 535 (7613):547–550.

Mehrez, Samia. 2010. *Egypt's culture wars: Politics and practice.* Cairo: The American University in Cairo Press.

Mejdell, G. 2006. *Mixed Styles in Spoken Arabic in Egypt.* Leiden: Brill.

Mesthrie, Rajend, ed. 1995. *Language and Social History. Studies in South African Sociolinguistics.* Cape Town: David Philip.

Mesthrie, Rajend. 2007. "Of coconuts and kings: Accelerated linguistic change among young, middle-class females in post-apartheid South Africa." International Association of World Englishes Conference, University of Regensburg.

Mesthrie, Rajend. 2015. "Towards a distributed sociolinguistics of postcolonial multilingual societies." In *Globalising Sociolinguistics. Challenging and Expanding Theory*, edited by Dick Smakman and Patrick Heinrich. London: Routledge.

Mesthrie, Rajend, Joan Swann, Anna Deumert, and William L. Leap. 2010. *Introducing Sociolinguistics.* Edinburgh: Edinburgh University Press.

Meyerhoff, Miriam. 2011. *Introducing Sociolinguistics.* 2nd ed. New York, NY: Routledge.

Meyerhoff, Miriam, and Naomi Nagy. 2008. *Social Lives in Language. Sociolinguistics and Multilingual Speech Communities Celebrating the Work of Gillian Sankoff.* Amsterdam/Philadelphia, PA: John Benjamins.

Meyerhoff, Miriam, Erik Schleef, and Laurel MacKenzie. 2015. *Doing Sociolinguistics. A Practical Guide to Data Collection and Analysis*. London/New York, NY: Routledge.

Milani, Tommaso M. 2015. *Language and Masculinities. Performances, Intersections, Dislocations*, New York, NY: Routledge.

Milroy, James. 2001. "Language ideologies and the consequences of standardization." *Journal of Sociolinguistics* 5:530–555.

Milroy, James, and Lesley Milroy. 1978. "Belfast: Change and variation in an urban vernacular." In *Sociolinguistic Patterns in British English*, edited by Peter Trudgill, 19–36. London: Edward Arnold.

Milroy, Lesley, and James Milroy. 1985. *Authority in Language: Investigating Standard English*. London/New York, NY: Routledge.

Milroy, James, Lesley Milroy, Sue Hartley, and David Walshaw. 1994. "Glottal stops and Tyneside glottalization: Competing patterns of variation and change in British English." *Language Variation and Change* 6 (3):327–357.

Milroy, Lesley, and M. Gordon. 2003. *Sociolinguistics: Method and Interpretation*. Oxford: Blackwell.

Minkailou, Mohamed, and Ibrahima Abdoulaye. 2016. "Investigation into Bamanankan-French Code Switching among University Students in Bamako." *International Journal of English Language, Literature and Humanities* 4 (8):178–194.

Mitsova, Sofiya. 2014. ""Nie sme ora estete" – Pohvati za izrazyavane na identichnost onlayn ['We are' or esthetics – Expressions of identity online]." In *Problemi na sotsiolingvistikata XI. Ezikat vav vremeto i prostranstvoto [Sociolinguistics Issues XI. Language in Time and Space]*, edited by M. Videnov, 302–308. Sofija: Mezhdunarodno sotsiolingvistichno druzhestvo.

Montgomery, Martin. 1994. *An Introduction to Language and Society*. London/New York, NY: Routledge.

Morales, J. Francisco, Mercedes López-Sáez, and Laura Vega. 1998. "Discrimination and beliefs on discrimination in individualists and collectivists." In *Social identity. International Perspectives*, edited by Stephen Worchel, J. Francisco Morales, Darío Páez and Jean-Claude Dechamps, 199–210. London/Thousand Oaks (California)/New Delhi: Sage Publications.

Morgenstierne, Georg. 1961. "Dardic and Kafir languages." In *The Encyclopedia of Islam*, 138–139. Leiden: Brill.

Morris, Jonathan. 2014. "The influence of social factors on minority language engagement amongst young people. An investigation of Welsh-English bilinguals in North Wales." *International Journal of the Sociology of Language* (230):65–89.

Mougeon, R., T. Nadasdi, and K. Rehner. 2010. *The Sociolinguistic Competence of Immersion Students*. Bristol/Toronto: Multilingual Matters.

Müller, André, and Rachel Weymouth. 2016. "Constructing and deconstructing Kachin and Palaung linguistic identities." Language, Power and Identity in Asia. Creating and Crossing Language Boundaries, Leiden, 14–16 March 2016.

Munson, Benjamin, and Molly Babel. 2007. "Loose lips and silver tongues, or, projecting sexual orientation through speech." *Language and Linguistics Compass* 1:416–449.

Murray, Georgina. 2006. *Capitalist Networks and Social Power in Australia and New Zealand*. Aldershot: Ashgate Publishing.

Musau, P. 2004. "Linguistic human rights in Africa: Challenges and prospects for indigenous languages in Kenya." In *New Language Bearings in Africa: A Fresh Quest*, edited by M. Muthwii and A. Kioko, 59–68. Clevedon: Multilingual Matters.

Myers-Scotton, Carol. 1998. "A theoretical introduction to the markedness model." In *Codes and Consequences. Choosing Linguistic Varieties*, edited by Carol Myers-Scotton, 18–38. New York, NY/Oxford: Oxford University Press.

Nababan, P.W.J. 1993. *Sosiolinguistik. Suatu Pengantar* [Sociolinguistics. An introduction]. Jakarta: Gramedia.

Nanda, Serena. 1999. *Neither Man nor Woman. The Hijras of India*. 2nd ed. Belmont, CA: Wadsworth Publishing Company.

Nederveen Pieterse, Jan. 2003. *Globalization and Culture. Global Mélange*. Lanham, MD: Rowman & Littlefield.

Needham, Rodney. 1972. *Belief, Language, and Experience*. Chicago, IL: The University of Chicago Press.

Nekvapil, Jiří. 2010. "Language cultivation in developed contexts." In *The Handbook of Educational Linguistics*, edited by Bernard Spolsky and Francis M. Hult, 251–265. Chichester: Wiley-Blackwell.

Nerbonne, John, and Wilbert Heeringa. 1997. "Measuring dialect distance phonetically." Third Meeting of the ACL Special Interest Group in Computational Phonology, Madrid.

Newman, Michael, and Angela Wu. 2011. ""Do you sound Asian when you speak English?" Racial identification and voice in Chinese and Korean Americans' English." *American Speech* 86 (2):152–178.

Nguyen, Dong, Rilana Gravel, Dolf Trieschnigg, and Theo Meder. 2013. ""How old do you think I am?": A study of language and age in Twitter." The Seventh International AAAI Conference on Weblogs and Social Media, Cambridge, MA.

Nida, Eugene A. 1949. *Morphology; The Descriptive Analysis of Words*. Ann Arbor, MI: University of Michigan Press.

Niedzielski, Nancy A., and Dennis R. Preston. 2000. "Introduction." In *Folk Linguistics*, edited by Nancy Niedzielski and Dennis Preston, 1–40. Berlin/New York, NY: Mouton de Gruyter.

Nilesh, Preeta, and Nilakshi Roy. 2016. "Fashioning authority and distinctiveness in India through language imperialism." Language, Power and Identity in Asia. Creating and Crossing Language Boundaries (14–16 March 2016), Leiden.

Norton, Bonny. 2000. *Identity and Language Learning: Gender, Ethnicity, and Educational Change*. London: Longman.

Nussbaum, Jon F., and Justine Coupland, eds. 2004. *Handbook of Communication and Aging Research*. 2nd ed. Mahwah, NJ: Lawrence Erlbaum Associates.

O'Shannessy, Carmel. 2005. "Light Warlpiri. A new language." *Australian Journal of Linguistics* 25 (1):31–57.

Ochs, Elinor. 1992. "Indexing gender." In *Rethinking Context: Language as an Interactive Phenomenon*, edited by Alessandro Duranti and Charles Goodwin, 335–358. Cambridge, MA: Cambridge University Press.

Ochs, Elinor, and Bambi B. Schieffelin 2012. "The theory of language socialization." In *Handbook of Language Socialisation*, edited by Alessandro Duranti, Elinor Ochs and Bambi B. Schieffelin, 1–21. Malden, MA: Blackwell.

Onze Taal. 2016. "Geschiedenis van Onze Taal." Stichting Onze Taal. Accessed 9 October 2016. Available at: https://onzetaal.nl/over-onze-taal/organisatie/geschiedenis.

Paltridge, J., and Howard Giles. 1984. "Attitudes towards speakers of regional accents of French: Effects of regionality, age and sex of listeners." *Linguistische Berichte* 90:71–85.

Pandit, Probodh Bechardas. 1955. "Linguistic survey of border lands of Gujarat." *Journal of the Gujarat Research Society* 14:57–67.

Panov, Mikhil, ed. 1968. *Russkiy Jazyk i Sovetskoye Obschestvo [The Russian Language and Soviet Society]*. Moscow: Nauka.

Papacharissi, Z. 2011. *A Networked Self. Identity, Community and Culture on Social Network Sites*. London: Routledge.

Páramo, M.L. 2002. "Uso de estrategias comunicativas de género en adolescentes [The use of gender communication strategies by adolescents]." In *'Género', sexo, discurso* ['Gender', sex, discourse], edited by A.M. Vigara Tauste and R.M. Jiménez Catalán, 311–376. Madrid: Laberinto.

Paulston, Christina Bratt, Scott Fabius Kiesling, and Elizabeth S. Rangel, eds. 2012. *The Handbook of Intercultural Discourse and Communication*. Malden, MA/Oxford: Wiley-Blackwell.

Paulston, Christina Bratt, and Richard G. Tucker, eds. 2003. *Sociolinguistics. The Essential Readings*. Oxford Blackwell.

Paveau, Marie-Anne. 2007. "Les normes perceptives de la linguistique populaire [Perceptual Norms in Sociolinguistics, Translated by Ellen Marriage, 2010; accessible through www.gutenberg.org]." *Langage et Société* 119:93–109.

Pedersen, Inge Lise. 2003. "Traditional dialects of Danish and the de-dialectalization 1900–2000." *International Journal of the Sociology of Language* 159:9–28.

Peirce, Charles Sanders. 1932. "Division of signs." In *Collected Papers of C.S. Peirce* edited by C. Hartshorne and P. Weiss, 134–155. Cambridge, MA: Belknap/Harvard University Press.

Pereira, Cristophe. 2007. "Urbanization and dialect change: The Arabic dialect of Tripoli (Libya)." In *Arabic in the City: Issues in Dialect Contact and Language Variation*, edited by Cathrine Miller and Enam Al-Wer. London/New York, NY: Routledge.

Petkovska, Viktorija. 2014. "The impact of sex discriminative language upon ELT." *Journal of Education and Practice* 5 (25):193–201.

Phyak, Prem. 2015. "(En)Countering language ideologies: Language policing in the ideospace of Facebook." *Language Policy* 14 (4):377–395.

Piller, Ingrid. 2011. *Intercultural Communication: A Critical Introduction*. Edinburgh: Edinburgh University Press.

Piller, Ingrid. 2016. *Linguistic Diversity and Social Justice. An Introduction to Applied Sociolinguistics*. New York, NY: Oxford University Press.

Pinker, S., and Ray Jackendoff. 2005. "The faculty of language: What's special about it?" *Cognition* 95:201–236.

Podesva, Robert J., Sarah J. Roberts, and Kathryn Campbell-Kibler. 2001. "Sharing resources and indexing meanings in the production of gay styles." In *Language and Sexuality: Contesting Meaning in Theory and Practice*, edited by Kathryn Campbell-Kibler, Robert J. Podesva, Sarah J. Roberts and Andrew Wong, 175–189. Stanford, CA: CSLI Publications.

Polivanov, E.D. 1931. *Za marksistskoe yazykoznanie [For Marxist Linguistics]*. Moscow: Federatsiya.

Pollock, D.C., and R.E. Van Reken. 2009. *Third Culture Kids: The Experience of Growing Up among Worlds*. Boston, MA: Nicholas Brealey.

Preston, Dennis R. n.d. "Language and Prejudice. Language myth #17." Accessed 13 November 2016. Available at: www.pbs.org/speak/speech/prejudice/attitudes/.

Preston, Dennis R., ed. 1999a. *Handbook of Perceptual Dialectology*. Vol. 1. Amsterdam/Philadelphia, PA: Benjamins.

Preston, Dennis R. 1999b. *Perceptual Dialectology*. East Lansing, MI: Michigan State University.

Preston, Dennis R. 2008. "Qu'est-ce que la linguistique populaire? Une question d'importance [What is Folk Linguistics? A matter of importance]." *Pratiques. Linguistique, Littérature, Didactique* [Practice. Linguistics. Literature. Didactics] 139/140:1–24.

Preston, Dennis R., and Nancy A. Niedzielski. 2009. "Folk linguistics." In *The New Sociolinguistics Reader*, edited by Nikolas Coupland and Adam Jaworski. New York, NY: Palgrave Macmillan.

QES. 2016. "The Queen's English Society. Good English Matters." Accessed 13 November 2016. Available at: http://queens-english-society.org/about-us/.

Queen, Robin M. 1997. "'I don't speak Spritch': Locating lesbian language." In *Queerly Phrased: Language, Gender, and Sexuality*, edited by Anna Livia and Kira Hall, 233–256. New York, NY: Oxford University Press.

Rickford, John R. 1986. "The need for new approaches in social class analysis in sociolinguistics." *Language and Communication* 6 (3):215–221.

Rickford, John R. 2016. "Foreword." In *Sociolinguistic Research. Applications and Impact*, edited by Robert Lawson and Dave Sayers, xi–xiv. London/New York, NY: Routledge.

Riigikantselei [State Chancellery]. 2012. "The Constitution of the Republic of Estonia (passed on 28 June 1992)." Accessed 13 November 2016. Available at: www.president.ee/en/republic-of-estonia/the-constitution/

Robertson, Roland. 1995. "Glocalization. Time-space and homogeneity-heterogeneity." In *Global Modernities*, edited by Mike Featherstone, Scott Lash and Roland Robertson, 25–44. London: Sage.

Romaine, Suzanne. 2001. *Language in Society. An Introduction to Sociolinguistics*. Oxford: Oxford University Press.

Romaine, Suzanne. 2003. "Variation in language and gender." In *The Handbook of Language and Gender*, edited by Janet Holmes and Miriam Meyerhoff, 98–118. Oxford: Blackwell.

Rosaldo, Michelle. 1984. "Words that are moving. The social meanings of Ilongot verbal art." In *Dangerous Words. Language and Politics in the Pacific*, edited by Donald Brenneis and Fred R. Myers, 131–160. Prospect Heights, NY: Wavelenad Press.

Rosenthal, Marilyn S. 1977. The Magic Boxes: Children and Black English. Urbana (Il.)/Arlington (VA): The ERIC Clearinghouse on Languages and Linguistics/Center for Applied Linguistics (CAL.ERIC/CLL) and The ERIC Clearinghouse on Early Childhood Education (ERIC/ECE).

Rumsey, Deborah. 2010. *Statistics Essentials for Dummies*. Hoboken, NJ: Wiley.

Rundell, Michael, and Gwyneth Fox, eds. 2002. *MacMillan English Dictionary for Advanced Learners*. Oxford: MacMillan.

Ryan, E.B., Howard Giles, and R.J. Sebastian. 1982. "An integrative perspective for the study of attitudes toward language variation." In *Attitudes Towards Language Variation. Social and Applied Contexts*, edited by E.B. Ryan and Howard Giles, 1–19. London: Edward Arnold.

Sacks, Harvey, Emanuel A. Schegloff, and Gail Jefferson. 1974. "A simplest systematics for the organization of turn taking in conversation." *Language* 50 (4):696–735.

Sadiqi, F. 2003. *Women, Gender and language in Morocco*. Leiden: Brill.

Saisuwan, Pavadee. 2014. "How do ladyboys talk?: The use of prosody among Thai male-to-female transgenders." Sociolinguistic Symposium 20, Jyväskylä, Finland.

Sankoff, Gillian. 2004. "Adolescents, young adults and the critical period: Two case studies from "Seven Up"." In *Sociolinguistic Variation: Critical Reflections*, edited by Carmen Fought, 121–139. Oxford/New York, NY: Oxford University Press.

Sankoff, Gillian, and H. Blondeau. 2007. "Language change across the lifespan, /r/ in Montreal French." *Language* 83:560–588.

Sano, Naoko. 2001. "'Gengoteki jinken' ni tsuite no hihanteki kosatsu [A critical view on linguistic human rights]." *Nagoya shiritsu daigaku jinbun shakai gakubu kenkyu kiyo [Journal of Humanities and Social Sciences of Nagoya City University]* 11:147–158.

Satyanath, Shobha. 2015. "Language variation and change. The Indian experience." In *Globalising Sociolinguistics. Challenging and Expanding Theory*, edited by Dick Smakman and Patrick Heinrich, 107–122. London: Routledge.

Satyanath, Shobha. 2016. "Hybridity, multilingualism, identity and change in Nagaland." Language, Power and Identity in Asia. Creating and Crossing Language Boundaries (14–16 March 2016), Leiden, 15 March 2016.

Savage, Mike, Fiona Devine, Niall Cunningham, Mark Taylor, Yaojun Li, Johannes Hjellbrekke, Brgitte Le Roux, Sam Friedman, and Andrew Miles. 2013. "A new model of social class? Findings from the BBC's Great British Class survey experiment." *Sociology* 47 (2):219–250.

Saville-Troike, Muriel. 1984. "What really matters in second language learning for academic achievement?" *TESOL Quarterly* 18 (2):567–590.

Saville-Troike, Muriel. 2012. *Introducing Second Language Acquisition*. 2nd ed. Cambridge, MA: Cambridge University Press.

Sax, Kelly. 2000. "Acquisition of stylistic variation by American learners of French: /l/ elision in the subject pronouns il and ils." Second Language Research Forum, Indiana University, Bloomington, IN.

Schieffelin, Bambi B., Kathryn A. Woolard, and Paul V. Kroskrity. 1998. *Language Ideologies. Practice and Theory*. New York, NY: Oxford University Press.

Schmidt, Richard W. 1986. "Applied sociolinguistics. The case of Arabic as a second language." *Anthropological Linguistics* 28 (1):55–72.

Schoenthal, G. 1998. "Introduction." In *Feministische Linguistik. Linguistische Geschlechterforschung* [Feminist linguistics. Linguistic gender studies], edited by G. Schoenthal. Hildesheim: Olms.

Schuerkens, U., ed. 2004. *Global Forces and Local Life-Worlds*. London: Sage.

Schumann, John H. 1978. "The Acculturation Model for second language acquisition." In *Second Language Acquisition and Foreign Language teaching*, edited by R.C. Gingras, 27–50. Arlington: Center for Applied Linguistics.

Schüppert, Anja, Nanna Haug Hilton, and Charlotte Gooskens. 2015. "Swedish is beautiful, Danish is ugly? Investigating the link between language attitudes and spoken word recognition." *Linguistics* 53 (2)375–403.

Schwarz, Norbet, and Gerd Bohner. 2001. "The construction of attitudes." In *Intrapersonal Processes (Blackwell Handbook of Social Psychology)*, edited by A. Tesser and N. Schwarz. Oxford: Blackwell.

Scollon, Ron, and Suzanne Wong Scollon. 2001. *Intercultural Communication: A Discourse Approach*. Oxford: Blackwell.

Sebregts, Koen Dirk Corné Jac. 2014. "The Sociophonetics and Phonology of Dutch /r/." Ph.D., Department of Languages, Literature and Communication, Utrecht University.

Selishchev, A.M. 1928. *Yazyk revolutsionnoj epokhi [The Language in the Time of Revolution]*. Moscow: Rabotnik prosveshcheniya.

Sharma, Rajendra K. 2007. *Fundamentals of Sociology*. New Delhi: Atlantic Publishers.

Shioda, Takehiro. 2011. "Constraints on language use in public broadcasting." In *Language Life in Japan. Transformations and Prospects*, edited by Patrick Heinrich and Christian Galan, 124–139. London/New York, NY: Routledge.

Shopen, T. 1978. "Research on the variable (ING) in Canberra, Australia." *Talanya* 5:42–52.

Shpilrein, I.N., D.I. Rejtynbarg, and G.O. Netskij. 1928. *Yazyk krasnoarmeitsa [The Language of a Red Army Soldier]*. Moscow/Leningrad: Gosizdat.

Sibata, Takesi. 1958. *Nihon no hōgen [Dialects of Japan]*. Tokyo: Iwanami.

Sibata, Takesi. 1959. "Subjective dialect boundaries." *Gengo Kenkyu* 36:1–13.

Sifianou, Maria, and Eleni Antonopoulou. 2005. "Positive politeness in Greece: The politeness of involvement." In *Politeness in Europe*, edited by Leo Hickey and Miranda Stewart, 263–267. Clevedon: Multilingual Matters.

Silverstein, Michael. 1979. "Language structure and language ideology." In *The Elements. A Parasession on Linguistic Units and Levels*, edited by Paul Clyne, R., William F. Hanks and Carol L. Hofbauer. Chicago: Chicago Linguistics Society.

Silverstein, Michael. 2003. "Indexical order and the dialects of sociolinguistic life." *Language and Communication* 23 (3/4):193–229.

Šimičić, Lucija, and Anita Sujoldžić. 2004. "Cultural implications of attitude and evaluative reactions toward dialect variation in Croatian youth." *Collegium Antropologicum* 28 (1):97–107.

Simpkins, Gary, and Charlesetta Simpkins. 1981. "Cross-cultural approach to curriculum development." In *Black English and the education of Black children and youth*, edited by Geneva Smitherman, 221–240. Detroit, MI: Center for Black Studies, Wayne State University.

Simpson, Paul. 1993. *Language, Ideology and Point of View*. London/New York, NY: Routledge.

Singh, R., J. Lele, and G. Martohardjono. 1988. "Communication in a multilingual society: Some missed opportunities." *Language in Society* 17:43–59.

Sloboda, M. 2010. "Menej používané jazyky v Česku: problémy rozvoja v jazykovo „homogénnom" národnom štáte [Lesser-used languages in the Czech Republic. Problems of development in a linguistically 'homogeneous' nation state]." In *Kevésbé használt nyelvek helyzete a Visegrádi Négyek országaiban [The Situation of the Lesser Used Languages in Visegrád Four Countries]*, edited by A.M. Papp, 38–55. Budapest: Országos Idegennyelvű Könyvtár.

Sloos, M., and A.A. Garcia. 2015. "Own variety bias." *I-perception* 6 (5):1–4.

Smakman, Dick. 2006. *Standard Dutch in the Netherlands. A Sociolinguistic and Phonetic Description*. Utrecht: Landelijke Onderzoekschool Taalwetenschap (LOT).

Smakman, Dick. 2012. "The definition of the standard language: A survey in seven countries." *International Journal of the Sociology of Language* 218:25–85.

Smakman, Dick. 2015. "The westernising mechanisms in sociolinguistics." In *Globalising Sociolinguistics. Challenging and Expanding Theory*, edited by Dick Smakman and Patrick Heinrich. London: Routledge.

Smakman, Dick, and Sandra Nekesa Barasa. 2016. "Defining 'Standard'. Towards a cross-cultural definition of the language norm." In *Prescription and Tradition in Language. Establishing Standards across Time and Space*, edited by Ingrid Tieken-Boon van Ostade and Carol Percy, 23–38. Bristol/Buffalo, NY/Toronto: Multilingual Matters.

Smith-Christmas, Cassie. 2016. *Family Language Policy. Maintaining an Endangered Language in the Home*. Basingstoke: Palgrave MacMillan.

Smith-Christmas, Cassie, and Tadhg Ó hIfearnáin. 2015. "Gaelic Scotland and Ireland. Issues of class and diglossia in an evolving social landscape." In *Globalising Sociolinguistics. Challenging and Expanding Theory*, edited by Dick Smakman and Patrick Heinrich, 256–269. London: Routledge.

Smyth, Ron, Greg Jacobs, and Henry Rogers. 2003. "Male voices and perceived sexual orientation: An experimental and theoretical approach." *Language in Society* 32:329–350.

Spolsky, Bernard. 2009. *Language Management*. Cambridge, MA: Cambridge University Press.

Stanford, James, and Dennis R. Preston. 2009. "The lure of a distant horizon. Variation in indigenous minority languages." In *Variation in Indigenous Minority Languages*, edited by James Stanford and Dennis Preston, 1–20. Amsterdam: John Benjamins.

Steger, Manfred B., and Paul James. 2010. "Ideologies of globalism." In *Globalization and Culture. Ideologies of Globalism*, edited by Paul James and Manfred B. Steger, ix–xxxi. London: Sage.

Stell, Gerard. 2014. "Uses and functions of English in Namibia's multiethnic settings." *World Englishes* 33 (2):223–241.

Stewart, William. 1968. "A sociolinguistic typology for describing national multilingualism." In *Readings in the Sociology of Language*, edited by Joshua Fishman, 531–545. The Hague: Mouton.

Stroop, Jan. 1998. *Poldernederlands. Waardoor het ABN Verdwijnt [Polder Dutch. Due to Which Standard Dutch is Disappearing]*. Amsterdam: Bert Bakker.

Suleiman, Yasir. 2003. *The Arabic Language and National Identity*. Washington, DC: Georgetown University Press.

Sunny, Neethu. 2013. "A Sociolinguistic Study of Malayalam in Cherukunnam." M.Phil dissertation, University of Delhi.

Suzuki, Takao. 2000. *Gengoken no kozo [Structures of Language Rights]*. Tokyo: Seibundo.

Švejcer, Aleksandr Davidovič, and Leonid Borisovič Nikol'skij. 1978. *Vvedenie v sociolingvistiku [Introduction to Sociolinguistics]*. Moscow: Vysšaja škola.

Swain, Merrill. 1985. "Communicative competence: Some roles of comprehensible input and comprehensible output in its development." In *Input in Second Language Acquisition*, edited by Susan M. Gass and Carolyn G. Madden, 235–253. Rowley, MA: Newbury House.

Tachibana, Shoichi. 1943 [1936]. *Hōgengaku gairon [Outline of Dialectology]*. 3rd ed. Tokyo Ikuei shoin.

Tagliamonte, Sali. 1998. "Was/were variation across the generations: View from the city of York." *Language Variation and Change* 10:153–191.

Tagliamonte, Sali, and D. Denis. 2008. "Linguistic ruin? LOL! Instant messaging and teen language." *American Speech* 83 (1):273–286.

Tajfel, H. 1974. "Social identity and intergroup behaviour." *Social Science Information* 13:65–93.

Tamasi, Susan L. 2003. "Cognitive Patterns of Linguistic Perceptions." Ph.D., University of Georgia.

Tanabe, Suketoshi. 1936. *Gengo-shakaigaku [Sociology of Language]*. Tokyo: Nikko Shoin.

Tanaka, H., and A. Sugiyama. 2011. "Language and power in business discourse." In *Language Life in Japan. Transformations and Prospects*, edited by Patrick Heinrich and Christian Galan. London/New York, NY: Routledge.

Tannen, Deborah. 1986. "Introducing constructed dialogue in Greek and American conversational and literary narrative." In *Direct and Indirect Speech*, edited by Florian Coulmas, 311–332. Amsterdam: De Gruyter.

Tannen, Deborah. 1990. *You Just Don't Understand: Women and Men in Conversation*. New York, NY: Morrow.

Tarone, E. 1998. "Sociolinguistic perspective on an SLA theory of mind." *Studia Anglica Posnaniensia* 33:431–444

Tempesta, I. 2000. *Varietà della lingua e rete sociale*. Milan: Franco Angeli.

Terborg, Ronald, and Virna Velázquez. 2018. "Mexico City as the capital of a multilingual country." In *Urban Sociolinguistics around the World: The City as a Linguistic Process and Experience*, edited by Dick Smakman and Patrick Heinrich. London: Routledge.

Thoegersen, Jacob. 2004. "Attitudes towards the English influx in the Nordic countries. A quantitative investigation." *Nordic Journal of English Studies* 3 (2):23–38.

Thomason, Sarah, and Terrence Kaufman. 1988. *Language Contact, Creolization and Genetic Linguistics*. Berkeley, CA: University of California Press.

Thompson, John B. 2003. "Editor's introduction." In *Language and Symbolic Power (by Pierre Bourdieu, 1991)*, edited by John. B. Thompson, 1–31. Cambridge, MA: Harvard University Press.

Thurlow, C., and K. Mroczek, eds. 2011. *Digital Discourse. Language in the New Media.* Oxford: Oxford University Press.

Tieken-Boon van Ostade, Ingrid, and Carol Percy, eds. 2017. *Prescription and Tradition in Language. Establishing Standards across Time and Space.* Bristol: Multilingual Matters.

Trudgill, Peter. 1972. "Sex, covert prestige and linguistic change in urban British English." *Language in Society* 1:179–195.

Trudgill, Peter. 1974a. "Linguistic change and diffusion: Description and explanation in sociolinguistic dialect geography." *Language in Society* 3:215–246.

Trudgill, Peter. 1974b. *The Social Differentiation of English in Norwich.* Cambridge, MA: Cambridge University Press.

Trudgill, Peter, ed. 1984. *Applied Sociolinguistics.* Edited by David Crystal, *Applied Linguistics Studies.* London: Academic Press Inc. Ltd.

Trudgill, Peter. 2000. *Sociolinguistics: An Introduction to Language and Society.* London: Penguin.

Trudgill, Peter, and Howard Giles. 1978. "Sociolinguistics and linguistic value judgments: Correctness, adequacy and aesthetics." In *Functional Studies in Language and Literature,* edited by F. Coppieters and D.L. Goyvaerts, 167–190. Gent: Story-Scientia.

Tsuda, Yokio. 1990. *Eigo shihai no kozo [Structure of the Dominance of English].* Tokyo: Daisaanshokan.

Turner, Terence. 1995. "Social body and embodied subject. Bodiliness, subjectivity, and sociality among the Kayapo " *Cultural Anthropology* 10 (2):143–170.

Tzitzilis, Christos. 2001. "Modern Greek dialects and modern Greek dialectology." In *Encyclopaedic Guide for the Language,* edited by Anastassios Christidis, 168–174. Thessaloniki: Center of Greek Language.

UNESCO. 2003. "Language Vitality and Endangerment." UNESCO. Accessed 19 May 2017. Available at: www.unesco.org/new/fileadmin/MULTIMEDIA/HQ/CLT/pdf/Language_vitality_and_endangerment_EN.pdf.

Vaicekauskienė, L. 2007. "English borrowings and social identity in Lithuania." In *Spritt österut: Språk og identitet* [Spread east: Language and identity], 50–66. Volda: Høgskulen i Volda.

Van Bezooijen, Renée. 1994. "Aesthetic evaluation of Dutch language varieties." *Language and Communication* 14 (3):253–263.

Van Borsel, John, Jana Vandaele, and Paul Corthals. 2013. "Pitch and pitch variation in lesbian women." *Journal of Voice* 27 (5):656.

Van de Velde, Hans. 1996. *Variatie en Verandering in het Standaard-Nederlands (1935–1993) [Variation and Change in Standard Dutch (1935–1993)].* Utrecht: Landelijke Onderzoeksschool Taalwetenschap (LOT).

Van der Haagen, Monique. 1998. *Caught Between Norms. The English Pronunciation of Dutch Learners.* Utrecht: Landelijke Onderzoekschool Taalwetenschap (LOT).

Van der Wal, Marijke, and Cor Van Bree. 2008. *Geschiedenis van het Nederlands [The History of the Dutch Language].* Utrecht: Het Spectrum.

Van Eeden, J. 1991. Ageing and seniority in a rural Xhosa community. Cape Town: HSRC/UCT Centre for Gerontology, University of Cape Town.

Van Engelenhoven, Aone, and Maaike Van Naerssen. 2015. "South-Eastern Asia. Diglossia and politeness in a multilingual context." In *Globalising Sociolinguistics. Challenging and Expanding Theory,* edited by Dick Smakman and Patrick Heinrich. London: Routledge.

Van Hoorde, Johan. 1998. "Let Dutch die? Over De Taalunie's dead body." *InfoNT2* 2:6–10.

Van Meurs, Frank, Brigitte Planken, Hubert Korzilius, and Marinel Gerritsen. 2015. "Reasons for using English or the local language in the genre of job advertisements: Insights from interviews with Dutch job ad designers." *IEEE Transactions on Professional Communication* 58 (1):86–105.

Van Nierop, D.J.P.J., Louis C.W. Pols, and R. Plomp. 1973. *Frequency Analysis of Dutch Vowels from 25 Female Speakers*. Soest: TNO.

Vargas, A., E. Lledó, M. Bengoechea, M. Mediavilla, I. Rubio, A. Marco, and C. Alario. 1998. *Lo femenino y lo masculino en el Diccionario de la Real Academia Española* [The feminine and the masculine in the Dictionary of the Royal Spanish Academy]. Madrid: Instituto de la Mujer.

Vertovec, Steven. 2007. "Super-diversity and its implications." *Ethnic and Racial Studies* 30 (6):1024–1054.

Vossler, Karl. 1925. *Geist und Kultur in der Sprache*. Heidelberg: Winter.

Vygotsky, Lev S. 1962. *Thought and Language*. Cambridge, MA: MIT Press.

Vygotsky, Lev S. 1978. *Mind in Society. The Development of Higher Psychological Processes*. Cambridge, MA: Harvard University Press.

Walker, James A. 2010. *Variation in Linguistics Systems*. London: Routledge.

Walters, K. 2003. "Fergie's prescience: The changing nature of diglossia in Tunisia." *International Journal of the Sociology of Language* 163:77–110.

Warner, Allen. 2015. "The future of creaky voice. Listener attitudes." *Schwa. Language and Linguistics* (12):45–57.

Watt, Dominic, and Carmen Llamas. 2014. *Language, Borders and Identity*. Edinburgh: Edinburgh University Press.

Watts, Richard J. 2003. *Politeness*. Cambridge, MA: Cambridge University Press.

Wegener, Philipp. 1880. "Über deutsche Dialektforschung [About German dialect research]." *Zeitschrift für deutsche Filologie* 11:450–480.

Wegener, Philipp. 1885. *Untersuchungen über die Grundfragen des Sprachlebens* [Studies on the basic questions of Language Life]. Halle a/d Saale: Max Niemeyer.

Wéi, Lǐ. 1998. "The 'why' and 'how' questions in the analysis of conversational codes-witching." In *Code-Switching in Conversation: Language, Interaction, and Identity*, edited by Peter Auer, 156–176. London: Routledge.

Weijnen, Antonius A. 1946. "De grenzen tussen de Oost-Noord-Brabantse dialecten onderling [The borders amongst East-North-Brabantian dialects]." In *Oost-Noordbrabantse dialectproblemen. Bijdragen en Mededelingen der Dialectencommissie van de Koninklijke Nederlandse Akademie van Wetenschappen* [East-North Brabantian dialect issues. Annals of the Dialect Committee of the Dutch Royal Academy], edited by A.A. Weijnen, J.M. Renders and J. Van Ginneken, 1–15. Amsterdam: KNAW.

Weijnen, Antonius A. 1947. "De onderscheiding van dialectgroepen in Noord-Brabant en Limburg [The dividing lines between dialect groups in Noord Brabant and Limburg]." Akademiedagen, Amsterdam.

Weinreich, Uriel. 1954. " Is a structural dialectology possible?" *Word* 10:388–400.

Weissberg, Robert, and Suzanne Buker. 1990. *Writing up Research. Experimental Research Report Writing for Students of English*. Englewood Cliffs, NJ: Prentice Hall Regents.

Westinen, Elina. 2011. "'Bättre folk'. Critical Sociolinguistic commentary in Finnish rap music." *Tilburg papers in Culture Studies*, Paper 16.

Whorf, Benjamin. 1956 [1940]. *Language, Thought, and Reality: Selected Writings of Benjamin Lee Whorf*. Edited by John B. Carroll. Cambridge, MA: Technology Press of Massachusetts Institute of Technology.

Wierbicka, Anna. 1996. "Contrastive discourse analysis and misunderstanding. The case of German and English." In *Contrastive Sociolinguistics*, edited by Marlis Hellinger and Ulrich Ammon, 313–344. Berlin New York, NY: Mouton De Gruyter.

Wierbicka, Anna. 2002. "Russian cultural scripts. The theory of cultural scripts and its applications." *Ethos* 30 (4):401–432.

Williams, M. 1994. "Motivation in foreign and second language learning: An interactive perspective." *Educational and Child Psychology* 11:77–84.

Winkler, Johan. 1874. *Algemeen Nederduitsch en Friesch Dialecticon* [General Low German and Frisian dialectology]. The Hague: Nijhoff.

Wise, H. 1997. *The Vocabulary of Modern French*. New York, NY: Routledge.

Wolff, Hans. 1959. "Intelligibility and inter-ethnic attitudes." *Anthropological Linguistics* 1:34–41.

Wolfram, Walt. 1969. *A Sociolinguistic Description of Detroit Negro Speech*. Washington, DC: Center for Applied Linguistics.

Wolfram, Walt. 1991. *Dialects and American English*. Englewood Cliffs, NJ: Prentice Hall.

Wolfram, Walt. 2004a. "Social varieties of American English." In *Language in the USA*, edited by Edward Finegan and John R. Rickford, 58–75. Cambridge, MA: Cambridge University Press.

Wolfram, Walt. 2004b. "The sociolinguistic construction of remnant dialects." In *Sociolinguistic Variation: Critical Reflections*, edited by C Fought, 84–106. New York, NY: Oxford University Press.

Wolfram, Walt, and Ralph W. Fasold. 1974. *The Study of Social Dialects in American English*. Englewood Cliffs, NJ: Prentice-Hall.

Wright, Joseph. 1898–1905. *English Dialect Dictionary*. Vol. 1–6. Oxford: Oxford University Press.

Wright, Sue. 2004. "Language rights, democracy and the European Union." In *Language Rights and Language Survival*, edited by J. Freeman and Donna Patrick. Manchester: St. Jerome Publishing.

WVS, World Values Survey. 2015. "Findings and insights." Institute for Comparative Survey Research. Accessed 13 November 2016. Available at: www.worldvaluesurvey.org/WVSContents.jsp.

Xu, Daming. 1992. "A Sociolinguistic Study of Mandarin Nasal Variation." Ph.D., University of Ottawa.

Xu, Daming. 2015. "Speech community and linguistic urbanization: Sociolinguistic theories developed in China." In *Globalising Sociolinguistics. Challenging and Expanding Theory* 95–106, edited by Dick Smakman and Patrick Heinrich, Speech Community and Linguistic Urbanization: Sociolinguistic theories developed in China. London: Routledge.

Xue, Steve An, and Jianping G. Hao. 2006. "Normative standards for vocal tract dimensions by race as measured by acoustic pharyngometry." *Journal of Voice* 20 (3):391–400.

Yaghan, Mohammed Ali. 2008. ""Arabizi". A contemporary style of Arabic slang." *Design Issues* 24 (2):39–52.

Young, Richard F. 1991. *Variation in Interlanguage Morphology*. New York, NY: Peter Lang.

Yuasa, I. 2010. "Creaky Voice: A New Feminine Voice Quality For Young Urban-Oriented Upwardly Mobile American Women?" *American Speech* 85 (3):315–337.

Yurramendi, Yosu, and O. Altuna. 2009. "Zuzeneko behaketaz hizkuntza-erabilera neurtzeko metodologiaren eredu matematikoa [A mathematical model for the direct observation of language use]." Accessed 28 March 2017. Available at: www.soziolinguistika.eus/files/txostena.pdf

Zemskaya, Elena, ed. 1973. *Russkaya razovornaya rech [Russian Colloquial Speech]*. Moscow: Nauka.

Zemskaya, Elena, ed. 1983. *Russkaya razovornaya rech. Fonetika. Morfologiya. Leksika. Zhest. [Russian Colloquial Speech. Phonetics. Morphology. Vocabulary. Gesticulation]*. Moscow: Nauka.

Zemskaya, Elena, M. Kitajgorodskaya, and N. Rozanova. 1990. "Osobennosti muzhskoj i zhenskoj rechi [Distinctive features of male and female speech]." In *Russkij yazyk v ego funktsionirovanii. Kommunikativno-pragmaticheskij aspekt [The Functioning of Russian]*, edited by T. Vinokur, 90–136. Moscow: Nauka.

Zemskaya, Elena, M. Kitajgorodskaya, and E. Shiryaev. 1983. *Russkaya razovornaya rech. Obschie voprosy. Slovoobrazovanie. Sintaksis. [Russian Colloquial Speech. General problems: Derivation, Syntax]*. Moscow: Nauka.

Zhang, G.J. 2002. *Yuyan yu Minzu Wuzhi Wenhua Shi [Language and Ethnic Material-Cultural History]*. Beijing: Minzu Press.

Zhuravlev, A. 1988. "Opyt kvantitativno-tipologicheskogo issledovaniya raznovidnostej ustnoj rechi [Quantitative-typological study of oral speech varieties]." In *Raznovidnosti gorodskoj ustnoj rechi* [Varieties of urban oral speech], 84–151. Moscow: Nauka.

Zimman, Lal. 2012. "Voices in Transition: Testosterone, Transmasculinity, and the Gendered Voice among Female-to-Male Transgender People." Ph.D. dissertation, University of Colorado.

Zwicky, Arnold M. 1997. "Two lavender issues for linguists." In *Queerly Phrased. Language, Gender, and Sexuality*, edited by Anna Livia and Kira Hall, 21–34. New York, NY: Oxford University Press.

Glossary

This Glossary contains general terminology that is not explained extensively in the text.

Anthropology The study of the diversity of human behaviour; human culture, societies, and physical development. The viewpoint is one of cross-cultural comparative study, holism and cultural relativism. See also **Linguistic Anthropology**.

Ethnicity A group of people (usually large) who share nationality, race, and/or cultural origins have their ethnicity in common. Language can be one of the identity markers of ethnicity.

Ethnolinguistic Related to the view of language as an aspect or part of culture, especially the study of the influence of language on culture and of culture on language. This word emphasises shared language as being the distinctive and dominant feature of an ethnic group, especially if other features of the group are less visible.

Folklore The body of knowledge of culture and beliefs of a people and the means through which they express these, like myths, legends, songs, proverbs, riddles, costume, dance, drama, and recipes.

Formal Linguistics Linguistics that treats language as a system with categories that are systematically and hierarchically related. Formal linguists tend to ignore vaguely defined and intuitive categories based on context of usage. Investigations revolve around constructing formal models that allow us to comprehend how various subparts or modules of the linguistic grammar function.

Ideology A system of beliefs that characterise a particular culture and which is reflected in behaviour, including language. Ideologies about language are part of this and may be referred to as 'language ideologies'.

Intra-speaker variation The variation that is typical in the language of individuals and which varies in different social contexts. One person speaks differently under different circumstances.

Inter-speaker variation The variation between speakers; every speaker speaks differently from other speakers.

Kinesics Body language. The use of body movements to communicate social information.

Language planning Efforts, usually by governments, to influence the acquisition, use, function, and structure of languages.

Lifespan change Change in an individual's language that occurs after the Critical Period.

Lingua franca A language form that is used for communication between people who do not speak each other's language.

Linguistic Anthropology The study of the diversity of human language and its relationship with social groups, values, and practices.

Linguistic marketplace The theory that certain language capabilities have a higher value in society than others and can be applied to benefit one's social position.

Linguistic Relativism The notion that language is not merely a means to express experiences but a vital part of those experiences, because it contains concepts, distinctions, and values that make people of different languages interpret reality differently. Also called the 'Sapir-Whorf hypothesis'.

Minimalism The hypothesis that Universal Grammar contains only the components and characteristics that are required to meet our conceptual and physical (pronunciation) needs. Universal Grammar is the theory that suggests that basic linguistic ability is language-independent because it is connected to the workings of the brain and therefore does not depend on language input from outside. Because human brains all over the world share their basic features, so languages share universal features as well.

Morphology The study of the structure or form of words, especially inflection and word formation.

Nation state A state, or nation state, is a political system in which a central government has the power over a delineated territory and can enforce laws, establish currency, collect tax, and maintain and use an army. It is an idealised independent unity with (perceived) shared traditions and histories of its inhabitants. Language is part of this tradition and history, and usually there is one dominant language that fulfils the role of state language.

Norm language The language that people consider to be the norm, usually within a country. This language could be called 'national language', 'standard language', or perhaps 'official language'. The qualities, social position, and actual usage in daily communication of this language vary across countries.

Optimality Theory A model of how grammars are structured, which started in the field of Phonology. Rather than studying rules that determine what is allowed in language, this theory uses constraints as a guiding force to structure grammar by looking at the language people receive (the input, the underlying form) and produce (the output; the surface structure).

Paradigm A system of social circumstances and belief systems that leads to a way of viewing the world.

Phonology The study of the systematic organisation of speech sounds.

Power One's hierarchical position relative to others that is associated with influence, control and authority. The use of certain languages (usually official languages) is associated with power, while other languages (minority languages, usually, and less official languages) are associated with less power.

Proxemics The study of the meaning of physical interpersonal space, posture, and tactile contact in human communication.

Psychology The scientific study of the human mind and its functions.

Social space The social world individuals live in, in which they communicate with other people for various reasons and in various ways.

Society A group of people (usually large) who live relatively close to each other, tend to enter into relationships with each other, and who share beliefs and behaviours.

Sociology The study of the organisation, functioning, classification, and development of human societies.

Speech event All social activities in which language plays a central role. This could be a long story that is being told to a group of people but also a conversation between two people, a condolence, a fight, or an apology. A speech event is the basic unit of the analysis of spoken interaction.

Style or **Speech style** Sociolinguistically relevant manner of using language. Style varies situationally and it varies from person to person and from group to group.

Stratification Systematic patterning. Sociolinguistic stratification is the patterning of linguistic and social factors. This term is associated with Variationist Sociolinguistics.

Syntax The study of the rules about the way the elements in sentences are organised.

Index

This index contains relevant terms as mentioned in this book. It does not contain phonetic or statistical terms. Where relevant, it is indicated whether an item refers to a language variety or style ('language'), a community of people or an individual ('people'), or a place ('place').